THE BATTLE OF THE STYLES

The Battle of the Styles

Society, Culture and the Design of the New Foreign Office, 1855–1861

Bernard Porter

continuum

Published by the Continuum International Publishing Group

The Tower Building, 11 York Road, London SE1 7NX

80 Maiden Lane, Suite 704, New York, NY 10038

www.continuumbooks.com

First published 2011

British Library Cataloguing-in-Publication Data
A catalogue record for this book is available from the British Library.

ISBN: HB: 978-1-4411-6739-2

Typeset by Pindar NZ, Auckland, New Zealand
Printed and bound in Great Britain

Contents

For Jasmine

Illustrations

Every effort has been made to trace copyright holders and to obtain their permission for the use of copyright material. The publisher would be grateful to hear from anyone not here acknowledged.

Preface

Buildings can be deceptive. The British Foreign Office in Whitehall, London, is a case in point. Looking at it today, and knowing when it was built (in the 1860s), it is natural to assume that it was designed as it was in order to emphasize Britain's great power in the world, now long passed. It is huge, heavy, dominating, vaguely Roman in its details, and topped off with statues of national heroes; all in all rather forbidding, even to new ministers – David Miliband, foreign secretary from 2007 to 2010, admitted to finding it 'intimidating' on his first visit; and so also, presumably, to most foreigners who have to pass through its doors and up its famously grand staircase. We know that it was Lord Palmerston, the great bully (allegedly) of British diplomatic history, who had it built, which must confirm this impression. Indeed, it seems so very obvious, simply from the *appearance* of the building, that few people have bothered to question this reading. 'It was built at the height of our Victorian imperial power,' boasted a BBC television programme about the work of the Office in February 2010, 'specifically to impress foreigners', and in a style chosen 'to proclaim Britain's status in the world'.[1] Of course it was. You only have to glance at it to see that.

But a glance is not enough. Examine the Foreign and Commonwealth Office (as it is now) more closely – the stones, the style, the original designs, the discussions that took place over these, and the more general historical context behind the whole enterprise: more general, that is, than merely 'the height of our Victorian imperial power' – and a very different picture emerges. At the very least, it cannot be as simple as the 'impressing foreigners' scenario; or, I would say, as dull.

For a start, let us look at the basic facts of the building's origin. These are pretty well known to architectural historians, though not, I think, more generally. The circumstances were these. In 1855 the British government decided it needed some new Government Offices, to replace, in the first instance, the Foreign Office, which was (literally) falling about its ears, and the War Office, which was inconveniently scattered all over London. (This was in the middle of a war.) So it held a competition, to help it pick a design. The outcome of that was messy; but the architect eventually chosen from among the winners was George Gilbert Scott, well known at the time as a 'Gothicist' – that is, one who sought to revive mediaeval principles of building – who had produced a Gothic plan. So it looked as though the new Offices would be in that style. Before this could happen, however, there was a change of government, and the aged Lord Palmerston became prime minister. Palmerston loathed Gothic. He could not get rid of Scott, who had already been promised the job; but he insisted he redesign the building in the 'Classical' style. Scott protested, but eventually caved in, to the disappointment – to put it mildly – of his fellow Gothicists. That was in 1861. (The row was known at the time, and is referred to in all the architectural histories of this period, as the 'Battle of the Styles'.) The result is the building that still stands in Whitehall today, housing not only the Foreign and Commonwealth Office but also the Home Office, and various other departments of state. If it had gone the other way we would have had something like the present very Gothicky St Pancras Station Hotel, also by Scott – and his riposte to the critics of his original Foreign Office designs. Opinions differ over whether that was a lost opportunity or a lucky escape.

It is an entertaining tale, more so than the histories of most architectural projects, though there are parallels. The controversy in the 1870s over the style of the new German Reichstag was one, in that case also won by the Classicists;[2] the debate over the design of a new Copenhagen City Hall in the 1890s was another, this time won by the 'national romantics', who can be seen as Denmark's version of the Goths;[3] and a third was the dispute in the 1920s over whether the British Raj's new capital at New Delhi should be Classical or 'Oriental', where the result was a compromise.[4] The most recent was probably the public row in 2009 between Lord Rogers and Prince Charles over the redevelopment of Chelsea Barracks, with Rogers being the Scott of his day, and Charles the Palmerston, and the ultimate victor there. (A case will be made out here for Gothic's being the 'modern' style in the 1850s.) In the case of the Government Offices the row was enlivened by various skullduggeries, hints of scandal, low farce, some quite good jokes – mainly from Palmerston, who used them to win over support in the House of Commons – and ungentlemanly language all round. The smell of ordure rising from the Thames also played a part. It was a lively affair, worth telling, perhaps, for that reason alone. (I shall be telling it, straight, in Chapter 1.)

But all this must detract from the *significance* of the building itself, in the form it ultimately took, if we want to infer from it something important about the character of Britain at this time. Its style was something of an accident. It could very easily have gone another way. Would a St Pancras Hotel in Whitehall have given off the same aura of imperial power and domination that Scott's final design is said to do? (That may be a matter of opinion. We shall be coming back to it.) In any case almost no one at the time said that British power and domination, or empire, or prestige, or whatever, was what they wanted the building to express. (Of course it might have gone *without* saying; but I think I can show not.) A significant number of MPs wanted no new building at all – foreign secretaries, they said, should use their own town houses for conducting their business – and a much larger number would have preferred the Foreign Office to be much more modest in scale than it turned out. The foreign secretary of the day – who was not Palmerston, as it happens, but Lord John Russell (Palmerston was prime minister) – had not cared what it looked like so long as it had a roof on to keep his clerks and secretaries dry. His permanent secretary – the top Foreign Office 'mandarin', that is – felt it was far too grand both for his liking and for its purpose. Most of the press of the time thought so too. Palmerston, though he was largely responsible for the way it came to look, never really liked it. The best he could say of it was that it would 'do'. Even its architect, Scott, virtually disowned it. Scarcely anyone beyond ministers and civil servants – and precious few of those – had taken any interest at all in the building while it was being planned and constructed, and those who had did so for a variety of reasons, very few of which had anything to do with the expression of British 'power'. It was not a popular building at the time, and has never attracted much attention subsequently: from foreign and provincial tourists in London, for example, who are mostly oblivious of it as they pass it on their way from Westminster (to see the abbey and the Houses of Parliament, which *are* much loved), to Trafalgar Square (to feed the pigeons). All this must mean that we should be wary, at least, before attempting to read anything important into – or even between the lines of – the present Foreign Office building alone.

The 'Battle', however, was something else. That *was* important, in two ways. The first is in an architectural historical context; where it is supposed, at any rate, to have marked a crucial stage in a wider war that had been going on for the previous 20-odd years between the advocates of the Gothic and Classical styles, for the architectural soul of England, no less. By the 1850s this had established Gothic as the dominant style for churches, colleges and, in its 'Jacobethan' form, for country mansions, but not yet for large urban secular public buildings (despite the new 'Perpendicular' Palace of Westminster; or even because of it). That was the new field the Goths were looking to conquer. The Government Offices, because of their size and importance, were the fortress they needed to topple in order to be able to march on. Both Scott and Palmerston saw it in these terms: Scott as a way of conclusively proving that his Gothic style was suited to every kind of building; Palmerston more apprehensively as the thin end of a wedge that would 'Gothicize the whole of London' if Scott won. So a lot was thought to depend on the outcome. Whether that outcome was as crucial as the contemporary battlers thought is questionable. It was undoubtedly a setback for the Goths, but not necessarily an irreversible one. There are several great public buildings still standing from after 1861 that were built in Gothic (or Gothic-*ish*); including, for example, the new Law Courts in London, much of the South Kensington museum complex, and Manchester Town Hall. (In much the same way, it seems unlikely that Prince Charles's blow to 'modern architecture' in the Chelsea Barracks affair will be a fatal one.) But Scott's defeat, or apostasy, certainly had some effect. We shall be discussing this – the aftermath of the Battle – in the final chapter of this book.

The second thing making the Battle over the Foreign Office worth studying is the light it sheds on the Victorian society of its day more generally, or at least on a part of it; and in particular on the relationship between that society and the artistic culture of the time, or at least a part of *that* – the architectural part. One reason for this is that it is so well documented. This is where the Government Offices affair scores over most other architectural projects of the nineteenth century (though not quite all). Unusually, it was the subject of widespread contemporary public argument and discussion, arising mainly from the fact that it was publicly funded, and so needed the sanction of the public, represented in this instance by parliament, to go ahead. So, there were debates in parliament about it, which can be read in *Hansard*; a public exhibition of the competition designs (over 200 of them) in Westminster Hall, which was apparently well attended; a flurry of pamphlets published on both sides of the argument; meetings of societies like the infant RIBA (Royal Institute of British Architects), which was riven over it, and rival deputations to the prime minister – all of this reported in the press; extensive and often heated discussions in the professional architectural journals; and newspaper leaders, periodical articles and satirical accounts in *Punch*; millions of words in all, approaching the issue of the style of the Government Offices from many different angles.

Further, and crucially: most of these angles were to do with the *associations* of the two styles, rather than 'purely' aesthetic considerations (design, proportion, 'taste' and so on), which is what links them overtly with 'society', and so makes them of particular interest to the social and cultural historian. It is not often that a single and relatively short-lived artistic controversy becomes the focus of such a wide range of contemporary societal attitudes, or 'discourses'. These included religious ones; political; social; national and imperial; gender-related; ideas about 'morality', 'truth', 'liberty', 'modernity' and 'progress'; and several others, including possibly some that I have not prised out of the material yet. These are often confusing, and confused. They also come at a confusing time in Britain's broader history, as 'crucial' and transitional a decade in many ways as it was in the field of architecture. It is for that reason that I shall not be offering a single overarching theory to account for the Battle; except that it – and consequently the Victorian culture and society that it (in part) reflected – *was* complex, and irreducible, therefore, to simple explanations. But it is Victorian society's complexity, after all, that made it so rich and fascinating; and also left us the brilliantly chaotic architectural heritage that it did.

The following chapters will attempt to reduce this chaos to some kind of order, albeit – inevitably – of a somewhat artificial kind. This will explain the loose ends and cross-references that will be found all the way through. Chapter 2 will be on the broader historical background of the 'Battle'; because although the Battle itself forms a necessary context for an understanding of the Foreign Office as it appears today, there lay a context behind that also, which it is essential to be aware of. Some of this, too, was political and social, rather than 'purely' architectural, which means that I shall sometimes stray from the latter, up some historical tracks which may at first sight seem to have little bearing on the question of architectural style, but which by the end of the book I hope to have persuaded readers are in fact germane. Chapter 3 will focus on English architectural history more narrowly.[5]

The following four chapters treat the various discourses that I have found fed into the debate, either overtly or, where I have been able to sense this, implicitly. These include, in Chapters 4 and 5, questions of national, class, religious, political and imperial 'identity'; in Chapter 6, the ethical qualities that were supposed to be reflected by the two styles; and in Chapter 7, the 'modernity' that – despite appearances – both styles claimed for themselves, and the wider debate over that. After all this, Chapter 8 may be thought to be throwing something of a spanner into the works by showing how, despite the wide range of these discourses, the debate was limited in its appeal, and in the interest most people took in it; which, mildly deflating as it must seem, is important if we want to get to the bottom of culture's relationship with society generally, and the way the former can be said to reflect the latter. Apathy and dumb philistinism are difficult to write about, because they do not leave cultural records; but it is important to be aware of them, if only to rein back any propensity we may have to exaggerate the social importance of various aspects of ('high') culture. A study of the 'Battle of the Styles' in its broadest context can, I think, help us to do this. I shall be discussing this and various other general inferences that may be drawn from this whole affair, as well as the legacy of the 'Battle', in my concluding Chapter 9.

This is, I think, an unusual book; a kind of hybrid of architectural and what might be called 'general' history, which I hope may be seen as its strength. Its weaknesses will stem from the fact that I am not a professional or practised architectural historian, as are (or were) those who have written about this event before, in particular Ian Toplis and David Brownlee, but also several others;[6] and the many more who have included an account of the 'Battle' in more general histories of Victorian architecture. I should like to make it clear that this account of mine is not meant in any way to supplant theirs, but only to supplement them. I have found no substantial errors, from my own researches, in either Toplis's or Brownlee's accounts, both of which are fuller than mine on certain aspects of the Government Offices affair, and may well be more accurate and sophisticated in their treatment of some of the more purely architectural or professional aspects of the story. I have approached the task of writing about this subject with some trepidation, as must any scholar trespassing into others' territories, so I am prepared to be corrected. I trust, however, that architectural historians reading this book, with all its flaws, may learn a little from it that augments their understanding of Victorian architecture, as I have learned an immense amount from them. My own background is as a historian of various aspects of British political and social history, in particular imperial, diplomatic and 'secret service'. I have always had a passionate interest in architecture, and Victorian in particular; the first extended paper I ever wrote, in fact, was for a school prize when I was 17, on 'Ruskin and Architecture' (it won); and I have twice dabbled in the subject since then, in a popular article (on Norman Shaw's Cragside in Northumberland) and a couple of pages in a book (on imperial culture). The Cragside article was enough, apparently, to qualify me for membership of the Society of Architectural Historians, but I

imagine the *real* (broader) society of architectural historians has stricter rules for
acceptance as one of them. I decided to research and write this book out of an
interest in the subject; because of a feeling that, at this late moment in my career, I
should allow myself the luxury of working on something that enthuses me rather
than topics that I mainly disapprove of (imperialism and espionage); and from a
belief that a bit of historical context, of the kind that I think I can supply from
my many years of toiling in the broader acres of the nineteenth century generally,
cannot be bad for any specialist.

It was at that point in my original draft of this book that my Preface was supposed
to end (before the acknowledgements). I thought I had made my purpose plain
there, and had, in particular, pre-emptively smoothed down any feathers that might
be ruffled by this incursion of mine into an area – architectural history – which
is not my normal field of experience and expertise. Specialist historians – and
others, I guess – can get quite proprietorial about their chosen patches, and
irritated when others venture into it from the outside. I know, because I have had
the same feelings about those who have dared to stray into my own major area of
imperial history: 'cultural studies' scholars, for example, and Niall Ferguson. But
it is an unworthy sentiment, and one that needs to be suppressed, in order to be
able to benefit from the new approaches and insights that the interlopers nearly
always bring with them. It was to help with this that I concluded, originally, with
that last paragraph, which was intended to express the humility and uncertainty
I genuinely feel in this field; my great respect for the architectural historians who
have written about the 'Battle' before me; and the fact that the present book is
not intended to challenge or supplant their work (except insofar as the latter very
occasionally get their general history wrong), but merely to supplement it. More
generally, I have been at pains throughout to stress that this is a book about the
contemporary debate on architecture, rather than the architecture itself. Hence
the title. One publisher to whom I originally submitted the manuscript realized
this, and rejected it as a result. 'I have enjoyed reading your chapter and outline,
but I'm sorry to say that this isn't really for us. The difficulty is that it is written
as history about architecture, rather than as architectural history.' That seems fair
enough to me. She was looking for 'architectural history', which this book, strictly
speaking, is not.

   One other publisher's reader, however, clearly did not 'get' this at all; which
is the particular reason why I now feel the need to labour the point again. I
understand that he is a specialist architectural historian. He certainly took offence
at what he thought to be my 'amateur' approach to his subject: a 'sideline' to be
'indulged in', as he called it. He accused me of a number of things: of having
'made his mind up on what he thinks Victorian architecture is, and that's that!',
for example, which I can't believe any more objective reader will be able to infer
from the book; and of putting forward a version of social history which is, 'to
be quite frank, off the wall', though to most other historians it will seem rather

conventional. The main ground of his criticism, however, was that the book was poor 'architectural history'; though when I asked him (through the publisher, as he asked to be anonymous) for examples of faults or errors, he did not furnish any; and when it was pointed out to him that it was not intended to be an architectural history as such, but an account and analysis of a cultural debate that just happened to revolve around this particular building, he responded by accusing me of dishonesty. 'I know what you're saying,' was his reply to the publisher (though it seems clear that it had not occurred to him before); 'but that's the point, I guess. It seems clear that what the author really wants this book to be is an architectural history of sorts – it is, in my view, architectural history *masquerading* [my emphasis] as "social history"'. Most readers, however, would see through this. 'I don't think he's fooling anyone'.

To which I feel I must protest here, emphatically, even indignantly – in case any other architectural historian might be tempted to approach this book in the same spirit – that I'm not trying to 'fool' anyone. This is a book about a *debate*, a 'battle'. It was a very revealing battle in its British cultural, social and political context, which is what mainly concerns me; whether or to what extent that context should be taken on board by architectural historians, in explaining the building of the time, is for them to say. My reader finished by downplaying the importance of 'context' generally for all 'art/architectural' historians; which may mark a very real difference between his sort and mine. Most other historians believe that 'context' is pretty vital – not that it explains everything, but that nothing can be fully understood without it. For example (to revert to the opening of this Preface): it is mainly 'context' that can tell us whether the new Foreign Office took the shape it did in order to express the 'imperialism' of its time, as is sometimes claimed; so that must be a matter on which the general historian is best placed to enlighten the architectural historian. If other architectural historians feel the way my reader does, then I would hope they might at least consider the possibility that 'good' – in the sense of truer, or more sophisticated – context is better than 'bad.' This is what this book attempts to provide: not the first, but a deeper and more elaborate account than exists, so far, of the surrounding context to the 1855–61 debate over the new government buildings in Whitehall. I trust that some architectural historians may find this illuminating. Even if not, however – if they adjudge that it sheds no light at all on the buildings of the 1850s and 1860s – it must shed some on the social, political and cultural life of the period viewed more broadly; which is my main interest here.

This intemperate reader's response, I have to say, surprised me, and is what first alerted me to the possibility that this book may be more controversial than I had any idea of when I wrote it. Hence this little addendum, to alert general readers to this. I don't want to give the impression that I see this book as a final word, about mid-Victorian architecture or anything else. Architectural historians, it now seems clear, will find things to criticize here, though not, I hope, as rudely as my hostile reviewer. If they can tell me where my architecture is wrong ('off the wall'), or my context unhelpful, I shall greatly welcome their feedback. But please don't accuse me of attempting to 'fool' you. I'm not; but merely trying – as a friendly neighbour from an adjacent wing in the great building called 'history' – to help.

Finally (before the acknowledgements, and while I am in defensive mode), a word or two about my *apparatus criticus*. This partly consists of quite a forest of endnotes, most of which carry the citations that are necessary to any serious work of historical scholarship to enable readers to check, independently, the scholar's sources. Because one of the concerns of this book is the *extent* of certain architectural opinions that were held in the 1850s and 1860s, many of these are multiple. (Almost anything is said *once*; that does not necessarily make it significant.) The endnotes are also used to elaborate on certain points made in the text; obviously ones that I regard as minor or secondary, otherwise the elaboration would come *in* the text; but I may be wrong about this, and this device will enable readers – once again – to decide for themselves about my priorities, and to follow up trails (or 'loose ends') that may be of more interest to them. Some of these are, I think, interesting *per se*, whatever their 'relevance'; so although the notes can be ignored, which is why they are all lumped together at the end, it may do readers no harm to take the occasional glance at them. (They represent a lot of work!)

The *illustrations* form another part of this critical apparatus. They have been selected in order to illustrate crucial points made in the text, so that readers can come to their own judgements about – for example – the range of architectural styles mooted for the Government Offices in 1857, and my characterizations of them. They are not chosen for their artistic quality, or in order to beautify the book. Some are taken from very defective sources – fading woodcuts in greying newspapers, for example – which my publisher was at first reluctant to use at all; but for most of them there were no alternatives, and I felt they were important enough as *evidence* to compensate for their deficiencies in other ways. I hope that readers will tolerate their poor quality, for this reason. They and the thicket of endnotes are all necessary grist to the historian's mill.

My first thanks for their assistance with this project must go to the British Academy, whose 'Small Research Grant' made the work for it possible. My good friends Professor Patrick Salmon, chief historian at the FCO (Foreign and Commonwealth Office), and Professor Theo Hoppen, emeritus professor of Hull University and an FBA, supported my application for that, and have helped in many ways since. John Mackenzie, whom I recommended to Continuum as a possible 'reader' for the book, even though we are – as the imperial history community knows – terrific adversaries on certain issues, but who is also highly knowledgeable on social and cultural history, and, I thought, a fair-minded and generous man, proved to be that in the comments he made on my manuscript, which I have found insightful and valuable. Naturally, I haven't accepted them all. Others who merit particular thanks are Katherine Jones, Justine Sambrook,

Cathy Wilson and Susan Pugh of the RIBA Information Centre and Drawings Collection (though I feel I must add a sour note of complaint here against its unusually high 'permission' fees, which will probably swallow up any royalties I earn from this book); the staff of the Victoria and Albert Museum Drawings Collection (whose fees are more reasonable); Karen Robson, Senior Archivist, Hartley Library, University of Southampton; Kate Crowe of the FCO, who gave me a wonderful and knowledgeable personal tour of the interior of Scott's building; Pamela Clark, Registrar of the Royal Archives; Jenni De Protani, Archivist of the Athenaeum Club; Glyn Hughes of the Meteorological Office National Archive – the last three of whom answered particular queries of mine enormously helpfully (the details are in the endnotes); the staffs of the Public Record Office (as I still prefer to call it); the British Library at St Pancras and Newspaper Library in Colindale; Hull City Reference Library (for its run of the *Builder*); the Brynmor Jones Library, University of Hull, especially Vivien in Photography; the Cambridge University Library; St Deiniol's Library, Hawarden; and Kungliga Biblioteket in Stockholm; and, for ideas exchanged between us, Mark Stocker, Preeti Chopra, Ian Morley, Sharrona Pearl, Gareth Atkins and Pedro Guedes. Sections of the book have been aired as papers at conferences and seminars at the universities of Cambridge, London, Yale, MacMaster and Texas (Austin), where feedback from audiences and other participants has been valuable, except in the case of the London one, of 'New Imperial' historians. The paper I prepared for them, incorporating some of the present Chapter 8, was later published as 'Architecture and Empire' in the *British Scholar*, vol. 2, no. 2, March 2010. I should also like to thank Robin Baird-Smith at Continuum for taking the book over after its original editor left the company, and for nursing it through the press. Kajsa Ohrlander will be glad the book is finished, as it kept us apart longer than either of us liked: there is not much work one can do on English Victorian architecture in Sweden. She has also advised me on the gender aspects of my subject, which are her area of academic expertise. My children Zoë, Ben and Kate and their partners have helped in ways they probably do not realize. Lastly, while this book was being completed, my first grandchild was born (to Zoë and Kelwyn), to whom *The Battle of the Styles* is dedicated, with a typical granddad's adoration.

Bernard Porter
Hull, Stockholm and Svartsö
19 April 2010

The Battle Joined

During the nineteenth century three great national buildings were erected in London: the Houses of Parliament in Westminster (1840–c. 1860), the Government Offices in Whitehall (1863–74) and the Law Courts in the Strand (1874–82). Each evoked public interest and controversy, much of it surrounding the *style* to be employed, in a period – embracing almost the entire century – when there was no consensus over this, and a huge gulf in particular between those who advocated the 'Classical' (or Italianate, or Greek, or Renaissance) style, or styles, and those who championed the 'Gothic' (or 'pointed'), and variants of it. All three buildings were affected by this controversy to some degree, but none of the others half so much as the middle one of them, the Whitehall buildings, where the row that erupted was popularly dubbed the 'Battle of the Styles'. It may not have been the most important or decisive battle in the more general architectural war it was an episode in; but it was the most public and spectacular. For that reason we shall begin with a straightforward account of it here – that is, of the 'Battle' as it was fought on the front lines, between 1855 and 1861, mainly in and around parliament – before moving *back*, in the following chapter, to place it in its historical context; and then going on to consider the various cultural, social and political discourses that informed it while it raged.

The original motive for rebuilding the Government Offices was the simple one of need. The business of the Victorian state was expanding.[1] The premises in which it was carried on were quite obviously unsatisfactory. Benjamin Hall, the First Commissioner of Works in 1857, thought that 'no public offices in the world' were 'so inconvenient or in so ruinous a state as our own'. He called them 'wretched abortions'.[2] Many were rented: 'the government', commented *The Times*, 'lives in lodgings'.[3] The worst was reputed to be the Foreign Office, an old house on Downing Street that was far too small for its purpose, and actually physically dangerous. If the government held any kind of reception there attended by more than a few foreign dignitaries, the floors had to be propped up from underneath with beams. The favourite story, repeated many times, was of how Lord Malmesbury had once narrowly escaped injury or even death when a ceiling fell in on the desk he had been sitting at just a moment previously.[4] This, as *The Times* pointed out, held the whole nation up to 'ridicule'[5] – especially when compared with the situation in Paris, which, as we shall see, it often was. The problem with the War

Office – the second department prioritized originally – was slightly different. This was that its various sub-departments were scattered all over London, making coordination difficult.[6] That could be serious in times of war. (Maybe it helps explain the British Army's notorious shortcomings during the Crimean conflict.)

The first official government report recommending a substantial rebuilding came in 1839, followed by another in 1854.[7] Architects, anticipating a great commission, started sharpening their pencils. As early as about 1844 Thomas Wyatt produced a design which would have used Inigo Jones's Banqueting Hall as its basis, extending it on one side and adding two towers.[8] The Banqueting Hall is of course only a small part of Jones's original scheme for a 'Palace of Whitehall', whose plans were apparently still extant. A number of people in the 1850s, including the great civil service reformer Sir Charles Trevelyan, thought they might be placed at the disposal of likely architects of any new building.[9] This seems so superficially attractive an idea as to make one wonder why it was not taken up more seriously. Much later Gilbert Scott complained that while his Government Offices were under way 'I had always thrown in my teeth . . . the magnificence of Inigo Jones's building'; but by then of course it was too late.[10] Following the 1854 report the government's official architect, James Pennethorne, was asked to draw up plans and elevations for a new building, with costs;[11] and one John Tarring, whom the *Saturday Review* described as 'a minor architect of obscure fame', also offered a design, apparently on his own initiative.[12] All these were in the Classical style; which may explain the *Saturday Review*'s put-down of Tarring: the *Review* was uncompromisingly pro-Gothic. (But we can see from this how the *tone* of the 'Battle' was already developing.) Both also followed the government line that if these new offices were to be replaced, they should also be brought together in a single block, near to the Houses of Parliament, for convenience. That would have the added advantage of removing many unsightly – typically London, poor, higgledy-piggledy – buildings from the area.[13] It was at this point that the idea of using the project to beautify the capital, make it at least comparable with some of the great cities of the Continent, also took hold – to Palmerston's alarm. ('I see in the Times today a flourishing account of an advertisement by Benjⁿ Hall to all Europe for Plans of new Buildings to cover half of Westminster. When was he authorized to invite competition for such plans . . .?')[14] If it was to be on anything like that scale, of course, the question of 'style' was all the more important.

First, however, ministers and bureaucrats had to get their political masters to agree to any rebuilding at all. To do that they had to pass the obstacle of the 'Radicals' in parliament, the low-tax party, who objected in particular to any government buildings that could be used for *entertainment*, as of course Foreign Offices in particular often are. Why should the taxpayer be expected to provide 'great rooms' where ministers could 'gossip and flirt', as the critics put it; did they not all have great houses of their own they could use for that?[15] (It was left to *The Times* to point out the very undemocratic implications of this: certainly up till then the post of foreign secretary had been virtually restricted to men who could afford large London houses, but did the Radicals want it to stay like that for good?)[16] There was also a 'wartime' consideration. During the period of this debate Britain fought two major wars, in the Crimea (1853–6) and India (1857–8), which were followed by a huge invasion scare, centring on Napoleon III's France. (Napoleon objected to Britain's giving refuge to terrorists, one of whom had just thrown a bomb at him.)[17] Was this the best moment to be squandering great sums on 'ornamental architecture', when they might be needed to repair the country's defences? Even Lord Palmerston argued this at one point.[18] At length, however, the Commons granted a miserly amount (£90,000) for the purchase of some of the *land* necessary, and the government could go ahead.[19]

It might have gone ahead with Pennethorne's design. He was after all the government's official architect, and clearly expected the contract to come his way. He was also a pretty good architect, judging by the few designs of his that actually materialized, and the many more that were thwarted.[20] He suffered, however, from several disadvantages. By the 1850s his position – formally 'Architect for Metropolitan Improvements' at the Office of Works – had been progressively weakened; partly due to the mid-nineteenth century's dislike of 'jobbery', which his post was supposed to represent.[21] This may also have damaged his professional reputation, which appears to have been unfairly low at this time; even among Classicists, but especially at the hands of the thrusting new Gothicists, who regarded him as the very symbol of the fusty old conservatism in architecture they so much deplored.[22] This was despite the fact that he did occasionally design in Gothic; but then 'true' Goths always disapproved of those who only did it as a sideline, as we shall see.[23] He may also not have had the talent for self-advertisement that was coming to be so important in this new, pushy age. As a result, he cuts one of the sorriest of the figures in the drama that was about to unfold. In May 1856 Pennethorne wrote to the Office of Works to ask what had become of the designs and elevations for the new Public Offices he had submitted many months before, and had been working on – under instructions from a previous commissioner – for at least three years.[24] It was only then he learned that the job had been taken away from him. Sir Benjamin Hall, the current commissioner, who had a particularly low opinion of Pennethorne,[25] had decided that the contract was to be put out to open tender, by public competition. Competitions, of course, were part of the new spirit of this capitalist age. Hall was ideologically in favour of them.[26] Architects were divided – their trade press was constantly debating the principle – but with a strong section favouring them, or at least preferring them to the old way of government patronage.[27] 'Competition is the great struggle for life', proclaimed the *Building News* in March 1860. Spurn it, and architects 'will lose their manly tone and vigour, their self-reliance and enterprise, and fall into a condition as helpless as that of the unprotected female.' (We shall be discussing the 'gender' aspects of this whole affair later.)[28] In August 1855 the *Builder* came out in favour of one for the Government Offices project specifically.[29] That was the course recommended by a report submitted to the House of Commons in

July 1856, and accepted by the government, with the terms of the competition announced in October.[30] Of course Pennethorne could have entered for that if he had wanted, but he chose not to.[31]

Perhaps it was just as well. In fact the Government Offices competition was thoroughly mismanaged. For a start, its terms were odd.[32] It was divided into three parts: one for a 'block plan' for the whole, within certain but not rigid limits (some took this as a licence to redesign almost the whole of west London; one even proposed draining the Thames and turning its bed into a flower garden);[33] a second for Foreign Office elevations; and a third for the War Office. Later on the judges introduced a new rule of their own, which was that no one entrant, even if he had competed in more than one category, could win more than one prize, or 'premium'.[34] (These ranged from £500 to £100.) This meant that the three main prizewinners might – indeed, were almost bound to – produce designs that were mutually incompatible: buildings that would clash with one another, and would not fit on the premiated ground plan. Luckily the government also made it clear that they would not necessarily be committed by the results of the competition, and certainly were not bound to give the contract to the competitors who came first in each class.[35] One of the reasons for this was that the entries were all supposed to be anonymous (though for many this was a fiction), and they did not want to have to engage an architect who, when they learned his name,[36] turned out to be 'of poor character'.[37] That was useful later in getting them off the hook when the overall winner of the Foreign Office competition turned out to be a duffer. Apart from this, the competition was open to architects of all nations, and foreigners, in fact, won two of the 15 prizes awarded.[38] (This was not inadvertent. The foreign entries were not difficult to spot; as well as the mansard roofs, most of them had street names written in French.)[39] Some in the profession protested against this, xenophobically, though for others it was a matter of national pride.[40] Another, better cause for professional resentment was the short time span allotted for the preparation of designs: about six months, or a few days more in the case of those from abroad.[41] (One enterprising British architect who couldn't quite make the domestic deadline went over to Paris to post his entry from there.)[42] Altogether there were 218 entries submitted, though some of them were multiple – alternative Gothic and Classical elevations for the same ground plan, for example[43] – and, at the other extreme, a few seem to have been mere rough sketches. There was no weeding out of no-hopers.

This caused difficulties when the entries were all put on public display in Westminster Hall in the summer of 1857. Superficially that was a success. Following private viewings for Prince Albert and then MPs – we do not know what Albert thought of it all, unfortunately[44] – the public flocked in (free),[45] and seems to have been generally enchanted by the beautifully drawn 'towers, domes, pinnacles, far-reaching corridors, Gothic arches, terraces, statues, with and without trumpets, fountains, triumphal arches' *etcetera* on display.[46] Newspapers were impressed by the depth and breadth of national architectural talent they appeared to reveal, quite unexpectedly.[47] But they could not really tell. Because there were so many drawings – over 2,000 in all – many were placed badly on the boards that were erected for them along the length of the Hall: too high for people to be able to examine properly, or in dimly lit corners, or next to other entries that put them at a disadvantage.[48] Although fairly strict regulations had been devised in order to facilitate comparability – all the drawings were to be to the same scale, for example – the treatment of the designs differed widely, with some drawn more delicately than others, and less shaded – shading was supposedly forbidden, but 'stippling' was a grey area[49] – which meant that their effect could be overpowered by more boldly drawn neighbours, or by the multiple entries: such as George Gilbert Scott's, who provided more than 30 views of his Foreign Office design alone.[50] There was no official catalogue of the exhibition, though one or two private ones appeared later.[51] Visitors were clearly confused. Some newspapers tried to make sense of it all, but failed: giving up after the first dozen or so exhibits, missing the best ones and frequently getting the ones they did feature – style, and so on – completely wrong.[52] Two honourable exceptions were the professional journals, which managed over several weeks to cover nearly all the entries, but even they confessed that they experienced great difficulties.[53]

This, however, was nothing by comparison with the problems that emerged when the judges were appointed – after the deadline for entries, so that competitors couldn't tailor their designs to their supposed preferences[54] – and the judging took place. The choice of judges was extraordinary. There were seven originally. Four were Scots.[55] They were chaired by the (Scottish) Duke of Buccleuch, chosen mainly, it seems, because he was a duke. Noblemen still had the reputation in Britain of being fair and honourable, which was supposed to be half the battle.[56] They were also of course greatly socially superior to architects.[57] Knowledge of or even more than a smattering of interest in architecture seems to have counted for less.[58] The duke's only connection with the subject was that he possessed a mansion in London – Montagu House – which he was presently rebuilding, in the French 'Second Empire' style. Unfortunately that same house gave him an obvious conflict of interest, standing as it did on or very near the proposed site of the new Government Offices.[59] After the panel's first meeting, Buccleuch resigned from it – though he gave another reason. A second aristocratic member of the panel, Lord Eversley, jumped ship a little later.[60] That left just one upper-class and four middle-class members: Earl Stanhope, president of the Royal Society of Architects; David Roberts, the water-colourist; Isambard Kingdom Brunel, the engineer; William Stirling, MP, the art 'connoisseur'; and William Burn.[61] Burn, another Scot, was at least a professional architect; unfortunately he was also Buccleuch's architect, the rebuilder of Montagu House, so could be said to have the same conflict of interest as the duke, and the same stylistic preference. A little way into their proceedings the committee co-opted a couple more architects, Samuel Angell and George Pownall, to advise them, but without voting rights. According to the *Athenaeum* these were necessary in order to be able to discriminate between really good designs, and 'architectural dreams and fairy-lands on drawing paper', which the 'amateurs' clearly could not.[62] But they were very obscure men (neither has found his way into any modern dictionary of architects),[63] leading the *Saturday Review* to speculate that their appointment may have been a 'practical joke'.[64] In the event, there is little sign that the amateurs took much notice of them.

One reason for this odd choice of jurors was an anxiety to be seen to stand outside the 'Battle' that was already raging then between the Classical and Gothic styles, as we shall see.[65] Scott had just begun to crusade publicly for the application of Gothic to secular as well as to ecclesiastical buildings,[66] which some contemporaries thought explained the bitterness that entered the debate around then. Before, there had been an uneasy truce; the Classicists had conceded the ecclesiastical ground to the Goths – they couldn't in fact do much else; virtually no one wanted Italianate churches any more – so long as they could still have public buildings, offices, street architecture, great houses and the like, to keep them in employment. This new front that Scott was opening up seemed to threaten their very living. (That was one, perhaps rather ungenerous, explanation.)[67] In 1855–6 there was a widely publicized row at the premises of the RIBA when William Tite, a moderately distinguished mainly Classical architect who was also an MP,[68] openly attacked what he called the current Gothic 'mania', and Scott snapped back, just as intemperately.[69] In this atmosphere it seemed politic to avoid judges who might be committed on one side or the other. Unfortunately that seemed to rule out anyone with any expertise in architecture then. (There were in fact some neutral experts, but the government may not have known of them.)[70] That left them with 'honourable' jurors, but in the main ignorant and impressionable ones.

They seem to have worked conscientiously. They were given a fortnight to peruse the designs after the public viewings finished. Burn and Brunel apparently started work at 6 a.m. each day.[71] The panel's report, issued on 26 June, was claimed to be unanimous. It also gushed about the general standard of the entries.[72] Seven prizes were handed out for the Foreign Office (numbered in order of merit); five for the War Office; and three for the block plans.[73] Out of the 12 prizes for elevations, four (or five, if you count Tudor) were awarded to Gothic designs, which was a creditable result in view of the fact that only around 20 out of the 163 *entries* (excluding the block plans) were Gothic.[74] (Why? was a question often asked. 'Where were the Goths?' We shall return to this later.)[75] That seemed to show that the panel had, indeed, been careful to maintain a balance between the two schools; indeed, it may indicate that this was their primary concern. It could also reflect the superior draughtsmanship of the Goths; Scott's in particular, with his 30-odd drawings, some of them very large, and 'marvellously executed' in 'every portion', according to the unofficial *Handbook Guide*.[76] Gothic, being a 'picturesque' style, was probably more suited to this. For critics, of course, this merely confirmed the danger of 'telling sketches, the curse of architecture';[77] which had been one of their chief objections to the competition system for years.[78] Of the 'Classical' winners, only one was *strictly* Classical: that is, Roman;[79] the others being mostly French 'Second Empire', or very close.[80]

Both the 'first' premiums, for the Foreign Office and the War Office, went to Classical designs: one French, the other more Italian Renaissance. The problem there, however, was that the winner in the Foreign Office category was an appallingly bad design, by a young architect whose best effort before then had been a plan for 'an Idiot Asylum at Reigate', which on the surface did not seem a very happy precedent for a Foreign Office – and that not even on his own behalf, but as an assistant in a previous firm; but really the jurors should have been able to tell from the drawings how hopeless he was.[81] In the upshot it was revealed that the experts *did*; for all their initial talk of 'unanimity', it is clear that the panel was seriously divided over this design at the very least, with Burn and the two expert assessors placing it only sixth (which itself seems generous).[82] Thereafter Coe and Hofland's design was quietly dropped,[83] being scarcely mentioned in the bickering which, as we shall see, went on about which of the premiated designs were *really* the best. Its chief significance probably lies in what it tells us about the taste and judgement of the group of men who were supposed to be adjudicating on this. 'A triumph of mediocrity', is how one modern architectural historian describes the result.[84]

This must be one of the worst-run public competitions in British building history. One of its most unfortunate results was that it gave no clear lead about who should build the new Government Offices, or in what style; unlike, for example, the Palace of Westminster competition 20 years earlier, where the style had been specified at the outset, and a clear winner had emerged.[85] So far as the 1857 Goths were concerned, though they had won neither of the main first prizes, it left them all to play for still. Their main champion, Gilbert Scott, had come only third in the Foreign Office class – or second if you disregarded Coe and Hofland; but it was later revealed that he would also have come second in the War Office competition if that arbitrary rule had not been invented, disallowing one contestant to be awarded two premiums.[86] Neither of the other winners in either class had come as high in the other. In Scott's eyes that gave him the overall lead. (He pushed his own cause shamelessly, incidentally, which wasn't considered quite cricket.)[87] He was also acknowledged to be the top Gothicist in both categories. With the whole competition so discredited, this was bound to lead to further confusion – and did.

For the moment, however, there was a brief hiatus, caused by another extraneous event – the Indian Mutiny, which broke out in May, and was cited by those who were lukewarm about the scheme anyway as another reason why it should be at least shelved.[88] At the same time it is clear that many MPs and even ministers had been rather taken aback by the grandiose character of so many of the exhibited designs, which they did not want at all. The *Building News* suggested competitors had been misled by the popular designation of the project as a 'Palace' ('of

Administration').[89] Lord John Russell and William Gladstone, for example, both thought the winning designs were overdone.[90] *The Times* was still in favour, but also turned off by all the ornamentation; what people really wanted, it opined, was 'a halfway house between a Gothic cathedral and a workhouse'.[91] In these circumstances further Commons bills to buy more of the necessary land stalled,[92] and the matter reached what Lord John Manners called 'a complete dead lock'.[93] Many assumed the whole scheme was sunk. At around this time Sir Charles Barry (the architect of the Palace of Westminster) tried to break the deadlock with a new design, apparently unsolicited, which would have covered the whole site – and more – with a magnificent domed Renaissance palace. It is unclear what became of this. (From the surviving drawings, it seems a pity that it was not considered.)[94] A rumour then began circulating that the government had turned to Pennethorne again, who had always promised to do it more *cheaply* than other architects; this scandalized the RIBA, who sent a strong protest in to the government, against the very idea that they might give the contract to someone who had not even competed for it.[95] 'We know of nothing more grievous and scandalous in the history of art', raged the *Building News*; which on another occasion accused the government of 'returning to its vomit'.[96] (Pennethorne may not have appreciated being classed as 'vomit'.) Scott also protested on his own account.[97] In fact the rumour was true;[98] but after this expression of outrage the government clearly could not persevere with poor Pennethorne.

For Gothicists the whole affair was ominous nonetheless. They had always felt that the cards had been stacked against them in the competition; that whatever the government assured them about its not taking sides in the Battle of the Styles, it was fundamentally prejudiced against them, and determined that a Gothic design would not win. This was one of the answers that Gothicists gave to the question: where were the Goths? – they were there, in the competition, they claimed, but *disguised* as Classicists because of these persistent rumours that they had no chance of winning in their true clothes. This suspicion was clearly on Scott's mind; in the pamphlet he produced to accompany his entry he claimed to know of many Gothic architects who had either abstained or produced Classical designs for this reason;[99] among whom, according to evidence given later – not necessarily reliably – were the first two prizewinners in the Foreign Office category.[100] The Pennethorne episode seemed to give substance to these suspicions. Combined with Palmerston's conduct later it proved in fact that while he was prime minister (as he was in 1857) Gothic really did not stand a chance.

Its best chance came a little later; and for another of those extraneous political reasons that kept intervening in this affair: the fall of Palmerston's Whig government over the 'Conspiracy to Murder bill' in February 1858, and its replacement (*sans* election) by a Tory one. (The Conspiracy to Murder bill came in the wake of the Orsini *attentat* against Louis Napoleon; it was meant to make it easier to prosecute refugees who plotted this kind of thing in Britain, but was widely construed as 'truckling' to the tyrant Napoleon.) The significance of that was that it brought Lord John Manners back to head the Board of Works, which was responsible for public building, and Manners was a dedicated Gothicist. (He even lived in a Gothic, or Gothick, castle.)[101] By this time the Indian Mutiny was just about blowing itself out, and although there were still frequent alarums of other wars – France, for example, was doing some sabre-rattling over the Conspiracy to Murder bill débâcle – it looked as though they might soon be able to afford some new Government Offices once again. Indeed, the potential cost actually fell substantially when the War Office was dropped from the plan, and replaced by the new India Office that was thought to be needed when the British government took direct control of the subcontinent, in September 1858. This was because the India Office would be entirely financed not by the British taxpayer, but by the poor Indians; which is why, incidentally, there were no significant debates in the British House of Commons over that. The secretary of state for India said he was happy to go along with the government's choice for the neighbouring Foreign Office, so long as his own departmental architect, Matthew Wyatt, was allowed some say. Manners therefore went ahead, and appointed yet another committee to enquire into the 'Public Offices' question, which reported that (a) so far as the two 'styles' were concerned there was little difference between them in practical terms – cost, light, ventilation, etcetera; and (b) he could appoint anyone from among the original competition winners he liked.[102] So he did, and gave the job to Scott;[103] who shortly afterwards reached an agreement with Wyatt over the India Office. (In a nutshell: Scott was to be responsible for the outside, in the interests of harmony with the Foreign Office; Wyatt was to design the interiors.)[104] The Goths were cock-a-hoop. The influential *Ecclesiologist* journal, which was not on the best of terms with Scott at this time – but he was after all One of Them – saw it as a 'great success' for 'the good cause' (of Gothic generally).[105] On the news of his appointment William Burges, just then at the start of his own brilliant Gothic career, wrote to congratulate Scott; but also predicted – not particularly presciently, for it was pretty obvious – that 'the pagans will be very savage indeed'.[106]

The most savage was Palmerston, who chose this moment to enter the lists personally against the Goths, with the first of his notorious onslaughts on their style in the House of Commons in February 1859.[107] The timing was such that many of his critics assumed he was just party-politicking – getting back, after his recent defeat, at his Tory foes. One commentator suggested that if Manners had come out in support of 'Tite and the Greeks', Palmerston would have taken the side of 'Scott and the Goths'.[108] That seems unlikely. Palmerston's gut distaste for Gothic appears real. He was also well briefed, in particular by Thomas Donaldson, the ultra-conservative professor of architecture at University College, London, and also the consulting architect for Palmerston's own Palladian villa at Broadlands in Hampshire, who plied him with some good arguments against Gothic (that it was the style of an age, not of a country, and in any case was not particularly 'English' in the form chosen by Scott);[109] which, however, were not the ones Palmerston chose to use. Those were a good deal shallower. One of his recurrent ones had to do with windows, which he claimed were inevitably smaller in Gothic buildings than Classical,[110] which he only had to enter almost any large late Gothic church to see was nonsense, and which Scott went to great pains to rebut by going around measuring up windows in a dozen leading Classical and a dozen leading neo-Gothic buildings in London, thus proving his point to his own satisfaction, to the 1858 select committee's,[111] and eventually – albeit reluctantly – to Palmerston's.[112] Palmerston's reluctance was obviously because he wanted to portray Gothic as dim and unen*light*ened. For the same reason he harped on about its Roman Catholic associations; characterizing it, for example, as a 'Jesuit' style, in the teeth of the plain facts that the Jesuits, first, were not around when Gothic was king, and, second, nearly always themselves built in 'Italian'.[113] His arguments against the 'national' claims of Gothic – whatever else might have been said against them – were similarly ludicrous: they had Roman remains all over England, he said; but 'I never heard of the Goths, the Vandals or the Saracens doing much in this country.'[114]

On the other hand some of his points may have struck home more seriously. The Goths were on very weak ground when they tried to rationalize Manners's preference for Scott over any of the original competitors who had been placed above him: the 'two second places make a first' argument. Palmerston delighted the Commons with an analogy for that which its sporting members will have appreciated: what if you decided the winner of a horse race on that principle?[115] To which it was perhaps a fair but not a particularly effective reply to ask him back: what if you tried to give the palm to a horse (meaning Pennethorne) that had not run in the race at all?[116] Palmerston's other ace card was the perceived deficiencies of the Chamber they were discussing these matters in. This, thought the pro-Gothic Lord Elcho, was 'at the bottom of the whole thing'; 'the fact that the building in which parliament assembled was of a Gothic character,' so giving people 'the idea that if they were to have a Gothic building, they would have simply a repetition of the Houses of Parliament.'[117] One very current problem was the building's ventilation, which simply did not work. In the summer all the Commons windows had to be closed to exclude the stink of ordure from the Thames. By all accounts the resultant heat was insufferable. Many MPs blamed this on the building's style. (It may be relevant in this regard that most of the key debates on this issue took place in midsummer.)[118] The Goths had their answers to this, the main one being that the Palace of Westminster was *poor* Gothic, very different from what was now proposed; but the distinctions between different 'Gothic' styles may have been too fine for many of their compatriots to appreciate.[119] All those silly arguments of Palmerston's may also have been effective in simply distracting his enemies, who found they had to spend their powder shooting in all directions in order to bring them down – and then again, when they thought they had winged them. They also amused the House.[120] He was no fool, was Palmerston, but he knew how effective foolish arguments could be.[121]

While all this was going on Scott prepared new drawings, in response to changes in the specifications (there was now to be no built-in residence for the foreign secretary, for example), which – together with a pasteboard model, a new departure – were exhibited in the House of Commons Library in July. Most commentators thought these were an improvement on his competition designs.[122] They were still, however, Gothic, and consequently anathema to Palmerston, who, very unfortunately for Scott, had returned to power in June. (That was after an election, the first one ever won by the 'Liberal Party', a new creation, or rather combination of factions.) Palmerston could now get his way, therefore, if he could charm the Commons into scuppering the Gothic plan; but he could not sack Scott, though he would have liked to, because the government was contractually obliged to him. His tactic, therefore – this is what it looks like – was to make demands that would force him (Scott) to resign. At the end of July Palmerston wrote to Scott insisting that he start over again with an 'Italian or Classical' design. He was sure, he told Scott, that 'an architect of his ability' would be able to cope, especially as the Classic style was so much 'easier.' If he had any problems, he suggested that Henry Garling – the War Office competition winner, and more practised in Classical – be drafted in to help.[123] When this got out it infuriated the profession in particular, which rallied strongly behind Scott; earlier it had been more neutral, but now its professional integrity was being challenged.[124] At the end of July a delegation of 'mediaeval' (that is, pro-Gothic) MPs met Palmerston to try to turn him; unfortunately it contained a spoiler, Edward Ellice, MP, who criticized the Scott design, but it is unlikely that the prime minister would have been persuaded in any case. According to one report he seemed 'unusually jovial and frisky' – relishing the battle, perhaps.[125] He had never seen in his life 'a more frightful structure' than Scott's latest design, he told the delegation (and the Commons a little later), and was pledged to resist the Gothic style to the last drop of his blood.[126] The ball was now in Scott's court.

Palmerston must have expected him to drop out, enabling a more compliant Classicist to be appointed. Scott after all was more than an architect who happened to build in Gothic; he was a zealot for the style. The *Explanatory Remarks* that he issued in conjunction with his competition entry had insisted that he was more interested in the triumph of the Gothic cause than in his own success, which was why he had not followed the example of so many of his fellows, and donned Classic garb in order to win.[127] Could there be any doubt about the implication, in this situation, of that? Most other Gothicists expected him to take the principled course of action, too. In contradistinction to Palmerston, they did not think that a 'good' architect could turn his talents to any style; that was a very dilettante way of regarding their art. Supporters suggested it was 'like going to a French master to be taught German'; or asking Landseer to paint a picture of the Holy Family; or suggesting that Palmerston switch to being prime minister of Russia.[128] (Or, suggested one pamphleteer, expecting to get a good Gothic building from a Classical architect. That was a clear reference, yet again, to the much-maligned Palace of Westminster, whose deficiencies were now widely believed to stem from the fact that it had been designed by a Classicist.)[129] *Building News* confidently asserted that *of course* Scott would not find it 'compatible with his professional standing' to relinquish Gothic; if he did, said the paper, 'public opinion . . . would not allow it'.[130] *The Times* – perhaps unexpectedly – advised Scott to 'take the commission in his own style, or not at all.'[131] Even Gladstone, trying to be helpful, wrote to Scott that he was 'quite certain' he would not hazard his 'reputation . . . for any particular employment'.[132] Unless Palmerston blinked, therefore, it looked as though Scott was destined to become a Gothic hero: bloodied, and in all likelihood defeated, but still unbowed.

To dissuade Palmerston from blinking – as if that were needed – a deputation of pro-Classicists waited on him a couple of weeks after the 'mediaeval' one, led by the architect–MP who had by now become Palmerston's chief lieutenant in his battle against the Goths, William Tite. (In a way Tite seems an odd choice for this role, having designed extensively in Gothic himself; but he took greatly against *this* Gothic design for this building, for which he thought 'the Italian moderately applied' would work better.)[133] Obviously the Classicists came away happier than the Gothic party had.[134] The event, however, marked a low point in relations between the two schools, when the Gothicists, and the professional press, chose to regard the Classical deputation as somehow *dishonourable*: 'the greatest scandal and disgrace ever inflicted on the profession', as *Building News* put it; an act of 'outrageous indecency', 'ungenerous and unmanly', motivated by 'mean envy and low jealousy', and with – the paper darkly hinted – a 'scandal' lying at its root.[135] (This may refer back to an earlier episode in Tite's career, when he was thought to have secured his most famous commission, for the Royal Exchange in London, by underhand means.)[136] The reason for this feeling in this case was that two of the unsuccessful 1857 competitors, Garling and the partnership of Banks and Barry, were represented among the deputation; which was widely regarded, therefore, as an attempt by the 'losers' to put a fellow architect out of work. Indeed, Tite virtually admitted this, in an article he published in one of the professional journals shortly afterwards, arguing that Banks and Barry should still be given the job.[137] A few months later Tite was put up for membership of the Athenaeum, but blackballed by a large majority. We cannot be certain that it was over this matter, but it seems likely.[138] To be blackballed by a London club, of course, you really had to be a cad.

In the meantime, Scott struggled. He clearly still wanted the commission desperately. In an effort to square it with what were generally understood to be his 'principles', he offered to make any changes in his design that were asked for, so long, presumably, as it remained 'Gothic' in spirit. He sought advice from Gladstone – now chancellor of the exchequer – who assured him of his support as the 'regularly appointed architect', but also confirmed Palmerston's view that this did not mean the government had to accept any design he (Scott) chose.[139] All this time, incidentally, Palmerston was reputed to be secretly negotiating with Garling, to take Scott's place when his position became untenable.[140] Several papers, indeed, were quite convinced that in the end the whole matter would be 'snugly arranged *sub rosa*', by the 'red-tapists'.[141] But it was not. Palmerston raised the heat on Scott by being rude: keeping him waiting interminably in a lobby, for example, for an appointment – Scott claimed he could hear him eating his lunch.[142] Scott did not take the hint, however, but instead backtracked – a little way. He submitted a new design (his third), not in strict 'Classic', but in a 'Byzantine' round-arched style. It was the nearest he could find, he claimed, to his Gothic one in terms of letting in *light*.[143] (The Classicists' obstinate insistence that their style was better for this still rankled.) Palmerston, however, liked this no better: 'neither one thing nor t'other', he called it; 'a regular mongrel affair.'[144] He submitted it to an informal committee of three experts, C. R. Cockerell, William Burn and James Fergusson – none of them Gothicists – expecting them to advise against it; in fact all they did was suggest a couple of small changes – less grouping of the windows, for example; now the complaint was that there was too *much* light[145] – which Scott immediately implemented; but Palmerston rejected it nonetheless.[146] Again Scott offered to compromise; all he asked for, he said, was *some* 'freedom' to design as he thought best – how unfortunate it would be, he suggested, if 'the public offices of a free country' were 'characterised by want of freedom in their character'.[147] If Scott's other arguments had made no impression, however, this appeal to Palmerston's radical patriotism – we shall be examining its meaning later – was not likely to; and he came to accept, after taking advice, the more feudal position that patrons – in this case Palmerston – did have the right to dictate a building's style.[148] So Scott gave in, and started working on a genuinely 'Italian' scheme, which he completed in the spring of 1861, and was exhibited in the Tea Room of the House of Commons early in July.[149] (Its windows, incidentally, let in no more light than his Gothic design would have done. H. S. Goodhart-Rendel suggests that he made them deliberately small, to make his point about this.)[150] It was this design which, after another bravura comic performance by Palmerston, was finally passed by the House of Commons on 8 July, another scorching day (76.3°F, with the Thames a pretty warm 66°F);[151] bringing the whole affair – this particular 'Battle' in the more general War of the Styles – to an end. The present Whitehall Offices mainly conform to it.[152]

Palmerston recorded in his diary that evening that it was a 'good debate'.[153] But its conclusion was almost the least satisfactory imaginable. The debate itself must have galled Scott, with most of the few compliments on his design coming from his enemies, and most of the brickbats from his friends. In fact it had very few champions: which, as Lord Elcho put it, was a kind of achievement: to have united both of the warring camps against it.[154] To the Gothicists it seemed 'dull', 'a mean design', 'monotonous'; none of this, his friends hastened to add, was Scott's fault – he was a 'great' architect, capable of much better things – but his style had been 'cramped'.[155] Lord Elcho (who had headed the 'mediaeval' deputation the year before) even claimed that it was Palmerston who was directly responsible for the design, and was now passing it off as Scott's.[156] For Classicists like Tite, on the other hand, it proved what they had always said: that a style was simply a style, and a good architect could turn his hand to any.[157] Palmerston's own praise was somewhat grudging: it was not a great building, he thought, but it would *do*.[158] The leading Classicist C. R. Cockerell sent Scott a ringing endorsement – 'Allow me to congratulate you, and that most heartily . . . in this glorious approachment [*sic*] to the new Foreign Office'; but it is not clear that this referred to the final version of his design.[159] Scott's own view can be inferred from the pamphlet he produced in 1860 (to accompany his 'Byzantine' scheme) whose argument throughout is to reiterate his commitment to Gothic, and present his later designs as reluctantly drawn out of him, and very second-best.[160] It is difficult to find any positive *enthusiasm* for them on Scott's part.[161] In 1864 he made a large-scale (and very beautiful) drawing of yet another Gothic design for the Foreign Office, with no hope now of its being built, of course, to exhibit at the Royal Academy as a 'silent protest against what was going on'.[162] It has claims to be the best of his Gothic versions, and the one most consistent with the *genius loci*. But it was too late for practical purposes. Later he used another commission, for the great Midland Railway Hotel at St Pancras, in order to show explicitly what he could have done in Whitehall if he had been given his head. It is not true (as is sometimes claimed) that this is simply his original Gothic design for the Government Offices transplanted; but it does bear some resemblances, and was intended to prove his point, about the suitability of Gothic for large secular purposes.[163] This was the outcome, then, of the pig's ear that the government – or rather, three governments – had made of this whole process: a building that satisfied neither it nor its architect.

There was also, of course, the question of Scott's 'treachery' – if that is not too hard a word for it. It was certainly seen in this light by some of his Gothicist colleagues. There can be no doubt at all about the *reason* for it. Scott wanted the money. In a memoir of this affair he wrote for his progeny, most of which was published posthumously in 1879 as his *Personal and Professional Recollections*, but not this passage, he tried to make it appear less purely mercenary.

> The work had been mine – and being mine belonged equally to my wife and family – and to give up what represented in the end about five and twenty thousand pounds which was placed by providence in my hands as a trustee for my family, seemed to me to be an immoral act.[164]

But he also made it clear that he remained 'perturbed' by the decision thereafter,[165] and, indeed, the number of times he felt he needed to return to it in his autobiography makes this very obvious.[166]

Better arguments could be made in support of him. He always insisted that he was not a fanatical or an ideological Goth, like, for example, the Ecclesiologists (of whom more later). His main ambition was to help in the development of a truly modern, English architecture, which theoretically might be done on the basis of any past style, but would simply be easier if it started off from something that was 'native'.[167] In his *Remarks on Secular and Domestic Architecture* (1857), intended to prepare the way for his Gothic bid for the Government Offices, he had shown himself really quite flexible in being prepared to draw from other traditions, including Italian quattrocento, for major secular buildings; including horizontal cornices, 'uniform ranges of arched windows', round-arched or even flat-topped windows if people preferred them, and doing away with gables.[168] Some of his friends argued that if the job had gone to a genuine Classicist it might have turned out even worse – Palladian, for example. (Palladian was Palmerston's absolute favourite style.)[169] Charles Eastlake pointed out, unanswerably, that 'from a practical point of view', resigning would have been 'Quixotic. Mr Scott would have been reckoned a hero, but we should not on that account have secured a Mediaeval Foreign Office.'[170] Looking at it in an entirely different way, *The Times* suggested that Scott's involvement might 'bring down the Palladian style itself upon the heads of his persecutors' – presumably (it is difficult to know how else to interpret this) because the resulting building would be so bad, or inconvenient.[171] Most on the Gothic wing, however, regretted Scott's decision. The *Ecclesiologist* thought he had been 'badly advised', and that he could have made things tricky for Palmerston if he had 'firmly declined'. One thing it was sure about: it would do Scott's *reputation* no favours at all.[172] 'As matters now stand,' wrote a Belfast paper even before his final capitulation – when he was simply bending – 'a considerable portion of the architectural body denounce the pliability of Mr Scott's genius as unprofessional and anything but proper'.[173] That was a widespread view,[174] and felt keenly by Scott himself in later years.

There may be one further excuse that could be made for his apostasy: which is that it did not mark a full conversion. It was George L. Hersey who first remarked on what he saw (others might not) as the essential 'Classicness' – 'its rhythm, its regularity, its cumulative repetition' – of Scott's first design, despite its Gothic details; by the side of which his accepted version appears – to Hersey – *more* Gothic: less 'regular', for example. 'It is as if,' Hersey goes on, 'to complete his insolent jest, Scott were giving Palmerston High Victorian Gothic in Renaissance dress'.[175] But that would appear to be a *very* subtle disguise, not to be penetrated until more than a century later; and there is, of course, no evidence that Scott meant it this way.

So the rout of the Goths was complete, in this battle at least, and to outward appearances; and largely due to the obstinacy of one man and the weakness and avarice of another. 'Italianate' it was. Building began in 1862; the India Office – the most splendid of the Offices internally, thanks to the involuntary generosity of the Indians – was ready to move into in 1867;[176] the Foreign Office in 1868; and new Home and Colonial Offices, completing the scheme, in 1874. There were complaints along the way, as there were bound to be: of poor plumbing, for example; smoking fires; defective lifts (a man was killed trying to repair one on 5 December 1868), an inconvenient 'corkscrew' staircase, and the difficulty of importing 'faggots', which may come as a particular surprise;[177] for which Scott was taken to task, perhaps unfairly, by a committee in 1876.[178] More substantially, many of the men who worked in the new government building obviously did not appreciate its magnificence: 'designed' as it had been, according to a report of 1869, 'upon a plan more of a palatial, than of an official character'.[179] Edmund Hammond, possibly the longest denizen of the two successive Foreign Offices (ultimately as foreign under-secretary), wrote to Scott shortly before moving in that 'I should have preferred less gilding and colour, but as the matter is settled . . . I will say nothing more.'[180] In the 1960s a plan to demolish the whole complex, and replace it with a 'modern' building, came to nothing, mainly because of financial constraints.[181] So Whitehall remains 'Classical', if only just.

It could easily have gone the other way. A less obstinate prime minister; a more principled architect; a different debating chamber; another time of year; less shit in the river; some better jokes on the Gothic side — and the Goths might have won. As it was, the result was an unsatisfactory compromise from everyone's point of view: a building that virtually no one at the time had wanted — not even the architect himself — or ever grew to love afterwards. Its 'style' was the result of a series of pure and in some cases quite ludicrous accidents. Nothing more than this, therefore, can be read into it. To repeat: the Foreign and other Offices in Whitehall look as they do not because they reflect certain dominant social and cultural discourses of the time they were built, but for almost entirely trivial reasons. (This sometimes happens, cultural historians should note, with cultural artefacts.) This cannot be said, however, of the 'Battle' that preceded the decision to build them in the 'Italian' style; which reflected the society of the day much more accurately, and in so many ways, though in the end it had little effect on the outcome. This therefore will be the main concern of this book, *rather than* the building; after a chapter that will endeavour to set it in its broader historical and cultural context.

2

A Hybrid Society

The 'Battle' over the building of the Government Offices took place at an interesting time in British history: a period of important developments, social, political, economic and cultural (as, to be sure, are most periods); many of which can be seen reflected, directly or indirectly, in the Battle itself. What follows in this chapter will be a survey of the most important of these, and the most relevant to our topic, as they appear to the present author. Obviously there will be a degree of subjectivity in the choice of significant historical trends and events presented here, which leaves it open to challenge; and some omissions, which others may wish to repair. On the other hand, that choice will be a fairly wide one, which explains and I hope justifies the length of this chapter, for a merely 'background' one. For Britain in the 1850s and 1860s was a highly complex, confusing and even contradictory society; this complexity was one of the things that were most reflected in the architectural debate of the time, and so requires to be discussed in some detail, if we wish to understand the latter in most of its aspects.

The most obvious characteristic of Britain in this period – one that no one could possibly challenge – is that it was an *expanding* society; which meant that it needed to be a building society too. Over these two decades, for example, the population of England and Wales increased by 4.8 million, or 26.8 per cent (from 17.9 million to 22.7 million). This was after comparable increases during the 20 years before. Reflecting this, the number of inhabited houses increased over the same period by a million, or nearly 30 per cent (from 3.3 million to 4.3 million).[1] On the surface, that would seem to create huge new opportunities for architects. We shall see shortly that the booming housing market did not have that effect exactly, or not to the extent that might be expected; but other 'building' repercussions of the expansion of the time did. Those repercussions were most obvious (so far as England was concerned) in the great new industrial cities of the North and the Midlands: metropolitan Birmingham, to give just one example, expanded from 233,000 inhabitants to 344,000 (47.6 per cent) between 1851 and 1871;[2] and in London. For London – where of course our debate focused – the 1860s was *the* great building decade of the nineteenth century, when, according to Sir John Summerson, it was 'more excavated, more cut about, more rebuilt and more extended than at any time in its history', with both its drainage system and its first underground railway built: the essential infrastructure for the mega-city it was rapidly becoming; acres of commercial properties; several great (overground) railway termini; miles of new sprawling suburbs; and, of course, the Government Offices.[3] In the provinces the growth can be seen materialized in the great town and city halls that went up in these years; offices; factories; banks and shops; public libraries; schools and colleges; slums, villas and mansions (for the industrial and commercial *nouveaux riches*); and also churches, which played a lead role, as we shall see, in the debate about the style of the Foreign Office, even though it was not one. So: more people, more buildings, small and great.

But this does not take us very far. For it was not a question of *simply* more buildings: of the kind, that is, that had been built up to then. This is because British society was changing at this time, as well as expanding. The main engine of both these developments – the expansion and the change – was of course the 'Industrial Revolution'; which is generally reckoned to have begun around the middle of the eighteenth century, and to have delivered its greatest benefits to the British economy in what used to be called the latter's 'golden years', between about 1850 and 1870. The term 'Industrial Revolution' describes the process whereby what before had been a mainly agrarian, small-scale industrial and commercial national economy became largely superseded by one based on large-scale and highly capitalized manufacturing, to a degree unparalleled anywhere else in the world at that time (though many other countries were to follow Britain's lead and, indeed, to overtake her later), and with enormous repercussions in almost every social, political and cultural field. One feature of it that obviously affected the landscape was the growth of the steam-railway system from the 1840s on, whose need for stopping places, or stations, directly impacted on architecture; but which also influenced the profession in other ways: without this means of travelling swiftly between his building sites, for example, it is unlikely that George Gilbert Scott would have been able to keep as many of his projects on the go at the same time as he did.[4] (His practice mass-produced buildings like Birmingham factories mass-produced pots.) Another very visible feature was the distinctive appearance of all those huge new manufacturing cities that suddenly sprang up in response to the industrial monster's voracious appetite for human labour to serve it. ('Monster' and 'beast' were metaphors employed much at the time, to emphasize the enormity of the change.)[5] James Steven Curl's *Victorian Architecture* (1990) carries a wonderful purple passage describing the physical impact of all this.

> Splendour, darkness, vastness, blackness, flaming chimneys, roaring steam-propelled trains hurtling through tunnels or over huge ravines on viaducts grander than anything the Romans had built ... gigantic docks, warehouses and ports, near basins crammed with great ships; and cobbled streets illuminated by the yellow glare of gaslight, alive with all the damp, malodorous, noisy, vital activity of humanity on the move, the make and in a state of perpetual motion and change ... It was no wonder that the faint-hearted commentators from comfortable homes were frightened out of their wits ... It was dangerous, noisy, dirty, visually stupendous, completely new, mighty, energetic, terrible, magnificent, busy,

lively, bustling and exciting . . . It was successful, it created wealth, it gave opportunities not dreamed of in some frightful rural slum, and it could kill.[6]

Curl may possibly over-egg its scariness. (Years of immersion in the widest possible range of nineteenth-century literary sources – newspapers, journals, memoirs, fiction, private letters and others – have not persuaded me that the middle classes were anything like as terrified as he paints them here.) But there can be no doubt that the visible face of much of Britain was transforming quite spectacularly in these middle years of the nineteenth century. This furnished the physical context for much of the new architecture of the time.

Two provisos, however, need to be made here. The first is that the impact of the Industrial Revolution was not quite so visible everywhere. The south of England, apart from London, mainly kept clear of it, though its denizens profited from it (*via* the stock market); with railway stations often deliberately placed on the outskirts of the prettiest towns (Cambridge is an example, to the great inconvenience of its inhabitants, apart from taxi drivers, ever since), most of the pollution coming from flatulent cows rather than factory chimneys, and the labouring classes still tending to live in hovels, rather than slums. The impact of the Industrial Revolution on the landscape was highly uneven, therefore; just as it was on the broader society of Britain, in ways that seeped through into its architecture, as we shall see. The second important qualification to stress is that even where this physical trans-formation of Britain *was* happening, many architects neglected to take advantage of the new opportunities it was offering up. The leading ones, particularly, did not. Nikolaus Pevsner remarked, 'sadly', on how none of 'the architects whom one knows' took any interest in working-class housing, for example (for 'we must never forget', as Robert Furneaux Jordan reminds us, 'that the main contribution of the Victorian age to architecture is the slum');[7] or, with a few exceptions, in the great new 'market halls, railway stations and exhibition buildings, the office buildings, stores and factories' that were so peculiarly characteristic of this time. These were left to 'outsiders': 'small architects', as Pevsner calls them, and engineers. 'The career of a *successful* architect remained devoted to churches, major private houses and major public buildings', as it had done for a century or more.[8]

This unevenness in the impact of the Industrial Revolution is important to be aware of, because it was one of the things lying at the heart of the debate over the style of the Government Offices between 1855 and 1861. It was uneven because it – the Revolution – had not yet been completed. (It is arguable that it never has been, in Britain at least.) Just as many geographical areas of England were relatively unaffected by it, so was a large part of her social structure. The aristo-cratic and 'upper' classes, for example, representing in the main a *pre*-industrial and pre-capitalist social order, were still very much in the game; partly due to some clever accommodations they had made with the rising, thrusting middle classes of the day, which had the effect of forestalling a more complete and even possibly bloody transfer of power between them (like they had had, or had been attempted, in France), and preserved much of the power and influence of the 'uppers', in the cultural as well as the political field. Briefly, it was done like this. The upper classes liked ruling. (It was what they were trained up for in their 'public' schools.) The middle classes did not – it was an 'unproductive' occupation, if you could not make money from it – but wanted Britain's economy, at any rate, to be ruled in a certain way. So they reached a rather extraordinary concordat with the 'uppers', which preserved both their interests almost intact. The middle classes permitted the upper classes to carry on ruling Britain, so long as they, for example, freed up markets: the abolition of the Corn Laws in 1846 was the iconic event here; and liberalized the state in various other ways. (Granting civil rights to religious nonconformists, and then later to Roman Catholics and Jews, was one instance.) Both sides had to give a little. The upper classes, in order to stay in employment, had to change their ideological spots. Palmerston, the hero (or villain) of our story, is a good example of this: aristocratic to the core (though his title was an Irish one, which is why he sat and joked in the House of Commons), but trained in 'political economy' early on – at the hands of a leading disciple of Adam Smith, as it happens.[9] This is why he and his ilk could remain so influential in a country otherwise so dominated by the middle classes; influential, that is, when it came to matters of architecture: for Palmerston's prejudices in this area were very definitely, as we shall see later on, those of his class.

It was not a wholly reliable influence, however. The concordat between the two classes did not bring an end to the incipient war between them. The uppers were still there in the 1850s, dominating; but they always felt – and genuinely were – under threat. The great historical trend of this time, after all, was still the *rise* of the middle classes: in numbers, wealth, political clout, and in terms of their ideology; which the upper classes might not be able to resist or accommodate for much longer. (Behind that lay the spectre of the rise of another class, the 'workers', which had reared its head ominously in the previous decade, as 'Chartism', but that seemed to have receded in the 1850s: partly because the radical middle classes deserted the Chartists, and partly due to the promise of prosperity that capitalism seemed to hold out to the workers, very briefly, at this time. As a result, 'Labour' plays virtually no part in our story.) As the middle classes grew more powerful they also became more self-confident and assertive. Architecture is one area where this shows. Until the early nineteenth century large-scale architecture, at any rate, had been almost entirely the realm of the social élite of English society – upper-class patrons, the higher clergy, Oxbridge dons; 'men of taste', as they usually called themselves. (Hardly any were women.) Then the middle classes started muscling in, for example in connection with the proud public buildings they craved for their new great northern towns and cities, and the private mansions that some of them now found they could afford. Early on they seemed content to follow the advice and taste of their 'betters', but this did not last; partly through distrust of the aristocratic associations – dilettantism, and so on – that they read into that taste. They began demanding an architecture of their own, more (relatively) democratic, therefore, and reflecting better their own class values. The 'men of taste', of course, thought they were 'taste*less*'. In fact this was not just a snobbish put-down but reflected a fundamental difference between the classes' conception of architecture and of art generally, with the middles preferring more tangible yardsticks than 'taste' to judge works of art by, like their 'associations'. We shall see later in this book that this was what the Battle of the Styles was largely about; to the disadvantage initially of Palmerston and his ilk, who were not used to fighting on this kind of ground.

Britain's essential hybridity at this time explains a great deal about our 'Battle'. If her society had been homogeneous, uniform, or even dominated by one particular group or set of values in the 1850s and 1860s, obviously there would have been less disagreement over how her buildings should look. Class was probably the main divider (though there is room for disagreement here), defined in terms of people's relations to the factors of production, as Karl Marx put it at around this time as it happens (he was of course living in London); or, less ideologically, whether they were landowners, entrepreneurs or wage labourers, or *leaned* towards one of those major categories. (The lines of demarcation were rarely precise.) The classes in Britain were housed differently; educated very differently, along almost apartheid lines; and could often scarcely understand one another when they spoke. They had startlingly different value systems, which was one reason for the incomprehension and often hostility found between them. They hardly even shared a sense of common nationality, whether that be British, English or anything else. Many in the upper classes regarded the working classes as being of an inferior 'race' (the word 'race' was used very loosely then), and were seen in their turn by both the working and the middle classes as an alien – 'Norman' – imposition on them.[10] 'Englishness', if it was mentioned at all, was defined entirely differently, with radically different values accruing to it, by each different class, and usually in a way that excluded – and was intended to exclude – the others. We shall see later that this created serious problems for those who hankered after a 'national' style of architecture for Britain in this period. There *was not* one that all the classes of Britain could agree on.

Class, however, was not the only divisive factor, though it probably had a bearing on the others. Mid-Victorian Britain was riven in other ways. One was by nationality. The United Kingdom, as is well appreciated now, but was sometimes overlooked in the nineteenth century, especially by the English, comprises four nationalities (at least), not just one. There were (and are) tensions among all of them, but especially between Britain (the mainland) and Ireland, manifesting itself in considerable civil violence on either side of the period we are mainly concerned with here, and eventually, of course, in (southern) Ireland's political separation from Britain. The cultural differences between England and Ireland were enormous; as they were also between England and Scotland, whose architecture in particular pursued a notably distinct path from England's. Most architectural

histories from this period, for example, devote separate chapters to it.[11] So far as
the Battle of the Styles was concerned, however, these differences featured scarcely
at all. There were no designs submitted for the new Government Offices in the
form of Scottish baronial castles,[12] and very few in 'Greek', which was the 'revival'
much favoured in Scotland at this time.[13] Most of the contemporary discussion
of architecture that featured 'national' considerations was highly Anglo-centred, as
we shall see in the next chapter. Mediaeval styles were favoured – for the Houses
of Parliament, for example – because they reflected *English* 'freedoms', established
(supposedly) before Scotland had joined in. This accounts for the Anglocentric bias
of this present book too. In most of the discussions that took place over the style
of the new Offices in 1855–61, the other three nations of the United Kingdom
were almost completely ignored. Nationality, in this narrow sense of the word,
was not a significant factor in the debate – overtly, at any rate. There are ways in
which it might have had an input. It could have fuelled *apathy* among Scots, Irish
and Welsh, for example, towards the whole enterprise. If so, however, it was not
much more so than in the case of the English provinces, especially the industrial
North. As we shall see later, the debate over the style of the Government Offices
was a very metropolitan one. The other nations and regions of Britain by and large
left London to it. That may have been a weakening factor; but it had little or no
bearing on the question of 'style'.

Other causes of division were more important in this context. One very obvious
one was religion. It was religion of course that marked one of the main differences
between Britain and (predominantly Catholic) Ireland. Britain itself was mainly
Protestant, but with several competing forms of Protestantism represented, all of
them with different names (the Church of England, Baptists, Methodists and so
on), and most of those also bitterly subdivided: on theological grounds ostensibly, but also reflecting other differences, like class. The 'established' Church of
England, for example, was mainly associated with the ruling classes of the time,
and with those who accepted their dominance; the 'nonconformist' churches with
the middle and working classes, and in some instances with political radicalism.
The Church of England also had certain privileges over the other churches,
which, however, were being swiftly whittled away in early Victorian times, with
the 'emancipation' of (Protestant) nonconformists (1828), Catholics (1829) and
Jews (1858). Both these two latter religious groups were fairly small in mainland
Britain, though Catholicism was a significant force in the west of Scotland and
north-western England (due to Irish immigration), and widely perceived to be
more of a threat to British Protestantism than its strict numbers would imply.
This was due to two factors: what was called the 'Papal aggression': Pope Pius IX's
decision to establish a Catholic episcopate in Britain in 1850; and a significant
movement in the Church of England to move back to 'Roman' doctrines and
rites – 'Anglo-Catholicism'. These actually provoked riots in England and Scotland
in the 1850s, with Catholic churches being burned down: some of this, however,
expressing hostility to Irish immigrants; and people rampaging over the wearing

of surplices by 'high' Anglican vicars.[14] There was also a major Christian 'revivalist'
movement at this time, its leading figures the preacher Charles Spurgeon and (a
little later) the hymn writers Moody and Sankey.[15] When the word 'revival' was
used in the 1850s, it usually referred to this.[16] Some of the religious associations
of the word are likely, therefore, to have attached to other contemporary uses of
it, for example in connection with the resurrection of older architectural styles.
Even without this, however, Britain's religious divisions were bound to enter
into the debate we are concerned with in this book, partly because so much of
the new public building of the period was of churches, and partly because many
of these sects were found overtly championing particular styles. Religion was a
powerful factor here, influencing both the choices of style that people made and
the *fervour* with which they pursued them: for mid-Victorian religious belief
could, sometimes, be quite fervent.

This 'hybrid' situation of Britain also had an impact on the dominant *values* and
discourses of the 1850s and 1860s. In particular, the newfangled industrial capitalism came with values attached to it, and provoked other values in opposition to
it; all of which can be traced in the architecture of the time. One of these was
'economy': or 'cheapness', or 'parsimony', or 'niggardliness', or any other of the
score of words that the mid-Victorian classes had for this, one of their favourite
virtues; which we shall see illustrated repeatedly in the Radical critique of any
kind of grandiose building for the Offices of state. Another was practicality, or 'utilitarianism', as it was often loosely called; which carried with it an anti-aesthetic
component, which we shall meet later; or, rather that proclivity, mentioned already,
to redefine artistic worth in terms of something (like 'associations') that could be
practically *measured*.

  Most of the other values that came with industrial capitalism went under the
generic term of 'liberalism', centring around the idea of 'freedom': the freedom,
that is, of the individual to speak, worship, buy, sell, write, travel and so on as he or
(sometimes) she liked. This is of course a familiar political term in our times too,
which may lead us to think we know what it meant then; but there are differences.
For example, today economic liberalism is usually associated with inequality, quite
happily apparently for its aficionados; in the mid-nineteenth century, however,
it was widely believed that the internal propensity of free-market forces was to
diminish disparities of wealth between rich and poor. (Many 'political economists',
as they called themselves, would accept the system on no other terms.)[17] A second
difference between Victorian and modern 'liberalism' is that the Victorians did
not generally surround it with the rhetoric of 'democracy', as later liberals did. It
was not that they were particularly anti-democratic (though some were); more
that they rated freedom *from* government more highly than the freedom to
participate *in* it. This affected architects' views of themselves and of their profession, which they went to great lengths to emancipate from the government
and aristocratic patronage they were coming to see at this time as detrimental

to their independence and their dignity.[18] (Poor Pennethorne was a victim of this.) Independence from and hostility to government were obviously likely to impact on any plans for building Government *Offices*; and did, as we shall see. 'In an economy running with such miraculous success on the laissez-faire principle', wrote Sir John Summerson, 'action by the government and expenditure by the government were always suspect, always opposed';[19] and with them, of course, any new projects for it to spend money on, and − in this case − from.

A third characteristic of mid-nineteenth-century liberalism was its powerful strain of *cosmopolitanism*. The expansion of Britain into the world in the nineteenth century is well known, of course, mainly in one particular form it took, that of 'imperialism'; which, however, was not the only one. Unless one suspects every Victorian traveller or trader in Africa of carrying a Union Jack in his or her Gladstone bag (which is certainly arguable: it depends how broadly you define 'empire'), many of the hundreds of thousands of Britons found scattered over the globe in Victorian times were there for a variety of other reasons; and were easily matched (if we exclude emigrants) by the numbers of those who were also to be found living, travelling and even settling in Continental Europe, who have received less attention from scholars recently, partly because it is less easy to see a train-driver in Belgium, for example, or a tourist in Paris, or a young architectural apprentice visiting his ancient Roman and Greek models, as an 'imperialist'. The Victorians themselves regarded this as evidence *not* of 'imperialism', but of a breaking down of national barriers, a peaceful coming together of the world's peoples; anticipated by the great Radical politician Richard Cobden as the inevitable outcome of global free trade;[20] and by Tennyson in his famous poem 'Locksley Hall' (1842), which dreamed of a time when 'the war-drum throbb'd no longer, and the battle-flags were furl'd / In the Parliament of man, the Federation of the world.'[21] Popular educators openly taught the delusions and perils of 'patriotism': though how widely this caught on is difficult to say.[22] Another source of 'cosmopolitanism' − this time an illiberal one − was the sense of common identity that British aristocrats felt with their Continental class-comrades, which was often closer than they felt with their own 'lower' compatriots. (This was why most British ambassadors abroad were aristocrats: it was felt they would get on better with the foreigners they needed to diplomatise with.)[23] The Great Exhibition of 1851 was supposed to be a celebration of this liberal-internationalist ideal.[24] More progress along these lines, and even nations would wither away eventually, with scarcely any roles remaining for their governments, either at home or abroad.

That, however, was in the future. In the meantime Britain needed to have a government, and a foreign policy to deal with all those other governments of the world which still lagged behind her in terms of liberal and cosmopolitan progress, which was virtually all of them, and which so endangered her own progress and, if they only knew it, theirs too. Lord Palmerston, while he was foreign (and prime) minister, revelled in this role of safeguarding 'freedom' throughout the world: freedom for Britain's citizens, exemplified in the notorious and indeed somewhat outrageous 'Don Pacifico' case (when he threatened Greece with bombardment in reprisal for damage done to a British Gibraltarian's property there); and more generally freedom of commerce, for every nation, though he had Britain's mainly in mind: in China, for example, where the Chinese were trying to stop the trade in opium; and *via* the eastern Mediterranean, which is the only rational explanation for Britain's participation in the Crimean War (1853–6). He also tried to spread British ideas of freedom, subvertly, in countries like Spain and Italy; in every one of these cases, however, only so long as it was virtually risk-free, either because his opponent was weak or because he had an ally who would take the brunt of the fighting from the shoulders of Britain's notoriously small and inefficient army.[25] (That is what gave him his reputation as a bully and a hypocrite.) So Palmerston needed a Foreign Office and a War Office. But not everyone agreed: not, for example, the many contemporary opponents of his Crimean War policy. And many of those who went along with that hoped that, as the world advanced and caught up with Britain, that need would recede. At the very least – though this is not the main way in which this bears on the question of architecture – this might be a consideration when the question of housing the war and foreign policy-makers came up.[26]

The reverse side of this expansion of Britain out into the world was the migration of tens of thousands of foreigners into her, from all over, but preponderantly other parts of Europe; due to the fact that Britain at this time had no way – no laws or executive instruments – to prevent their coming in, or to expel them.[27] This was one of the most distinctive and remarkable features of Victorian Britain, applying even to the most violent of 'political refugees' (today we would call them 'terrorists'), for whom Britain was an automatic asylum: meaning that they did not even have to apply for the status. This was even when Britons did not particularly like these incomers; though some of the former – the most radical of them – felt the same sense of cosmopolitan identity with them that Britain's aristos did for *their* class abroad.[28] Most Britons were inordinately proud of this, to the extent of actually toppling one ministry that was suspected of targeting refugees.[29] That was in 1858, right in the middle of our Battle, therefore, and with important collateral effects on the course of it, as we have seen. The presence of all these foreigners in Britain, in a wide range of roles – not only refugees, of course, but also beggars, criminals, shopkeepers, wives, language tutors, artists, entrepreneurs, doctors, professors and the principal librarian of the British Museum, among others – contributed to the highly cosmopolitan atmosphere of London, where most of them lived, and where the Battle of the Styles was of course focused. In the 1850s, perhaps more than at any other time in British history before the present, cosmopolitanism was in the air.

Underlying all this liberalism was a belief in 'progress' that was all but universal in Victorian Britain, even among the oldest of fogeys, who believed *in* it – i.e. that it was happening – even while they deplored it, as some of them did. Indeed, one could hardly avoid it, with, for example, all these new 'steam engines' hurtling around the country at an oh-so-dangerous 30 miles per hour. It was industrial capitalism of course, that lay behind the railway boom of the middle of the nineteenth century; and it may also have affected – fuelled, if it did not originate – the idea of 'progress' in other ways too. Capitalism is an inherently dynamic system, always expanding and possibly *requiring* to expand in order to sustain itself; which was the aspect of it that Marx thought would cause it to implode ultimately. In the meantime, however – in our period, of the 'Great Victorian Boom', so-called – it seemed to be benefiting everyone, or to be promising *future* benefits for everyone, which was almost more important, and is what persuaded the working classes to put their earlier primitive 'socialism' aside for a while (about 30 years) while they waited for that promise to be realized. As a result, nearly everyone was a 'progressive' in the mid-nineteenth century. This involved, then, believing not only that things were getting better but also that they were *bound* to; that there was a fundamental law of history that determined that it inevitably moved, in a forward direction, albeit in stages, once the brakes were taken off; a theory (akin to dialectical materialism) which is sometimes attributed to Marx, or perhaps Hegel, but in fact was part of the common discourse in the Britain Marx made his home in during the 1850s. The only difference was that the Victorians believed that economic liberalism would bring them gently to the final stage of this 'progress', or what in more recent parlance is known as the 'End of History',[30] whereas Marx had that implosion in view. One important aspect of this, however, which we shall see reflected in the architectural debate, was that it gave the mid-Victorians a *future*, which would be different from their past. Not all societies have this.

The other aspect of this idea of 'progress' which is significant, and relevant, is that it assumed a state of constant *change* in everything, whether for the best (as liberals thought) or not. The world was not static. Even human biology was not static, but 'evolving', as a number of scientists had established even before Charles Darwin came along to suggest a reason for this ('natural selection') in his famous *On the Origin of Species*, published in 1859 – which as it happens comes right in the middle of our Battle. Science and technology were also self-evidently 'evolving'; as also were Britain's social institutions: her laws, political arrangements and so on. Other countries' were not; but it was the accepted wisdom in Britain then, among Conservatives as well as radicals, that it was her politicians' awareness of those inevitable trends, and their statesmanlike adaptation to them, that explained what was perceived as Britain's political success – certainly her stability – in this period. This was what marked her off from her neighbour France, for example: that she 'progressed' in an evolutionary rather than a revolutionary way; 'naturally, equably, and surely', according to *The Times* in 1848; 'not by an alternation of frenzy and trance, but by the uniform and simultaneous action of all parties in the State.'[31] This also has an important bearing on the Battle of the Styles. To anticipate a little: it explains why both sides needed to argue that their styles were 'progressive', not 'revivals' in any more static sense; and, secondly, gave the Goths an advantage here, at least theoretically and in the short term: maybe unexpectedly.

The 1850s and 1860s marked the high point of this liberal ideology in Britain; a very special time, therefore. The turn was quite sudden, reflected in the political confusion that was a special feature of the 1850s: the period that saw an old Tory–Whig–Radical political system breaking down and re-forming into the Liberal–Conservative one that was to dominate the remainder of the century, the bumpy transition to which helps explain all those sudden changes of government in the later 1850s that had quite significant, if fortuitous, repercussions on the Battle – Palmerston's return, for example, in June 1859. The middle-class campaign to implement its cherished 'freedoms' – especially of trade – had begun earlier (in the old Whig days), and with considerable legislative success, but little sign as yet of the general happiness that was supposed to ensue. The 1840s were marked by severe economic depression, famine in Ireland and a working-class revolutionary movement on the British mainland that threatened to go far beyond mere 'liberalism'. Then the clouds lifted. The 'Great Victorian Boom' took off. That may have been over-egged at the time: it was a period of very irregular and uneven economic growth in reality; but again, as with all these 'discourses', it is the myth that matters more. Two great events seemed to corroborate it – one of them featuring a famous building. The first was a negative one: Britain's *escape* from the otherwise near-universal political conflagration that took hold of the rest of Europe in 1848, which escape was almost universally attributed to her 'freedom': that is, to her people's *feeling* free enough not to want to rebel. When the 1848 revolutions were suppressed, many of the revolutionaries fled to Britain, where they yet again seemed to confirm the value of Britain's new liberal approach by posing no danger to *her* at all. That, said Palmerston proudly, was because Britons were too 'well-governed and contented' to be subvertible by them.[32] This was the reason he would also have given for the death of native socialism then. The second great event was the 'Great Exhibition of the Works of Industry of All Nations' which was famously held in Hyde Park just three years later, in the face of dire warnings from the Continental autocrats that the huge crowds expected there might be exploited and fired up by those selfsame refugees – one foreign police report had European communists allying with American Roman Catholics to set bombs off in London; another claimed Karl Marx (!) was plotting to assassinate the Queen – but of course with no harm coming to Britain from that either.[33] As well as this, the Great Exhibition served to emphasize Britain's by now quite obvious economic lead over the rest of the world, which was also thought to indicate that she had got things roughly right. All the most impressive machines and industrial products on show were hers. The building itself (Joseph Paxton's 'Crystal Palace') could be seen in this category too: a triumph of engineering, rather than of design. So far as design, or art, was concerned, Britain did less well. But that was thought to be not necessarily a bad thing either.

This was because of another 'value' that was widely thought to attach to liberal capitalism at this time, which was 'philistinism'. How widespread this was in early Victorian Britain is hard to tell. Philistinism will not of course be reflected in the contemporary cultural record, because if you were dismissive of culture you did not generally contribute to it. There is one exception: an early Victorian businessman, Samuel Laing (senior), whom bankruptcy forced into exile, which he then spent writing travel books of a philosophical and *very* philistine bent. He stands out in the extensive travelogue *genre* of this time by rating the countries he visited in *inverse* proportion to their artistic achievements (Norway was his favourite), and devoting much of his texts to sneering at every manifestation of 'high' culture, but especially large and ornate architecture, as typical of more backward and 'effete' – that is, aristocratic – times.[34] That was one characteristic middle-class way of responding to 'culture'; which is not to say, of course, that philistinism was an exclusively middle-class trait. There were plenty of upper-class philistines too; for example, probably most of the hunting and shooting set. And the huge majority of the over-worked, underpaid, continuously pregnant, cultur-ally starved working classes will have been philistine by default. Obviously, that was likely to be a spoiler when it came to debating a building to grace Whitehall, rather than a merely utilitarian one. As we shall see, many parliamentary Radicals wanted just that.

They did not have to be philistines to take this line. Many of them were not so in their own communities; especially the northern English industrial towns, where the true glories of nineteenth-century middle-class architecture are to be found: in their great town and city halls, for example, where the industrial bour-geoisie's proud enthusiasm for fine, monumental and intrinsically *non*-utilitarian architecture can be read in every stone. The reason for this must be that the middle classes identified more with their localities than they did with their nation; or rather, as Tristram Hunt has shown so well, with a conception of their nation that was local rather than centralized: a loose 'Saxon' confederation of free commu-nities, which the rise of at first civic and then industrial capitalism had enabled to break free from the tyrannical centralization that the 'Normans' had imposed on them all those centuries before.[35] That would explain why, as we shall see later (in Chapter 7), the middle classes were less than enthusiastic about the newly planned 'Government Offices', whatever 'style' they might be built in. These represented another kind of nation from the urban middle classes': centralized, bureaucratic, the home of the dreaded Normans, fundamentally unfree. And if the more extreme of the liberals were right – those who believed that all government would wither away eventually – they were ultimately doomed to obsolescence in any case.

If *this* Britain had a sense of national identity, of the sort one might expect to be reflected in a great national building, it was not a very national*istic* one. Middle-class Britons were proud of their individual and local liberties, fought for over the centuries in parliament – which is why that institution *was* worth com-memorating in stone; of their love of peace, even though this seems to go against all the evidence: these years after all saw two of the three most serious wars of Victoria's reign, but both defensive (of course) in the eyes of contemporaries; of their *inter*nationalism, which the 1851 Great Exhibition was supposed to exemplify above all; and – this in particular – of their *progress*, manifested in their technological achievements, their booming prosperity and the continual expansion of their 'liberties': but *not*, significantly, in their art, which was not regarded as necessarily a 'progressive' area to be proficient in. Mid-nineteenth-century Britain, philistinism and all, represented the future for all the world; one that would spread 'naturally', through its demonstrable virtues and Britain's example; and so did not need to be pushed by her, which was why she did not go about it imperialistically – or 'formally' imperialistically, at any rate. (The existing dependent colonies were usually regarded as regrettable obligations inherited from less enlightened times.)[36] It had already been planted quite freely in the US and in Britain's remaining 'settlement' colonies, with green shoots of it starting to be discernable even in Continental Europe – specifically at this time, in parts of northern Italy.[37] Today we tend to regard this as 'imperialism' of a kind, which it may have been (it depends on your definition);[38] but the fact that it was not regarded as such then means that empire was unlikely to form a part of liberal Britain's conscious national self-image; and so less likely to be explicitly commemorated in the new Government Office buildings in Whitehall.

Not everyone in 1850s Britain, however, was a liberal; and the proportion of the latter who believed all that stuff about the state withering away and universal peace and the rest was almost certainly a small minority. Of course minorities can exercise a disproportionate influence over societies and cultures, especially if they represent 'rising' trends, if they are cleverly organized, and if the resistance to them appears to be on the defensive. (Look at Thatcherism – the new, harder form of economic liberalism that dominated the 1980s. How many people then really shared that ideology?) In this case the middle classes, dominant and rising as they were, clearly did not speak for all early Victorians. If they had done, there would probably have been (again) less of a Battle over the style of the new Government Offices than there was: not no Battle at all, because one of the distinguishing marks of the new liberalism was the variety of opinions and tastes it permitted and encouraged within its own belief system, but one that gave little room to overtly or implicitly anti-capitalist discourses, which were a prominent feature of the Battle as it was actually fought, and were the other main cultural product of the Industrial Revolution – this time *provoked* by it, in reaction. In earlier and later times this kind of critique came mainly from working-class socialists; in the 1850s, however, it was associated more with the remnants of the older political and social order in Britain: the one that the liberal middle classes were so keen to supplant, but had not done so yet by a long chalk, and, indeed, were never to completely. It was basically 'Tory', and even reactionary; but no less radical for that. (It should go without saying that reactionaries can be radical too.)

The Tories saw a different side of middle-class free-market liberalism from its champions. Where the latter saw freedom, equality, progress and even eventual

Utopia, the Tories thought they detected the destruction of community, no less: the undermining of respect for authority and station on the one hand, and of a proper sense of social responsibility on the other; the enslavement of everyone, high or low, to mere money, or what Thomas Carlyle called the 'cash nexus' (Marx picked up the phrase later, but it was originally a Tory one);[39] men serving machines, rather than vice versa (there is a famous passage in Charles Dickens's *Hard Times* describing this – Dickens was another Tory, of course);[40] the breaking up of settled populations in the English countryside and Ireland to feed the 'beast'; people struggling individually for survival rather than helping each other on; a cold utilitarianism made especially unlovely by the aggressive philistinism that accompanied it; and – as some of the outward and visible signs of all this – workhouses for the poor, 'panopticons' for prisoners[41] and the streets of shockingly mean slum dwellings that disfigured the new industrial conurbations, thrown up by the 'swarm of speculating house-builders . . . who practically view architecture as a trade', as Scott called them,[42] mocking the pretensions of all those grandiose city halls. It was a powerful and seductive catalogue of evils, bound to be influential on its merits, probably, quite apart from the fact that it also clearly served the class interests of most of the people who were compiling it.

Not all of these were upper class – Dickens certainly was not, for example – and some of them were as critical of the record of that class in the past as they were of the new industrial bourgeoisie; but in the absence at this time of a significant socialist alternative to the latter, the old order and its representatives, somewhat sanitized and idealized, furnished the only banner to rally the anti-capitalist forces behind. That of course made them appear 'backward', which is usually a disadvantage for any political or social movement; and also hitched them to a number of tendencies they might not have chosen to be associated with otherwise – certainly not if they had been able to be socialists. The *echt* aristocracy's snobbish dismissal of 'trade', and its sense of *noblesse oblige*, could be easily recruited to the anti-capitalist cause, for example; but along with that came notions of hierarchy, power, authority – all the paraphernalia of 'Normanness', in fact – that might not be quite so welcome to the more radical social reformers. Similarly, the 'High' Church in Britain, ranging from the majority of the Established Church through 'Anglo-Catholicism' to Romanism itself (to which a significant number of English converted, highly controversially, in the 1840s and 1850s), were the staunchest in support of the traditional social values that were thought to be threatened by liberal capitalism at this time; but get too close to them and you could find yourself polluted by the irrationalism, superstition and (again) authoritarianism that were perceived to go along with them, as well, of course, as the 'smells and bells'. If you took Thomas Carlyle on board – the most powerful critic of free marketism before Marx and Engels – you might be touched with his overt racism, imperialism and worship of 'heroes'. It was the same with architecture. Aristocrats and priests (but perhaps not Carlyle) often had strong views about this – spending most of their time, as they did, living and praying in it. These came with the anti-capitalist territory, too.

Not that the architecture followed uncomplicatedly from the anti-capitalism. In what follows we shall not find preferences for styles breaking down as simply as this – all middle-class liberals opting for one style, and Tory paternalists for another. Social and political considerations certainly came into the picture, but they could lead to radically different choices for different individuals: Tories opting for Classical, for example, because it was more 'ordered', even 'imperial'; *or* for Gothic (or more likely Tudor) because it took them back to the good old days when their class properly looked after its peasants. Education was also a factor. Most upper-class Britons then were brought up on the Greek and Roman 'Classics', either privately or at their Public schools, which of course gave them a taste for those ancient styles, but also, and perhaps more importantly, imbued them with a particular view of the nature of political society as *static*, rather than dynamic and developing. The important thing about Greek and Roman history was that it was finished, all done and dusted, rounded off. It could be mined therefore for the direct lessons it taught for the present day. Boys came out of the 'public' schools prepared to govern the lower orders, both at home and in the colonies, on those principles alone. British history – the kind the middle classes were keener on – taught something entirely different: a more dynamic process of development, or 'progress', which had not stopped yet, and might never do. That of course was unsettling to both conservatives and reactionaries, who at this moment in time dominated the anti-capitalist camp. Classical architecture therefore symbolized stability of one kind; Elizabethan mansions, together with mediaeval churches and colleges, another, warmer sort. That is, until Gothic came to be interpreted as a 'developing' style, like Britain's history, when it lost some favour among the reactionaries. (We shall come on to this in a later chapter.) This is why anti-capitalists are to be found in both the Gothic and Classical camps; and why Goths could be either 'conservative' or 'progressive'. The picture is complicated; but it is all fundamentally rooted in the social conditions of the day.

Then there was History. In all these discourses the 'Middle Ages', or at least different perceptions of them, were prominent; as they were, of course, in the 'Battle' this book is mainly about. For centuries the mediaeval period had been reviled as one of superstition and barbarity; and still was by many of the disputants in the 'Battle', including of course Palmerston, and this pamphleteer: '[w]e can scarcely hint at the turbulence, violence, ignorance and cruelty of those times, and at the ribald jests and indecent buffoonery . . . in no age is the female sex spoken of with so much bitterness and contempt', or was the clergy so 'dissolute', the state so cruel, poverty so abject . . . and so on. Contrary views, said this writer, were 'illusive . . ., derived from poetry and romance', unrelated to reality.[43] He was probably right about this; but 'illusory' views, or myths, had been growing for nearly half a century now, until by the 1850s they dominated. Mediaeval history was experiencing a great resurgence of scholarly and popular interest, which was beginning to reveal some unexpectedly bright and progressive aspects of the period: Magna Carta; the first English parliament; the rise of 'free' towns and cities; the guild system, and so on. The thirteenth century was supposed to be the crucial period here (this is important architecturally, as we shall see); but several historians were pushing the origins of England's 'freedoms' back further, to a Saxon age of free local government: 'witenagemots', and such like; which had the effect, or it may have been the intention, of giving them a *racial* aspect: attributing English liberty, typically, to the northern European 'Teutons' in their forests.[44] Since then the development (or 'progress') of what was seen as a peculiarly English kind of polity had been almost continuous, albeit with some blips: the Norman Conquest and the Stuart 'usurpation' being the main ones, which, however, had been surmounted, usually by means of good old English popular revolt.[45] This, note, was a highly radical, even democratic, use of the mediaeval 'myth', quite different from the feudal-paternalistic one that people like Augustus Welby Pugin (as we shall see) appealed to, though they could complement each other in some respects. Both readings, however, had one implication, which we shall find was highly relevant to the debate over the Revival of the architecture of the Middle Ages. 'The England in which we live,' wrote E. A. Freeman, one of the leading historians of the English Constitution, in 1872, 'has, in its true life and spirit, far more in common with the England of the earliest times than it has with the England of days far nearer to our own ... We have advanced by falling back on a more ancient state of things; we have reformed by calling to life again the institutions of earlier and ruder times'.[46] Therein lay the seed of what we shall later see was the 'progressive' case to be made for Gothic architecture.

Of course this does not explain everything, even in this nuanced way. Other factors also came into the Battle of the Styles – though none of them, I would contend, entirely without socio-political roots, or at least links. Individual genius may have been one: the sheer quirkiness of many Victorian buildings is surely explicable in no other way; in this case, however, the fact that architects were allowed to be quirky could have a social explanation.[47] Fashion and imitation are another: a style suddenly becomes 'trendy', so everyone wants a house (or whatever) built in it; but why the attraction of that style in particular, and then? Foreign influences – arising, that is, from *other* social contexts – are of particular importance in the period under discussion in this book, when, as will be seen later, the idea that English buildings should particularly express English traditions was beginning – under the influence of cosmopolitanism – to wane, and architects and their patrons suddenly started looking abroad for models: to France, Flanders, northern Italy and even Byzantium. (Elements of all these styles are to be found in one or other of Scott's designs for the Government Offices.) Again, however, architects and architectural theorists invariably came up with socio-political arguments for these choices: for Venetian Gothic, for example, on the grounds that it expressed Venice's fifteenth-century commercial greatness, which could be seen to stand for Britain's similar greatness in the nineteenth century.[48] It is difficult to find many architectural preferences in the mid-nineteenth century that were not *justified*, at any rate, in broader social, political and ethical terms. The reason for this is that the Victorians, as we shall see later, demanded 'serious' reasons for espousing a style. But of course those reasons may have been merely excuses. John Ruskin may have liked Venetian Gothic simply because it was pretty. (Some of his more serious arguments are rather thin, and would fit other styles better.) Of course he could not say that; but this may have been another, hidden general factor in this great controversy – simple personal taste.

3

Early Skirmishes

Just as the debate over the style of the new Government Offices took place against a particular social and political background, so it also had an architectural historical context of its own. The Battle of the Styles did not appear suddenly out of the blue. For a few years now a wider war had been waging between the two great 'historical' styles of the nineteenth century. This needs to be summarized (briefly) at this point in the book, before moving on to see how the Battle of 1855–61 fits in or on to it. Specialist architectural historians will be familiar with all this (if I have it right); cultural and general historians, however, may not.

There is probably no need to go very far back in England's architectural history for this purpose; except to say that in the Middle Ages English building had conformed to the north-western European tradition of 'Gothic' architecture,[1] though with certain small peculiarities of its own,[2] until around the late fourteenth century, when it metamorphosed into what is called 'Perpendicular Gothic', which is a very distinctively English style (no other 'Gothic' country copied it); until that was superseded by the 'Renaissance' or revived Roman style, albeit very much later there than in most of the rest of Europe. This tardiness, as we shall see shortly, was thought to be highly significant in the later Battle over the style. Even after it was formally superseded it is possible to follow traces of 'surviving' Gothic right through, to the point where the style was consciously 'revived' again, sometimes in the work of 'Classical' architects, like Sir Christopher Wren, usually peculiarly, and sometimes unsuccessfully. ('Tom Tower' at Christ Church, Oxford, is usually and properly admired; Hawksmoor's clumsy twin west towers of Westminster Abbey, often at this time misattributed to Wren, not so much.)[3]

The Gothic 'revival' proper is generally reckoned to date (of course it depends when you think the 'survival' ended) from the later years of the eighteenth century, and as a rather trivial thing. 'Gothick', as it was more often spelled then, was taken up as little more than a toy, indulged in mainly by grown men and women who could afford such toys: rich country-house-builders bored by the dull Georgian boxes of their neighbours, or leisured antiquarians. It was seen as an occasional picturesque admixture to the dominant Classical style of architecture, not a serious rival. It was much informed by the romantic and sometimes grotesque taste of *some* of the age: 'the witchery thrown over the middle ages by the writings of Sir Walter Scott', for example,[4] and of the even more lurid 'Gothick' novelists;[5]

which to the rest of the age made it seem all the more trivial. It was up there with Chinoiserie and Turkish pavilions, and sometimes even confused with them, satisfying exactly the same craving for the 'picturesque', or the exotic.[6] (Indeed, it is worth noting, in view of the emphasis that has been placed on Western 'Orientalism' in recent years, how much more popular 'Gothick' was. When the English sought their exotic thrills, it was usually far back in time, rather than far away.) Perhaps surprisingly, in view of later developments, it did not catch on widely for churches as yet.[7] There was no way the style could be thought to pose a threat to the established Classical mainstream, any more than the Prince Regent's 'Indian' Pavilion in Brighton did. The less exotic examples – mainly country houses for the gentry – were in a comfortable style later dubbed 'Jacobethan', based on sixteenth- and seventeenth-century models, and with enough 'Classical' features – symmetry, for example, horizontality and very flattened 'points' to the windows – to be not too disturbing to conservatives.[8] *Quâ* 'Gothic', all this was terribly superficial, only very rarely indicating any understanding at all of the true principles behind the original style. This comes out in contemporary explanations given for the pointed arch – for most people Gothic's main distinguishing feature – which included its resemblance to the shape of two hands joined in prayer, or to an upturned Noah's ark, or to branches meeting in an avenue of trees, or to wickerwork; or intersecting *round* arches; or the fact that people simply liked spiky things.[9] The best-known surviving monuments of this early Gothick are probably Strawberry Hill in Twickenham – built by a Gothick novelist: 'the sneering, sceptical Horace Walpole', as one 'Aunt Elinor' called him;[10] and much of Windsor Castle. It is an interesting movement, well worth studying in its own right,[11] and which may even be considered to have produced some attractive buildings: if one is broad-minded enough. The mid-Victorians generally were not. They thoroughly despised these gewgaws; especially the serious Goths among them. By the 1850s the Gothic Revival had turned into something almost entirely different; which is why we need not spend much time on its 'Gothick' prelude here.

There are a couple of threads, however, connecting this Revival with the later one. One is negative. Goths of all (modern) ages were reacting against what they took to be the existing architectural poverty of their country and times. Almost every British commentator in the years around 1800 agreed that their nation's architecture had fallen very low by then: since the deaths of Wren (1723), Vanbrugh (1726) and Hawksmoor (1736), say; and some suspected that even at its height in the later seventeenth-century English 'Renaissance' architecture was not really a patch on contemporary building in most European (and even Latin American) countries. It was certainly not as jolly. England had her 'Baroque' phase, but that, with a few exceptions (Vanbrugh's early Blenheim Palace, for example) had nothing of the exuberance that you find in Italy, Spain and southern Germany; positively resisting, in Chris Brooks's delightful phrase, 'the naughty curves of the rococo'.[12] By contrast with the Neumann brothers in Bavaria, for example, Hawksmoor is really very dour. 'England,' as Nicholas Taylor puts it, 'preferred chastity'.[13] That was a lack.

Classical architects might have supplied it, but did not. Country-house-building became simpler and duller during the later eighteenth and early nineteenth centuries, following Palladian patterns slavishly. London's major recent public buildings in the Classical style were widely considered to be feeble. George IV's earlier attempt, with the help of John Nash, to achieve a more 'imperial' look for London ('imperial' in this context, incidentally, having less to do with 'imperialism' as the word is understood today than with his own grandiosity), was generally unappreciated even in George's own time, resented as it was for its extravagance, while at the same time despised for its superficial theatricality.[14] Things had not improved since then. 'The sepulchral Bank, the chilly Post-Office, the insignificant National Gallery, and that most unpalatial of buildings, Buckingham Palace' – all dating from the 1820s and 1830s – 'do not, I think, awaken in our breasts any warm feelings.' That was Gilbert Scott, who of course was biased, but his view was widely shared, especially in the case of the National Gallery (Wilkins, 1832–8).[15] (Prince Charles's famous campaign in 1984 to save the Gallery from being disfigured by a modernist 'carbuncle', as if it were a masterpiece, would have raised a wry smile from contemporaries. Many of them might have welcomed a carbuncle or two.) Middle-class suburban housing consisted of rows of square-windowed stuccoed terraces, sometimes dignified with porticos (as in Nash's Regent's Park Terrace), but again, deadly boring. (Speculative building for the underclasses was obviously worse.) *Chambers's Information for the People* (1842) castigated just about all recent Classical English architecture as 'spiritless and mean';[16] as did, for example, the *Quarterly Review* in 1837, which even took on Edinburgh's New Town, and Bath.[17] 'The greater part of the last age,' wrote the historian Edward Freeman in 1849, was, architecturally speaking, 'an entire blank'.[18] Similar judgements are to be found in contemporary editions of the influential *Encyclopaedia Britannica*; and, indeed, almost everywhere else one looks.[19] Such sweeping dismissals of 'modern' architecture are common in any age, of course – it probably has something to do with the ubiquity of architecture, coupled with ignorance; but it is astonishing how widespread this view was in early nineteenth-century England. The Victorians' attitude to Georgian London, for example, was 'mostly and for most of the time one of utter disgust . . . Any opportunity of displacing some part of it was greeted with glee.'[20] This remained a constant theme in the 1850s,[21] and, indeed, has generally been confirmed by modern architectural historians (which is rare with past 'modern' styles). 'Just imagine yourself living in late Georgian London,' wrote John Summerson in 1949. 'Imagine a city in which every street is a Gower Street, in which all the "great" buildings are by smooth Mr Wilkins, dull Mr Smirke or facetious Mr Nash.'[22] When Kenneth Clark published the first post-Victorian history of the neo-Gothic movement in 1924, albeit an unsympathetic one, this was the only rational excuse he could find for reviving Gothic at all: 'we must remember that men will change a good shape for a bad one from no other motive than the desire for change.'[23] Unfortunate as their choice was in the nineteenth century, therefore, it was understandable in view of what they had then.

At the time, only Gothic seemed to offer relief from this. What other alternatives were there? As it happened, some Classical architects dabbled in Gothic too, as a kind of 'second language'.[24] (We shall see that this was much frowned upon by later Goths: changing styles like overcoats, as though they were 'only' 'styles', nothing more serious; but for the moment architects had few problems with this.) That was where they turned when they wanted to be fanciful. A prime example is William Wilkins, the designer of the much-reviled National Gallery, who also, however, built in (late) Gothic in Cambridge: King's College 'screen', for example; and the New Court of Corpus Christi. People must have *enjoyed* those more.[25] They might be *impressed* by Downing College – another of Wilkins's Cambridge designs, this time in Greek – but that was not the same.

It was about then that another factor entered the picture: the notion, which was already beginning to develop during the 'Gothick' phase but mainly flourished in the 1820s and 1830s, that 'Gothic' was a quintessentially *English* way of building, 'natural' to the country, which therefore should be readopted on patriotic grounds. Maybe that was why English Classical architecture was as inferior as it was: the country was not really *suited* to the style. That could be the underlying reason for that long delay in taking it up, and the persistence of the old style thereafter.[26] This was the first *serious* argument for championing the style: the first one to create a threat for the dominant Classicists, therefore; and the second of our 'threads' leading from Gothick with a 'k', to neo-Gothic without.[27] It has even persisted into modern times: Robert Furneaux Jordan, for example, could still be found claiming in 1966 that Classic was 'an imported art', by contrast with Gothic, which was 'born in the flame of the English spirit ... Deep in English soil ... the sap of Gothic was being nourished.' This was his reason for believing that a 'Gothic Revival, sooner or later, was quite inevitable.'[28] For a time in the early nineteenth century you had English writers claiming that Gothic was actually invented in England, whence it spread to the rest of Europe;[29] but that was always a difficult argument to sustain (especially when France was opened up to travel again after the Napoleonic Wars, and people could visit the real birthplaces of Gothic, like the Abbey of St Denis), and the patriotic argument eventually fell back on England's sharing the credit for the style with others; or on 'Perpendicular', as the one indisputably national variant of it.

This was one of the reasons why the 'Gothic or Elizabethan' style was stipulated in the 'exceptional case', as Scott called it,[30] of Britain's *most* 'national' building, the new Houses of Parliament, in the competition set up for that in 1835; together with the fact that the only part of the original building to have largely survived the fire that had consumed the rest of it, Westminster Hall, was in that style, as was the very adjacent Lady Chapel of Westminster Abbey; plus a popular association of the original period of that style with the winning of Britain's 'freedoms'; and possibly a suspicion of 'Classical' for this particular purpose due to its contemporary republican connotations, in the US and France. There was also some complicated and unprincipled politicking, eerily anticipating that over the Government Offices 20 years later, and which might have had an entirely different outcome – a Classical building by Robert Smirke was the most likely one – if certain cards had been played differently.[31] (So, just as Scott's Italianate Foreign Office was not inevitable, so neither were Barry's Gothic Houses of Parliament.)

As it turned out, however, the Palace of Westminster seemed terrifically national and patriotic, and has always been 'one of the most popular and beloved buildings in the world' (*as* a building, that is, not necessarily for what goes on inside it).[32] Nearly a century later, at the peak of the modernist reaction against all things Victorian, the president of the RIBA, no less, could describe it as 'surely the most beautiful group of modern buildings in Europe.'[33] The modern architect and writer Reginald Turnor called it 'one of our few really popular buildings', and 'shuddered' at the thought of how it might have turned out if the fire had come 20 years later, and the commission had therefore 'fallen into the hands of Scott, Butterfield, Street, or – the shudder becomes a paroxysm – Waterhouse'.[34] But that, of course, was not what Scott, Butterfield and the rest thought. By their time, whatever the 'public' felt about it, among the architectural *cognoscenti* the Palace of Westminster's reputation had catastrophically collapsed. 'Long before the building was completed,' wrote Kenneth Clark (construction was still continuing in our period), 'no serious Gothic Revivalist dared to praise it.'[35] The reasons for this (aside from MPs' practical objections)[36] were that its 'Gothic' features were now seen as merely a pastiche on what was basically a Classical design: Barry was basically a Classical architect, after all; and taken from a period of Gothic architecture that was now regarded as a decadent and even an immoral one. 'To despise it for its Palladian symmetry and multiplicity of corrupt ornament' became, as John Summerson put it, 'a mark of sophistication'.[37] However much the people may have loved it – indeed, perhaps *because* they loved it – men of taste, or principle, were bound to disagree.

This was when the Gothic Revival started to get really serious. It began with Augustus Welby Pugin, ironically in view of the fact that he provided most of the detailing for the Palace of Westminster; but even he had not realized how corrupt a style the Perpendicular was until he had thought it through. (His own early buildings are in Perpendicular.)[38] Pugin's contribution to the Revival of Gothic in Britain, apart from inspiring the fashion for little Gothicky villas that can be seen in every English suburb today, was to give it a high *moral* purpose; imbue it, in fact, with nearly all those ideas – about its being a more religious style, more functional, more structurally honest, closer to 'nature', more progressive, more satisfying for the masons who built in it, more expressive of communitarian values, fundamentally more *human*, therefore, than the cold, alien and alienating, artificial, deceptive, mechanical paganism that had been foisted on them all those centuries before – which we shall see being pursued and elaborated so eagerly in the debates of the later 1850s (which is why there is no need to go into detail about them here). None of these characteristics fitted Perpendicular half as well as they did earlier Gothic styles (especially 'Middle Pointed', generally thought to be the purest form); which may have been a blow for English patriots, but, as Pugin showed, when it came to the 'serious' matter of architecture there were holier grails to be followed than the narrow 'English' one.

In fact Pugin saw Gothic as a way of reinvigorating English society, no less; restoring to it the communitarian values that, in his opinion, the Renaissance and Reformation had all but destroyed. *Contrasts: A Parallel between the Noble Edifices of the Fourteenth and Fifteenth Centuries and Similar Buildings of the Present Day; Shewing the Present Decay of Taste*, his first great book on this, by juxtaposing drawings of ideal mediaeval townscapes – church spires, almshouses, infirmaries – with what he took to be their modern equivalents – utilitarian factories, workhouses, slums, prisons: it was all a bit unfair (and not very well drawn)[39] – illustrated the social transformation he wished to achieve far more vividly than mere words could have done; and also clearly demonstrates, for us, that the evils he was really resiling against were mainly those of industrial capitalism. It also implied two other things, both of which were to become problematical. One was that England, if she were to reform herself in the way Pugin wanted, needed to return to Rome, as he himself had done in 1834. This created presentational problems, at the very least, at this time of particular tension between Catholics and Protestants – the 'Papal Aggression', and all that. Protestant Goths, who included all the major architects lined up on that side of the Battle of the Styles in the 1850s, had their work cut out for them to resist the 'Papist' slur, repeatedly thrown at them by Palmerston, for example; and were not helped by the fact that so many other of the most fanatical and dogmatic champions of the style were High Church Anglicans – 'Puseyites', for example, and 'Ecclesiologists' – thought to be teetering on the edge of the pit that led to Rome. Or, it should be added, by Pugin's perceived insanity – he was committed to Bedlam – shortly before his death in 1852. ('It is not to be wondered at!' wrote the severely Protestant Basil Clarke, some time afterwards.)[40] That is one reason why Gothic also needed John Ruskin, its other main champion in the early 1850s, but as anti-Catholic as Pugin was pro.

The second implication of those drawings in *Contrasts*, and, indeed, Pugin's open belief, was that the transformation had to be total. This applied to architecture as well as to society. It would not do just to build a few Gothic churches, say, among all the Classical boxes. (The 'modern' townscapes in *Contrasts* have one or two of those, survivals from the original Gothic age, albeit with their spires usually broken off.) Britain needed to have a style that united her, just as every other society in history had done. We shall be picking up on the 'totalitarian' implications of this later.[41] Yet again, this can be seen as a response to the social *dis*unity that had been one of the effects of the Industrial Revolution on Britain, explaining (as it certainly did, in part) the confusion of architectural fashions at that time; by contrast with the more harmonious England that was reflected in, say, 'Middle Pointed' (in Pugin's opinion, of course). All this was revolutionary, marking the end, for the Goths, of any idea that theirs was 'merely a style', to be picked and chosen according to personal preference; and the beginning of an all-out war with the Classicists.

Indeed, there can be no doubt that in this war – the wider war in which our Battle was just one engagement, albeit the most exciting one – it was the Goths who were the original aggressors.[42] This may explain why the Classicists were so slow to muster their defences: the onslaught took them by surprise. It happened quite suddenly. (Sir John Summerson gives a very precise date for it: 1857.)[43] First Gothic had been just a bit of fun; then it was taken up more seriously for churches and Oxbridge colleges – often as a side-interest for Classically trained architects (like Barry). By the 1840s the Classicists had more or less conceded that territory to the Goths, in a kind of two-state solution, with themselves still holding on to the urban secular. It always needs to be borne in mind in connection with the Gothic Revival, in view of the greater publicity it has always enjoyed, that the majority of buildings erected in this period were probably 'Classical'.[44] Some Classical architects occasionally designed in Gothic too. This kept them in employment. But the Goths were not content with that. Round about 1850 – not much earlier – they decided they could conquer the whole land. At about the same time, and as a result of the more serious turn that the Gothic Revival had taken, it began to be argued that Classical architects should not be allowed to build in Gothic even if they were willing to, because they could not have absorbed the 'spirit' of the style. Look at Barry's pastichey Palace of Westminster, the 'serious' Goths said.[45] Several books and pamphlets were also produced – one of them by Scott – to show that 'middle' Gothic was as suited to secular buildings as it was to churches.[46] This was clearly ominous for the Classicists, threatening not only their principles (which there is no reason to believe were not genuine) but also their jobs.

Which is where our story begins: at the precise moment when the Goths were starting to move on from the mainly ecclesiastical territory they had so successfully carved out for themselves in the 1840s and early 1850s, to take on the whole secular world. Before them now stood the Government Offices: the greatest secular building one could imagine; a worthy test of the pretensions of their style to suit any function; and – possibly – the prize that had to be taken if they were to march on. Their loins were girded, with their books and pamphlets and magazine articles sharpened and strapped to their sides. They were in the ascendant, their little victories marked all over the land: a town hall here, a new church there – and there, and there. On the other side, the Classicists seemed less well prepared – why, they had scarcely produced a pamphlet for years – but were the army in possession, and so a formidable foe. And they had the old Palladian Palmerston on their side, of course; though they were not to realize the importance of this yet, until the Battle got under way, the political terrain suddenly shifted, and, like Macaulay's Horatius, he was able to hold the Government Offices bridge for the Classical cause virtually on his own.

4

A Grand and National Work

From the time it was decided to group a number of Government Offices on one large Whitehall site, it was obvious that this was going to be a Great National Building. There were not many of these in London, as it happened: the Houses of Parliament obviously; plus Westminster Abbey and St Paul's Cathedral. Others were either too small (the original War Office in Horse Guards Parade), or too frankly undistinguished (Buckingham Palace), to qualify. So this seemed a good opportunity to add to them. A Great National Building, by definition, had to be more than a mere set of offices for ministers and civil servants to work in. For a start it had to *represent* the nation: that was the 'national' part of it. Secondly, it needed to *celebrate* it; to be worthy of the 'greatness' of the nation it represented in this way. These were two of the considerations that bore on the vexed question of its style.

Both, however, were problematical. One simple reason for this is that not everyone participating in the debate in the 1850s did want the new building to be 'celebratory'. The reasons for this will be explored later (in Chapter 8), but it is important to bear it in mind at the outset. Those who hankered for a 'grand and national work', in the words of the Duke of Newcastle;[1] or one 'worthy of a great country' (the *Morning Advertiser*);[2] or 'a *chef d'oeuvre* of the nineteenth century' (the *Ecclesiologist*);[3] or 'the crowning achievement of the century' (A. J. Beresford Hope);[4] or 'a monument of architectural genius' (*Building News*);[5] or, quite simply, 'the most magnificent building of the age' (Hope, again),[6] were in a minority. *Blackwood's Magazine* insisted that 'the final reputation' of any nation depended 'as much, perhaps more, on the structures which they have reared as on the writings they have produced, or the conquests they have gained.' (As proof of this he instanced the ancient Assyrians, Babylonians, Egyptians and Greeks.)[7] But not everyone agreed. And for those who did, there were other difficulties. One was a simple, but perhaps an intractable, one. Even if they had wanted to, and irrespective of the 'style' chosen (which we shall come on to in a moment): was it *possible* for Britons to build 'great'?

The signs were not auspicious. We saw in the last chapter how low most Britons' national self-regard *vis-à-vis* architecture had fallen for years now. This had not changed. Scarcely anyone in the country in the 1850s – certainly not those with any interest and expertise in the subject – believed that England was any good at architecture. London especially was a mess: a 'howling wilderness of stuccoed stupidities', as one warrior in the 'Battle' put it,[8] with most of its public buildings regarded as 'wretched abortions' by another, Benjamin Hall, MP, in 1857.[9] Gilbert Scott thought that most of London's recent buildings were 'a disgrace to a civilised country'.[10] This touched a patriotic nerve, because of the contrast it seemed to present with most other European capital cities at this time. Foreigners visiting London, wrote one (English) critic, 'regard with astonishment' its 'feeble, insipid [and] spiritless' character – this by comparison with Britain's wondrous 'works of utility, our bridges, canals, tunnels, railroads' and the like.[11] Nearby Paris was the most commonly cited contrast: before 1850 a city not unlike London in many ways, with its narrow filthy winding streets, for example, but just then being gloriously renewed by Baron Haussmann under Napoleon III's patronage.[12] 'Every traveller abroad', wrote a correspondent to one of the professional journals in 1857, 'comes back enraptured with the architectural beauties of Continental cities and deploring the meanness of our own metropolis.'[13] It was true. Cultivated cosmopolitans had been saying this for years.[14] With the advent of cheap excursions to Paris in the 1850s (Thomas Cook started package tours there in the summer of 1855), knowledge of Paris's superiority began to seep down the social scale.[15] In regard to national architecture, William Tite told a meeting of the Royal Institute of British Architects in 1855, most foreign nations 'put us to the blush'.[16] His and all the other *cognoscenti*'s views may have been jaundiced. 'Cultural cringe', especially in relation to France, was a common English phenomenon at this time. Others noticed and deplored this; like W. M. Thackeray, who satirized it as a form of 'travel snobbery'.[17] But it persisted. The overwhelming impression made by the new Paris is reflected in the profusion of 'French Second Empire' designs among the Government Offices competition entrants, and its winners. (This, incidentally, was the current favourite style of William Burn, the only architect among the judges.)[18] Some of us, long after the event, might want to put a word in for at least a handful of mid-nineteenth-century British architects, as worthy of comparison with the best of their Continental contemporaries.[19] On the other hand the various contrasts that were drawn by the critics were, objectively, telling. By the side of so many great foreign cities – not only Paris but also Vienna, Rome, Berlin, St Petersburg, the new Washington – London could appear very tawdry indeed.

How had this situation come to pass? Or, as one critic put it, *after* the Westminster Hall exhibition: how was it that a nation that had been 'so prolific in heroes and statesmen, in philosophers and philanthropists', could only *build* in a way that attracted 'the contempt of Europe'?[20] (Most experts thought the exhibition showed no improvement at all. If this was the cream of English architectural design, wrote one 'Quilp' in the *Building News*, many must be wondering what the skimmed milk could be like.)[21] Opinions as to the root causes varied. The old cultural élite, predictably, pointed to the simple lack of 'taste' to be found among the rising middle classes; the 'illiterate patronage', as the élitist John Summerson called it later, 'of the industrial age'.[22] Robert Furneaux Jordan may be right to claim that these people 'were not always the philistine upstarts they have been painted'; but there can be little doubt that their 'taste' was generally different from the old guard's: 'they preferred the obvious to the subtle, the grand to the simple, ornament to proportion'[23] – and *associations* above all.

Other scapegoats were trotted out. Pugin blamed utilitarianism, as we have seen.[24] Coventry Patmore thought the fault lay with 99-year leases, which discouraged solidity and permanency.[25] Others blamed capitalism generally (or 'money-grubbing');[26] individualism – with people preferring to live in pigsties of their own, as Patmore put it, rather than share substantial buildings with others;[27] government patronage: poor Pennethorne came in for a great deal of vituperative criticism on these grounds, quite unfairly, but the point being made was an ideological one;[28] poor education, which had not mattered so much when patronage was in the hands of the small élite that *was* educated, but did now;[29] 'doting antiquarianism';[30] and fashion.[31] The architect E. B. Lamb thought poor self-regard on the part of his fellow professionals had something to do with it. 'It is a humiliating truth, but truth nevertheless, that very low views – utterly derogatory to it as art – are entertained of Architecture, *both by those who follow it as a profession* and by the public.'[32] Goths, of course, blamed the 300-year tyranny of the Classical *style*; Classicists the unsettling new penchant for Gothic. It also partly depended on when you dated the start of the decline: the Reformation (Pugin), the Renaissance (Ruskin),[33] the Great Rebellion (Gilbert Scott),[34] or Strawberry Hill. A particular obstacle in London's case was English property laws that made large-scale planning like Haussmann's in Paris virtually impossible: 'they manage such things better in France', as one critic put it;[35] though there was also another, less negative, side to this, as we shall see later. (In a nutshell, France had got its fine architecture at the cost of its 'freedom'.)[36] Some were defeatist from the beginning. Pugin, for example, thought it would be 'impossible to do much good' while England remained Protestant.[37] The *Daily Telegraph* also, but for other reasons, believed the problem was 'irremediable'.[38] One hoped not – if one had any feeling for architecture, at least.

If this situation was to be remedied – if it could be – there was obviously a lot of work to be done. Some was. There were attempts to improve architectural education: a new Chair of Architecture instituted at London University in 1841, for example;[39] occasional lectures at the Royal Academy and the London colleges;[40] a new school of architectural design set up by one C. B. Allen under the auspices of the fledgling (and radical) Architectural Association in 1851, which, however, struggled thereafter;[41] and a professional syllabus and exams proposed (but not implemented for a while).[42] Also in 1851 an 'Architectural Museum' was founded, initially in a warehouse in Canon Row, Westminster, though it moved several times. In 1854 Prince Albert was persuaded to become its patron, but used the opportunity, according to Scott, 'to read us a not very complimentary lecture on the state of architectural education in this country, which he described as contemptible in the extreme'.[43] (They did these things better in Germany.)

Despite its royal patronage, however, the museum was beset with difficulties from the start, and struggled financially; mainly because it was felt to be, in the words of the architectural historian James Fergusson, 'too exclusively mediaeval to perform, even in a limited sense, the functions of an institution to improve the taste of the nation'.[44] That was due to the fact that the original idea behind it had been the rather narrower one, of aiding the training of craftsmen in what its neo-Gothic founders took – but not everyone agreed – to be 'the national style'. One effect of this was to divert government funds from it to the far more catholic architectural collection that the new South Kensington (later Victoria and Albert) Museum was currently assembling, based originally on the old Crystal Palace exhibits.[45] Another educational initiative was the award of prizes to promising architectural students, which also, however, quickly turned partisan. (It started in August 1860 with the announcement of a 'Pugin Travelling Fund' to promote the 'true principles of mediaeval architecture'; to which William Tite immediately responded with his own prize for 'the author of the best set of sketches or suggestions in the Italian style of Architecture, for Public Buildings adapted to modern wants'; which was then capped by Sir Francis E. Scott's new 'Prize of ten guineas for a design for some Civil Building, in the style of the Thirteenth or Fourteenth century' . . . and so on.)[46] Beyond this, public taste in historical architecture was boosted by the richly illustrated 'Handbooks' published in these years by Fergusson and others;[47] and at a 'lower' level by some excellent surveys, again well illustrated with woodcuts, in the characteristic serial 'cyclopaedias' of the time, produced for the working (but usually consumed by the aspirant lower middle) classes of society.[48] It was not much, but it was something to be going on with. And it was necessary, if British architecture was to rise to a level where the 'greatness' of the British nation could be adequately commemorated in its public buildings.

So far as *style* was concerned – the other chief problem for the enthusiasts – this gave virtually no guidance at all. A great national building had to be big, of course, and well designed. Implied in much of the grand language surrounding it was that it should be 'monumental'. One or two commentators suggested it needed to have a prominent vertical feature, like a dome or tower.[49] Virtually everyone agreed that any statuary affixed to the buildings should be illustrative of British history, rather than Classical.[50] Beyond that, however, architects and their patrons were left to their own devices and preferences. What architectural style the new Government Offices should be in depended on two other considerations: what particular *qualities* of national 'greatness' it was thought they should be commemorating; and, of course, what styles there were to hand. But neither was straightforward. We saw in the last chapter how muddled Britons were in the ways they collectively regarded themselves; divided as they were by region, religion, gender and class, far more than they were united in any kind of common 'nationality'. Identities were shifting, too; especially the balance of domination and influence between the upper and middle classes in Britain, which was particularly delicately poised in this decade (the 1850s), so that one cannot even talk of a 'dominant' social discourse then. Each grouping had a different idea of what Britain, or England, stood for, several of which were incompatible with one another. So, some Britons admired themselves for their religion, others for their rationality; some for their modernity, others for their traditions; some for Britain's military and naval exploits, others for her pacifism; some for the great British Empire, others for the fact that they had put all that 'imperial' nonsense behind them. (This was reflected in their differences over what kinds of English 'heroes' should be commemorated in the friezes and statues surrounding the new Offices.)[51] Each of these alternatives had different stylistic implications, at a time when the situation on the architectural stylistic front was just as muddled.

What was called the *genius loci* – the spirit or associations of the precise location of the new building – did not help much either. In the case of the Houses of Parliament this had been a big consideration: to ensure they blended in with the structures surrounding them, especially the surviving parts of the old palace, like Westminster Hall, and Henry VII's Chapel just over the road. 'In all architectural plans,' Sir Robert Peel had argued then, 'one of the most indispensable attributes was congruity.'[52] Goths tried to make the same case for a Gothic Government Offices;[53] but it was obviously less convincing here, with the site being just that much further away from the abbey and the palace, and nearer, in point of fact, to the Classical buildings of old Whitehall, including Inigo Jones's Banqueting Hall. 'There must be incongruity,' as the *Building News* put it, '*somewhere* between Whitehall and Westminster.'[54] Really it depended which way you looked: up the new Parliament Street, or down. And, of course, on whether you believed 'congruity' was a virtue in any case. Lord Elcho's argument for having a building that *stood out* against its neighbours was that it would avoid the 'monotony' that he, for one, found in Edinburgh's (Classical) New Town.[55]

One way of sidestepping these vexed issues was archaeological. It is a common practice of national movements in modern times to help forge their identities through the discovery and reinvention of past traditions: literatures, customs, styles of building and the like; but this is usually a recourse of national*ist* movements in opposition to foreign tyrannies; which was not Britain's, or at any rate England's, situation in the 1850s. Both sides in the Battle of the Styles did occasionally try to present the issue in this way: with Classicists painting Gothic as a Roman Catholic imposition, for example, with the emphasis on the 'Roman', and the Goths in their turn regarding Renaissance architecture as a product of Italian cultural imperialism (as it was *not* called then); but that is not the same as having a colonial jackboot on your – Irish, say, or Indian – neck. Gothic – the obvious historical candidate for a truly indigenous style – did not quite have the purchase that this would have given it. It also had some other drawbacks as a 'national' style, as we shall see.

Nonetheless, Gothic's 'English' claims were certainly sounder than those of any other style. The controversy over where it had exactly originated still rumbled on in the 1850s, but only desultorily, with scarcely anyone believing any longer that the English had 'invented' it, and everybody happy to cede primacy to the northern French – or possibly the 'Saracens', but independently.[56] German Goths, incidentally, were less happy about this, resisting the French (and even more Islamic) claims 'frenziedly' for years, and in the end only managing to square them with German national pride by the trick of defining the 'Franks' as Germans *really*. 'If the Gothic could not be German because it was French ... then France, the birthplace of the Gothic, must itself be German.'[57] The nearest the English Goths got to this was by emphasizing the closeness between England and France in the twelfth and thirteenth centuries, which made Gothic a shared achievement in a way.[58] One or two claimed it had reached its 'highest form of perfection' there, whatever its origin: 'the Gothic of England,' wrote the historian J. H. Parker, 'is more perfect, more systematic, better proportioned, more consistent, than that of any other country.'[59] It was also occasionally spoken of more generally as a 'Teutonic' style, at a time when many English counted themselves as Teutons.[60] A more securely 'patriotic' way might have been to base the revived style on 'Perpendicular', the one indisputably English Gothic variant of them all; which some contemporaries favoured (including the leading historians who engaged in this debate),[61] though not the *cognoscenti*, for reasons we have touched on (and shall return to). This aside, however, Gothic was – as Coventry Patmore put it – 'the only style which England has had any part in inventing or improving.'[62] The clincher may have been the argument from the weather: Gothic was clearly better suited than the Classical, wrote G. E. Street, to England's 'cold, dark and chilling' climate; 'who ever saw Englishmen really enjoying a portico in England?'[63] The main proofs here were the large windows that the 'Decorated' and then the 'Perpendicular' styles enabled, to let in the sparse northern light; and the high-pitched roofs, for the northern rains and snows to run off.[64] In fact there could be almost no doubt at all about Gothic's historic English credentials, so long as the English were prepared to share them with others – and vice versa. Hence the transnational eclecticism of Scott's first design for the Foreign Office. Gothic may have been English, but it was not narrowly English. In fact, in the eyes of Edward Freeman, one of its chief glories was that it *transcended* nationality.[65]

In any case, people instinctively *sensed* it was 'their' style, claimed the Goths; 'something which they feel to belong to their own race and their country',[66] one that had 'sprouted forth of itself from the souls of our forefathers';[67] 'our National Style'.[68] In fact, some said, it always had been: one should not be misled by that 300-year gap. That had only occurred because the Classical élite had cruelly taken Gothic away from the people; despite which it had remained close to their hearts, surfacing in the occasional 'survival', or in the 'real style of architecture, rude but quite genuine' – barns, for example – that 'lingered on' in the countryside, where the Classicists' claw could not reach.[69] The idea that the Classical style had been *imposed* on England, unwillingly, was a powerful one.[70] All the Gothic Revival was doing, therefore, was reawakening a slumbering giant; or, by another way of looking at it, releasing the people from their Classical chains. How many people opted for Gothic *simply* because of its English historical credentials is hard to tell. There was certainly a surge of interest in both English history and ancient English buildings at this time (stimulated in part by Pugin's artist father), which may have had this effect.[71] And the argument was felt to be seductive enough by the Classical camp to be worth trying to counter.

Palmerston tackled it by arguing, in the final Commons debate of the Battle, that in fact 'the real aboriginal architecture of this country was mud huts and wicker wigwams', which were then supplanted by Roman, long before the Goths came along: which the Goths thought was silly, but was in fact quite ingenious, and did, indeed, give Classical a considerably longer pedigree in Britain. Palmerston also claimed that the later Classical (Renaissance) style very soon became naturalized, in effect, by the genius of Inigo Jones, Wren and Vanbrugh.[72] That could also be said to be true. The problem with this line of argument, however, was that it still did not alter the fact that Classical was an alien imposition (on the first occasion), and an import (on the second). (Yes, admitted one Goth in 1860, Classical remains in Britain preceded Gothic; but with them they were 'only the evidences of ancient humiliation'.)[73] But then you could argue that Gothic essentially was too. In fact, wrote a contributor to *Building News* in 1860, reviewing a pro-Gothic pamphlet, Gothic was found in southern France a century before it appeared in England; had been brought there by the crusaders from the East; and so far as England was concerned had been imposed on her by her Norman masters.[74] A better argument, rather more frequently aired, was that Gothic was not the style of a nation or region so much as of a historical period; and of a pretty unenlightened – dark, feudal, superstitious – period at that. If it was English *then*, it was certainly not English now.[75] In other words, archaeology alone could not clinch the argument.

This was why the 'patriotic' argument for Gothic needed to go further. One way was to associate the age of the original Gothic with institutions the English could be particularly proud of; which meant, of course, cleansing it of all those 'dark, feudal and superstitious' associations. That was difficult, especially in view of Pugin's open fondness for dark, feudal superstition; but not impossible. The alternative to the 'feudal superstitious' scenario was the 'winning of English freedoms' one: the view of the thirteenth century, in particular, as the period of Magna Carta, Simon de Montfort's parliament, the gradual liberation, through 'incorporation', of England's great commercial towns and cities, and (a little later on) the Peasants' Revolt and the Lollards; the period, in other words, in which the 'real' England was heroically struggled for, against her feudal tyrants.[76] This was not a new idea, but can be traced back at least to the revolutionary years of the seventeenth century, constituting what Chris Brooks has dubbed the 'gothic [political] semantic' that he believes was largely responsible for the style's survival, underground, right through the years of dominant Classicism.[77] As it so happened – but not fortuitously, the Goths believed – the thirteenth century was now broadly coming to be accepted among experts as the highest stage in the development of the English Gothic style: that is, early and Middle Decorated; and the point where it first began evolving indigenously and separately, rather than being still subordinate to, or linked with, France.[78] And there was a further architectural link. This period of mediaeval 'freedom' was commonly seen as having been rudely interrupted in the sixteenth and seventeenth centuries, when England's over-mighty monarchs returned; or, as the pro-Gothic historian Edward Freeman put it: 'the old power of the bold heart and the strong arm' was supplanted by 'the plotting head and the cunning tongue'.[79] He was referring to the Tudors; but the Stuarts were universally seen as worse.[80] And it was the Stuarts, of course, who had brought the Italian Renaissance to Britain.[81] Simple coincidence?[82] The patriotic Goths thought not.

It is worth reiterating this *radical* appeal of mediaevalism, whose attraction to so many people in the mid-nineteenth century might otherwise be attributed to sheer reactionism, which is what on the surface it looks like. Capitalism was also a factor here. It could be argued that the Stuarts introduced that to Britain too, though this is highly questionable (simply because so many other reigns have an equal claim), and was not, in fact, argued at the time. Nonetheless, much of the appeal of the Middle Ages rested on its *pre*-capitalist characteristics; its innocence of all those 'modern' features – in architecture, the shoddy speculative urban build-ing of the eighteenth and early nineteenth centuries, but more broadly the greed, cold utilitarianism, alienation and soullessness: the virtual destruction of 'society', in other words – that we have seen formed many people's abiding impression of modern industrial capitalism in those (mainly) grim times. In the absence of a convincing contemporary 'progressive' (or socialist) challenge to this, the Middle Ages began to appear strangely alluring to those who sought alternatives. This was whence a number of architectural Goths quite openly came; men like W. J. Cockburn Muir, for example, whose Battle manifesto, *Pagan or Christian?* (1860), was full of fulminations against 'the god of gold', and of appeals to the superior spirituality of England's surviving 'nobles, . . . almighty burghers . . . and villeins of labour', whom he relied on to rescue not only England's architecture (which the book was about) but also her whole society.[83]

Muir reads very feudally, and also religiously; but you did not need to be as backward-looking or Puginesque as this in order to be inspired, socially or archi-tecturally, by the Middle Ages. There were contrary indications to be inferred there too. They are strongly implied in all that talk about Gothic's being the 'people's' mode of building which was then snuffed out by the 'élite'; the same élite, in fact, that had also robbed the people of their *political* liberties under the Stuarts. 'Liberty', indeed, was one of the two most common associations claimed for Gothic in the mid-nineteenth century, together with religion, of which more later. Political liberty was only part of it. Gothic builders had also been more *soci-ally* free: ruling themselves (in their guilds), and so able to express their creativity; so making the erection of the great mediaeval cathedrals, for example, labours of love for all concerned, unlike the alienating labour of the present day.[84] That was one of the things that made Gothic *intrinsically*, as Scott put it, 'the most free and unfettered of all styles'; less regimented, that is, by rules, conventions, 'orders' and strict models from the past. 'The true characteristic of the style is *liberty*'.[85] It was a rose-tinted picture, of course, so far as the genuine Middle Ages were concerned; but it furnished an ideal that was radical as well as reactionary. Even when the socialists returned to the political scene again in the 1880s, some of them took up with it: William Morris, of course, most famously.[86]

It was a powerful case, appealing to the new Liberal and democratic national identity that was forming quite powerfully (among certain classes) in Britain at this time. How radical it was perceived to be, even before Morris, is demonstrated by a public meeting that took place at the Architectural Museum in London in July 1858, when the sharp political differences between Goths and Classicists broke out in a furious row over just this question. The museum was founded to educate craftsmen in the building trade, as we have seen; to which end its trustees took great pride in their tolerance in allowing them in 'in their working clothes without obstruction'. At this meeting, however, one member of the audience went further, suggesting that, by this means, 'servile' workmen might be turned into 'free' ones, like in the Middle Ages; and be given the credit they would then deserve for the buildings they helped create. Gilbert Scott went along with this. That, however, was going too far for the Classicists present, who took strong exception to this downgrading of the 'genius' of the individual architect, to the undeserved benefit of 'mere' artisans.[87] This seems to have been a common view on the Classical front. Later William Tite, the scourge of the Goths in the Commons, insisted that architects needed to be 'scholars and gentlemen', not mere craftsmen.[88] On another occasion, in a talk to the RIBA, he recalled how, as part of their apprenticeship years ago, aspiring young architects were supposed to spend three years in a carpenter's shop. 'He could hardly conceive how three years could be more completely wasted.'[89] Architects designed; craftsmen simply carried out their orders. That was the natural order of things, which Gothic threatened.

It may also have been felt to threaten a wider natural order. One of the problems with Gothic, in the eyes of upper-class Classicists, was that it seemed peculiarly *dis*orderly: not bound by the same clear rules and conventions as Greek and Roman, and hence (in those same eyes) not bound by any rules at all; or even − as was apparently one view in the eighteenth century − simply 'the capricious whims of a disordered imagination'.[90] It may or may not be significant in this regard that the word the Classicists used to categorize the different stages of their style was '*orders*' (plural) − Doric, Ionic and Corinthian, with some authorities adding two transitional ones − which must have sounded reassuring to those who put a high premium on 'order' in other senses. So important was it, in fact, that it was probably the main incentive to the neo-Goths' discovery, or invention, of some 'orders' of their own early in the nineteenth century, to match the Classicists'. Thomas Rickman is usually credited with being the first to divide mediaeval Gothic into 'Early English', 'Decorated' and 'Perpendicular', in 1817;[91] but the attempt to 'rationalize' and so in a way control Gothic goes back beyond this.[92] Unfortunately for the advocates of 'order', however, Gothic's 'stages' could also be taken to denote something else: development, or 'progress'; which for conservatives was not half so reassuring. It was for this reason that the Reverend J. L. Petit, despite his own great love of Gothic, came down in 1861 in favour of Classical as the national style of the future; on the grounds that its essential *stability* would counteract Gothic's 'restless tendency to change'.[93] One does not need to read much between the lines of that, in these very uncertain times, to detect some social and political as well as aesthetic apprehension there. Francis E. Scott accused Palmerston of opposing Gothic because it valued individuality and liberated the workman, so running 'counter to official doctrines of precedent and routine'.[94] Palmerston never said this directly, but it would fit both his aristocratic character and the times. There can be little doubt that Gothic was a socially dangerous style; or was perceived to be; or was presented as such by those who wanted to commend it to Radicals. It may not have helped that most Gothic architects in the 1850s came from the middle classes – even the lower middle classes (Scott's father was a minor clergyman, Street's a small solicitor, Butterfield's a shopkeeper) – which, however much they might have to fawn on the upper classes (for commissions), made them inherently unreliable.[95] There was, then, a political dimension to this Battle. Classical represented the order so beloved of Britain's traditional ruling classes; Gothic, the unpredictable energy of the middle classes they served.

This being so, then, how could either style be regarded as genuinely 'national'? For another *desideratum* for any 'national' style of architecture is surely that it be universal, or at least predominant; fit for every function in that society, and expressing in some way the 'identity' of every person in it. That is how the 'great' styles of the past and of other civilizations appeared, as the Goths kept pointing out: Greek, Roman, mediaeval European, Islamic, Hindu, Sino-Japanese; as 'catholic' styles, all-embracing, expressing the whole of those societies, not just classes or factions within them, as seemed to be the case then in England, and so 'national' in that sense. Of course there were alternative ways of looking at these: as fashions *imposed* from above by élites, and so representing hierarchies rather than peoples, for example;[96] but most neo-Goths did not see this, save in the case of England's own 'Classical' phase. Many of them were greatly exercised over England's deficiencies in this respect. Gilbert Scott, for example, deprecated the 'unnatural severance of civil from ecclesiastical architecture' then. 'No age of the world', he claimed, 'has ever . . . made use of a style for one class of buildings different from what it applies to others'. 'Our architecture . . . must be universal in its applicability. The style which is best for the church, must be equally so for the palace, the court of justice, the market, and the dwelling-house'. And lastly (this comes at the very end of his pre-Battle manifesto on the applicability of Gothic to public buildings): 'we must unite, one and all, in one steady, unflinching effort, constant, untiring, and in the same direction'.[97]

It is that 'same direction' that is the key phrase there. Nationality seems to have been at the root of it. It was not that Gothic was an intrinsically superior style to every other, in Scott's view, at any rate; but that it was the one most likely to rally the nation around it. This was thought to be important not only for the social and political reasons that have been suggested already – Scott gave no sign that these were ever any concerns of his – but also in order to legitimize the style and even the age historically. Past civilizations, it was pointed out, had always been defined by their ancient remains; indeed, often these were the only evidence modern scholars had to place and date them. What then was the archaeologist of the future going to make of the enormous stylistic confusion *he* found (or of course she, though that would have seemed less likely then) when he dug down to where they were now?[98] And if nineteenth-century English civilization – or any civilization, for this was not an exclusively British concern[99] – could not be straightforwardly verified by its archaeological record, could it really be said to qualify as a 'civilization' at all? At the root of this troubling idea lay the Victorians' new sense of 'history', which we shall be returning to later. In the present context, however, it added to the urgency for a *single* national style.

There was of course a tension here: between many Goths' association of their style with 'freedom' – and, for example, Scott's own resentment at the prime minister of 'a free country' daring to clip his (Scott's) wings[100] – and the fairly rigid boundaries to this 'freedom' that he was implicitly advocating here. In an earlier chapter this was characterized as a kind of 'totalitarianism'.[101] The main motive behind it seems to have been this one, to create a 'national style'. But a 'national style' (singular) for as free, pluralistic and highly individualistic a country as England was then may have been too much to hope for. How was it to be enforced, asks Chris Brooks; 'Art-police roaming the land, dawn-raiding architects' offices after a hidden stash of Doric details?'[102] We shall come on to some other ways that were found of solving this conundrum later (in Chapters 6 and 7); but only, as we shall see, by abandoning altogether the idea of a common English style.

Gothic was also supposed to express Britain's *religious* identity. Some of this related to particular features of the style: its verticality, for example, by contrast to Greek horizontality, was supposed to express striving towards God;[103] or to the style's supposedly superior 'honesty', of which more later.[104] But it was also based on history, yet again. Here lurked one obvious problem, however, if the middle classes were to take to it as the Goths hoped they would.

That was its obvious association with Roman Catholicism, both because of its origins in a Catholic age (and if you insisted that 'origins' were important you surely could not pick and choose among them – take the place, Anglo/France for example, but skip the religion); and also because of its great champion Pugin's fanatical Catholicism,[105] and his insistence not only that Gothic was a Catholic style, *rather than* an 'English' one,[106] but also that its revival would inevitably bring

Britain back to Rome.[107] That did not go down at all well in a country that largely defined itself in terms of its Protestantism. It was seen as an incubus right from the start. In 1843 *Fraser's Magazine*, for example, wished Pugin could have been at least a little more 'discrete' over this;[108] 'Verax' in the *Builder* in 1857 believed the 'Puginites are doing more harm to Mediaeval art than all its direct opponents' (and also, incidentally, that the *Ecclesiologist* had 'made more perverts' – that is, converts to Rome – 'than any other means of proselytism');[109] and the historian E. A. Freeman felt that the stigma associated with Pugin was still holding Gothic back eight years after his death.[110] Charles Eastlake pointed out, rather waspishly, that if 'reverting to the habits of our ancestors four or five centuries ago was to be a necessary condition of the Revival,' as Pugin had insisted, 'no one could be blamed for declining to sacrifice the comforts of advanced civilisation for the sake of architectural taste.'[111] Even Pugin might have found it a trial, Basil Clarke suggested much later. 'He was an extremely sensitive person, and could not have stood the life of the Middle Ages for a week.'[112] There was also a practical side. Protestant services emphasized the sermon more than liturgy; which made the traditional *plan* of a Gothic church, with its chancel, rood screen, crossings, high roofs, aisles and pillars (especially the last), unsuited to more modern and 'rational' forms of worship – the 'Service' as Charles Barry emphasized, of '*Common Prayer*'[113] – where congregations wanted to hear what their ministers had to say.[114] In Catholic times that had mattered less than the symbolism and mystery. (Or 'fopperies' and 'mummeries', if you were unsympathetic.)[115]

The Catholic association certainly put a lot of Protestants off. One was the evangelical minister Francis Close, for whom 'the pointed arch – and the fretted roof – and the gloomy crypt – and the secret stairs – and stone altars – and elevated chancels, credence tables . . . painted windows, the reredos, the trypticks, the reliquary' – all the features Pugin so much doted on – were 'the emblems of a gloomy, false, idolotrous, and persecuting worship, from which we were mercifully delivered at the blessed Reformation!'[116] One problem for Protestant Goths was that this was not an exaggeration, as witness this response from one very distinguished High Churchman at the time: 'I will not shrink from uttering my firm conviction that it would be a gain to this country were it vastly more superstitious, more bigoted, more gloomy, more fierce in its religion that at present.'[117] Charles Spurgeon even claimed that Gothic was invented by the Devil, by which he meant the Papists, and as a result built his own famous London 'Metropolitan Tabernacle' (opened 1861) in a very strict Classical Roman style – and one that enabled him to be seen and heard from every part of it.[118] Palmerston, of course, in his battle against a Gothic Foreign Office, milked these 'associations' for all they were worth: comparing Scott's original designs with 'monkish piles', 'nunneries' and a 'Jesuit college', even though – as several exasperated Goths pointed out – the Jesuits in fact post-dated Gothic, and nearly always built in Baroque.[119] But Palmerston knew which buttons to press. That left Protestant Goths, of whom Scott was one, with a great deal to do to take away the smell.

It could be done by ridiculing Pugin. There was a lot of that.[120] Perhaps he was not as important to the Gothic Revival as he seemed to be; which was one way of detaching that great movement from his religion. This of course was import-ant, at a time when an English identity was widely felt to be incompatible with a Catholic one. The solid Anglicanism of men like Scott, Street and Butterfield (Scott was the son of a Church of England vicar), and Ruskin's virulent anti-Catholicism (and anti-Puginism), were a help here.[121] Protestant Goths also had some fairly good arguments. One was to point out that, quite apart from the Jesuits, the more traditional modern British and Irish Catholics currently preferred Classical, which was true. (It was generally the converts who went for Gothic.)[122] Another was to ask why, if Gothic was an *essentially* Catholic style, had it taken 1,200 years from the foundation of the Church for Catholics to think of it?[123] But these were just debating points. A better case was probably the one that sought to relocate the style in the genius of the ordinary English people, rather than in their religion at the time. It was they who – *pace* Tite – had actually built the great mediaeval churches and cathedrals, after all. They had had no choice but to be Roman Catholics then, of course; if, that is, that is what they really were.[124] Ever since Elizabeth's time English theologians had been claiming – in order to justify the Henrician Reformation – that the Church of England's roots and mediaeval history were in fact far more 'Anglo-Saxon' than Roman. It followed – for those willing to listen – that so was Gothic.[125] With one bound, the Goths were free.

But not completely. Gothic's 'high' religious associations never entirely went away. Most Victorians were not 'high', and distrusted the dim religious atmos-pheres that pervaded many of the newer churches built from about the mid-1840s on: William Butterfield's famous All Saints, Margaret Street (1849–59), for instance; and William Burges's beautiful St Mary's, Studley Royal (1871–8).[126] That these churches did not call themselves 'Catholic' hardly fooled those who, in the 1850s more than at almost any other time, suspected Roman*isms* almost more than they suspected Rome; with even the wearing of a surplice by an Anglican clergyman being seen as the thin end of a sinister Papist wedge.[127] In much the same way the Gothic style was seen by some as 'a stalking-horse', 'behind the curtain', for the Revival of Romanism.[128] Some of the fanaticism and dogmatism that had accompanied the Gothic Revival in the 1840s, and could still be read in the 1850s, for example in the pages of the liturgy-obsessed *Ecclesiologist*, also did not greatly appeal, to a people which regarded itself (despite the anti-Catholicism) as usually more relaxed over these things. Even 'enthusiasm' was a derogatory term more often than not.[129] One solution to this problem, adopted briefly by more Evangelical Anglicans in the earlier nineteenth century, was to build in a late Tudor form of Gothic, which had the dual theological advantage of impec-cable Protestant credentials (it was the dominant style, after all, of the English Reformation), and of being lighter in tone, with all those large windows – more 'en*light*ened', therefore. It was also more unambiguously 'national'.[130] But then, of course, 'Perpendicular' was not 'Gothic' enough for the enthusiasts, either religious or professional, for reasons we shall come on to later.[131] Another lasting legacy of these early battles over Gothic in churches was to associate the style *with* churches, almost exclusively; partly because of the sheer accident – as a number of Goths pointed out – that in Britain it was almost only the churches that survived from the Middle Ages (apart from castles, and who would want to emulate them?);[132] and partly because the early neo-Gothic fanatics were usually church-builders. That, in fact, was the main stumbling block that Scott needed to overcome in advocating the style for as brazenly secular a building as the new Government Offices were.

He may not have helped his cause by making his Gothic designs as eclectic as he did. This was despite the motto he attached to them (all the anonymous entries were distinguished by short tags, usually in Latin or Greek), which seemed to present the 'celebration of the achievements of our country' as its major selling point.[133] Many people assumed that the very point of establishing an English 'origin' for Gothic was to justify an English Gothic style. This was the firm view of the historians Freeman and Parker, for example: that modern Gothicists should keep strictly to domestic mediaeval models, unpolluted with foreign (and especially Venetian) admixtures;[134] although Freeman did allow one rather curious exception to this, which was that it was alright if they copied details from buildings that stood on England's mediaeval European trade routes.[135] Scott's first two designs, however, were covered with French, Flemish and Venetian details, with the third, of course – the 'Byzantine' one – being even worse. Just about every contemporary commentator remarked on this: on how 'foreign' they looked.[136] So, if the main argument for Gothic was that it was the 'national style', as the *Building News* asked in 1860, why did Scott not choose a more 'national' form of it? Surely by not doing so 'the plea of "nationality" falls to the ground.'[137] Another pro-Goth thought that if he would only revert to a 'manly' English design Palmerston must accept it.[138] (That was highly unlikely, of course.) And Scott was not the only offender in this regard. Most of the other Gothic designs submitted in the competition were the same.[139] Indeed, one of the most striking features of this whole exercise is how very few of the entries reflected, or were intended to reflect, an English or British 'national identity'. (Most of the Classical entries, too, were basically Italian or French.) It seemed not to be important; to the architects, at any rate.

The reasons for this were simple, and significant. Architects were not nationalists. The Classical ones never had been, as the term 'Classical', referring to ancient Greece and Rome, implies. Italy had always furnished their models, and was the source of the architectural education of those who could afford to travel there (which is why Classical architects were usually Tite's 'gentlemen'). Their style was proudly international: or as international as their travels usually took them at that time. So were their aristocratic patrons, as we have seen.[140] Goths, by contrast, had started out as nationalists, but by the 1850s had turned their backs on that. One who did not, William Burges, claimed this was because Italy in particular was so much more warm and pleasant a country to travel and sketch in than England;[141] which sounds over-cynical, but is given some credence by Ruskin's admission in the *Seven Lamps* that the reason why he did not study his own national Gothic more closely was that he 'found it impossible to work in the cold interiors of our cathedrals'.[142] But there were more principled reasons too. One was the English Goths' conception of their style as *progressive*: to which we shall return.[143] It could not stay the same, but had to develop. The more it developed, however, the more it would depart from what people might recognize as 'English', because of their familiarity with the mediaeval English forms of it. Just copying those – often advocated in the earlier stages of the Revival, but only so that architects could get inside the 'spirit' of the style – was no longer acceptable. The mediaevals did not do it – otherwise they would not have had Early English growing out of Norman, Decorated out of Early English, and so on. Secondly, dull 'copyism' had always been one of the charges they had thrown at the Classicists (sometimes unfairly). Thirdly: they were 'artists, and not mere antiquaries', as Street protested in 1859.[144] They had to be allowed to spread their wings, experiment, be original. One way of doing that was to look abroad for features that might be grafted on to their English style, to improve it: which is what after all the mediaevals had often done. 'Polychromaticism' was the most visible foreign – Italian – import in the 1850s, and the one that provoked the most complaints about 'un-Englishness'; the use, that is, of varied colours of stones, or other materials, in bands or patterns. To deny themselves these improvements, as they saw them, on narrow nationalistic grounds seemed pointless; especially as narrow nationalism played very little part in their own architectural ideologies.

This may have had something to do with the fact that they were artists, and artists tend to be more cosmopolitan than general populaces. That will explain the gulf between them and many of their lay critics on this question, with all the criticism of 'foreignness' coming from the latter and from Classicists, and none from any major Gothic architect. Artists had always been open to foreign influences. Composers aped Mendelssohn and Brahms, slavishly, and invariably dully. Sculptors took their models from ancient Greece, coldly. Painters sought inspiration in the pre-Raphael Florentines, and in nature, which was global. Art recognized no frontiers. Architects were no exceptions. Confining themselves to English models would cramp their style. G. E. Street was the one who argued this most forcibly, in opposition to what he regarded as the narrow parochialism of the historians, Freeman and Parker.[145] Architects travelled far and wide across Europe for new ideas, therefore, and for any good models they could find. None of the leading contestants in the Government Offices competition, Classical or Gothic, was a narrow nationalist in the sense demanded by those who wished the building to look English through and through. There may have been a disjunction between 'culture' and 'society', or certain elements of the latter, here.

On the other hand, the 1850s were – as we saw in Chapter 2 – an unusually 'cosmopolitan' period of British history more generally, with the discourse, at any rate, of internationalism going far beyond the artistic élite. The fact that English Gothic architecture suddenly went 'foreign' at this time – Basil Clarke dated the breakthrough to the Lille Cathedral competition of 1855, which set in train a great fashion for 'French' Gothic in England[146] – could have reflected this. Both British society and English architecture were especially cosmopolitan in the 1850s and 1860s, before both reverting to a more narrow nationalism thereafter.[147] There is likely to have been a connection. At the very least, it is important to be aware that the 'Battle of the Styles' came at this specific period in the history both of British society and of English architecture, when narrow national considerations appear to have been less important than they might have been before, and afterwards.

The place of 'nationality' or 'national identity' in the debate over the architectural style of the Government Offices in the later 1850s is more complicated, therefore, than may appear at first sight. Obviously an early stumbling block is the building itself. However 'foreign' some of the Gothic designs for the Offices were, the version that was finally built was far more so. There is nothing – apart from the statuary – remotely 'English' about it; its clear and only model is Italian Renaissance. Even compared with other 'Classical' styles employed in Britain in previous years it was incongruous: Greek and Roman had at least some claims to have become 'naturalized' through use there over many decades; and French Renaissance was swiftly becoming the 'naturalized' – or at least fashionable – style just then. But then we have already dealt with this difficulty. The finished style of the Government Offices was the product of a series of accidents. It reflected *no one*'s preferences. Very little can be inferred from it, therefore; apart from Palmerston's anti-Gothic prejudice, which was probably related to *one* contemporary discourse in British society, but an aristocratic, rather than a national, one. And even that only explains why the building is not Gothic; not why it is Italian.

Gothic's 'English' credentials of course were far better, which makes it appear likely that they were one of the prime reasons for its aficionados' championing of it during the Battle. That, however, was only true up to a point. Gothic's indigenousness was certainly one of the claims that was made for it; but that was contested (albeit weakly), and it was certainly not the only aspect of the style that appealed. If it was an 'English' style, it only represented certain sections of the English population: male middle-class liberals mainly (though with many exceptions); and a limited range of English values, like 'liberty', which were mainly associated not with the nation but with a class: or, rather, *with* the nation but only *by* that class. As well as this, the way the style was developing in the 1850s was carrying it away from its purely English roots, into more cosmopolitan channels, to the discomfort of those (like our historians) who had originally championed it for its 'Englishness', and now felt betrayed. That sense of betrayal, or at least of puzzlement, may have been shared by others beyond the circle of the *cognoscenti*: this is one of those areas where it is possible that 'culture' did *not* reflect, in any truly representative fashion, the society of its day; but we have little evidence for this, either way. (We shall return to this, in the Conclusion.) Cosmopolitanism, however, was another leading discourse of the time (indeed, of this time in particular); which may furnish another link between all the Gothic designs premiated in the Government Offices competition, with their prominent French, Flemish and Lombardic features, and the broader culture they sprang from. Most champions of Gothic certainly felt that nationality was an inadequate rationale on its own for the Revival of the style. It was certainly a far less leading motive than it was for the contemporary German neo-Goths, whose great cause at that time was the completion of Cologne Cathedral, in its original style, as a 'monument to the German spirit, German power, and German concord'.[148] If that had been said of a Gothic Foreign Office, or, indeed, any neo-Gothic building in England, it would have sounded ridiculous. We shall see (in Chapters 6 and 7) that many believed Gothic represented much more *universal* values, which in their books easily trumped the 'patriotic' one. By their own way of looking at it this made them *inter*nationalists.

The apposition, however, is false. You can be an internationalist and a patriot at the same time: if, for example, your internationalism fuels your patriotic pride. Britons certainly felt inordinately proud that they, *as a nation*, had put aside – or grown out of – the narrower sorts of nationalism that they so despised on the Continent, which made Britain more welcoming of, for example, French and Lombardic forms of Gothic architecture than the French and Lombards would have been of English ones,[149] just as she was of French and Lombardic immigrants to her shores. If the values the Victorians admired so much in Gothic buildings were 'universal', still they could be proud of the fact that it was England, in the modern age, which had rediscovered them, and in many instances was responsible for diffusing them globally. The 'imperialist' implications of this will be discussed in the following chapter. After that, it will be argued that 'morality', 'modernity' and 'philistinism' were also crucial factors in the Battle; but these too need to be seen in conjunction with the fact that Britons tended to regard theirs as the most moral, modern and even proudly philistine nation in the world. So although the present chapter has focused on 'nationality', it certainly has not exhausted the issue. It is involved in all the other discourses that the Battle of the Styles throws up; just as, however, all those other discourses are involved in it.

5

Worthy of our Imperial City

Mid-nineteenth-century Britain, of course, was not only, or 'merely', a nation (or even four). She also ruled a considerable empire, including the hugely populous India. One might have expected that to have been reflected in the contemporary debate over the Government Offices, and in the building as it eventually turned out. One modern school of thought in particular will be expecting this: the one that holds that 'imperialism' was the dominant discourse in Britain throughout the nineteenth century, reflected (at the very least) in every aspect of her culture. This of course is the 'theory' associated mainly with the late Edward Said, though he was not the first to think of it.[1]

In fact Said's work generally steers clear of architecture, with a few pages on it in *Orientalism* (1978) – 'Orientalist' buildings, after all, are easy to spot – but none in his other seminal work in this area, *Culture and Imperialism* (1993).[2] Likewise, John Mackenzie's great series of 'Studies in Imperialism' – concentrating largely on imperialism at home – carries very few architectural titles.[3] The two exceptions to this (both articles), arguing for a significant 'imperial' component in the new Government Offices as they were eventually built, rely heavily on the *assumption* of a wider 'imperialistic' discourse in the mid-nineteenth century than may in fact have been the case.[4] Generally, however, the 'New Imperial History', one of whose most valuable contributions to our understanding of the Victorian empire has been to reveal previously neglected domestic repercussions, has left architecture pretty much alone as yet. This *may* be because it shows fewer imperial markings than do other areas of contemporary British life. Whether or not Said was right about the 'imperialization' of British culture generally (which is disputed by some historians),[5] architecture appears to have missed out on it. This clearly requires to be explained, if it is true; or to be examined more closely, if not.

The imperial significance *in practice* of the new Government Offices is indisput-able, and must – one imagines – have been obvious at the time. The first two departments planned to be housed there, the Foreign and War Offices, were both explicitly concerned with Britain's relations with the outside world. When the War Office dropped out in December 1858, it was the India Office that replaced it. You could not get more imperial than that. A little later the Colonial Office was added. Surely it must have occurred to someone in the 1850s that what they had here was the makings of a great imperial edifice, which ought to express, therefore, that aspect of Britain's national character, as well as all those others: freedom, history, religion and the rest.

And of course some did pick up on this. Here, for example, is Sir Charles Trevelyan, the great mid-nineteenth-century reformer of the civil service, among whose arguments for giving the government 'a beautiful range of public buildings' to conduct its business in was this:

> . . . this city is something more than the mother of arts and eloquence; she is the mother of nations; we are peopling two continents, the Western and the Southern Continent, and we are organising, christianising and civilising large portions of two ancient continents, Africa and Asia; and it is not right that when the inhabitants of those countries come to the metropolis, they should see nothing worthy of its ancient renown.[6]

Trevelyan knew his British Empire intimately, having served in India for 13 years before he took up his home civil service job, and returning there in 1859 as governor of Madras: indeed, he was as famous a reformer there as he was in Britain; so we would expect this of him. But his imperial experience also made him atypical. Few of his fellow Britons shared it with him. Those who did were often inclined to keep it to themselves. 'Anglo-Indians' in particular were something of a special caste in Britain, when they deigned to live there; sticking to their own kind socially, and largely insulated from the more mainstream values and cultures of the metropole.[7] Besides, if we look at it closely, we shall see even Trevelyan's argument was not a particularly 'imperial' one. He was not saying that the new buildings should express the spirit of the empire, but the growth of English 'freedoms', that old chestnut – this is clear from the passage that precedes this[8] – in such a way as not to disappoint any returning colonials. They were a means of celebrating Britain to the peoples of her empire; not the empire to the Brits.

In the more public 'Battle' over this issue, the *desideratum* that the new building should reflect Britain's empire – or her international power and influence, or any other of the words and phrases that were often substituted for the 'e'-word in this period – occasionally features, but less often than we might expect. For 'A Cambridge Man', for example, one of the best reasons for consolidating the public offices on a single site – this was a *practical* argument, therefore – was that they now had to administer the 'public affairs of an empire whose branches reach from Europe into Asia, Africa, America, and Australia, and whose commerce extends to every corner of the globe.'[9] The *Leeds Mercury* thought the same consideration should affect the new building's *style*, which must be 'not unworthy of the centre of the richest city and the greatest seat of empire in the world'. That is more celebratory.[10] A letter to *The Times* in 1857 similarly pleaded for an edifice 'worthy of our imperial city'.[11] 'Great Britain is the richest empire on the globe', commented the *Illustrated London News* in the same year; 'she has one imperial metropolis . . . if, therefore, there are any ten acres on the globe that ought to be covered with externally imposing and conveniently constructed public edifices, they are those adjoining Whitehall.'[12] Other examples could be cited; but not very many.[13] Even the Indian Mutiny, which broke out in the very middle of this debate, could not turn the discussion there. (The main way it bore on it was to strengthen the hands of those who felt they could not afford a new building, while the war against the Indians was going on.)[14] Imperial references really do need to be winkled out of the contemporary texts. Many of them are ambivalent, including some of those just quoted: hitching the word 'empire' to another one celebrating the *wealth* of Britain, which is usually put first, with the implication – surely – that this is a source of greater pride; and not always clearly signifying 'empire' in the sense the word is used today. (It was sometimes employed to describe the four nations of the United Kingdom alone.)[15] This does not entirely dispose of the question, as we shall see shortly; but it is worth noting the avoidance of the term 'empire' during the debate over the building that was supposed to lie at the hub of it, and of any explicitly 'imperial' arguments for it.

It may also be worth emphasizing at this stage that none of this necessarily means that the mid-Victorians, or many of them, did not value their empire; only that they did not think it should be celebrated in stone. Other aspects of their national life they *were* prepared to celebrate in stone (or sometimes superior brick). Their religiosity was one, obviously. Local autonomy was another, represented as we have seen by all those glorious town halls going up all over the north of England at this time. British 'freedom' was another, and was the main quality supposed to be represented in the style of that other great national building of the nineteenth century, the new Houses of Parliament – which incidentally also has nothing particularly 'imperial' about it, though one might expect it to have; with the historical scenes depicted in its frescoes, for example avoiding colonial events almost wilfully.[16] All this tells us, however, is that the Empire could not compete with other national assets or characteristics *as a subject for architecture*; no more.

There were special reasons for this. One was that the British were in a state of denial about their 'empire' at this time. That was not what they felt they were about. The word itself, and its derivative, 'imperialism', were far more likely to conjure up negative associations than positive ones, for reasons that had little to do with the British variety, but more with the tyrant Napoleon III's. (Napoleonic 'imperialism' was believed to be an actual military threat to Britain during much of the 1850s.)[17] It may also have put some of them against the 'Second [French] Empire' style of architecture that was so fashionable among the upper classes then – the 'e'-word there again, as well of course as its Frenchness. That was one reason for avoiding overt imperial associations. Another was that the mid-Victorians simply did not recognize as such the 'imperialism' they did practise. They were not *deliberate* imperialists. India had come to them (or rather, to a private British company), accidentally, and in the bad old days. All they wanted now was to trade with folk. Since their time the use of the word has been broadened out to include all kinds of activities that it would never have occurred to them to categorize as 'imperialistic', including Britain's commercial dominance, and her Christian missionary enterprise, for example; but they were not to know that. Britain's wealth and her commercial expansion did occasionally feature in the debate, and could perhaps be regarded as a euphemism for empire.[18] Alternatively, it could be argued that the imperial significance of the new Offices was so obvious at the time as not to require stating.[19] So the debate over the new Government Offices could have reflected an imperialism in fact, if not in name.

If so, however, it reflected it in curious ways. Our unstated assumption so far has been that an 'imperial' architecture must be grandiose; but that may not be how many mid-Victorians saw it. Cultured cosmopolitans regretted the dowdiness of Britain's capital city, as we have seen, but some of their compatriots actually valued this. It meant that they had their priorities right, and probably contributed to their prosperity. Britons invested money in industry and commerce rather than wasting it on gewgaws. They were a 'practical' and 'rational' people, wrote an anonymous pamphleteer in 1857, and wanted nothing to do with foreign architectural 'Utopias'.[20] (This will have been a reference to Napoleon III's reconstruction of Paris.) Here we find the word 'imperialism' coming into the debate again, but with negative associations. Britain would never be able to emulate the French example, wrote A. J. Beresford Hope (otherwise an architectural enthusiast), 'unless we please to accept an *imperial* regime in lieu of our free institutions'.[21] Almost everyone sneered at the most ornate designs offered in the competition. 'What do we want with the Hôtel de Ville from Paris in order that a few hundred clerks may execute their daily tasks?' asked *The Times* in 1859. 'The colonies may be ruled from a building which is without the Pavillon de Flore at one extremity and the Pavillon Marsan at the other.'[22] In parliament there were many who failed to see the need for a new building entirely, as we have seen already, and shall mention again. None of these commentators was necessarily an anti- or a non-'imperialist'. *The Times* was certainly not. Its empire, however, was struck from an entirely different mould from other kinds; one that could not or did not need to be marked in this way.

This may be one reason (among the other, more accidental, ones) for the mediocrity of the Offices that emerged from this debate. They are not a particularly 'imperial' building; or at least (because this must involve subjective judgements) not as imperial as they might have been. Evidence of 'imperial symbolism' in its detailing and statuary, for example, is – as M. H. Port observes – 'hard to find . . . Here is no sense that symbolic sculpture will strike dread into barbarian hearts, or fill brave Britons with martial ardour.'[23] The only exception is the India Office part of the complex, inserted into the general plan in the wake of the Mutiny, whose external elevation followed the boring pattern of Scott's Renaissance Foreign Office next door, but whose internal arrangements (by Matthew Digby Wyatt) were far more grandiose, and certainly 'imperialist' in just about every sense imaginable. (The great covered 'Durbar Court' is justly famous.)[24] Even so, it was not imperial enough for one or two commentators; like, for example, Beresford

Hope's *Saturday Review*, which greatly regretted that an opportunity to 'make the structure express the union which links the races of Hindostan to this Anglo-Saxon empire' had been subordinated to the need to blend with Scott's 'sham Italian' Foreign Office next door.[25] (Ruskin may also have been disappointed with this, as we shall see.)[26] Whether this was a widespread view, however, we cannot know, because the new India Office – unlike the others – was scarcely discussed publicly or even noticed at the time. There were two simple reasons for that. The first was that nearly all the 'imperialism' *was* internal, and so only seen by favoured (and usually imperial) guests. The second was that the India Office was not financed by British taxpayers, which would have been the only reason for raising it in parliament. It was free – to them. (The poor Indians paid for it.) So Britons took no notice. In the case of the Foreign Office they did take notice, but scarcely ever from an overtly imperial viewpoint. Indeed, the overwhelming impression one gets from this whole debate is that reflecting Britain's imperial status, whatever that might be called, was not seen as important. At the very best, it came fifth or sixth in the pecking order of contemporary discourses informing the debate.

When it came to the stylistic debate of the 1850s (the 'Battle' proper), overtly imperial resonances are fainter still. If either of the two warring styles could be said to be the more intrinsically 'imperial', then it had to be the Classical, because of its association with the Roman Empire. Of course it could be identified with Republican Rome too, which is how, for example, the Americans have usually taken it: hence Washington, and dozens of state capitols in the US; but in Britain's case this was less likely, because of the nature of her relationship with Rome in the distant, but still familiar, past. This was sometimes brought up in connection with the Classical style, but never in its favour.[27] Usually those associations were kept quiet, or used as an argument against. One critic's rejection of the Classical style of architecture on the grounds that it aroused folk-memories of 'ancient humiliation' in Britain, cited earlier, is one example.[28] There is a notion in some historical quarters, including among architectural historians,[29] that the Roman Empire was a popular model for the British in the nineteenth century, which it may have been in some quarters and in some (later) decades of that century; but not in the middle of it, when this particular debate suggests that the *imperium Romanum* was in rather bad odour generally. (Greece was different; less obviously imperial, and so more respectable in a liberal age.)[30] One recent precedent – George IV's 'Roman' ambitions for London, resulting in all those cheapskate pillared terraces around Regent's Park – did not help.[31] Coventry Patmore associated Roman architecture with pride, power, insolence and luxury; and its reproduction in Britain with the English ruling classes and their public schools.[32] It was in the public schools, of course, that the 'Classics' were mainly taught, to the almost total exclusion of any native English history and literature; and from which most of Britain's rulers, both home and colonial, emerged. These associations did Roman architecture no favours, except of course among the dominating élite. They were thought to be one of its attractions to Palmerston.[33] Most of his compatriots, however, would probably have gone along with Patmore. We cannot know for sure; but it may be why the very obvious (surely) Roman 'imperial' parallel was not pursued more.

Roman architecture was also thought to be *aesthetically* inferior to the sublime Greek from which it was derived – cruder, more superficial, simply uglier; but this was not unconnected with Rome's imperial role. The architectural historian James Fergusson, for example, blamed Rome's artistic inferiority squarely on her fatal diversion, under Augustus, away from art and into imperialism. He also felt that there was a direct lesson for Britain here. (And Fergusson, incidentally, knew his British Empire.)[34]

> We are fast verging to a state of wealth and luxury almost equal to that of Rome before she fell under the dominion of her emperors; and if we are to remain a mere money-making, power-accumulating people, undignified by any higher pursuit, our fate must be hers … Still … it is not too late to elect. The path of Athens is open to us as that of Rome.[35]

It did not follow from this that everyone would choose the Greek way, even when Rome's architectural downside was pointed out to them. As we shall see later, many Britons took positive pride in being – like the Romans – men (usually men) of action, not mere art.[36] But architects and the architectural *cognoscenti* could not be expected to feel this way. At the very least, there was thought to be a tension here between art and empire; which was bound to react adversely on the best-known imperial style of the past, and might make it unlikely – even contradictory – for 'empire' to be reflected in the architecture of the day.

More important, however, were certain other qualities or 'associations' that were supposed to attach to Classical architecture, and the contrast these afforded with the Gothic style. Many of these can be seen to have had a bearing on the 'imperial' question, though they did not essentially derive from it. Rather, they are likely to have reflected other discourses that impacted *on* imperial perceptions, or were common to them, in various – often conflicting – ways. The association of Classical with domination or 'ruling' is the example cited so far; but that had other resonances too. For a start, it connected with some of the very powerful class discourses of the period – the notion of the 'Norman yoke', and all that – which obviously had far more to do with the domestic social turbulence of the period (just after Chartism),[37] but affected attitudes to empire too. Classical architecture had a special symbolic role here. It was not simply through accident that that style had become associated with the ruling élite in Britain: their school syllabi, the Palladian fashion in villas, and so on. It also expressed a particular kind of ideology: of order, hierarchy and permanence, which the upper classes carried through to their ruling functions, abroad as well as at home. Classical was an *ideal* style, unsurpassed since Greek times, and unsurpassable. In much the same way, the ancient politics that Britain's future rulers studied in their public schools taught them all they needed to know about how to rule, in any place or time. (Most of

Britain's colonial rulers incidentally came from this class, just as we have seen her domestic rulers did, and for the same reason: the middle classes were off doing much more worthwhile things, like making money.) In this sense the rulers' empire, when they got out there, was 'Classical'. Their task was, simply, to *order* it, on age-old lines, probably 'till kingdom come.

The significance of this becomes clearer when we contrast the Gothic way. Gothic had no obvious 'imperial' associations – unless one went back to the Holy Roman Empire, which in any case built in Romanesque during its most active phase. Most of its non-religious associations, both mediaeval and modern, were local: city and town halls especially. (Indeed, it is for this reason that Ellen Morris feels that Scott's first design was so badly fitted for what she regards as its primary imperial role, with its 'primary topological symbolism ... based in structures connected with civic purpose, like town halls.')[38] Beyond that, from almost the beginning (after, that is, its initial, trivial 'Gothick' stage), Gothic was championed as a 'progressive' style of architecture; one that in its original manifestation had developed continually and rationally, and which consequently was capable of further adaptation, unlike Classical, to any new demands the present and future might throw up. (We shall be returning to this.) It was also a notoriously irregular style, balanced but rarely symmetrical; its forms growing out of its function and materials; dynamic and thrusting; Christian, of course, as against the pagan origins of its rival; built from the ground up, by honest craftsmen happy in their work, rather than imposed from above by dull Palladian pattern-makers, and so at least – as we saw in the previous chapter – quasi-democratic.

Although this cluster of 'Gothic' values gave no clear guidance on imperial matters, it implied some different ways of looking at the latter from the Classicists'. If British society was seen as changeable and 'progressive', it followed – unless you were a racist – that non-British societies were at least potentially equally so. That had implications for the way they were ruled, or the way the middle classes thought they ought to be; or for the images the latter created of the empire, in order to reconcile it with their liberalism. (Some did not, but always opposed colonialism outright.) Simply 'ruling', the Classical method, was not enough. Britain needed to develop her subjects, in a progressive way. Colonial rule had to be adapted to that. Until very recently it had also been thought that her subjects needed to be Christianized too: until the Indian Mutiny, provoked, it was widely felt, by just that policy, rather discredited that. These were not especially 'Gothic' ideas, but they were similar, because they grew in the same ideological, social and economic soil that had given rise to the latter. It is this that makes it instructive to compare them; and then to contrast both of them with the Classical-Tory cluster on the other side. In particular, it throws into relief the domestic imperial confusion that reigned at this time; unsurprisingly, it should be said, in a period of such intense (though generally non-violent) class warfare in Britain: between the upper and the middle classes, that is. Classical *versus* Gothic mirrored this; and also the two classes' very different imperial discourses.

So far (to recapitulate), we have not discovered many ways in which the Empire or imperialism are likely to have impacted on the architecture of this period. They scarcely featured in the debate over this important range of new government buildings, most of which was quite clearly rooted in other contemporary discourses which had no essential connection with empire at all. The buildings themselves (aside from the India Office) show very little physical sign of any imperial input into them. Less surprising, perhaps, is the absence of any influence the other way around: of architecture impacting on contemporary British perceptions of empire and imperialism, which one would not expect; although of course neo-Gothic architecture in particular did have an enormous impact on building in the British (and one ex-British) colonies, and consequently on the colonials' perceptions of the empire, as we shall see. The best we have been able to do – apart from highlighting this lack of a causal connection, which may be thought to be still a highly significant finding, despite its negativity – is to show the shared contexts of certain architectural and imperial notions; which may help us to understand both better.

However, we are not done yet. English architecture was not a closed shop. It was certainly affected by the fact of Britain's presence and expansion in the world. The error may be to regard that presence and expansion as necessarily or exclusively 'imperial', when it was not. Of course, this depends largely on your definition of the word (and its derivatives), which can be anything you like (it is only a word, after all); but which in my view, and as I have argued elsewhere,[39] loses much of its utility and its analytical cutting edge if it is employed too broadly, to describe relationships between peoples and people in which there is no element of domination. Many of Britain's and her citizens' relations with the rest of the world were of this kind. What underlay them in the nineteenth century was not usually a desire for dominance, but a more neutral curiosity, initially, derived in great part from the massive commercial expansion that Britain (almost alone) achieved in the immediate wake of the Industrial Revolution, and the movements of Brit*ons* throughout the world that followed from that. Another factor was foreign immigration into Britain. The scale of this 'outward-lookingness', as it might be termed, was enormously greater than in the case of any other nation – certainly any European nation – at this time, making Britain the most cosmopolitan country of the nineteenth century, and possibly ever. It is this that should be emphasized, and not the 'imperialist' channels into which, for one reason or another, much of this 'outward-lookingness' was turned. Contemporaries certainly emphasized it more, at what we have seen was a high point of internationalist thought and feeling in Britain; indeed, it was one of the principal reasons for any national pride they may have felt. Regarded in this light, the international aspects of mid-nineteenth-century society and culture make far more sense. For a start, they will include a European dimension, which both the parochial and the 'new imperial' schools of British historiography usually leave out. In fact Continental Europe and, to a lesser extent, the US were far better known – certainly more fully covered in their newspapers – than any of those parts of the world Britain was currently colonizing, which so far as most stay-at-home Britons were concerned were generally just blank spaces on the map. 'Cosmopolitanism', therefore, or 'outward-lookingness', are safer characterizations of this phenomenon than 'imperialism'; and of its influence on mid-nineteenth-century architecture in particular.

We have already seen the evidence of this, in the range of styles that were employed in the competition for the Government Offices, very few of which were 'English' in a strict sense, although plenty of English models were available. These included Scott's original Gothic entry, which was full of exoticisms. That was controversial, as we saw; but most people – architects in particular – seemed entirely relaxed about using foreign models or details for their designs. Nor did it seem to faze anyone at this time – it would have been different earlier – when it came to be generally accepted that the origin of the totemic feature of one of their favourite and most native styles, the Gothic pointed arch, might in fact have been a 'Saracenic', or Arab or Muslim, importation.[40] (There is one exception that I have found: a Classicist who blamed the decline of mediaeval architecture on this alien influence.)[41] Apart from that, however, most architects' exoticisms were Continental European, with just the occasional dash of Eastern flavour – Byzantine, for example, *via* Venice; but then architects' and architectural writers' travels at this time did not often take them beyond their own continent. And there was one important exception, whom it is worth dwelling on briefly, for the more he can tell us about the relationship between Britain's architecture and her worldwide presence.

James Fergusson (1808–86)[42] was the author of the fullest and best-known history of architecture of this time, in several large and profusely illustrated volumes, two of which appeared during the course of the Government Offices controversy.[43] He was also directly involved in the Government Offices in two ways: first as a competitor, though his design was not one of the favoured ones: it can best be described as 'free' Classical but with some 'Oriental' hints;[44] and second as one of Palmerston's advisers in the matter of Scott's 'Byzantine' version during that affair, though the former appears to have taken little notice of his advice.[45] The interesting thing about Fergusson is that he started out not as an architect or an architectural writer but as an indigo planter in India, where he first developed his interest in architecture through the study of, in particular, the ancient cave temples of Orissa in Bengal.[46] He branched out from there into Indian architecture more generally, and then Islamic, both of which he admired greatly, albeit discriminately. No modern writer has been able to find any trace of 'Orientalism' in its derogatory meaning, or condescension, in his work, the Indian volumes of which remain in print today in India.[47] Those volumes make no comments on the British Raj in India, except to castigate it for its lack of respect for his beloved Indian architecture; 'wherever our influence extends,' as he says in one place, 'we have destroyed.'[48] Just once, later in his life, he came out with some unflattering remarks about the Indians' capacity for self-government, which must reveal prejudices that had been simmering for years, though in this case they were provoked by one particular Indian's accusation against him, which was certainly unjust, that he *had* been condescending.[49] That, however, had no bearing on his views of their architecture, which did not require a capacity for self-rule to make it some of the most magnificent ever built. (After all, the great mediaeval builders were not self-governing, either.) It was from this unusual starting point that he eventually launched himself into European architecture, his volumes on which appeared in 1855 and 1862. There is much that is idiosyncratic and just plain wrong about many of Fergusson's ideas. (For a start, he thought the Romans had built Stonehenge.)[50] But they were not Eurocentric. Rather, they reveal a breadth of vision about the subject that was peculiar to him in one way (he was *sui generis*), but not entirely atypical for the time. This may be one of the less acknowledged by-products of Britain's expansion into the world in the nineteenth century: a broadening of *empathy*, too, which is not found so much in more self-contained nations.

Fergusson's general view of architectural style was that it should grow naturally from people's social and material situations, and from their 'ethnicity', which he had some more strange views about: such that the 'Celts', who inhabited Asia Minor as well as the regions usually ascribed to them, were superior artistically to the 'Aryans', or Indo-Europeans, including both the Greeks and the English.[51] This was 'true style', as opposed to what he called the 'imitative or copying' ones; which in his view included Roman and European Renaissance architecture, as well as what he saw as the 'strange mania for copying debased European art' by modern Indians, to which we shall return.[52] This in fact was not so very far removed from the Gothicists' position in the 'Battle of the Styles', which was that Gothic had, in its time, been 'natural', whereas revived Classical was artificial. It might have been expected to place Fergusson on the Gothic side in that Battle, but did not, because he felt – quite logically – that reviving Gothic now was just as false; and in fact he was no practical help at all when it came to this particular great question of the day, because he believed – again, perfectly logically, but exasperatingly for his admirers – that it was hopeless trying to anticipate, let alone devise, a future 'natural' style.[53] Nonetheless, he thought they could learn much from the Indians in this connection: not of course by copying from them – that would be 'a crime'; but in order to 'widen our basis of observation' in the pursuit of a new style of their own (there we have the 'outward-lookingness'), so enabling them to see their architecture from the outside, and from the point of view of a style which was still 'living and growing'.[54] It was a question of vitality. Indian architecture still had it, in abundance; European architecture did not.

It is of course possible to see this as patronizing, in a sense. There is a tradition, going back at least to the eighteenth century, of Westerners purporting to admire more 'primitive' societies for the freshness, naturalism, morality and so on of their lives and cultures: the 'noble savage' trope, for example; but who would run a mile if they were asked to live like noble savages themselves. The 'real' India, or Africa, or wherever, was romanticized, but not in a way that did any real favours, in the modern world, to its peoples. We find a lot of this in British imperial thinking and practice later on: as in the common post-Mutiny disdain for 'educated Indians', or 'babus' (Fergusson's assailant was a 'babu'); and the early twentieth-century administrative philosophy of 'indirect rule', which aimed to preserve and rule through 'indigenous' customs and institutions. Sharp-eyed watchers-out for tell-tale 'imperialist' hints in the cultural attitudes of nineteenth-century Britain are probably right to be suspicious of this.

On the other hand, one cannot really dismiss as 'patronizing', advice which the adviser genuinely believes should apply to him- or herself too. Fergusson certainly did; more to the point, however, is that this idea that English architecture should become more indigenous and natural – more 'native', if you like – was a deeply rooted one among the whole 'Gothic' community of the time, from Pugin to Ruskin; before it was taken up by the Arts and Crafts Movement towards the end of the century. Essentially this was another part of the contemporary reaction against modern industrial capitalism, and in particular factory mass-production, which were seen as the cause of the destruction of craftsmanship The solution was to revive the latter. But that was easier said than done. By this time there were, supposedly, few remnants of it left in England to revive. This is where the colonies came in. Capitalist imperialism had not yet succeeded in wiping out craftsmanship there. So Ruskin's architectural protégés, T. N. Deane and Benjamin Woodward, went recruiting in Ireland (a quasi-colony) when they wanted old-fashioned craftsmen to beautify their new, Gothic, Oxford Museum (1855–60).[55] India was another place where genuine craftsmanship survived, as Fergusson had found, and as the Indian galleries at the 1851 Great Exhibition wondrously revealed. In 1860 the Architectural Museum in London acquired a large collection of original Jain temple carvings to put among its Greek and Gothic casts, obviously because they were much admired.[56] Tim Barringer has given this trend – the recapturing of old skills and cultures from the imperial periphery – the name of 'Colonial Gothic': 'colonial', that is, in the *anti*-imperial sense, as in 'colonial resistance'.[57] Insofar as this can be seen as an important influence on the course of the Gothic Revival (and it certainly did not need India to remind the Goths of 'craftsmanship'), it was not an 'imperialist' one. 'Imperial', perhaps. Or, better still, another product of Britain's 'outward-lookingness'.

There was also, however, a payback to this. While Britain used her colonies for a certain amount of inspiration when it came to her architecture, she also shipped her architecture out to them, in a big way. It was a little like – though this should be regarded only as a simile, not a substantial point – the way she imported raw cotton from India, then made it up into fabrics in Lancashire, to be exported back to the subcontinent; in that case to the great detriment of India's indigenous textile industry. Whether the export of her architecture to India (and elsewhere) had anything like this effect is difficult to say, without a great deal of research. Fergusson thought it did. He greatly deplored the fashion among rich Indians for building mock Italianate villas for themselves, instead of houses in their own national styles. Of course this was mainly their choice, and even understandable. 'It was natural, perhaps, that they should admire the arts of a race who had shown themselves in war and policy superior to themselves; but it was fatal to their arts, and whether a Revival is now possible remains to be seen.'[58] That looks like a typical effect of 'imperialism'. But of course Italianate villas were not devised or designed to this imperial end, and certainly were not forced on Britain's colonial subjects. If they were a result of 'imperialism', then it was a very 'informal' kind: the imperialism of (bad) example, or influence. They also did not represent Britain's favoured style of building in her colonies, from the 1850s onwards. That style was the Gothic.

The spread of neo-Gothic architecture out from Britain into the wider world in the second half of the nineteenth century is remarkable. It was not of course confined to British colonies. Continental Europe also took to it in a fairly big way. So did the United States: in its prestigious college buildings, for example (both Yale and Chicago universities have Magdalen College towers),[59] probably because Gothic signified prestige. This is especially notable because Britain had never before been regarded as a *cultural* trendsetter, partly because she appeared so inferior to Continental countries artistically. This at any rate was the widespread opinion in Britain itself, among both the *literati* (as they were called), who of course regretted it, and those who, perhaps perversely, rejoiced in it. (They were the ones who thought actions were better than art.)[60] Neo-Gothic architecture, however, is the one exception to this. England was indisputably the world leader in this genre. France and Germany, despite the former's better claim to leadership of the original Gothic style, never took to it so early or enthusiastically. But on the occasions they did, it was often to English architects they turned for designs, at least initially – George Gilbert Scott among them.[61] One can call this 'cultural imperialism' if one likes; but it was a very 'soft' kind, unconnected with any element of 'power': neither expressing it, nor requiring any more overtly imperial form of power to back it up. It was more a matter of what D. C. McCaskie has termed '*in*culturation' (as opposed to 'acculturation'): other peoples sucking in artistic fashions, rather than having them imposed on them.[62] If one insists on using the 'i'-word for this, one is diluting it very thinly indeed. (And one would have to apply it to Renaissance Italy.)

Of course it was different in the British colonies, where British colonialists of one kind or another – government officers, capitalists, settlers, *etcetera* – were responsible for most of the major building, and where consequently the cultural imperialism involved was 'harder'.[63] Hence the Gothic-style buildings erected in the colonies during the second half of the nineteenth century: from the great cathedrals, churches and universities of Sydney and Melbourne, for example, some by English and others by Australian architects, but all reflecting their common

cultural heritage; through Canada's extraordinary neo-Gothic parliament building in Ottawa – the style there partly chosen to link British North America
with the fount of its 'liberties' in Westminster;[64] the imposing university and
'Victoria' railway terminus buildings in Mumbai, which obviously did not reflect
the Indians' cultural heritage, or not entirely; through to the hundreds of small
churches, especially, scattered all over Britain's dependent colonies, sometimes
in rather crude forms of Gothic (through lack of resources), but recognizably
'pointed' all the same. In the case of the settlement colonies there is no mystery
about this: Gothic architecture simply – as Thomas Metcalf puts it – 'reassured
their inhabitants that, even though far from "home", they remained British.'[65]
One should not underestimate the deep imperial loyalties of most British settlers
in the nineteenth century. It is only fairly recently that Australians, for example,
have come to refashion themselves historically as a 'subject' people of the British
(and so a country that had its architecture 'imposed' on it).[66] Elsewhere it was
different. But in any case, neo-Gothic architecture was one of the most visible
signifiers of the British presence throughout her empire; up there with afternoon
tea, arrogance and cricket.

Of course this does not mean that it was inherently, originally or essentially
'imperialistic', any more than tea, cricket and arrogance were. (Well, perhaps
arrogance.) We have seen that the 'Battle' over architectural styles in the mid-
nineteenth century was fought with hardly a hint of 'imperialism' entering the lists
at all – certainly not as significantly as the many other discourses, and 'accidents',
that determined the victors in that. We have also seen, however, that the value
systems that were associated with the two major warring styles could *inform*
imperialism, in different and even contrasting ways. Classical was the 'dominating'
style. It expressed authority, rigidity, power. Gothic did not, to the same degree.
It is significant, therefore, that Gothic became so ubiquitous a style in Britain's
colonies; by contrast with England, as it happens, where it was *never* the majority
style, after the Goths lost their Battle over the Government Offices in 1861. This
may largely have been a simple matter of artistic or emotional taste: exiled Britons
found Gothic prettier, or – for the homesick ones – more familiar. (We should
not allow ourselves to be over-seduced by 'deeper meanings'.) On the other
hand, the arguments that were made at the time to justify the transplantation of
what was, despite its possible 'Saracenic' influences, clearly an essentially European
style, beyond Europe, and beyond the European 'races', suggest another reading.
Gothic expressed – or rather, could be used to express – simply a different *kind*
of imperialism from the rigid, authoritarian, Classical one. It partly hinged on its
being a fundamentally 'natural' style – 'natural' to all peoples, therefore; and partly
on its flexibility. The next couple of chapters will elaborate and try to explain
these two crucial justifications for the use of Gothic in such buildings as the
Government Offices. They also, however, had clear imperial implications, which
we need to note briefly here.

The first derived from Gothic's universalist pretensions: the idea – among advanced Gothic theorists, at least – that the style was *not* just an English or European one, but expressed fundamental 'truths' that were applicable universally. This way of thinking always carries the seeds of imperialism within it, though they are not necessarily imperially sown, and do not always flower imperially. (Some cultures are happy to keep their 'fundamental truths' to themselves.) What can turn them imperialistic is when people with the power to do so decide that universally applicable principles should be universally *applied*; with the universalism acting both as their justification for this, genuinely or otherwise, and as a way of blinkering them to its 'imperialist' attributes. (After all, they are only trying to enlighten, not to control.) Many 'imperialisms' have either started or been sustained in this way, from the Iberian conquest of the Americas (Catholicism), through Napoleon's (Enlightenment), to the American Neo-Conservatives' in the early 2000s (markets and democracy). The worldwide spread of neo-Gothic, of course, was nowhere near as portentous as these events; nor was it instrumental – so far as we can see – in furthering Britain's own contemporary 'formal' imperialism in any significant way. Other 'universalist' principles were far more important. At most, it may have been symptomatic of these: of many Britons' beliefs, first in general principles *generally*; and second that *they* had discovered them. The 'imperial' implications of this were probably insignificant, and certainly not a prime reason behind the support for Gothic in the mid-nineteenth century. But they were there.

There was one more imperial implication to this, however. Gothic universalists of course did not argue that Gothic as it appeared in Britain, or even in Europe, was applicable universally; but only that the style, in this more relaxed perception of it, as merely a body of 'principles', could be *adapted* anywhere. This was because of its capacity for 'progressive development'; which was the thing that laid it open to accommodation to other cultures than the one it was rooted in. Its propagandists were very insistent over this. Gothic, wrote one of them, 'is applicable, not only to all purposes, but, with some modification, to all climates . . . It would not be exotic even in the tropics.' After all, 'Saracenic', which was really only an 'inflexion' of Gothic, flourished there.[67] In 1859 the *Building News* spoke of the 'elasticity and almost universality of Gothic architecture, which does not consist alone in pointed arches, clustered columns, and floral ornaments, but in its useful and practical character, in its constructional truth, and in the broad measure of liberty which it accords to all who practise the style.'[68] Gothic in other words was not simply a 'style', and certainly not one over which England wished to claim any sort of 'ownership'; but a body of principles, applicable anywhere, and which if they were applied everywhere would produce a rich variety of indigenous styles.[69] This could be said to mirror another strand in the complex web that constituted British imperial ideology in the later nineteenth century: the more 'liberal' sort, which saw Britain's role as facilitating the free development of her colonies, eventually, in their own ways.

So far as colonial architecture was concerned, this is largely what happened. In Britain architectural theorists, especially those associated with the *Ecclesiologist* magazine, busily set to work to begin adapting the Gothic style to other climes. In 1856 the *Ecclesiologist* even produced a design for a prefabricated iron church to be shipped out to the tropics, which showed remarkable flexibility in view of its principled opposition to the use of iron before then.[70] In fact when Gothic reached the colonies it did often diverge quickly and substantially from the English pattern: least of all in the countries of Anglo-Celtic settlement, including the US, as we have seen (all those Magdalen towers); but quite substantially in India, for example, where the greatest monuments of Victorian neo-Gothic would look just as 'Oriental' if they were transported to an English setting, as they seemed English in Mumbai. This can be read in several different ways. George L. Hersey sees it thus: '"Gothic" possesses itself of the styles, now denatured into partial vocabularies or dialects, of other cultures. By incorporating the best in them, and by removing their indigenous structures, it exploited them and dominated them.'[71] For Tim Barringer, on the other hand, 'read rightly, the colonial Gothic style implied a profound critique . . . of . . . the forms of authority on which British power in India rested.'[72] But that was how British imperialism very often worked. Anglo-Indian Gothic was expressing one – more 'liberal' – form of it, as against the 'authoritarian' one. Perhaps the best way to regard these Anglo-Indian Gothic buildings, however, is as a form of architecture essentially 'negotiated', as Preeti Chopra has put it, between the two cultures and sides.[73] As such they fully expressed the 'progressive' spirit of neo-Gothic, far better than, for example, the mere homesick copyism more typical of the Australian colonies. It is this that makes them – in Chris Brooks's opinion – 'high Victorian Gothic's outstanding imperial creations';[74] and also some of the most telling, about the ambivalent and complex nature of the British imperial process itself.

One of the reasons why the new Government Offices were projected and built was to enable the government to take care of all the new business that was coming its way, to which the colonies contributed, but not in any exceptional or much remarked-upon way. The style of the building had nothing at all to do with the empire, except of course the decoration of the India Office part of it, the decisions on which involved nobody apart from the small Anglo-Indian élite that had commissioned it, at the expense of their Indian subjects. In the widespread discussions over the remaining Offices – which had, as we saw, almost no impact on the outcome, which was stitched up between Palmerston and Scott – imperial considerations were barely raised, either as reasons for building them at all, or as arguments for building them in one or other particular style. Britain's status as an imperial power, therefore, had almost no bearing on the project; at least not ostensibly. (For we do need to leave the door slightly open for coded references; or for the possibility, unlikely as it might seem, that the only reason it was not mentioned was that everyone accepted it without saying.)[75] Lastly, we need to remind ourselves again of the highly fortuitous nature of the ultimate decision, to build in Classical rather than Gothic, before assuming – as one commentator does

– that the latter style stood almost no chance in view of the fact that 'the imperial status of the nation demanded a symbol of international legibility', which could be 'afforded by [a] classicized style alone'.[76] In fact, Gothic *could* have won.

This may seem odd to us, even counter-intuitive; but it was not atypical of most of the nineteenth century. The empire only began to be celebrated monumentally in Britain itself towards the very end of that century; and to be plausibly reflected in the style of other buildings later still, with the advent of 'Edwardian Baroque'.[77] As well as this, London boasted almost no 'Oriental' architecture in this period, at least in its public buildings, which, if there had been more of it, might have been seen as another way Britain's empire was reflected in her culture. (This, however, can be read two ways. It could be a sign of imperial arrogance. On the other hand, if the India Office had been topped off with a Hindu dome, or some other feature, it would probably be regarded today as insufferably Oriental*ist*. One cannot win here.)[78] It should be repeated here that this does not prove, on its own, the unimportance of the empire to Britons in the mid-nineteenth century. There may be evidence for that; but this is not it. There are better reasons for this neglect. The first has to do with the nature of the British Empire at this time, at least as perceived at home: unassertive, apologetic, cheaply run, in denial, sheltering behind other terms (so as to avoid the 'i'-word), distorted by other value systems than essentially or obviously imperial ones: unlikely, therefore, to dominate the discourse or (more accurately) discourse*s* of the day, in competition with other spirits of the age. The second relates to the nature and place in Britain at this time of 'culture', meaning in this context 'artistic' culture; which was hardly ever a reliable indicator of the broader society it was rooted in, as we have seen. The fact that the mid-nineteenth-century empire is not reflected in the metropolitan architecture of its time, therefore, is more likely to indicate apathy towards architecture than towards the empire. (We shall be returning to this.)[79]

This then is a *cul-de-sac*. But there are other ways of relating these two phenomena. One is to see what the architecture of this period can tell us about the *forms* of contemporary imperialism; not through any way in which the former might have been affected by the latter, or vice versa, but in the ways that both reflected discourses that were independent of each of them, but nevertheless underlay them both. The 'Battle of the Styles' shows how contested they were *vis-à-vis* architecture; they were in the imperial field too. We have seen how there was a 'Classic' way of ruling, and a 'Gothic' way: in other words, how the domestic discourse that inclined the British upper classes to rule authoritarianly also inclined them towards Classical Revival architecture . . . and so on. There was also, incidentally, a 'plague on both your houses' way: that of the 'free-trade' imperialists, who did not really want to 'rule' their markets at all, but only to be allowed to trade with them, and involving as little as possible of the government interference that was symbolized by the building of 'Offices' for it. We have also seen elements in *Gothic* architectural theory, especially, which reflected other imperial discourses: cosmopolitanism, for example (all those Flemish and Byzantine features in Scott's original drawings);

anti-capitalism and anti-modernism ('Colonial Gothic'); and 'Liberal Imperialism', whose equivalent in the sphere of architecture was the export abroad of the universal principles of Gothic, to be developed indigenously thereafter. All of these constituted alternative discourses, which had nothing originally to do with either architecture or imperialism, but affected both, commonly.

6

The Lamp of Morality

Scratch almost any middle-class Victorian and you would find a moralist under-neath. (Scratch a little deeper and you might well find a hypocrite.) We should not underestimate the bearing of this on the debate over the style of the new Government Offices in the 1850s. Both sides saw themselves as crusaders, bat-tling for 'right' and the 'truth'; rather than merely people with different aesthetic preferences, or even identities. Hence the ferocity of the contest. Of course this could have been merely a cover, conscious or not, for less elevated motives, such as stylistic preferences that were really socially determined, or simply whimsical; but few of the participants in the 'Battle' would have admitted to that. For them this was a deeply serious matter; involving, as most of the greatest Victorian debates did, some quite fundamental questions of morality.

'Seriousness', or 'earnestness', was one of them.[1] For many middle-class Victorians, this was a moral *desideratum* in itself. All else was frippery, superficiality, play; alright in their place – the nursery, for example – but elsewhere only to be indulged in guiltily. So far as English architecture was concerned seriousness had been a leading feature of it since at least the Stuarts, by comparison at any rate with other countries' architectures, where 'fancy' played a larger role. This may be one of the reasons England never took to Rococo; or – with one exception we shall come on to shortly – to the kinds of delightful fancies that adorn so many seventeenth- and eighteenth-century public buildings even in a city like Copenhagen (in case we thought this was a northern thing). Why this was so is difficult to fathom. The English were not blind to 'fancy' generally, as much of their literature attests. Maybe it was the fact that literature was a matter of choice for them, as buildings – together with food, another area in which the English were notoriously unimaginative – were not. So they had to be taken seriously. Two historical influences may have been the Puritanism that unseated the Stuarts (temporarily) in the mid-seventeenth century; and then the succession of very dull royal patrons who replaced them (permanently) after 1689.

A more crucial factor, however, was probably the rise in Britain of the practical and productive middle classes, especially in the early nineteenth century. Their antipathy to 'fancy' is well known, if only through the character of Thomas Gradgrind in Dickens's *Hard Times* (1854): a caricature, of course, but with some basis in truth.[2] Another of their antipathies was the upper classes, and especially the aristocracy; which as it happens were the classes responsible for virtually the only *un*serious English architecture of the eighteenth and early nineteenth centuries, as well as for the dull, boxy stuff: all those Gothick makeovers, for example; and aptly named 'follies'; and the occasional 'Orientalisms'. The two leading serious architectural theorists of the day, Pugin and Ruskin, both deplored aristocratic luxury, Pugin blaming it for the collapse of the tower of Fonthill Abbey, for example;[3] and Ruskin for the decline of Venice, no less.[4] This was also thought at the time to explain the greater prevalence of this kind of thing in Continental countries, all of which (including Denmark) were more socially backward than Britain – more aristocratic, therefore.[5] The ethical dimension to this was plain. Fancy meant pleasure, which at worst was a sin in itself, but even at best offered temptations to sin, as exemplified in the common middle-class image of the typically amoral aristocratic lifestyle, which was not entirely unmerited; and a waste of productive time. One of the charges laid against upper-class Regency architecture by *Blackwood's Magazine* in 1836, for example, was that it was frivolous, and so – and it was *Blackwood's* that made the connection – 'unchaste'.[6] Such moral seriousness – one modern architectural historian calls it 'the dreadful Victorian guilty conscience'[7] – may have been a particularly British characteristic at this time; which in the view of Henry-Russell Hitchcock helps explain why 'High Gothic', the 'serious' version of the style, caught on so much more in Britain and her settlements than elsewhere.[8]

Respectable architects, and anyone with a serious interest in architecture, needed to distance themselves from 'frivolity'; which also meant – for the two ideas were closely connected – rejecting the notion that architectural style was simply a matter of personal choice, or 'taste'. 'Let me protest warmly', wrote G. E. Street in 1852, 'against the too common method of argument in this matter, which seems always to assume that the question between the two styles is merely one of taste'.[9] That also of course had another advantage for the middle classes, who were always being told by their 'betters' that they *had* no taste, yet were scarcely ever helped by them to acquire it; but who in any case rather resiled against qualities that could not be measured or quantified. This, claimed most anti-Goths of the nineteenth century and after – usually rather sneeringly – was why they became so reliant on extraneous yardsticks to judge art by: like its 'associations', or its archaeological verisimilitude, or the ethical principles that lay behind it; all these could be measured, in a way that true 'taste' simply could not.[10] Classicists generally stuck with 'taste' right through the 1850s, which is why we find so relatively few *manifestos* on their side of the argument over the Government Offices affair; it was in the nature of 'taste' that you could not explain it to others, and to try to meet the Goths on their own 'associationist' level would have been to concede half the ground to them. To the Goths the Classicists' whole approach appeared superficial. It was they, for example, who happily turned to Gothic (or Gothick) occasionally when their aristocratic patrons demanded it, or sometimes (like William Wilkins) hopped lightly and equally between the two styles; in a way that you never found the leading Gothic architects of the mid-nineteenth century doing: putting up the occasional Classical building as a diversion from their main work, for example – at least until Gilbert Scott shocked most of his co-Goths in 1861 by agreeing to do exactly that in the case of the new Government Offices.[11] Palmerston's advice to Scott on that occasion, that if he were as good an architect as everyone said he was he should be able to design in any style, was exactly the attitude the Goths rejected.[12] For them, the question of style went far deeper than that.[13]

The problem they had at the beginning of the 1850s, however, was that of the two major competing styles it was the Gothic that had seemed to be used least seriously up to then: either for play (in all those follies) or in superficial cladding (Windsor Castle); usually at the behest of aristocrats; nearly always by Classical architects as a sideline; with no true understanding of its structural principles; often in 'false' materials – plaster moulded to look like stone ribbing, for example; and usually for *theatrical* effect: another word summoning unfortunate associations in the minds of solid middle-class folk. It was partly for this reason that most of the earliest fruits of the Gothic Revival in England came to be quite brutally repudiated by the new generation of Gothic architects; up to and including the Palace of Westminster, as we have seen.[14] Two reasons for this we have mentioned already: MPs' grumblings at its practical inconveniences,[15] and its choice of *Perpendicular* Gothic, which was now thought to mark a falling-off in the original development of the style;[16] but there was another objection too. It was (again) not *serious* Gothic. Its architect was not a genuine Goth, but a distinguished Classical architect, Sir Charles Barry, who occasionally dabbled in the style. Its Gothicisms were all in the detail. A common way of describing it was as 'a Gothic skin over a Palladian skeleton'.[17] Indeed, this is what positively recommended it to some Classicists;[18] but obviously could not to the new generation of Goths. Even the great Pugin's involvement, as the man responsible for the skin, could not save it. Pugin had been a theatrical scenic designer in his youth – and apparently succumbed to many of the moral temptations of the life, which if the moral middle classes had known about it would certainly have borne out their suspicions of the theatre;[19] and some thought this showed in the palace's elevations. According to James Fergusson's rather cruel assessment of Pugin, 'the theatrical was the one and the only branch of his art which he perfectly understood.'[20] For J. H. Parker the new parliament building evoked 'shame rather than pleasure'.[21] Gothic was not a style to be employed superficially. That was dishonest. (We shall return to the question of 'honesty' shortly.) It should grow from conviction. That was one of the Goths' main complaints against their adversaries: not simply that they had chosen the wrong style but that they regarded style as a *matter* of 'choice'. This was the first moral objection to Classical, even before the associative and intrinsic aspects of the two styles themselves came into play.

There was also a gender aspect to it. 'Frivolity', the mere following of fashions, and even the theatre, were commonly associated with women at this time, and 'seriousness' with men, who were – it is important to note – almost the only participants in this 'Battle'. Architecture was of course a particularly masculine art form, according to the conventions of the day; involving as it did lots of muscle power – digging, heaping stones on top of one another, climbing ladders, brick-laying, carving – even if the actual architects did very little of this themselves. So far as it is possible to establish, no woman entered the competition for the design of the Government Offices in 1857, and none is to be found commentating on it, unless it was pseudonymously.[22] There are indications that women were interested in the debate, enough for many of them to be spotted at the exhibi-tion in Westminster Hall, as we shall see,[23] and at other meetings to discuss the issue: one at the Architectural Museum in July 1858, for example;[24] and another at a lecture in January the same year, 'attired as if they were at the Opera', as the *Builder* commented afterwards – to its readers' patronizing amusement, no doubt.[25] If they contributed to the discussions, they were never reported. Male speakers expressed the hope that they would nonetheless influence the debate, in 'silent yet powerful ways', through their menfolk.[26] If so, it was assumed it would be in a Gothic direction, as that would give them scope for 'embroidery'.[27] Apparently the Classicists had no use for soft furnishings.

Gothic, however, was not otherwise essentially their realm. If they went for it, it would be for the same reasons that attracted them (supposedly) to strong men. One interesting aspect of the Battle of the Styles of the 1850s is the gendered *language* often used in it.[28] We have come across one or two instances already: the *Building News*'s advocacy of architectural competitions, for example, on essentially 'macho' grounds.[29] The word 'battle' itself might be thought to be another; in the nineteenth century, of course, only men fought. In this case, however, the Battle bore many of the characteristics of a war between the sexes, with Gothic cast in the 'male' role, Classical in the 'female'. (This, incidentally, was not how the styles and sexes had always paired off.)[30] Gothic was vigorous, bold, free, manly and explicitly 'masculine'.[31] A lot was made of thrusting towers and spires. For Ruskin, 'masculine' is almost his highest term of approbation for a building or a decorative feature.[32] Any 'false' aspects of buildings – we shall be coming on to this shortly – were characterized as 'effeminate'.[33] In the famous book 2, chap-ter 5, of *The Stones of Venice*, 'The Nature of Gothic', 'Savageness' leads Ruskin's list of the 'characteristic or moral elements' of the style.[34] Gothic might have feminine features; but they needed to be kept in their place. The 'ogee' was the most problematical of these in the eyes of some Goths (the sides of the ogee arch curve back on themselves before they meet); such as Scott's friend and patron the Reverend Thomas Stevens, who regarded it as 'mean, weak, dishonest' and so less 'manly' than the straightforward Early English arches he insisted on;[35] and Beresford Hope, whose comments on it in 1858 appear to associate it quite clearly with feminine sensuality and seduction, which required to be controlled. Early on, he wrote, the mediaevals had toyed and dallied with their darling until they made it the symbol of weakness and luxury; but in its due subordination, such as we find in the later of the two archways at Bury St Edmunds, there is no one who will not feel that the introduction of the ogee was a splendid contribution to the resources of architecture.[36]

It is difficult to avoid a gendered reading of that, even if we accept that what seem to us to be its clear sexual connotations may not have been so obvious, or intended, in Hope's less prurient time. Ruskin, who regarded the ogee as a 'degraded' form, thought it might have been an 'Arab' importation originally, which would explain a lot.[37] By contrast with the (generally) 'masculine' Gothic, Classical architecture was nearly always described and championed at this time in terms of repose, beauty, prettiness, purity, chastity, delicacy, effeteness and effeminacy.[38] Even its characteristic symmetry reflected the way women parted their hair – in the middle.[39]

All of which is simply to point out that this particular 'moral' dimension of the Battle – 'seriousness' – was a partly gendered construction, significantly influenced by contemporary perceptions of the essential roles of the sexes, and mainly by *men's* (the architects') perceptions of them. That is as well as the 'middle-class' and (possibly) Puritan factors. Whether 'seriousness' would have been as leading a moral *desideratum* if men had not been so dominant in mid-Victorian society is, of course, difficult to say, and even dangerous to hypothesize, if it perpetuates the assumption that the 'feminine' is less 'serious' intrinsically.

We have alluded to some of the more overt moral associations of Gothic already. Religion was the first: useful because it had always been a Christian style (apart from that early Muslim input), by contrast with the originally 'pagan' Classical; but also problematical, because of the *denomination* of Christianity it could be associated with. Of course, modern Classical architects were not pagans themselves; but that in a way only made it worse: Goths were at least celebrating a deity they believed in, rather than (by implication) gods and goddesses who meant nothing to them.[40] That was more honest. Gothic's association with the 'truths' of Christianity gave it a certain advantage, though not a crucial one, as we shall see; partly because the obverse of this association was a reputation for *religiosity*, much played on by Palmerston, which acted as something of a brake on its spread from the ecclesiastical to other fields. People did not necessarily want to work or play in churches. This, together with the Catholic problem, is why the 'holiness' of the style was rather downplayed in this particular battle, which was over a very non-religious building, of course, and whose further objective was, quite overtly, to establish Gothic's secular credentials more generally.

This was where the *social* morality associated (allegedly)[41] with Gothic came in useful. Pugin's *Contrasts* was telling here: the plate illustrating modern and mediaeval 'Poor Houses', for example – the first like a prison, the second like a mews – illustrating vividly, if highly tendentiously, the superior humanity of the

Gothic way.[42] Ruskin too was quick to read immorality in Classical; for example, in 'Central Renaissance' architecture, which revealed the 'pride', 'infidelity' and 'indulgence' that lay behind it in every stone. Indeed, '[t]he whole mass of architecture, founded on Greek and Roman models', was 'utterly devoid of all life, virtue, honourableness, or power of doing good. It is base, unnatural, unfruitful, unenjoyable, and impious ... an architecture invented, as it seems, to make plagiarists of its architects, slaves of its workmen, and sybarites of its inhabitants.'[43] It was also immodest, with Classical architects concerned only with '*showing off what they could do*, instead of *carrying out what was required.*' (This is Pugin, and his italics.)[44] 'Slavery' was also one of the targets of G. E. Street's onslaught on the neo-Greek St Pancras parish church (1820); specifically 'Greek female slavery', which presumably referred to the statues holding up the roof of the ersatz Erechtheum on its north side.[45] The 'slavery' Ruskin alluded to was because of the miserable lack of freedom and therefore pride that Classical craftsmen were permitted to take in their work, which could be *seen*, claimed both Pugin and Ruskin, in the dull mechanical products of that work, unlike the obvious joy that Gothic artefacts expressed. There was of course a strong anti-industrial capitalist agenda underlying this, expressed quite openly in the work of both writers. Freed from his 'alienation' (as Marx would have called it), the architectural craftsman could express his humanity again.[46] Not only joy but also 'strength of will, independence of character, resoluteness of purpose, impatience of undue control' and (a little later) 'humility', 'magnificent enthusiasm' and 'unselfishness of sacrifice': all these could be easily inferred from the best Gothic craftsmanship.[47] Working in Gothic obviously made men better (and women embroiderers too, no doubt). It was but a short step from this, though a drastic one, to claim that only independent, humble, unselfish and so on men could produce good architecture; an idea that G. E. Street seems to have gone along with, though he was careful to point out that virtue by itself was no guarantee of good art. Bad men could not build the best buildings, but good men could design rubbish.[48] Beyond that, Coventry Patmore held that even *walking* among good buildings could make people better.[49] The link between morality and Gothic architecture was not watertight, therefore, but it was pretty close.

That was if you thought 'morality' should come into the picture at all. On the Classical side they generally did not, which is why one does not find so many moralistic arguments in favour of the Classical style, as aesthetic and practical ones. If that style had a broad ethical basis at all, it was founded on the idea of 'reason'; the product of the fifteenth-century Renaissance that had also given birth to neo-Roman architecture, after centuries of what the Classicists regarded as barbarism and superstition, not, in their case, morality.[50] Some on the Classical side used that to link Gothic with Catholic and monarchical tyranny (an obvious association, really), so reversing the Goths' libertarian argument for their style.[51] As well as this, one or two of them tried to make something of their style's 'feminine' virtues: its 'purity' and 'chastity', in the words of the *Edinburgh Review*.[52] Another suggested that the five (Classical) 'orders' might have been 'laid down by God'.[53] One George Wightwick had the interesting idea that Gothic should not be used for secular buildings because it was too good and holy for it – it became 'degraded' when put to 'common' use.[54] In this way Gothic's ethical superiority could be turned against it. But that was not a common argument.

The commonest moral line from this camp, however, was to charge the Goths with dishonesty, for pretending they were what they were not: that is, products of the Middle Ages, not of modern times. The very idea of 'reviving' past styles was moral anathema to many. (Classical did not count. It was a long time now since that had been 'revived', since when it had changed out of all recognition. It was the 'modern' style.)[55] Most neo-Gothic houses, wrote the Reverend Thomas Hugo, were 'unrealities and shams', 'hypocrites in plaster', exercising 'an immoral influence' on all associated with them.[56] *Fraser's Magazine* railed at the 'ridiculous pretension and masquerade in a person without a pedigree rearing a brand-new mansion intended to look like a relic of the feudal times' (though one suspects that 'without a pedigree' is the key phrase there).[57] 'Baby-house towers and turrets,' mocked *Chambers's Journal*; 'battlements where no battle can be waged – niches in the walls for dolls instead of statues – what can be in more pitiful taste?'[58] Classicists found plenty of this exhibited among the Gothic entries for the Government Offices competition: 'no better than so much architectural masquerade – the mere playing at Mediaevalism', as a contributor to *Building News* put it in 1857.[59] (Sometimes the play could be dangerous. One particularly virulent anti-Goth wrote of 'disease-engendering sedilia' in neo-Gothic chancels.)[60] Several critics charged Pugin with 'dishonesty' for exaggerating the 'contrasts' between Gothic and 'modern' in the famous illustrations to his book of that name: which was certainly fair comment.[61] That was potentially the most wounding blow that could be dealt the Goths; for whom the clinching moral argument for their style was its intrinsic 'truth'; perhaps, as Michael Bright alleges, 'the most important aesthetic value of the age.'[62]

The idea here was that Gothic buildings openly revealed their functions and structures, as Classical buildings did not. Indeed, the latter style seemed almost designed to do the opposite, with its curtain walls, false windows, internal arrangements distorted to fit in with the requirements of external symmetry, unnecessary porticoes, brick facades plastered to look like stone, and so on. Goths spared no one in their condemnation of these artifices. Ruskin called them 'trickery and dishonesty', and railed against them mightily in chapter 2 of the *Seven Lamps of Architecture* ('The Lamp of Truth') (1849).[63] Scott at one point seemed to attribute them to the capitalist spirit of the age, or, at least, to its seamier side: 'The same unsoundness and want of principle which leads to frauds and wholesale forgeries among commercial men . . . revels unchecked in our architecture'.[64] A particular target was Sir Christopher Wren's St Paul's Cathedral, mainly on account of the 'false' dome suspended underneath its external one, fooling people looking up from the crossing that they were seeing the inside of the latter. Wren had thought he was being very clever here (without the internal dome it would have been like looking up into a chimney); Pugin, however, called it 'a mere construction for effect'.[65] Classicists generally did not dispute this – how could they?[66] – but usually excused it, on the grounds that the structures of buildings, which were usually ugly, *should* be hidden. That was the whole purpose of art, wrote one of them in 1857, using a gendered simile for this, yet again: likening 'architecture' to 'the charm which the modesty of retirement – nay, concealment, throws over the female character.'[67] The Goths – it followed from this – preferred their (masculine) buildings nude.

The idea that architecture should express structure and function was an old one,[68] but started to be applied to Gothic at the beginning of the nineteenth century.[69] From the 1840s onwards it came to be associated particularly with Pugin, who was the one who added this 'moral' patina to it. It was the first of the 'two great rules for design' that he adumbrated (in italics) at the very start of his *True Principles* (1841): '*that there should be no features about a building which are not necessary for convenience, construction, or propriety*'.[70] In Ruskin's *Seven Lamps of Architecture*, this came out as 'the Lamp of Truth'.[71] But that was just a general principle. To use it in support of Gothic in particular, one needed to show that Gothic fundamentally abided by it. After centuries of regarding it as, at best, 'merely' picturesque, a number of authorities in recent years had been progressively revealing what Ruskin called its 'lost structural principles',[72] which seemed to achieve this. The talismanic 'pointed arch' was an example. Early on this had been widely regarded as simply a 'romantic' deviation from the round-arched norm – all those explanations that attributed its origins to praying hands, for example, or forest avenues.[73] Now it was seen in another light. The mediaevals had hit upon it as an *engineering* solution to the problem of bearing great vertical weights, more effectively than the round arch, whose weakness lay in its middle section (or keystone), which of course the 'point' did away with. So it was rational; indeed, was the most rational way possible of bridging high gaps.[74] Ruskin called it 'the *only rational* architecture',[75] which will have come as a surprise to those brought up on the belief that 'rationality' only came in with the Renaissance. Most important for the Victorians, however, was that it represented what many of them were now coming to call 'constructional truth'.[76] Others used words for it like 'honesty', 'reality', 'naturalness', 'science' and 'common sense'.[77] This was essential for the Goths to establish, in order to do away with the notion, which if Scott is to be believed was still around as late as 1860, that Gothic's origins were somehow 'occult'. (That was in a series of lectures he delivered at the Royal Academy early that year on 'The *Rationale* of Gothic Architecture'.)[78] But it was the 'truth' aspect that gave it its moral appeal.

So, in a similar way, the mediaevals had not hidden or disguised the great flying buttresses that were necessary to take the lateral weight of the great stone vaults that covered the greatest of their churches, but simply ornamented them; or tried to flatten the roofs that were needed to cover these, but instead made what they could, decoratively, of their steep pitches; or obscured the seams of their vaults, but instead picked them out in ribbing; or covered the necessary bracing of humbler, wooden roofs, but emphasized it, for example with 'angels'; or even attempted to drain their roofs and towers modestly, but instead flaunted their celebrated 'gargoyles', for the final extrusion of the rainwater, and lovingly and often grotesquely carved them. (It is easy to imagine mediaeval stonemasons having great fun here.) If a Gothic building looked like stone, it was stone; brick was left as brick; wood as wood. Usually, too, form reflected function: a church looked like a church, a manor house like a manor house, a castle like a castle, a humble peasant dwelling like a hovel; and, going into a Gothic building, it was as you would expect it to look from the outside. In particular, no especial value was placed on 'symmetry': facades could be symmetrical, as was the case with many – but certainly not all – great cathedral west fronts; but they would not be forced into symmetry if the requirements of the rooms behind suggested some other form.[79] Today this would be called 'functionalism' or 'structuralism'. Indeed, it is, by historians today looking for the origins of 'modern' architecture, who usually generously acknowledge Pugin's influence here, in spite of how different his buildings look from 'modernist' ones.[80]

Lastly, mediaeval *ornamentation* was supposed to be always 'true', though in another way. Ornamentation might have been thought to be a tricky area, for Gothic theoreticians who placed so much weight on structure and function, which ornamentation, of course, has nothing to do with. Yet almost every mid-Victorian Goth valued 'decoration' highly, and most of them insisted that it was an essential – indeed, a defining – element of architecture, distinguishing it from mere 'building', for example, or engineering.[81] Obviously there were social reasons why architects, struggling for status both as professionals and as 'artists', should want to put some distance between them and these 'lower' occupations. But there may have been something else behind it too; a quite fundamental aesthetic problem arising out of the 'functional' view of architecture: which was, what to do with features that were (or were generally thought to be) ugly intrinsically? (Factory buildings and water-closets were sometimes cited as examples.)[82] Or were the functionalists saying that 'truth' was beautiful *per se*? Ornamentation – of factory chimneys and lavatory bowls, for example – was a way of getting over that. So long, that is, as the ornamentation did not pretend to be something else – that everyone knows that the chimney one sees from the train approaching Leeds is not really Uccello's tower in Florence – in which case it would be deception, and so wrong.

Pugin's way of reconciling ornamentation to his 'constructionist' principles was by insisting that it had to be subordinated to structure, the second of his 'great rules'; and also to function: '*the external and internal appearance of an edifice should be illustrative of, and in accordance with, the purpose for which it is destined.*' (This is another 'principle' he thought it necessary to italicize.)[83] Ruskin offered one interesting suggestion along these lines in the *Seven Lamps*: that East India House in Leadenhall Street be decorated with 'bas-reliefs of our Indian battles, and . . .

carvings of Oriental foliage', and sculptures 'composed of groups of Indian life and landscape, and prominently expressing the phantasms of Hindoo worship in their subjection to the Cross', so reflecting its function far more clearly that was the case at present. (It looked like an ordinary Classical-style English mansion.) But then its successor in the 1860s, the new India Office, as we have seen, was scarcely an improvement in this regard.[84]

There was another way of expressing 'truth' in ornamentation, however; which was by insisting that it was modelled on 'nature' so far as possible. Nature in the mid-nineteenth century could be regarded in two ways: as God's perfect creation, and so unimprovable;[85] or as the ultimate example of structural adaptation to need. (Here we have 'Darwinism', or, rather, the general intellectual climate that gave rise to Darwinism, kicking in.) This marked a huge difference between Classical and mediaeval decoration, with the Classicists sculpting identical urns and bunches of grapes everywhere, taken from pattern books, while the mediaevals took, as Street expressed it, 'nature as their guide' – the Victorian *view* of nature, that is, less ordered than the eighteenth-century one;[86] 'went into the meadows and the woods and culled all that was most beautiful in colour and in form, and applied it to the use of art.'[87] (Even many of the most grotesque of those gargoyles probably looked 'natural' to them, living at a time, of course, when physical deformities were common.) That was especially important to Ruskin, as one might expect if one had read *Modern Painters*.[88] It was a kind of 'truth', too.

Of course there were problems with all this. There is in fact quite a lot of 'deception' to be found in some genuine mediaeval buildings: walls giving the impression of solid masonry but filled with 'clunch', inside, for example; or with bits of iron hidden in them, for strength. Even some of the 'natural' foliage so much admired on the capitals of mediaeval columns proved difficult to track down precisely: the nearest Gilbert Scott could find to it, for example, was 'common parsley'.[89] One or two of those gargoyles will not have been true to any 'nature' their sculptors could possibly have seen, at least while sober: griffins, dragons, devils and the like. Then there was the question of what was 'natural' and what was not, with almost every conceivable shape being found somewhere in nature – crystals, for example. 'Pigs' snouts' was another one provocatively thrown at the Goths at the time; and 'entrails' later on.[90] Ruskin got over this by ruling that a shape was more 'natural' in proportion to how common and visible it was, which ruled crystals and entrails out, and generally favoured curves, 'since there is hardly any common natural form in which it is possible to discover a straight line';[91] but this could also be said to sanction the striped polychromy that architects like Street and Butterfield were so fond of, on the grounds that they resembled sedimentary layers.[92]

So far as 'honest' construction was concerned, too, there were some obvious borderline cases. Did paint, whitewash, gilding and marble veneers count as 'deception', for example? Not, ruled Ruskin, if there was no disguising the fact that these *were* paint, gilding and the rest.[93] But that surely was a matter of

perception, not of objective truth. Then there was the question of iron, over which
Goths never could agree, as we shall see in the next chapter. (Logically it should
have been accepted as a 'natural' material, but was often not.) Another great row
blew up in the 1850s over 'restoration', which strictly speaking could be regarded
as a form of deception, first because it was not true to the 'spirit' of the craftsman
concerned in carrying out the work, and second because what it left behind
could – indeed, was designed to – fool people that it was the genuine thing. 'Do
not let us talk then of restoration', railed Ruskin in the *Seven Lamps*. 'The thing
is a Lie from beginning to end.' If a building was crumbling, then let it crumble
away. 'Accept it as such, pull the building down, throw its stones into neglected
corners, make ballast of them, or mortar, if you will; but do it honestly' – that word,
again – 'and do not set up a Lie in their place.'[94] George Gilbert Scott, of course,
as the leading 'restorer' of the age, rather disagreed.[95] Little of this bears directly on
the controversy over the style of the Government Offices in the 1850s, but it does
all illustrate the centrality of these moral issues in that controversy. It could also
illustrate the hypocrisy. Some of Pugin's and Ruskin's arguments seem specious.[96]
A number of critics wondered whether Ruskin's preference for the relatively non-
structurally 'honest' Venetian was really consistent with his own principles, or just
a personal preference masquerading under them.[97] And there were times when
the two great men's masks slipped, to betray a far more superficial, romantic, and
therefore 'amoral', preference for the simply picturesque underneath.[98]

Lastly: however sound Gothic's claims to be an 'honest' style might be, surely
it was not the only candidate? That was certainly Scott's generous view: 'far be it
from me to say that this honesty of treatment belongs exclusively to Gothic architecture. *It does not.* It is the leading principle of all true architecture'.[99] Another way
of looking at this – just a semantic contrivance, really – was to stretch the word
to cover anything that was 'constructionally true'. Gothic architecture, wrote one
correspondent to the *Building News* in September 1859, 'does not consist alone
in pointed arches, clustered columns, and floral ornaments, but in its useful and
practical character, in its constructional truth, and in the broad measure of liberty
which it accords to all those who practise the style.' So anything that conformed
to these principles could be called 'Gothic'.[100] This was also Pugin's theoretical
position.[101] Others, while not going quite that far, liked to emphasize the style's
flexibility: its character as 'the most pliant and accommodating of all styles,' as *The
Times* acknowledged (unexpectedly) in 1859.[102] This, as we shall see shortly, was
the main reason for advocating it as a modern, secular and even universal 'style',
or (more properly) mode of building, in the 1850s. But if that was indeed one
of its virtues, how far could it be allowed to flex? And why, then, that narrow
insistence, on the part of many neo-Gothic builders and ideologues, which we
have noticed already and shall return to, on *thirteenth-century English* as the only
true *point de départ* for the present day?[103]

Still, there can be no denying the general force of this particular kind of
argument from 'morality'. 'Truth' was relatively straightforward, or seemed to

be, compared with the moral *associations* – Christianity, happy workers and the rest – that were also supposed to boost Gothic's case, and did so to an extent; but could also be ambivalent, controversial and potentially alienating, as we have seen. For at least one commentator it was its 'truth' that made Gothic essentially 'Christian': the connection being that Christianity itself embodied 'truth';[104] for others, however – getting the best of both worlds – it could liberate it *from* its Christian associations, 'secularize' and so universalize it.[105] It was also a fundamental English virtue, or supposed to be: the 'English gentleman' reckoned to be 'straighter' than his foreign equivalent; his financial transactions utterly trustworthy ('an Englishman's word . . .' – in theory, that was); 'cheating', for example at cards, almost the ultimate crime among the upper classes; dissembling for any purpose – in order to 'spy' on dissidents, however dangerous, to give one little-known instance[106] – almost unthinkable; and so on. Ruskin referred to this at one point, expressing (or feigning) surprise that so 'upright' a nation could be so 'deceitful' in its architecture. (At another point, feeling more generous, he included all the northern European 'tribes' in this.)[107] To a people brought up with these kinds of values (however much they were honoured in the breach) the idea of 'honesty' in architecture was bound to strike a chord. It was comparatively easy to achieve: '[w]e may not be able to command good, or beautiful, or inventive, architecture,' wrote Ruskin; 'but we *can* command an honest architecture.'[108] It was also easy to measure: by sticking a nail into a column, for example, to see if the marble effect really was marble, or a veneer; or by comparing a sculpted leaf with a natural one. Lastly, it was a highly *useful* point, when it came to the matter of extending Gothic to the secular field; which of course was the larger issue at stake in the great Battle of the Styles.

The argument from structural and functional 'truth' was important in this context because it saved the Gothic style from being bound to a particular genre of building, such as churches. If it was a style essentially based on functional need, it followed that it could be adapted to any purpose. Indeed, it had been in the Middle Ages, as the champions of Gothic pointed out, entirely fairly; the only reason one got the opposite impression in England was that it was almost only churches and colleges that had survived there from the Middle Ages. (Apart from castles; and who would want to copy one of those, in the middle of Whitehall?) This, however, was purely accidental. England had had urban Gothic buildings once, but they had disappeared as a result of 'redevelopment': the subsequent rebuilding of the towns and cities they had stood in, as they throve and expanded economically.[109] Abroad, in less progressive countries, you could see what they had probably looked like: in the street architecture of Lombardy and Venetia, for example, revealed by Ruskin; and the great mediaeval town and cloth halls of northern France and Belgium, which were Street's favourite precedents.[110] All this went to demonstrate what W. J. Cockburn Muir called 'the truth and beauty of the Gothic . . . – that it moulds itself readily and naturally to all uses.'[111]

If, that is, it was the right sort of Gothic. This is where the emphasis on the thirteenth (actually, the late thirteenth and early fourteenth) century came in. If truth, honesty and fidelity to nature were to form the main case for neo-Gothic, then their model needed to be the stage in the evolution of the original style when those qualities had been at their height. In the 1850s nearly all the leading Gothic theorists agreed this was 'Middle Decorated'; after which the style was supposed to have degenerated, into the over-exuberant 'Flamboyant' in France, and the formalistic 'Perpendicular' in England. It was this that blocked off what might otherwise have seemed to be the most obvious path for the 'revival' to follow: taking up Gothic again at the *latest* point in its development, as had been done in the case of the Palace of Westminster. There was nothing much that could be done now about that, save to regret it, as a 'splendid failure' at best.[112] The objection to it now was not merely that it was inconvenient; or a superficial 'pastiche'; but that the style chosen for it was a decadent one in any case. In other words, even if Barry's Perpendicular had been better, truer to its original fifteenth-century models, it still would not have done. 'No architect of the present day', wrote Coventry Patmore, 'would think of designing upon [that] plan'.[113] Nor did they, as we have seen, when it came to the Government Offices competition, none of whose premiated entries was in Perpendicular. Ruskin regarded the style – not just Barry's building – as 'detestable'.[114] Already by 1852, claimed Street, it had been 'rejected as worthless by all who have studied most or know most about ecclesiastical work.' He particularly disliked its 'stiffness, hardness, and sameness'; its 'abuse of the greatest element of architecture in this age – the pointed arch', by flattening it; and its 'departure from nature in sculpture and the like.'[115] In other words, it had lost Gothic's original virtues; the ones that commended it to contemporaries both morally and in practical terms.

It was in order to regain those virtues that the leading Gothic architects of the day fixed on the thirteenth century as their '*point de départ*'.[116] That was the term used widely at this time, to indicate that they should use 'Middle Decorated' not as their *model*, note, or at any rate for very long, but simply as a means of returning to the point where they could recover the 'spirit' of the style, before then moving it forward along 'truer' paths than the one it had taken from the later fourteenth century on. 'Models' were for Classicists, to copy artificially; Gothic architecture was more evolutionary than that. It sprang from needs, which changed over time. This was why there was not a perfect Gothic style, nor ever would be; other styles 'attained perfection' wrote one Richard Simpson in 1859, but 'Gothic never did so; it always left a place for longing.'[117] Because it evolved (or should evolve) naturally, its future course could not be anticipated; which of course raised difficulties when Classicists asked the Goths what it would look like in, say, 20 or 50 years. 'I should have thought,' wrote Street in 1859, in response to this point, 'that by this time we were all agreed that Gothic architecture was a natural growth, and in no sense an invention'.[118] So far as morality was concerned, 'natural' progress easily trumped artificial 'perfection'.

To recapitulate: the main moral virtue of Gothic, certainly for its professional devotees, was supposed to lie less in its *associations*, like the Christian one, which were merely fortuitous – though these may have been what recommended it to its more lay supporters – than in its 'truth' as a style. By that was meant its fidelity to structure, function and material; and beyond that to 'nature', in two senses of the word: the 'natural' forms around them (*'in* nature'), and the idea of 'natural' development. 'Cast away the mysticism', was Ruskin's advice to a lecture audience in 1858; Gothic was not 'the architecture of a tradition, but of fact and stern reality.'[119] Modern critics have cast doubt on the genuineness of this as a motive, regarding 'Gothic rationalist theory' as 'mainly a costume' or 'justification' for a style that was really preferred for 'religious, sociological or nationalistic reasons',[120] or alternatively because, 'to put it quite plainly, they' – the English – 'liked the way it looked';[121] which it may of course have been (who can truly tell?), but is not borne out by the general *zeitgeist* of the time, in which 'truth', 'reason' and 'progress' were at least as important considerations as religion, society and nationality. It was these features that made the style so 'almost universal', to quote one critic (the one who thought it did not need to be pointed to be Gothic),[122] or 'comprehensive and Catholic', in the words of another.[123] It is why, as we have seen, the British felt they could transplant their Gothic (suitably adapted) to their colonies, without any great sense of incongruity.[124] As Ruskin again put it: 'Gothic was an art for England *and the world*'.[125]

So: Gothic could be applied anywhere. That was one thing. It was only a short step on from this, however, to saying that it *should* be applied *everywhere*; that no other style – or none yet discovered – shared its legitimacy, so no other should be allowed. This was one of the factors contributing to the incipient stylistic 'totalitarianism' that was noticed in an earlier chapter of this book, where it was the social factors behind it that were highlighted: the hope that a 'common' architecture might heal a fractured society.[126] What the 'morality' argument did was establish which architecture that should be; which was obviously, for believers, the 'truer' of the two main ones on offer, in preference to the showy, artificial, deliberately deceptive Classical. If you believed all that stuff about 'honesty' and the like, and thought architecture was important, you *had* to want to spread it everywhere. It is interesting that nearly all those who complained about the coexistence of two major styles in England, one for church buildings and the other for secular – pointing out, for example, that this sort of thing was unheard of in any other great civilizations[127] – were Goths; not Classicists, who by now had come to accept the demarcation, and the resultant mix. That was because Classicists did not think in this kind of moral way. A style *was* simply a style, a thing to be picked and chosen; one might be preferable to others, for certain purposes, but none was superior *per se*. One commentator even argued in 1857 (albeit unusually then) that the more styles an architect could master, the better any of those styles would be in his hands; 'the true architect is bound ... to make himself strictly master of all ... In my humble judgement, the best Gothic architects are those who are also good Classic architects'.[128] The Goths, however, would have none of that. All the expansionary aggression, therefore, came from them, as it had from the beginning: 'today the Government Offices, tomorrow the (English) world'. In the light of this, Palmerston's worry that if Scott won over the Foreign Office it would open the way for him and his like to 'Gothicise the whole of London' may not have been quite so unreasonable as it might be natural to assume, coming from a joker like him.[129]

In fact there was never any chance of that, for reasons that will be explored in the next two chapters. Gothic ideologues of the sort mainly featured here were a tiny minority in the mid-nineteenth century, even of those who favoured the Gothic style generally. The *Daily Telegraph* called them a 'sect'.[130] Their moral seriousness, while *characteristic* of the mid-nineteenth-English middle classes, was not typical. To many people it appeared hypocritical. Scott, for example, was not universally trusted. He professed to be following high principles in his buildings, of structural 'truth' and 'development'; but at least one critic could see none of these when he looked – just 'copy and guess'.[131] In view of this, Scott's deeply *un*principled *volte-face* over his Government Office designs in July 1861 should have come as no great surprise. Maybe, however, this might be regarded as *more* typical of his place and time; if, as suggested at the start of this chapter, hypocrisy was also an ingredient in the complex mix that made up the English 'national character'.

7

An Architecture for our Age

At first glance it is difficult to recognize 'modernity' in either of the two styles that battled it out over the possession of the new Government Offices in the 1850s. Outwardly the debate was all about which of two very old historical periods and peoples they should reflect. On the one side stood the ancient Romans (or sometimes Greeks), in their phalanxes and breastplates and little skirts; on the other, the only slightly less ancient Goths, wild and barbarous if you opted for one view of them, chivalric and mounted on white horses if you preferred another. Many of the ensuing skirmishes focused on the comparative qualities of these two civilizations: the Romans' superior rationality, learning, order, *virtù*, etcetera; pitted against the mediaevals' faith, hope and charity, if you took the second version, or their rough, happy 'freedom', if you took the first. The question was, or seemed to be: which of these much older cultures should Britons look to, as the main inspiration for their architecture – and perhaps their lives.

It is this that makes the 'Battle' appear a somewhat backward-looking, anachronistic and even nostalgic event in retrospect. One common notion is that the Victorians went back to these periods and styles of architecture out of discontent and disillusion with their own age; from a desire, that is, to retreat from a scary, stressful present – all those newfangled railway engines hurtling along at 30 miles per hour – into a more stable and comfortable past, when God was in his heaven, the squire in his manor house and all was right with the world. That was on the Gothic side. Similarly, much of the support for Classical architecture is supposed to have reflected the craving for stability and order at an increasingly unstable and disorderly period of history. Both signalled a reaction against the (Victorian) present; a crumbling of confidence in contemporary times; a feeling of inferiority in the face of those earlier civilizations; and a lack of cultural self-confidence, even in this age of unprecedented 'progress' in so many areas: technological, obviously; but also 'moral' in the eyes of many.

While there is something in this, and may have been even more in it for earlier (Gothic) times, it distorts the full significance of the mid-Victorian Battle of the Styles only to see it in this reactionary light. It was not how most of the participants in the debate regarded it. Indeed, one of the major claims made by each side was that its style *was* 'modern' and 'progressive' – usually in contrast to the style championed by the other side. 'Modernity' was important to mid-nineteenth-century architectural theorists; far more so, as a *desideratum* for any new style, than 'nationality'. 'The great question is,' as Professor T. L. Donaldson expressed it in 1847: 'are we to have an architecture of our period' – not of our nation, note; 'a distinct, individual, palpable style of the nineteenth century?'[1] Which indicates that, despite appearances, both styles' champions were highly influenced by – indeed, found it almost impossible to avoid – the far more dominant 'progressive' discourse of the day.

This was partly because of the criticism and even scorn that the Goths in particular encountered at the time, on exactly these 'anachronistic' grounds. We have seen how Lord Palmerston played this card repeatedly and shamelessly, combined with the anti-Catholic one: as when he characterized Gothic as suited only to 'monk-ish piles': 'all very well for our ancestors', perhaps, but inadequate for the present day.[2] 'Why should we go back to the rude architectural forms and arrangements of a comparatively barbarous period?' asked one of his strongest supporters in the House of Commons. 'Are only the men who had their floors covered with rushes, their lights in horn lanterns, and who carried their glazed sashes about with them on their pack-horses, to be studied, copied, venerated?'[3] Charles Dickens's *Household Words* carried a witty satire in 1850 on what it called the 'retrospective principle', directed specifically against the Pre-Raphaelites, but in terms that could equally well apply to architecture. (What next? it speculated. A 'Pre-Newtonian Brotherhood'? A 'Pre-Galileo Brotherhood'? A 'Pre-Agincourt Brotherhood', for music? A 'Pre-Henry-the-Seventh Brotherhood', to take Britain's social and political arrangements back to Mediaeval times?)[4] You might just as well, suggested the *Building News* in 1857, propose to 'grind old women young again.'[5] 'Architecture should reflect the spirit of the age.'[6] Was it not really quite deplorable, wrote one Edward Tarbuck, that in that great age of progress, 'while other classes advance,' the architects' 'eyes and minds are constantly turned back'?[7] Gilbert Scott regretted that they did not yet have an architecture 'worthy of the greatness of our age'.[8] Austen Layard, the famous archaeologist who was also a Liberal MP at this time, remarked on how 'strange' it was 'that in this nineteenth century we had made so little advance in the art of architecture.'[9] And so on. There was something very wrong here. The Victorians' disparaging successors, in the more assured 'modern' age that followed, were not the first to sense this.

It clearly worried the Goths and Classicists themselves. Hence the concentration of most of their propaganda *not* on the supposed superiority of the ages whose architecture they were proposing to revive (or sustain) but on those styles' essential *modernity*: again, despite appearances. 'I am no mediaevalist', insisted Scott, even before Palmerston launched into him on these grounds.[10] This applied even to those who did hanker for olden days, of whom Pugin is the leading example;[11] but who also advocated Gothic because it was a 'progressive' style, capable of being 'developed' and carried forward in modern times, just as it had been in the Middle Ages – at least until the fourteenth century, when the purists thought it had fallen off.[12] After Pugin this was almost the most common pro-Gothic argument of all.

The general idea was that the Renaissance (or in Pugin's case the Reformation) had interrupted this process of logical development, replacing it with a static style, capable only of imitation. ('The Italian style,' commented Scott, 'has produced nothing new for many a long day.')[13] It was rather as though the developing science of astronomy had been cast aside for 300 years in favour of astrology: in which case it could have been argued that the only way to resume the path of 'progress' was to return to the point where the interruption had occurred, and go on from there. This is how most Goths looked at their architecture. Middle-period Mediaeval was a necessary starting point (or *point de départ*). They needed to go back there in order to get the hang of those long-defunct principles of true architectural progress again. Once they had mastered these, however, they could move on.[14] Some thought they had just about reached that point now (the 1850s), including the *Ecclesiologist* – the strictest guardian of Gothic's integrity up until then – for which the stage seemed to be set for what it called '*inventive imitation*' to take over.[15] Eventually, it thought – and other Goths agreed – they might even come to surpass the mediaevals.[16] When that would be, however, and how exactly it would look, they could not possibly say; as was inevitable with a 'naturally developing' style of architecture. (We shall return to this.)

What all Goths agreed on, however, was that their favoured style was capable of development in ways that would come to express the nineteenth century; 'truthfully symbolising', as Scott put it, 'the greatness which belongs to our period in the history of human progress'.[17] (It may be worth noting here that in many ways this was the opposite of Pugin's view: that society had to adapt to the Gothic.)[18] Scott was particularly insistent on this, and that his original Gothic designs for the Government Offices were in fact 'modern' in this sense.[19] In some ways it is difficult to disagree with this. Nothing quite like a 'Government Offices' had ever been called for in the Middle Ages, yet the mediaeval style of architecture had proved to be eminently adaptable to this most modern of purposes. Even the windows were fine, according to Charles Buxton, MP: 'as large as any windows in London';[20] which, if you did not believe him (as a Gothic partisan), you would have to trust the word of Sir Joseph Paxton on: the builder of the Crystal Palace, which was of course the most windowed structure in history. (We have seen how important the 'windows' point was to Scott.)[21] Paxton had studied the designs in detail, he told the House of Commons in 1859 (he was now a Liberal MP), and found them perfectly fitted for their task in every way, as well as, he added – though he did not claim any particular authority in this area – 'beautiful'.[22] The *Building News* used the word 'utilitarian' to describe the design (positively).[23] That word will have struck a contemporary chord. 'One of the characteristic features of our age,' Scott had written a little earlier, 'is its *practical character*.'[24] Today this may imply something rather simpler than Scott's spiky palace; but a thing can be useful and ornate too. It certainly convinced the *Building News*, against its initial feelings – 'for we confess that our tastes and sympathies rather incline us to what is not strictly Gothic' – that a Gothic Foreign Office would work. Thereafter the *Building News* shifted its influence and weight heavily behind Scott. If Scott's designs 'are now to be set aside to please the caprice or prejudice of a noble indi-vidual,' it warned, 'the nation will be losers.'[25] It was the practical modernity of the plan – the aspect of it that the anti-Goths had most doubted, or pretended to doubt – that had persuaded it. This must be counted a great achievement for Scott, who had done all that could have been expected of him to demonstrate that very point. It should have been enough to win him the commission. Unfortunately, that was to reckon without 'the caprice or prejudice of [the] noble individual' who stood in his way.

The other 'progressive' chord that the Gothicists tried to tap was the techno-logical one. One of the great discoveries of the early Gothic Revival, as we saw, had been that mediaeval buildings were built as they were not in order to look picturesque, let alone barbaric and mysterious, or through a simple ignorance of the 'correct' (Classical) rules, but in obedience to solid and scientific structural principles which were in many ways far in advance of what later replaced them. The obvious example was the pointed arch, which revolutionized the craft of building *high*. The tallest mediaeval cathedrals are in fact masterpieces of structural engineering,[26] comparable at any rate with the great iron and brick bridges and viaducts that were some of the proudest achievements of the eighteenth and nineteenth centuries, and, indeed, almost a defining icon of 'modernity'. G. E. Street went so far as to claim that, despite its antiquity, the pointed arch was 'the greatest invention in construction which ha[d] ever been made.'[27] Once discovered, Coventry Patmore agreed, it '*rendered all previous styles for ever obsolete*.'[28] How much more 'modern' could you get? It was a clever argument. In one bound it freed Gothic from the anachronistic associations that were likely to chain it down in the eyes of 'modernists'. It made it into a *rational* style, closely akin to engineering, albeit with a few more (literal) knobs on. And it lay it open to further technological development, just as bridge-building was (outside the pointed-arch department), with a view to taking in the new functions the nineteenth century was bound to demand of it, and the new materials it was providing. One might even bring in iron: the modern material *par excellence*. Why, wrote Coventry Patmore, with iron you could raise the height of a typical Gothic spire another 500 feet![29] Or span huge areas, as the railway-shed-builders were famously doing just them, and as the architects Deane and Woodward did more Gothically, and controversially, with their Oxford Museum in 1855–60.

The English Goths' 'progressive' claims were important to them. They were not, incidentally, shared by German neo-Goths, who were in the main more rigid, conservative and 'archaeological'. August Reichensperger, their great guru, was quite shocked by the *Ecclesiologist*'s turn in the 1850s away from 'strict' Gothic to a more developmental form, and in particular its guarded support for iron; which provoked a furious letter from him in 1856: 'we know, by experience, how danger-ous the charm of that word ['progress'] is, particularly in the domain of Christian art'.[30] That must be related to the more conservative nature of German society

generally (in its little mini-states) at this time. Of course – to look forward a little
– Gothic turned out *not* to be the 'progressive' way, with the reaction against it that
set in during the twentieth century, and the switch – eventually – to assertively
anti-historicist styles. But this is not to destroy the Goths' claim to 'modernity'
entirely. If the style itself came to be seen as far from 'modern', the underlying
principles behind it were not. Indeed, as several later architectural historians have
acknowledged, 'they lay the foundations of modern architectural theory': that is,
'functional planning, honest use of materials and expression of structure'; which
the twentieth century simply clothed in different ways.[31] It may be difficult to
discern beneath the busy decoration and associative features of Scott's first Foreign
Office drawings; but there was more than a glance to the future there.

That was neo-Gothic's stab at being 'modern'. The Classicists' strategy was very
different, and less inventive. They may have been taken by surprise at the start.
This was because they had not regarded theirs as an anachronistic way of building
originally. It was not seen as a 'revival', though of course it had been originally (at
the Renaissance), but rather as simply the established style of the day, and so 'modern' in that sense. It is what the phrase 'modern architecture' usually implied at
that time; in the mouths of Palmerston, for example, and of most of his co-stylists.
What was all this agitation for a 'modern' style? They had a modern style, like it
or not. 'However mean and miserable it may be, *Modernism* is our fate.' By that the
Building News meant the 'English Renaissance' (or 'Wrenaissance')[32] style: Italian
originally, but modified for English purposes by Inigo Jones and Christopher
Wren.[33] 'That Classic architecture . . . did not originate in this country, is an
indisputable fact', admitted *Building News*. But by now it had 'taken such firm root'
as to have become the English style in essence. If you wanted a more up-to-date
version of it, you just had to look over the Channel, to the 'Second Empire' style
gracing Paris and now so favoured by the upper classes in England (as well as by
very many of the entrants to the Government Offices competition), which was
certainly no copy of any past mode of building, but a true 'development'. Either of
these styles, according to the *Building News,* 'bears upon it the stamp of *modernism*,
in contradistinction to *mediaevalism*, and that ought to be some recommendation,
even a pretty strong one.'[34] If there was to be adaptation or 'progress' to meet the
requirements of the modern age, it had to be based on that. 'The only question to
be decided is simply, – what is the style of the day? On that we must advance.'[35]
'No one appears to have yet realised the truth,' noted Tarbuck, 'that the right *point
de départ* is the present.'[36] 'Depend upon it,' agreed the *Builder*, 'we must "accept
the situation", and that which is must be taken as the foundation of that which is
to be: on this, purified and improved, we must engraft and incorporate.'[37]

 And it could be done. Classicists were a little late on to this; but at length
they came out fighting, with evidence that their style was at least as 'adaptable'
to modern requirements as Gothic, or even more so – so long as they got out
of the old 'copying' habits of the past, and got inside its 'spirit'. (That of course

was exactly what the Gothicists were saying about their own style. In fact Scott claimed it was the Goths who had shamed the Classicists into taking this on.)[38] Matthew Wyatt, Scott's collaborator on the India Office, was one Classicist who believed as strongly as any Goth that architecture needed to 'progress', in his case from the *point de départ* of Italian Cinquecento.[39] C. R. Cockerell, probably the best English Classical architect of this time (it is a pity he did not have a go at the Government Offices), was absolutely sure of Classic's ability to 'progress', and even, for example – for he was immensely impressed by the Crystal Palace – to incorporate all the implications of iron.[40] Work along these lines, and they would see 'of what classic architecture is capable . . . the universal fitness it possesses for the requirements of a rich, enlightened, and progressing nation.'[41]

Again we have the insistent need to appear 'modern', *not* 'historical', though in a different way. The argument for Gothic was that it was an intrinsically 'progressive' style. That for Classic was that it was the *established* style: modern, therefore, by virtue of its prior possession of the territory. It was the most up-to-date style when the Goths appeared on the scene. (It was different, incidentally, with one small adjunct to the main Classical army, the 'Greeks', who had had a proper 'revival' a little earlier, and whose argument for 'modernity' was a little different. Greek was 'modern' because it was perfect and timeless. So there was no need for it to adapt. You occasionally get this kind of argument deployed in favour of the Roman.[42] But by the 1850s the Greek movement had rather fizzled out.)[43]

Whether or not these arguments for the 'modernity' of their favoured styles were in any way valid is none of our concern. (They were somewhat contrived, in any case.) More important is that both Goths and Classicists felt obliged to make them. Another significant point is that they do not seem to have been found widely convincing. Classic's case to be the 'modern' style because it was 'established', for example, was bound to be undermined by the increasing 'establishment' of Gothic, which several Goths in the later 1850s felt handed this argument to them.[44] Another problem for both sides, but especially the Goths, was that they tended to fall down in their practical implementation of these 'modernist' principles, leaving the material evidence of their modernity somewhat lacking. Too many neo-Gothic churches still simply aped mediaeval models; 'while raving about the development of a new and vigorous style,' as the president of the Liverpool Architectural Society put it in 1858, '. . . they are doing nothing but copying.'[45] Three years later Professor J. H. Chamberlain, of the future Birmingham University, 'took occasion to protest most warmly against the pernicious error from which architects are not yet free – that the highest merit of modern Gothic consists in the exact reproduction of ancient forms, instead of applying old principles to modern wants and materials.'[46] That was letting the side down.

Others were doing it by backsliding with regard to 'modern materials'. Iron was a particular difficulty, with Ruskin being famously entirely against its use,[47] and others seeming to change their minds on it from one year to the next. Coventry

Patmore, for example, a supporter of iron in 1857, by 1858 had come to regard it as a 'Frankenstein' monster that could destroy architecture.[48] Street opposed it in 1852, but had then come round to supporting it by 1860. His reason for disapproving of it originally was 'because I do not believe that it is architecture at all. It is simply engineering.'[49] That highlights another undoubted obstacle in the way of the 'modernization' of architecture: the snobbish attitude of the architectural profession towards the engineers who should have been their partners in this. (Architecture was an 'art'.)[50] They scarcely ever collaborated. If architects used iron, they handled it themselves; and engineers prettified their structures with their own architectural details. The lack of communication between the two professions can be seen quite starkly at the point where St Pancras Station's huge iron train shed, designed by William Henry Barlow, abuts on to the back of Gilbert Scott's extraordinary Gothic Railway Hotel: quite brutally, without any attempt, even, to marry them.[51] When Victorian Gothic became new and 'original' in other ways (and, incidentally, there is no way one can mistake most 'High Victorian' buildings, including St Pancras Station Hotel, for mediaeval ones), it could appear ugly.[52] 'Modern' Gothic was very much let down by its practitioners.

Even if the practice had been better, however, it might not have satisfied many architectural aficionados at the time. The 'Battle' between these historic styles was widely felt to be too narrow, too fanatical and in some circles too frankly ridiculous for the whole of England's architectural future to rest on it. Remember, the Victorians were by and large intolerant of 'zeal'. Pugin and Ruskin, the great high priests of the Gothic Revival, may have alienated more people than they won over to their zealously cherished style. The 'impertinent fun' that Palmerston enjoyed at the expense of Gothic[53] also put serious students of architecture off. They became even more antagonized when the debate got bitter and personal. An understandable reaction to this was to dismiss both sides, impatiently: 'a plague on both your styles, say we.'[54] 'We must look far beyond the squabbles of schools, and the antagonism of tastes, that are so loud and energetic in the present day.'[55] The 'plague on both your houses' camp may in fact have been larger than the Gothic or the Classical ones. There is no way of telling. (Rejection is usually expressed silently.)[56] What we do know about, however, is those who rejected Gothic and Classical for other alternatives.

These were the people whose craving for a 'new style' ran deeper than the 'Battle' might suggest. The nineteenth century was *so* new, they thought, that it deserved something better than cold Roman or warmed-up Gothic. A distinctive age should have a distinctive architecture. 'Every major period has established its own architectural style,' wrote the great German architect Karl Friedrich Schinkel in 1830; 'so why do we not try to establish a style for ours? Why should we always build in the style of another period?'[57] Indeed, this was as much a matter of concern on the Continent, where in 1861 a congress gathered (in Antwerp), specifically 'to consider why the nineteenth century had no distinctive architectural style'.[58] How many in England thought this was a problem is difficult to know; Peter Collins suggests it may have been just a few 'architectural historians and journalists' − not even the majority of practising architects, and certainly not their clients, or the 'public'.[59] And Ruskin, perversely, was right against the whole idea. ('It does not matter one marble splinter whether we have new or old architecture. The forms of architecture already known are good enough for us, and for far better than us.')[60] Still, the 'new stylists' made their presence felt. Gilbert Scott thought the 'Gothic Renaissance' should take much of the credit for this; it had, he claimed, 'at least, set people thinking'. But it was a deeply problematical thought. Most concerned people would probably have agreed with Scott that what he called 'a spick-and-span new style' was a chimera. 'No age of the world has ever deliberately invented a new style . . . every development of art must have a foundation, − to attempt a pure invention is vain.' That was why he went for his Gothic base.[61] If you rejected that, however (or the Classical), where should you go for inspiration?

One possibility was the new building materials (or potential building materials) that had been developed in recent years; new materials, that is, used as the basis for new styles, rather than simply pressed into service for older ones, like those iron Gothic spires. As early as the 1830s the Dutch-Scottish designer Thomas Hope, after mocking the historical 'copies' he saw all around him in England, had argued for making 'the new discoveries, the new conquests, of natural productions unknown to former ages, the models of . . . an architecture which, born in our country, grown on our soil, and in harmony with out climate, institutions, and habits . . . should truly deserve the appellation of "*Our Own*"'.[62] 'This is an age of new creations,' wrote a much younger architectural Turk, Thomas Harris, in 1860; 'steam power and electric communication, neither the offshoot of any former period, but entirely new revolutionizing influences. So must it be in architecture if it is to express these changes.' Reviving old fashions 'will not suffice'. New functions and new materials required an entirely new style.[63] Harris and many of his contemporaries thought they had been given a tantalizing glimpse of this, in Joseph Paxton's Great Exhibition building (the 'Crystal Palace') of 1851.[64] That employed iron and plate glass *essentially*, not just as ancillary to a more traditional design, stimulating quite an interest on the margins of the architectural profession.[65] And there were other models. Lewis Cubitt's highly functionalist King's Cross Station (1852), right next to St Pancras, and with the frontage and shed integrated far more successfully than in the latter case, was one. Northern factories and warehouses furnished others. There was no shortage of architectural writers puffing these as the potential bases of a truly 'modern' style. Some seem quite prescient, though of course that was likely to have been a matter of luck. For example, one 'E. J.' looked forward (in the *Building News*, 1859) to an architecture of the future that was functionally planned, bereft of 'heavy ornaments' and 'puerile decorations', and full of 'light, air and space': which could almost be late twentieth-century Scandinavian.[66] One of the pamphleteers involved in the 'Battle of the Styles' recommended looking to 'the engineering works of the day' for inspiration, 'because they do express the spirit of the present age.'[67] The architectural historian James Fergusson was attracted to modern brick factories and warehouses.[68] One problem with this was the common prejudice of the time that equated architecture with decoration. Without it, it was 'mere' building.[69] But there was no reason why more 'modern', functional buildings could not be decorated too. Even King's Cross Station has one or two 'architectural' features.

Throughout the middle years of the nineteenth century there were people try-ing to work out a distinctive style for the times, based on the 'new' materials, like iron. (Other new materials capable of shaping a 'style' were plate glass; and – a little later on – concrete[70] and aluminium.[71]) The main one of these was William Vose Pickett, whose distinctive line was that iron required a completely new style to be developed *from* it, just as past architectural styles had developed from the nature of their materials, and from the constructive and functional needs of their times. This went beyond Paxton and Cubitt. (But not beyond Pugin, perhaps, if it were possible to imagine him embracing this logical conclusion of his 'True Principles'.) Among the distinctive new features that Pickett believed iron would contribute to this style were: curved forms; suspension; and what he called 'Protean Effects' – moving shadows. He also embraced its possibilities of mass production. Such a style would clearly reflect the spirit of the present age, and might even turn out to produce more beautiful buildings, he thought, than ever known before. They would emphatically not be Gothic; indeed, he was positively insulting about the prefabricated Gothic 'iron church' that W. Slater designed for the Ecclesiological Society, for export to the colonies, in 1856. 'Iron and analogous materials are here completely in fetters . . . Mr. Slater's is a stone church built in iron and not one composed on purely metallic principles.' He called it 'frightful'.[72] Pickett took out patents, put on at least one exhibition of his ideas and wrote indefatigably to various organizations, capitalists and even Prince Albert to get his plans taken up. Most of these (including Albert) were sniffy; some journals made fun of him: but not all. His ideas, however, got nowhere, partly because (apparently) he could not draw, and so could not show what they would look like, and partly because he was about 50 years ahead of his time.[73]

Other more practical revolutionaries fell by the wayside. Thomas Harris's actual buildings, for example, appear disappointingly conventional in the light of his early principles: mock Tudor for mansions, a kind of stripped-down Georgian for warehouses.[74] Even concrete, where it was used, seems to have been generally poured into neo-Gothic moulds.[75] The Crystal Palace had far less of an influ-ence on future architectural thinking than many had hoped at the time, though more, perhaps, than is implied by H. S. Goodhart-Rendel's witty assertion that its only impact was to make 'every householder long to have a bigger and better conservatory'.[76] More to the point, perhaps, was that very few of the country's better-known architects 'were ready to come to terms with iron' and the other new materials, despite the backing that some gave to them in principle. Nikolaus

Pevsner cites the case of Gilbert Scott, who in 1858 wrote that 'metallic construction is the great development of our age', yet still deliberately hid it in his own buildings – St Pancras Station Hotel, for example, and the Albert Memorial.[77] 'Architects', wrote Sir John Summerson, 'talked of a new style but had little to show'.[78] 'Such a contrast between theory and performance is frequent amongst Victorian architects' (that is Pevsner, again).[79] According to one modern authority, they were 'far too busy fighting the "Battle of the Styles" at the end of a cul-de-sac', leaving the real 'spirit of the age' in the hands of the engineers.[80] One suspects that the architectural profession's desperation to be accepted as such, rather than as a 'trade', may have had much to do with this. More charitably, it may simply have been that these new materials were not yet *ready* to bear – literally as well as metaphorically – a new style. Iron, for example, hit a practical snag in the 1850s when a number of iron-framed buildings burned down, which was just what they were supposed not to do.[81] And concrete's time did not come until the development of the ferro (iron-strengthened) variety in the 1890s.[82] So we should probably not make too much of these single swallows. Summer would be a long time a-coming.

This, however – 'modernism' as we know it – was not the only alternative to Gothic and Classical being mooted at this time. Most people interested in architecture still saw it in terms of 'features' and 'decoration'; and so the main debate going on outside the 'Battle' was over what features should be added to their buildings to make them look more 'modern' in their eyes than Gothic or Classical. This of course was problematical. Where did one get these features from? With so many choices available – 2,000 years of several European cultures, plus the many others that were opening up to Britain through her travels, trading and ruling in the wider world – it was hard to know where to start. Obviously, not everyone would want to start in the same place. 'We pick and choose and argue about it; one man likes one style, one another.'[83] There were no recognizably and indisputably 'modern' artistic styles anywhere. One authority even doubted whether any were possible; it was at least 'questionable', he wrote in 1860, 'whether the phraseology of architecture . . . was not exhausted long ago.'[84] There is no evidence that *this* was a widespread suspicion:[85] if it were then it would say a great deal about the mid-Victorians' view of History, which we shall be coming on to shortly; but everyone agreed that new styles could not be invented, just like that. 'Those who cry out so loudly for originality, for the "Deus ex machina" to make his appearance and invent a new style of architecture by his own original genius, only prove that they have not studied the history of the art.'[86] That was not how styles were made.

Usually in the past they had simply grown. It had happened 'naturally': needs, materials, technological discoveries and the social environment giving rise to new ways of building, or modifications of them, without people thinking about them overmuch. That was how the great original styles of the past – Greek, Gothic, Hindu, Islamic and (probably) native American[87] – had originated and then developed. In this way, they were bound to reflect and express their peoples and their times. This was how many of those in the 1850s who were discontented with contemporary 'copying' would have liked English (and European) architecture to proceed from that point on. One of the problems with this, however, as we have seen, was that there was no undisputed *point de départ* to develop *from*, with all the breaks in the English architectural tradition that had taken place over the past 400 years; but another was that even if a single *point de départ* had been agreed, no one could have been expected to predict how things would go from that point on. It was in the nature of 'natural' development to be unpredictable; it was why, for example, Doric Greeks could not have foreseen Corinthian, or the Normans the pointed arch, or – to jump for a moment to two other contemporary fields in which similar natural evolutionary ideas were dominant – *Homo erectus* could not have predicted *Homo sapiens*, and Karl Marx was still unable to say, right up to his death, precisely what the 'socialist' stage of human social development would look like. This made rational sense, but it was also a singularly unhelpful idea, for practical architects. James Fergusson, who was constantly being asked what he proposed to put in the place of the 'copying' styles he so much derided, put it frankly in 1849.

> The answer is a simple, though scarcely a satisfactory one, as it is merely – I do not know. But if anyone reflects a moment, he will see that it is impossible I or anyone else could know, without, at least, the gift of prophecy; for the very essence of progress is its procession towards something we do not see now, and the essence of invention is finding out what we do not know, and what could not be before known.[88]

(He also pointed out, soberingly, how very long it took for any 'true' style to develop: a thousand years, for example, for Gothic to develop out of Roman.)[89] Fergusson was in fact the most exasperating of guides when it came to the 'architecture of the future': seeming to want to base it on modern factory buildings at one moment,[90] but at others advocating, somewhat feebly, a modified 'Italian',[91] and producing himself (though he was not a practising architect) a mainly 'Roman' design, albeit with an 'Oriental' air, for the Government Offices.[92] That was just confusing. Other recommendations were simply vague.[93] And if they were ever illustrated, it was often with far more conventional designs than one might expect from the radical language used.[94] But was not that only to be expected, if Fergusson's warnings about the impossibility of *inventing* the future were true?

As a result many architects, unable to strike out in really original ways, and uncomfortable about going back, even in order to go forward again, were left with that myriad of previous and existing styles to plunder; the only way to harness which in any even semi-disciplined way was to admit them *all*, eclectically. Eclecticism was in fact the major alternative building style – alternative, that is, to Classical or Gothic – in the mid-nineteenth century. (It was sometimes called 'astylism', or 'latitudinarianism'.)[95] It generally meant mixing styles in one and the same building, rather than allocating different styles to different *kinds* of building, which was another possible usage of the word (and of course the actual situation in Britain then).[96] Several of the entries for the Government Offices competition were rag-bags of different stylistic features. In some a single style stood at the base of it – typically Renaissance – but with a plethora of features from other traditions stuck on. (Cuthbert Brodrick, the greatYorkshire architect, was a master of this style.)[97] Others claimed to be trying to merge, or synthesize, Gothic and Classical: vertical features from the one, perhaps, ingeniously reconciled with the other's horizontality.[98] Beresford Hope, one of the most enthusiastic (and richest) Goths in the 1850s, but also a highly flexible one, came to favour a disciplined form of eclecticism towards the end of that decade.[99] Others were more anarchic. A number of young architects not only built in this way but also wrote 'eclectic' manifestos and pattern books. Most publications of this period bruiting a 'new architecture' were of this kind.[100]

Purists of course hated it. Pugin, with his Catholic respect for orthodoxy and discipline, lambasted what even in his time he saw as 'a confused jumble of styles and symbols borrowed from all nations and periods.'[101] Street thought it was a disastrous trend. 'Impoverishment of genius has been the result.'[102] 'Our English Architecture is just now an Architecture of "shreds and patches"', wrote W. J. Cockburn Muir in 1860; a 'general *pot-au-feu* of all known and possible Architectures'; a 'chaos-region'.[103] And here is Robert Kerr in 1865: current architecture 'exists in utter bewilderment. Much learning hath made it mad.'[104] The *Builder* felt that unless they reversed this, and returned to 'unity of style', architecture would lose 'the high position that may be destined for it'.[105] (There we have the professional architect's need for *status*, again.) By and large, eclecticism has not weathered well critically; Sir John Summerson, for example, claimed it was mainly resorted to by 'the stupider architects', and 'with preposterous results'.[106] But at the time it seemed one way out of the 'modernist' impasse; until 'Queen Anne' came along, to open up another path.[107]

In fact eclecticism may have been the most 'modern' way to go. Several writers pointed out how well it fitted with the values of that age: individualism, democracy, tolerance, curiosity, anti-authority, global travel and commerce; and also with some of its problems. Cockburn Muir, who disapproved of it, linked it in with the 'want of fixity' of the time, by which he meant their current social and political convulsions.[108] Edward Garbett, who also did not like it, nonetheless thought it was the first genuinely 'national style' England or any country had ever had; for all previous ones had been 'the styles of classes, priesthoods, and corporations', whereas eclecticism embraced everybody, in all his or her individuality, and hence the democratic, or vulgar, reality of modern Britain.[109] Looked at more positively, in an age of free trade – one of the great new ideals of that time, from which all kinds of good were confidently expected – was it so very unreasonable, as the Scottish architect Robert Anderson put it rhetorically to an Edinburgh audience in April 1860, to expect 'free trade in the arts of the past'?[110] Their very liberties, wrote J. Henry Stevens, meant that patrons and architects were bound to have very different ideas and tastes. Uniformity of style was only possible in either autocratic societies, like the Catholic Middle Ages, where they could be imposed, or insulated ones, where people knew no others.[111] Modern architecture, argued S. Huggins of the Liverpool Architectural Society in 1858, was bound to take 'a variety of shapes analogous to our present complex civilisation, and reflect the hues of different orders, professions, pursuits, and interests.'[112] 'Had the Victorians not had something of an eclectic temperament', writes Michael Bright, 'they would never have been so hospitably receptive' to this range of styles in the first place.[113] We might add that eclecticism expresses very well the 'hybridity' that was mentioned, in Chapter 2, as one of mid-Victorian Britain's fundamental social and political characteristics. Indeed, claimed Huggins, *progress* was contingent on it; which made 'eclecticism' intrinsically the most progressive 'style'. The problem was not that there were 'too many styles, but too little art'.[114]

Obviously, the kind of consensus that the battlers were demanding – Scott, for example, who wanted them all to unite around Middle Pointed – though it might be tidier, would not express any of this half so well. For, as the architect Robert Kerr put it in 1865:

> We live in the era of *Omnium-Gatherum*; all the world is a museum ... And while critics demand, not without contempt, why is it that our age has not a *Style of its own*, like all other ages! – How could it have a style of its own in such circumstances? Or otherwise, let us answer, if it has no style of its own in one sense, it has in another a very notable style of its own, and a very novel one, – the style of this miscellaneous connoisseurship, – the style of instinct superseded by knowledge, – a state of things characteristic of our age – and not in architecture alone – as no other state of things can be characteristic of it.[115]

Eclecticism expressed this. As also, it could be said, did the *Battle* of the Styles in the 1850s and early 1860s; far more so than the clear victory of one or other of the battling styles themselves, or of any of the alternatives on offer, could possibly have done. In this sense, it is the very confusion and chaos of the Victorians' architectural achievement that gives their age, certainly in retrospect, a *kind* of unity; comparable, in Henry-Russell Hitchcock's happy metaphor, to that of complex orchestral music, 'after the harpsichord-like efforts of the previous century'.[116]

This whole debate raised questions for the Victorians about the nature of 'History', no less, which went further and deeper than the relatively simple one of comparing two historical periods. Although it is dangerous to talk about 'dominant' discourses in any complex society, and especially one as 'eclectic' as her architecture was revealing mid-nineteenth-century Britain to be, there was pretty widespread agreement then that 'History' was fundamentally a matter of 'progress', and in certain broad 'stages' – an idea that Karl Marx, of course, took up at around this time. This is so familiar an idea to us now that we may need reminding how relatively new it was in the early nineteenth century. Earlier concepts of the historical process had generally seen it as static, circular or even in decline from a past 'golden age'. Something like this still infused the historical education Britain's upper classes received in their public schools, using ancient Greek and Roman sources almost exclusively. By the 1850s, however, the idea of 'progress' had all but triumphed. It lies at the core of Macaulay's great *History of England* (1849–61), though he did not invent it;[117] and by now had trickled down into most popular histories and schoolbooks.[118] It had received a great boost from recent events: such as the rapid growth of liberalism and prosperity in Britain; the toppling of *anciens régimes* in Europe; the spread of 'freedom' beyond Europe, sometimes in revolt against imperialism (the Americas), elsewhere with its help (India); and the 'opening up' of 'dark' regions of the world, especially to the twin 'lights' of true religion and commerce. Darwinism – or, rather, the intellectual environment in which evolutionary theory emerged – may have given it a fillip.[119] In Britain the middle classes were especially enamoured of it, largely because it seemed to embody the spirit of capitalism so well; but the other classes also took to it, with the very satisfactory side-effect – or maybe this was its real hidden purpose – of making them generally optimistic (so the working classes forgot about socialism, for example), and thus less likely to cause trouble for the state. That is why the ruling classes came round to it. Its main dynamic was the advance of 'freedom'. The 'stages' it was seen to pass through were, first, 'primitive' (though in a way this was an *a*historical stage); second, 'ancient'; third, 'feudal'; and lastly 'modern', or capitalist. There was usually assumed to be a kind of inevitability about this. It is often called the 'Whig' view of History.[120] This was a particularly powerful discourse in the 1850s and 1860s: between, that is, the economic 'depressions' of the two flanking decades; in other words, at the precise moment of the Battle of the Styles.

Which is what rendered things so difficult for those who wanted to *revive* styles that were associated with previous historical 'stages'; and made it so crucial, therefore, that they establish their 'modernity'. 'If there is one lesson more conspicuously written than another on the page of history,' declared one critic, 'it is – continual progress. "On, on!" is the cry that rings throughout time.'[121] 'The great drama of history does not admit of encores ... Streams do not flow back to their sources.'[122] This was irrespective of how much one might admire any of the styles in question. The Reverend J. L. Petit, for example, sincerely regretted this, holding Gothic in genuine affection, but believing nonetheless that it could not be 'revived'.[123] The particular problem here was that Gothic was not merely anachronistic but represented a whole previous 'stage'. Several anti-Goths made the point that if you revived thirteenth-century architecture you would need to revive other features of that stage too, like feudalism – which of course was impossible. (Though in fact this was exactly what Pugin wanted.) 'If we could forget the invention of gunpowder,' wrote Fergusson, 'and induce nations to revert to bows and arrows and plate armour, – if we could ignore the printing-press and all its thousand influences, or persuade ourselves to believe that the steam-engine is still only the dream of some crack-brained mechanic, – then indeed we might restore the Middle Ages,' and Gothic Architecture with it. But that was what it would require.[124] Styles were the products of their times. Face it, commented *Building News* in June 1857: 'the Plantagenets have vanished – Victoria reigns.'[125] 'Revived' styles flew in the face not only of 'history' but also of the fundamental, almost scientific, processes of historical development.

Which, by the mid-nineteenth century, had reached a particularly distinctive 'stage'. The obvious differences from previous stages had to do with technology, capitalism and 'liberty'; but another lay in its self-consciousness (or rather, that of the people who lived at the time) *as* a historical 'period', through its awareness of those earlier ones; against which, indeed, it mainly defined itself. One product of this was that idea of 'progress'. Another, however, was a certain inevitable confusion, born of all this new knowledge of earlier times, and the *choices* it presented to artists for the first time. This was entirely new. 'Our ancestors,' as *Fraser's Magazine* pointed out as early as 1843, 'experienced no perplexities of this kind: having shaped out a style for themselves, they carried it on progressively, till it either wore itself out, or at length subsided into some other.' The only instance of a 'sudden break-off' had been the adoption of 'Italian' in early modern times; and that was effected by general agreement. 'There was no theorizing on this subject – no inquiry, consequently no doubt, no misgiving': nothing like they were experiencing then.[126] Scott picked up on this point during the Battle. 'The peculiar characteristic of the present day, as compared with all former periods,' as he wrote in one of his Battle manifestos, 'is that we are acquainted with the history of art. . . . It is reserved for us alone, of all the generations of the human race, to know perfectly our own standing point, and to look back upon a perfect history of what has gone before us.' That, he concluded, was 'amazingly interesting to us as a matter of amusement and erudition, but I fear it is a hindrance, rather than a help, to us as artists.'[127]

Indeed it was. Scott, and most of the others on both sides of the debate, clearly hankered for the time when all artists knew their stylistic place, and no others; before the essential innocence of that situation was destroyed by all this *knowledge*. How wonderful it would be, mused William Burges a little later, 'if some kind fairy could make a clean sweep of all our existing buildings and all our books on architecture'; then, 'left to our own resources, we might do something of our own.' But 'fairies have long ceased to exist.'[128] On the other side of the Channel the French architect and theorist Eugène-Emmanuel Viollet-le-Duc was enjoining architects to 'forget everything that was accomplished before our time. Then we will have a new art'; but with the rather discouraging proviso that, 'however difficult it is for man to learn, it is much more difficult for him to forget.'[129] Charles Eastlake made an interesting analogy with the transition from innocent, instinctive childhood to a more widely aware adulthood; again, regrettable in some ways, yet necessary. Their present situation *vis-à-vis* architecture (this was in

1872) he likened to an 'awkward' adolescence.[130] That explained a lot. It also made it highly unlikely that a new 'Victorian' style would emerge 'naturally', as most theorists of the day believed all previous (and foreign) styles had done[131] – but only because of the huge advantage they had had, of blissful ignorance. In this sense, the nineteenth century marked the end of architectural history:[132] of history, that is, as an almost seamless garment, with each of its stages, and the 'transitions' between them, marked by its own distinctive style. (Some feared it might mark the end of *art*, even: if the 'phraseology of architecture', for example, really was 'exhausted'; or if – as some believed – art was a characteristic of a more 'backward' stage of history entirely.)[133]

Others besides Scott lamented the anarchy this had thrown up. For example, in the case of all previous architectures, you could date any building by its style; but no longer. What looked like solid fourteenth-century could easily have been put up just a couple of years before. In fact that is rarely so; those of us today who are knowledgeable about Victorian buildings can usually spot them immediately, and even date them pretty accurately, within a decade or two. Architecture cannot shed its 'history' so easily. But the general point may be a valid one. The very idea of a 'historical style' was one of the casualties of this new *post*-historical age of enlightenment and knowledge.

Each side in the 'Battle of the Styles' fought hard to establish its exclusive 'modernity'; but that may have been a hopeless task. This was not necessarily because good or at least convincing 'modern' cases could not be made out for both sides. The problem lay in trying to create a single or even dominant style for the times at all, a 'Victorian' style, like all those other 'historic' ones; simply because history had moved on from there – to a 'stage' that could not be expressed in this way. As much as the Goths and Classicists tried, therefore, and may even have succeeded, in liberating themselves from the anachronistic histories that were associated with them, they both remained entrapped within an anachronistic historiography.

1. The old Foreign Office, c. 1850. *Illustrated London News*, July 1861.

2. The Palace of Westminster, still under construction in 1857.
Photograph by Roger Fenton, in G. Baldwin (ed.), *All The Mighty World*
(Yale University Press, 2004).

3. Sir George Gilbert Scott. *Illustrated London News*, 13 April 1858.

4. Viscount Palmerson at around the time of the 'Battle'. *Illustrated London News*, 21 January 1860.

5. Scott's original third-placed design for the Foreign Office. RIBA Drawings Collection; reproduced with permission.

6. John Tarring's early unsolicited design for new Government Offices, 1854.
Builder, 6 December 1854.

7. Thomas Wyatt's 1844 design for the completion of the Banqueting House.
RIBA Drawings Collection; reproduced with permission.

8. James Pennethorne's design for the new Government Offices, 1855.
RIBA Drawings Collection; reproduced with permission.

9. Robert Kerr's unplaced, but apparently popular, design for the Public Offices.
Builder, 26 September 1857.

10. Sir Charles Barry's design for a 'Government Palace' presented to parliament in 1857,
but after the Westminster Hall competition. RIBA Drawings Collection; reproduced with permission.

11. James Fergusson's unrated design for the Government Offices.
V&A Drawings Collection, with permission.

12. The Westminster Hall exhibition of entries for the Government Offices competition, May 1857. *Illustrated London News*, 9 May 1857.

13. The Manchester Art Treasures Exhibition, 1857. *Illustrated London News*, 9 May 1857.

The prize-winning designs in the Public Offices competition, 1857.

14. First in the Foreign Office category, by H. E. Coe and H. H. Hofland.
Builder, 1 August 1857.

15. Second in the Foreign Office category, by Banks and Barry.
Builder, 8 August 1857.

16. Fourth in the Foreign Office category, by Deane and Woodward.
Illustrated London News, 3 October 1857.

17. Fifth in the Foreign Office category, by Bellamy.
Illustrated London News, 3 October 1857.

18. Sixth in the Foreign Office category, by Buxton and Habershon.
Illustrated London News, 24 October 1857.

19 Seventh in the Foreign Office category, by G. E. Street.
Illustrated London News, 24 October 1857.

20. First in the War Office category, by Garling. *Builder*, 1 August 1857.

21 Second in the War Office category, by Boitrel D'Hazeville (detail).
Illustrated London News, 29 August 1857.

22 Third in the War Office category, by Rochead. Sketch based on
Illustrated London News, 3 October 1857.

23. Fourth in the War Office category, by Prichard and Seddon. *Builder*, 22 August 1857.

24. Fifth in the War Office category, by Brodrick.
Illustrated London News, 3 October 1857.

25. Sixth in the War Office category, by W. G. and E. Habershon.
Illustrated London News, 21 November 1857.

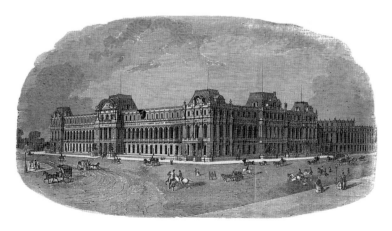

26. Seventh in the War Office category, by Dwyer.
Illustrated London News, 26 November 1857.

27. Scott's third, 'Byzantine', design for the Foreign Office.
RIBA Drawings Collection; reproduced with permission.

28. Scott's final Italianate design for the Foreign Office.
RIBA Drawings Collection; reproduced with permission.

29. The present-day Government Offices. Author's photograph.

31. The title page of Scott's great manifesto pleading for the suitability of the Gothic style for secular buildings (2nd edn).

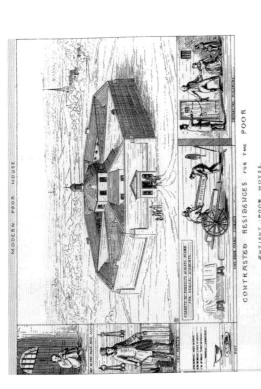

30. One of Pugin's famous 'Contrasts' between modern and 'Gothic' times. From A.W. Pugin, *Contrasts* (1837).

32. St Pancras Station Hotel, by Scott, 1865–74.

33. King's Cross Station, by Lewis Cubitt, opened 1852. Author's photograph.

34. G. E. Street's Royal Courts of Justice, begun 1866. *Illustrated London News*, 20 January 1872.

8

Not the Most Interesting Public Question of the Day

Ultimately, the most significant thing about the Government Offices debate may have been how insignificant it was. In architectural circles of course it was quite an event, although even there, as we have seen, the terms of the discussion – 'Gothic *versus* Classical' – were felt to be unhelpfully narrow. In parliament the debates were very few, short and ill-attended,[1] and concentrated mainly on practical matters, including the very practical matter of whether there should be any new Government Offices at all. Much less time was spent on how they should *look* – the question of 'style'. The same was true of discussions behind the scenes; M. H. Port finds that 'in the 160 pages of evidence elicited by the 1858 committee on Foreign Office reconstruction, about twelve are devoted to questions of style, and that chiefly in terms of cost or convenience.'[2] Only a handful of MPs spoke in these debates, usually the same ones repeatedly. These included just eleven who were definitely on the Gothic 'side', and seven on the Classical.[3] As for the rest, the *Art-Journal*, bitterly ruing the result of the final vote, was probably correct to say that most MPs were 'incompetent judges', who 'knew nothing whatever about architecture', and so were easily swayed by 'influential prejudice'.[4] No ministers apart from Palmerston, a couple of foreign secretaries and chancellors, and of course successive commissioners of the Board of Works (whose responsibility the new building was), joined the debate. Searches in the private papers of the leading politicians of the day reveal almost no interest in the question at all.[5] 'For my part,' wrote Lord John Russell in January 1860, '*I care not* when a new Foreign Office is built [as to] *whether the stile* [sic] *is Gothic or Italian*': but only that *something* got built, to protect his clerks.[6] *The Times* opined in August 1859 that there was, perhaps, 'no subject whatever upon which there is so much difference and so much strength of opinion as the rival claims of Italian and Gothic architecture.'[7] But it was a difference and a strength of opinion confined to a very small number of men.

Outside parliament the level of interest appears to have been even lower. The pamphlet campaign was vigorous, but thin, with only about a dozen pamphlets issued all told.[8] The same is true of the press. With the exception of the professional journals, the *Ecclesiologist*, *The Times*,[9] the *Illustrated London News* (because the subject was so pictorial), and one weekly paper that happened to be edited by a (Gothic) zealot,[10] there was almost no comment on these issues in the periodical literature of the time, except to mock the whole affair.[11] The working-class press avoided the issue completely.[12] This was unusual even for artistic events, for it so happens that we have a comparator here: exactly contemporaneously with the Westminster Hall exhibition of designs, Manchester was hosting an 'Art Treasures' exhibition which attracted far more attention in the press, both provincial (as one would expect) and metropolitan.[13] It also attracted at least ten times as many visitors; 'over one and a half million', according to Tristram Hunt.[14] We cannot be sure about attendance at the Westminster Hall show; if an official count was made it has not survived, and contemporary press reports are contradictory. The two main professional journals claimed a figure of around 9–10,000 for the first day (Monday 4 May), but this cannot have been much better than a guess.[15] The daily press – less interested, one would think, in boosting it – was less precise. Several accounts claimed the hall was 'thronged';[16] but it would not take many to throng what is not all that big a hall, with all those screens, carrying the drawings, taking up so much space – and women's skirts so wide. Even by the most inflated estimates it is impossible to imagine the exhibition – held over five weeks, four days a week – attracting more than 150,000 *in toto*. (It could have been half that.) Some reports remark on its popularity among 'all classes', including 'a large number of mechanics', and 'even' women;[17] but these are contradicted by others commenting on the 'painful' *absence* of 'ouvriers'. (One reason for that was that it was only open during working hours.)[18] Granted a buzz of curiosity at the beginning, one pamphleteer noted how sharply attendances fell off quite soon afterwards: 'the Exhibition, as a whole, has fallen flat indeed'. 'In most quarters,' he went on, 'the Exhibition seemed to have been entirely lost to public attention'.[19]

In the light of this, the *Building News*'s happy confidence at the end of it all that the Exhibition had done what the professionals had always hoped it would – raised architecture from a 'mystery' to be appreciated only by the '*cognoscenti*', to the level of 'a national and popular art' – looks like whistling in the wind.[20] It is even possible that most architects – even 'serious' ones – were not much interested, as opposed to architectural theorists and historians: a very small band. They just got on with their jobs.[21] On this matter most historians have clearly been misled by the shrill noise the battlers made at the time. 'The significance of the struggle in the fifties', writes Stefan Muthesius, 'was that interest in the matter went beyond the small circles of connoisseurs . . . into what one must call public opinion in a much wider sense.'[22] No. Peter Ferriday claims that 'never before or since had the interest in contemporary architecture been so great.' *That* might be true; but only among the memberships of local architectural societies, on which this claim is based; and with reference to *churches*, which is what the societies mainly studied.[23] 'The motive power' behind the whole debate, writes Halsey Ricardo, still 'came from the book-reading classes.'[24] It is for this reason that we simply cannot tell, for example, which 'side' most people took in it. (Claims have been made for both: Kenneth Clark believing that the 'ordinary man' was on Palmerston's side;[25] Eve Blau that 'popular opinion . . . was overwhelmingly in favour of Gothic.')[26] What evidence there is suggests that they did not care one whit. This must be important. If we want to infer any broader meanings from this debate – about 'Victorian' attitudes to architecture, for example, or about nineteenth-century culture and society more generally – it must be hugely relevant that the 'Battle of the Styles' of the 1850s and early 1860s, over such a nationally important building project as this, seems to have left the great majority of the nation's people so very cold.

Of course there were special reasons for it in this case. The parliamentary debate itself was one. This was conducted on such a low level as hardly to inspire an intelligent interest in the issue. It was Palmerston who mainly brought it down, of course: the *Building News* slammed his arguments as 'twaddle and bosh',[27] and even *Punch*, which might have been expected to enjoy his jokes, described his humour as that of the 'dunce';[28] but he was not the only one. 'Like a crib from a comic history of architecture', was how one pamphleteer characterized the contributions of one William Coningham, M.P.[29] The *Building News* saw the whole debate as similarly 'comical', 'puerile' and 'calculated to make us Englishmen look wondrously small in the eyes of foreigners'.[30] Some found it over-partisan: the charge here being that neither side was genuinely interested in 'style', but only in scoring party political points.[31] Other aspects of the debate also put people off. Some saw it as simply an unseemly scramble between architects for jobs. The 'scandal' surrounding the 'Classical' delegation that visited Palmerston in August 1859, however much it may have been puffed up,[32] typified the extraordinarily bad 'tone' that afflicted much of the rest of the debate: '*odium architectonicum*', the lord chancellor of the day called it.[33] Another alienating factor was the zeal – even 'fanaticism' – of the Gothic camp in particular.[34] The word 'revival' (as in 'Gothic Revival') may not have helped here, associated as it was at this time mainly with evangelical religious movements, like the Reverend Charles Spurgeon's.[35] Victorians generally distrusted 'enthusiasm' – except the enthusiasts, of course. The *Building News* was not alone in believing that all this could turn people off architecture generally.[36]

There was also the circumstance – alluded to already – that this was not the kind of building to attract people's enthusiasm naturally. In this it differed from the Houses of Parliament, which had rich and mainly positive associations for the Victorians, as a symbol (for most of them) of their fundamental national character: the 'freedoms' that the English had fought for from Simon de Montfort's time on, and still looked to parliament to defend and extend. Government 'Offices' had no such ring about them. Even the more elevated nickname sometimes given to them of a 'Palace of Administration' (to go with the 'Palace of Westminster') fooled no one.[37] They were the abode of bureaucrats, or 'functionaries' as they were often called then; of unelected civil servants presided over by appointed – and usually aristocratic – ministers, charged with ruling them, the people, which no one liked; taxing them, of course; and dealing and fighting with foreign countries, which most people in the 1850s saw as regrettable necessities at best. It may have been this that largely accounted for what Sir John Summerson identified as 'the mid-Victorian hatred of official architecture and, indeed, the fear of public money spent on architecture at all' which he claimed was 'at its height in the 1860s'. (One illustration he gave was a stipulation attached to a competition for a new poor asylum in Stepney, that the design should possess 'no architectural pretensions whatsoever'; though that may have been on the grounds that the poor did not deserve architecture.)[38] There was also a Northern (English) prejudice involved here. Prince Albert put his finger on it when he adverted to the 'increasing dislike of the large provincial Towns to the monopoly in London of great institutions to be paid for by money collected by the general taxation of the Country', of which the Government Offices were one.[39] Except in very exceptional circumstances, only the functionaries would ever see the inside of these buildings – be able enjoy Wyatt's great 'Sultan's Court',[40] for example, as at present the 'people' were allowed to marvel daily at Pugin's House of Lords. The Government Offices just did not engender affection. And it probably helps to love something, in order to care what it looks like.

Lastly (among the special reasons for apathy in the case of the Government Offices project), there were other distractions. It should be remembered that this period (1855–61) was a particularly eventful one in British and world history. It embraced two out of three of the Victorians' most serious and dangerous wars – the Crimean War and the Indian Mutiny – together with the constant perceived threat of a French invasion, and some highly important domestic political developments: including the formation of the Liberal Party, a new campaign for the extension of the parliamentary franchise and a great builders' strike in the summer of 1859, which was bound to interest the working classes, in particular, far more than the question of how the edifices the builders were supposed to be building should *look*.[41] As if this were not enough, Continental Europe was shaking down into nation states, often dramatically (Italy in particular), and the US was splitting apart. The years 1859–60 also saw one of the most celebrated murder trials of the century.[42] None of this furnished ideal conditions for the calm and thoughtful consideration of architectural questions. Indeed, some MPs thought the perils of the day should rule it out altogether. Napoleon III could strike at any moment, one of them pointed out in February 1859; which made that the very worst time to be debating 'ornamental architecture'.[43]

But there was more to it than this. It was not as though these circumstances undermined an interest in architecture that had been there before. The worst they did was probably to hinder the burgeoning of such an interest, which was one of the things it had been hoped the project – and in particular the Westminster Hall exhibition – might arouse. But that was always unlikely. Contemporary British (or at least English) apathy and ignorance about architecture were widespread, and deeply ingrained. The debate about the Government Offices reflected this, without essentially changing it.

Watching the visitors in Westminster Hall in May 1857 tended to confirm this. For a start many of them appear not to have been interested in the buildings at all so much as in the 'block plan' section of the competition, which told them where the new roads, bridges and embankments were planned to be – where they could walk or drive, that is, rather than what they might see. This was the main concern of many of the press reports, too.[44] So far as the 'elevations' were concerned, most visitors apparently went for the most picturesque drawings rather than the best designs[45] – though we have seen that this was a failing of the official judges also;[46] and for the most 'fantastic' schemes rather than the most practical ones, in line with the vulgar popular taste in most things.[47] Ignorance was rife, with one visitor (a Reverend) reporting meeting two 'well-dressed' men at the exhibition who were under the impression that 'the most purely-English of the designs' (that is, mediaeval Gothic) was an 'outlandish exotic' produced by one of the foreign competitors.[48] Of course we cannot necessarily trust this testimony either. Much of it smacks of snobbery. It was mainly furnished by members of the architectural *cognoscenti*, who were likely to look down their noses at the taste of the 'gaping Cockneys' in any case,[49] and even, one suspects, to secretly welcome the latter's ignorance. (It boosted their own sense of superiority.) But the impression they gave is also corroborated by press reports of the exhibition – in those few newspapers that began listing and describing the exhibits before, in most cases, giving up quite early[50] – which are full of egregious errors and howlers. Styles are confused almost ludicrously, for example.[51] When they try to pick winners they are almost never the ones that were chosen by the judges: which is not necessarily to their detriment, of course (the judges made some pretty poor choices, as we have seen), but does seem to reflect what the *cognoscenti* saw as the popular preference for 'showy' over more meritorious designs.[52] Obviously this does not apply to the professional papers; but they were less representative of common, or even middle-class, opinion than were the ordinary dailies and Sundays. There is not much sign of a broad-based architectural expertise or even interest there.

In fact there never had been, if one was to believe most architectural writers, who for years had been making exactly the same points about public taste as came up in connection with the Westminster Hall exhibition. Genuine *cognoscenti* were rare. The *Building News* reckoned that 'Westminster Hall would hold the whole of the public [in Britain] who take any sincere, unaffected interest in architecture' – once of course the 'gaping Cockneys' and the crinolines had been moved out to make room.[53] It went almost without saying that the '*common* mind' had 'no taste' in these matters, as the *Edinburgh Review* put it in 1837,[54] and 'scant interest' in the subject, according to the *Quarterly Review* in 1854. The latter also made the point about the *superficiality* of the public's taste in architecture; most people, it wrote, did not 'look for anything beyond what is apparent at a hasty glance.'[55] No one, however, thought this was confined to the lower orders. The *Gentleman's Magazine* remarked on how ignorance of and disinterest in architecture affected most MPs also (which would explain the low attendances at the 'Battle of the Styles' debates), and even 'educated persons' generally, who tended to 'consider it merely an architect's question, which is a great mistake'.[56] Even the upper classes, claimed Francis Scott, knew more about their horses than about their houses.[57] (Was this a sideswipe at Palmerston?) Edward Freeman thought this degree of ignorance was peculiar to architecture, among all the arts; which would explain the greater popularity of the Manchester Art Treasures Exhibition: architecture never did 'hold in public estimation the position which is so justly allowed to painting and sculpture.' (This was at the same time, he also noticed, that every ignoramus seemed to feel free to have an opinion on it.)[58] Charles Eastlake remarked on this too: 'the enormous disadvantage under which it [architecture] labours, when compared with other arts, in regard to popular interest.' One reason he gave was that you could not exhibit buildings in galleries.[59] This was a national failing, not one confined to a particular class.

One general reason often adduced for it was quite simply the poverty of England's existing architectural heritage, which was supposed to have dulled people's sensitivities in this field. It was all those boring eighteenth- and early nineteenth-century boxes and uniform grey London terraces that had done the damage. We have seen that nearly everyone at this time agreed on the poor state of the most recent English architecture.[60] Obviously this would have an impact on taste. Coventry Patmore thought it was scarcely surprising that this was so low in view of the buildings the English saw around them daily.[61] Gilbert Scott's explanation was the same.[62] Bad buildings were bound to sap public enthusiasm for architecture generally. The danger was, of course, that this could also work the other way around. Another reason for poor taste was the lack of any kind of 'art education', at all levels of schooling from elementary to public. 'Art' was never considered to be a thing that should be 'taught' at all in the nineteenth century (at least not to non-practitioners), with the possible (but very minor) exception of ancient Greek and Roman art in the élite public schools; one or two experiments in art schools, at a tertiary level; and that new Architectural Museum set up in London in 1851.[63] *Chambers's Journal* also complained in 1848 of the absence of educational books on architecture, especially for working-class readers; which, however, was not quite true, and was a little odd to find *Chambers's* asserting, in view of the fact that one of the best contemporary popular accounts of architecture was to be found in Chambers's own *Information for the People*, a kind of serial encyclopaedia intended for the 'lower' orders, published six years earlier.[64] (But of course few of the working classes had time to read at this time, after their exhausting working days and weeks, even if they could.) There were also some short single-volume guides to English architecture in circulation;[65] and then of course James Fergusson's wide-ranging and richly illustrated but also fairly expensive and occasionally idiosyncratic three-volume history of world architecture, published between 1855 and 1862.[66] When the Battle of the Styles broke out this was just about the only comprehensive book on architecture available to English readers; but it was very recent indeed, of course, and so unlikely to have percolated into the general culture yet; and did not get up to modern times – that is, post-Renaissance – until after the fighting was over.

These could be said to be accidental and unfortunate obstacles in the way of a proper appreciation of architecture in mid-nineteenth-century Britain. But there were also deeper ones. To some commentators the situation appeared 'irremediable',[67] for a number of reasons, mostly social. General philistinism – more general, that is, than simply with regard to architecture – was held to be one. For James Fergusson, art in Britain at that time (this was in 1862) appeared as 'little more than a dead corpse galvanised into spasmodic life by a few selected practitioners, for the amusement and delight of a small section of the specially educated classes'.[68] Even the 'specially educated classes', however, were not reliable. It was they, after all, who had erected all those grey Palladian boxes in the eighteenth century which now appeared so boring to middle-class architectural enthusiasts (and a few of their own number); in the face of whose revulsion many appeared to be withdrawing from the field of 'art' entirely: for example, to spend time with their hounds. 'To be an artist in Britain,' wrote Fergusson, again, was now 'to be eccentric and exceptional among the upper classes', where 'proficiency in Art' was now a matter of 'reproach'.[69] And if the uppers felt this way, believed some, there was little hope for the rest. *Blackwood's Magazine* for example thought good building depended on a strong aristocratic presence in society: from which it followed, incidentally, that the US – born of an anti-aristocratic revolution – would never have a great architecture.[70] Fergusson did not agree with that, and predicted – or at least hoped – that the rising middle classes would save the situation in Britain, their 'industry and virtue' (he was one of them himself) giving rise to a new and genuinely native British art, rooted in the soil.[71] By the 1850s the middle classes were definitely in charge, economically and politically, if not quite socially yet. (The date of the handover is conventionally placed some time between the Great Reform Bill of 1832, and the repeal of the Corn Laws in 1846.) So the onus now rested on them.

For some, however, that was part of the problem. Nikolaus Pevsner's main explanation for what he saw as the artistic 'atrocities' of this period was the rise of this class, 'who had not enjoyed the aesthetic training of the Age of Taste nor had the leisure to acquire aesthetic appreciation in later life.' This led them to 'scorn' most art; or else to admire it – as we have seen – only for its external associations, which were more easily grasped. Hence their admiration – if they had any at all – for 'revived' architectural styles; simply because it was easier to tell whether a building was a good imitation of a familiar one, than whether it was aesthetically good.[72] This was the common 'Classical' view in the nineteenth century. It was of course – however much truth there may have been in it – highly élitist, snobbish and disparaging. It infuriated the middle classes, understandably.[73]

This was not all. As well as their lack of 'taste' the middle classes were seen as bringing with them certain positive values, quite aside from 'industry and virtue', that were even more directly antipathetic to 'art'. A major one was 'what you call Economy, but what is in reality Niggardliness', as one writer put it in 1860;[74] or, to express it yet another way, 'the sordid, money-grudging spirit' of the new bourgeois age.[75] Clearly that militated against grand building, especially if it was decorated, which many saw as a prerequisite of 'architecture' (otherwise it was *merely* 'building');[76] it was the main argument, for example, of those debaters in the House of Commons – middle-class to a man – who opposed any new Government Offices building at all. Some of them thought the money would be better spent on hospitals for the poor, or Irish schools.[77] Most, however, believed it would be better not spent at all, or at least by government, which had no moral right to the money in the first place, except for very fundamental purposes (national defence was the one that nearly everyone agreed on); mainly because, in the phrase famously attributed to Gladstone at around this time, money was best left to 'fructify in the pockets of the people' – to create wealth privately, that is, in the bright new free-market way. This had nothing to do with any *shortage* of money, incidentally. There were some who argued this: that, in the words of the *Daily News* (during the Crimean War), 'we have spent too much in demolishing Sebastopol . . . *to have much left* for beautifying London';[78] but that was nonsense. Britain was the richest country in the world, as more than one architectural enthusiast pointed out;[79] of course the means were there if they needed them. That, however, was the wrong way of looking at it. Britain was rich *because* she was 'economical'. Spending her money on non-necessities – in this instance 'architecture' – would only impoverish her: not just of the net cost of the non-necessities but of the amount that that money could have 'fructified' if left in private hands. It went almost without saying that government buildings did not fructify. That was another reason why the 'economists' distrusted the Whitehall scheme so much.

This was not just a 'radical' view. Such was the insidious influence of free-market ideology in the mid-nineteenth century that almost every commentator on this affair was touched by it to some degree. It lay behind much of the scorn that was liberally poured on the more 'utopian' of the designs in the competition, for example: such as those several who went far beyond their briefs to attempt to beautify Westminster generally, with 'palatial architecture, surrounded by a fairy park, [and] umbrageous walks washed by a silver Thames'; it was 'to be hoped,' wrote the sarcastic author of this description, 'that John Bull has not quite lost his character as a practical man' so as to fall for that.[80] 'We ought to be proud,' said Sir Francis Baring in the House of Commons, 'of the *simple* manner in which we carried on the State business'.[81] The *Morning Advertiser* claimed it was this – a certain modesty in their public buildings – that fitted the English national character best.[82] It marked the nation's maturity: that it did not try to compete, for example, with inferior countries in architectural grandiosity, regarding (as M. H. Port puts it) 'such petty one-upmanship with disdain'.[83] Even *The Times*, as we have seen, shied away from too much display.[84] Sir James Pennethorne's modern biographer suggests that this may have had something to do with the utilitarian way the busy English regarded cities generally. 'There was no tradition of elegant street life as there was on the Continent. Streets were to be hurried through, not lingered in.'[85] Lastly, from the middle-class provinces, the *Liverpool Mercury* was even blunter. 'The respective merits of Gothic, Palladian, Italian and the other orders of architecture are not the most supremely interesting public question of the day,' it asserted at the height of the 'Battle'. 'We do not want to make the erection of a new Foreign Office subservient to "the encouragement of the fine arts", or to any other collateral purpose.' All they desired was a serviceable, cheap 'and at the same time, of course, a *reasonably* handsome building'. The *Mercury* clearly felt that 'reasonably handsome' was a generous enough concession to 'art'.[86]

For some people that appeared to augur the death of architecture. It was hard to see middle-class patrons encouraging fine building with these kinds of values; trusting to individual wealth, that is, to 'fructify' into great art. Even Fergusson admitted that they would need to be properly educated first.[87] Without that, the prospects were dire. They could be glimpsed already, in the new middle-class suburbs, which most architectural writers scorned – partly because so few of them were designed by architects. Instead they were given over to 'speculative builders' *pretending* to be architects (these were the great villains of many a diatribe against middle-class housing),[88] acting on the instructions of the typical client whose only aims were 'to follow his own fancy, and to work for the gratification of his own senses' rather than any higher purpose, and usually in tow to some passing fad or fashion of the day. (This was the architect G. E. Street.)[89] But was not this to be expected from a 'nation of shopkeepers', 'money-grubbing', concerned only for cheapness,[90] where nothing was built 'unless it promises a good dividend', its people inherently 'shortsighted, selfish, stingy and rapacious',[91] and individualistic to a fault: in short, from the new culture of *capitalism*, whose relationship to architecture was bound to be crucially different from the old aristocratic or 'feudal' one?

This seems a damning indictment, especially presumably to readers of this book (because they will be 'cultured'); but it was not taken that way by everyone. Many Victorian English wore their philistinism proudly. It is hard to say how many and how proud they were, because the philistines themselves generally did not usually write about these things; it was an aspect of their function *as* philistines, in fact, not to write about anything at all, unless it had a practical purpose, which writing about art – even negatively – obviously did not. Arty people often commented on their countrymen's philistinism in order to criticize it (like Fergusson when describing the upper classes), but rarely empathetically, in a way that might help us to understand it, which they clearly did not. Usually they attributed it to vulgarity, poor education and the absence of good models to inspire people: the implication being that it was due to some sort of *lack*. But there was more to it than this. A constructive and rational argument could be made out for philistinism too. This is never quite spelled out in the debate that took place over the new Government Offices in the 1850s; but it is hinted at there.

This is in connection with the comparisons that were repeatedly made at that time between London and Parisian architecture, nearly always to the former's artistic detriment, as we have seen,[92] but with another side to it too. That side was political. In London such a fundamental makeover as Haussmann's of Paris would be impossible not only because of the Englishman's inferior 'taste' but also because of the rights of property it would hit up against. Louis Napoleon was clearly able to ride roughshod over these. Was that an acceptable price to pay for even the best architecture? Beresford Hope, for one – the architectural enthusiast Beresford Hope – thought not. 'If they liked to take France with its constitution let them take it,' he told an audience in 1861; 'but he for one was satisfied with the British constitution, and with London as it was'. (According to one press report he was applauded at this point.)[93] That was a good way of getting one over on the French, without having to compete with them on their own artistic terms. Okay, so they were better at architecture. But there were better things to be better at than architecture. 'Freedom' – the British Constitution – was one.

One could think of others. Manufacturing useful things and creating wealth were two that would have particularly appealed to the Victorian industrial middle classes. Imperialists might have other ideas. 'Book-learning didn't get me round the world,' Charles Kingsley has Sir Francis Drake say in *Westward Ho!* (1855) – 'book-learning' here can stand in for the whole range of 'high' culture; 'book-learning didn't make Captain Hawkins, nor his father neither, the best shipbuilders from Hull to Cadiz; and book-learning, I very much fear, won't plant Newfoundland.'[94] For Thomas Carlyle, Britain's great material achievements were their own best 'art': 'thy Epic, unsung in words, is written in huge characters on the face of the Planet – sea-moles, cotton-trades, railways, fleets and cities, Indian Empires, Americas, New Hollands: legible throughout the solar system.'[95] Britons prided themselves on being *practical* men (it was the men they usually had in mind here), rather than artists and thinkers, and all the better for it: could they have invented the steam engine, or become as prosperous as they were, or adventurous, as well as 'free', if they had frittered their time away cultivating 'art'? Samuel Laing (the elder), a rare philistine thinker (but only because philistines did not usually think), went so far as to argue, in some detail, that art was positively deleterious to what he called the 'civic virtues' – debilitating, effeminizing, giving young people ideas above their stations and so on: worse than merely a distraction, that is; and that the progress of nations could be precisely measured by how *little* 'high culture' they had. France's superior architecture, therefore, was a sign of her backwardness.[96] Of course (again) we cannot know how widespread this way of thinking was; but it is consistent with much of the evidence, including many of the comments already quoted on the entries for the Government Offices competition in 1857; and it must be significant that none of Laing's reviewers found anything unusual or objectionable in the 'philistine' parts of his books.[97]

It also fits in with an extraordinary argument adumbrated in a lecture on architecture that was delivered in London in January 1858: extraordinary because it came from the mouth of John Ruskin, the doyen of architectural critics; and because it would seem, if taken seriously, to undermine everything else he had ever written about the importance of art. January 1858 was of course a time when

Britain was fighting for her imperial life in India, egged on by some grotesque and racist anti-Indianism (especially in the press) at home. Ruskin was very much affected by this, painting the Indians as cruel, treacherous and even 'fiendish' in this lecture; but he was aware too of the Indians' tremendous achievements in architecture. (He must have read Fergusson.) He also greatly admired the bravery and superior morality of the Highland Scottish regiments that were pitted against the mutineers: in this case, however, emanating from a society that had very little of what he would term 'culture' at all. Broadening his gaze, he also observed that throughout history 'artistic' nations (like India) had invariably been conquered by inartistic ones (like the Scots). The conclusion this seemed to be heading towards was that art (including architecture) was essentially degrading and weakening, just as Laing had claimed. This clearly troubled Ruskin. At the end of his paper, reported the correspondent whose account of it appears in the *Builder*, 'the lecturer ... proceeded to reply to the difficulty he had [with his own argument], but the answer was of too subtle a character to be seized in our notes.'[98] That was no wonder. It will have taken a deal of subtlety for Ruskin to extricate himself from the philistine implications of that.

Philistinism, as a product of capitalism, was undoubtedly a powerful discourse in mid-Victorian society, and one of the things that distinguished that society from most of its Continental neighbours'. It must account for much of the relative lack of interest there was in the arts in England, including architecture, then; and *may* help explain why – though this of course involves subjective judgements – England was so artistically impoverished by comparison with other European cultures in the nineteenth century; '*das Land ohne Musik*', for example, in the jaundiced eyes of one of her later German critics.[99] Yet we should not run too far with this; nor, indeed, with any too broad generalization about a society as complex and uneven as the English – even English capitalist society – was then. If we did, it would be difficult to account for the many substantial and in most cases very non-utilitarian public buildings that *were* built in England at this time.

A simple list should make the point. Leeds, Northampton and Halifax town halls; the old Hull City Hall (now demolished); Leeds Corn Exchange; St George's Hall, Liverpool; Manchester Free Trade Hall and Assize Courts (demolished); dozens of great churches, university buildings and major railway termini; Scarisbrick, Aldermaston and Mentmore halls (or 'houses'); the old Public Record Office in Chancery Lane; the Palace of Westminster (the finishing touches): all these were either being designed or were still under construction during these years of 'Battle' (1855–61); impressive buildings, all of them; most of them fine ones; a few even possibly 'great'. As Palmerston pointed out in 1863: 'if anyone will go to Liverpool, to Leeds, to Manchester, to other great towns, he will see buildings of the most beautiful description erected, not under the control of government, but by persons employed by the municipalities themselves.' (The 'not under the control of government' is the crucial phrase here.)[100] Extend the period by 20 years on either side, and we take in St George's Hall, Liverpool; Manchester Town Hall; the Law Courts in the Strand; the British Museum; Truro Cathedral; much of the South Kensington site; and at least a dozen more.[101] Extend it another way – 'downwards', socially and in terms of size – and we net literally tens of thousands of chapels, post offices, small commercial buildings, villas and terraces, all showing definite 'architectural' features (that is, decoration), which were often despised at the time by the *cognoscenti* but are far more appreciated today – unless it is only the better ones that have survived.[102] That is not a bad haul for a period of public apathy over architecture. It may even be better than most Continental countries could claim at this time, certainly in quantity and possibly also qualitatively; for many of the stylistic insecurities that Britain experienced then dogged them too. There is no way that mid-Victorian Britain could be dubbed a '*Land ohne Arkitektur*'. The idea of a national discourse of 'philistinism', therefore, does not quite seem to tally with the solid evidence on the ground.

But then 'discourses' often do not. This is for a number of reasons. One is that they are usually uneven, seldom uniform or 'hegemonic'. Mid-nineteenth-century Britain, for example, was the home not only of Thomas Gradgrind and his ilk[103] but also of men like Dickens, his creator, who deplored his cold, narrow capitalist values; of thousands of what might be termed pre-capitalist 'survivals' – aristocrats, squires, vicars, philanthropists, Catholics, Tory paternalists, country people generally; and also of many capitalists themselves of a far more generous and 'cultured' kind. These last may have been that because of the still pervasive influence of the 'old order', who still ruled the *cultural* roost in England, and whom Martin Wiener blames for the capitalists' backsliding from a purer kind of political-economic value system from the 1850s on. (This is the phenomenon, stated crudely, of successful entrepreneurs using their hard-earned wealth to buy into the leisured classes; which explains many of the great new private mansions that went up at this time.)[104] Many of them, before they backslid, lived in the great new cities of the north of England (and Scotland), where, as we have seen, most of their tribal loyalties lay, and most of their greatest public building enterprises were concentrated; designed not merely for 'use' but also to express their local – not national – pride.[105] Hence the great new city halls, corn exchanges, law courts, libraries and so on of the age. And hence also the middle classes' *disinterest* in the Government Offices, which could be seen to express neither personal aspiration nor local pride, but rather, if anything, elements – central bureaucracy and taxation – inimical to both.

The other main reason why dominant social and cultural discourses are not always reflected in the products of art, in this case architecture, is that art is not always subjected to them. Even in the case of architecture, which can be said to be the most public of the arts – in the sense of being the most difficult to avoid – it does not follow that it expresses public concerns as much as, possibly, it should. That is because the public does not usually commission it; and because those who do are not generally representative of the public, especially when that public is broadly apathetic. How can they be, when the act of commissioning would seem to require some *interest* in the matter, at least? So, in the cases of nearly all the great buildings that went up in the 1850s and 1860s, it was small minorities of people who generally determined what they looked like, especially in terms of style: the Camden Society for churches, for example; a few rich men for great houses; 'speculative builders' for little houses; committees of judges – often deferential to the 'cultured' class – for municipal buildings; and – for the new Whitehall Offices that this book is mainly about – a single, opinionated, old-fashioned and obstinate old lord. That was an extreme and exceptional case. But the general point it illustrates is valid. It was well expressed at the time by James Fergusson, in the very midst of the battle – just six months, in fact, after the Westminster Hall exhibition of designs that was hoped to do so much for the public's awareness of architecture. Obviously that had not worked. Architecture, claimed Fergusson, was still 'the privilege and the exclusive property of a small and limited class of persons. . . . *rather than becoming the expression of the nation's wants and feelings*'.[106] That marked the gap between mid-Victorian society and this aspect of culture, at least. Society was not interested enough in the building, or even the debate about it, for it to be truly and broadly reflected in the latter.

Hence the appearance of the Government Offices as they were eventually built; the most striking feature of which – if 'striking' is the right word for it – is how dull they are. There is no central feature: no clearly marked entrance or entrances, for example, only a single, stubby tower, and no dome. (Most of the Classical entries in the original competition had had either towers or domes, or both.) It is more 'massy' in appearance than Scott's original light sketches suggested, but that is the only external aspect of it that impresses. The old India Office part of it (now incorporated into the FCO) is more ornamented than the old Foreign Office part; but otherwise there are no significant features to distinguish the four original Offices from one another, apart from their friezes and roof-level statues, which scarcely anyone notices; and of course no element of fancy. The interiors are gorgeous (and gorgeously restored recently); one of them even has a Gothicky detail – pointed vaults at a kind of clerestory level in the 'Locarno Room' – which was apparently added by Scott after Palmerston was safely dead.[107] Otherwise, however, they are dull and repetitive. They are, in other words, *merely* offices, scarcely different from the hundreds of large office blocks that have been put up in London subsequently, except for their deeper windows and heavier mouldings. They were something of a disappointment at the time, even to Palmerston, who was so largely to blame for them, and to Scott, who seems to have put little love into them; and they remain a disappointment today. They certainly do not merit the name 'Palace' that was wishfully conferred on them before Scott's final designs effectively quashed that notion; and are not the proud monument of British architectural art that the profession and *cognoscenti* had so much longed for when the project was mooted in the first place. Geoffrey Tyack calls them 'one of the architectural tragedies of the nineteenth century'.[108] This is how they should be 'read' by historians wishing to infer more general conclusions about contemporary British (or English) society from this particular cultural production: not through its stylistic details, which were accidental; nor even through the 'great' debate over it – the 'Battle' – *on its own*, though that can be illuminating, as I hope to have shown; but mainly through that Battle set in its *context* of general apathy; which is what allowed such an accidental building to be built. It may not have celebrated contemporary England, as many would have liked; but in another sense it reflected the country pretty faithfully. It was probably what she deserved.

9

A Change for the Worse

It had been billed in some quarters as the great battle for the architectural soul of England, but in its outcome it was probably not that. The way the debate had been conducted, and then settled, made it difficult to read anything really significant into it: about the architectural preferences of the English, for example, or what style fitted their national 'identity' best. The immediate outcome was a great new 'Classical' public building, which was a setback for the Goths, to be sure; but the Government Offices were not *so* important, or talismanic, as to be likely to set any kind of precedent for any other public buildings that might come after them. Everyone – anyone, that is, who took any interest at all in the matter – knew about Palmerston's mischievous part in the whole affair, which was as likely to put them off the style he had insisted on as to make them want to adopt it as a model. Most people were also aware of Scott's ambivalent attitude towards his own creation, which he was never shy of voicing; asked, for example, by a select committee in 1877 whether he thought Palmerston's insistence on the Italian style had meant 'a change for the worse', his reply was: 'I think quite so.'[1] All this was bound to undermine any influence the style of the new building might otherwise have had, as an example to be followed, on English (or British) public architecture in the future.

In fact the reputation of the Government Offices never seemed to recover, quite, from the problems that had surrounded their birth. They had a few polite reviews in the professional press when they opened for business (*seriatim*),[2] but were mainly ignored. They were the continual object of complaints by those who had to work in them. Over-ornamentation was a common one,[3] which could be reasonably attributed to the architect, though Scott preferred to shift the blame for this on to his brief: 'all my earlier instructions on the subject led to the idea that a very palatial building was required. After I had carried out the first portion . . . I was told that we ought not to have done that; but my first impressions were that that was wanted, and I aimed at it';[4] other complaints, like poor plumbing and inadequate ventilation, were the sorts that are usually raised about new buildings – and never old ones, as Scott testily remarked[5] – and sound more like normal teething troubles. Nonetheless, it is worthy of note how some critics directly attributed these, too, to the *style* of the building – the fetid air that was trapped under its high Classical ceilings, for example; in a way that is reminiscent of the accusation that used to be made against Gothic, that it – the style – was responsible for the smells in the House of Commons. Scott was quite happy to go along with this. 'Assuming that these complaints about an upper layer of stagnant air, and so on, have any foundation, you impute the blame, not to yourself, but to those who compelled you to change your style,' Beresford Hope put to him at that 1877 select committee hearing. 'You may say so, indirectly', Scott replied (uncannily anticipating a famous character in a 1990s BBC TV series); 'but I would not wish to throw the blame on anyone.'[6] If conditions in the building improved after that, they deteriorated again later. By 1968 they were so bad – 'tatty, physically dirty and lacking in facilities', the lifts inoperative, the 'lavatories . . . ancient, unreliable and unsalubrious', half the rooms 'freezing cold' and so on[7] – as to lead the government of the day seriously to consider demolishing them. It seems not to have anticipated the opposition this provoked among contemporary conservationists, and which helped save the building in the end; indeed, to be splendidly restored in the early 1990s.[8] By then, however, it was ancient enough to have accrued 'historical associations', which will have compensated for its aesthetic deficiencies.[9] Modern opinion over the building mostly concurs with Sir John Summerson's judgement, that 'it is not one that counts for much in the history of English architecture'.[10] The best that can generally be found to be said in its favour is that, with all its mediocrity, at least it 'spared us a St Pancras in Whitehall'.[11]

Scott, too, never really recovered his reputation. He won several more important commissions, including that Midland Hotel at St Pancras, the Albert Memorial and the new Glasgow University; all of which, however, were widely criticized and even ridiculed at the time, not just later;[12] and in professional circles he seems to have been regarded as 'at best a middle-brow'. One authority suggests that this was why he lost the Law Courts commission, which he coveted, to Street, who was seen as a superior Goth and more principled.[13] Scott's *un*principled change of mind over the Government Offices will have contributed to this. He was knighted in 1872 (his sovereign's thank-offering for the gorgeous shrine he had built for her beloved and still much-missed consort), and granted the great privilege of a funeral in Westminster Abbey six years later. Even on that occasion, however, he must (if he was looking down on it) have felt miffed by the dean's less than full-hearted eulogy to his memory. 'Others may have soared to loftier heights,' said Dr Stanley, 'or produced special works of more commanding power; but no name within the last thirty years has been so widely impressed on the edifices of Great Britain, past and present, as that of Gilbert Scott.'[14] (So, 'never mind the quality, feel the width'.) Then, when Victorian architecture became almost universally reviled in the early twentieth century, and Victorian Gothic most of all, his stock of course sank with that; but lower, one feels, than most of his contemporaries', and with his rehabilitation taking much longer than theirs, when the tide began to turn again, very slowly, from the 1930s on. 'A man of great talents', acknowledged Kenneth Clark in 1928; adding, however, stingingly, that 'these were not specifically architectural'.[15] His success, agreed H. S. Goodhart-Rendel – the first twentieth-century architectural historian to have a good word to say for any

Victorian Gothic – was due to 'talents other than artistic', and especially his ability to pander to popular vulgarity.[16] 'Will anyone admire the works of Scott?' asked Basil Clarke in 1938. 'It is hard to believe that they will, for there is nothing in particular in them to admire.'[17] The anti-Gothic Reginald Turnor painted him in 1950 as typically Victorian in his self-confidence, ability to make money and smug morality, but with only 'an enormous output of bad and indifferent architecture' as his legacy.[18] Henry-Russell Hitchcock faint-praised him as 'a most "correct" if uninspired Revivalist'.[19] And so on.[20] Jokes are still made about his St Pancras hotel and Albert Memorial. So Scott has not worn well, even by comparison with his co-Goths. It may take the removal of the builder's hoardings from around St Pancras – now, as these words are written, being beautifully restored and converted to other uses – to remedy that.

Of the other main actors in the drama, Palmerston died in 1865, three years before his Foreign Office was completed; still no doubt believing – as he had offered as his 'impartial [sic] opinion' at the end of that crucial debate in the Battle in July 1861 – that 'the Gothic [had] been entirely defeated' by his intervention.[21] If that was meant to refer to a broader field of conflict than just this one building, it was a somewhat premature gloat. Gothic in fact flourished in the area of public secular building in the 1860s and 1870s, producing not only Scott's aforementioned St Pancras Hotel (1867–74) and Glasgow University (1870–9), and Street's London Law Courts (1871–82), but also, for example, Scott's Leeds General Infirmary (1863–9); Waterhouse's Manchester Town Hall (1868–77); and, if one takes a fairly broad definition of 'Gothic', much of the South Kensington exhibition site, including Waterhouse's Natural History Museum (1873–80): major buildings all. Indeed, for this period (c. 1860–80), unlike earlier and later, Gothic dominated, with only Captain Fowke's Victoria and Albert Museum (1866–70) and Albert Hall (1867–71), and Sir Charles Barry's Halifax Town Hall (1860–62), representing the Classical camp in the field of public secular architecture, and even in these cases somewhat idiosyncratically. (The 'V&A' is more Romanesque, aptly perhaps for a military man; and the silhouette of Halifax's central tower really quite Gothicky.)[22] So, after the disappointment of their Foreign Office débâcle, it did not take long for the Goths to pick themselves up.

Hence Charles Eastlake's confidence in 1872, when he came to publish his pioneering *A History of the Gothic Revival*, that the battle was almost won by then, and by the Gothic cause, with the Classicists 'in a decided minority'.[23] One or two problems remained: mainly the squabbles *among* Goths as to which variation or 'period' of their style to favour, and the occasional 'fitful gusts of private bias and public caprice' that blew across their bows; but he expected these to be overcome, and the style to 'burn long and steadily' in the future. The major question mark hanging over it, and which the Government Offices project had been supposed to address – was Gothic only suited to churches? – had now been triumphantly settled by all those subsequent buildings; so that Gothic's adaptability to secular purposes was fully acknowledged, and, indeed, was now 'probably a strong plea in its favour'.[24] In the short run, therefore, Palmerston could not have been more wrong.

But the tide was to turn; starting, as it happened, in Eastlake's time. The year after his book came out T. G. Jackson, an architect himself, noticed how among his younger colleagues – even those who had been zealots for Gothic in the past – there were those 'on whose palate modern Gothic begins to pall'.[25] It seems to have been a fairly general phenomenon. 'George Edmund Street awoke one morning', wrote H. S. Goodhart-Rendel 60 years later, 'to find his flock all scattered – scattered, as it has proved, beyond recall'.[26] Almost every architectural historian since has noticed this shift in the 1870s,[27] and the physical record attests to it. There is little agreement, however, as to the reasons for it. 'Something happened,' wrote Goodhart-Rendel, again. 'I cannot discover exactly what, but I suspect that Mr Richard Norman Shaw was at the bottom of it.'[28] Other historians blame the fake-mediaeval excesses of the new Law Courts: 'an unpopular building', writes Joseph Kinnard, 'before it was started';[29] but then fake mediaevalism had not been an obstacle to the appreciation of architecture (the Palace of Westminster, for example) before then. There were clearly deeper underlying causes too. The decline of religiosity – or at least of 'High' Church religiosity – is one; religiosity was important to the ecclesiastical branch of the Revival, and may have spilled over.[30] The rise of democracy is another, after the 1867 Reform Act, though the precise effects of this need to be inquired into: it does not quite work to say that it shifted local government priorities to social housing, for example, because plenty more monumental civic buildings were erected after this time, usually now in Classical or eclectic styles. (And prestigious architects still did not generally stoop to working-class housing in any case.) The return of overtly nationalistic and imperialistic considerations into British politics in the last quarter of the nineteenth century almost certainly had something to do with it, to which we shall return shortly. (It has important implications for one of the main arguments of this book.) Another factor, however, *could* have been the taste left by the Battle of the Styles of the 1850s: not the result of it, nor any of the arguments adduced on either side, but the spirit in which it had been fought.

We have seen (in Chapter 8) how cold that left most people at the time of the Battle itself. They had not cared greatly which side won. What seems to have grated with them was the ultra-serious turn it took, especially for the Goths, with their moralism and, yes, religiosity, applied to what for ordinary people was the *not* very serious matter of how their physical environment should look. Palmerston had played cleverly on this in those witty interventions of his in the House of Commons; capped off at the very end of the Battle with this gloss on the whole affair: 'Sir, the battle of the books, the battle of the Big and Little Endeans, and the battle of the Green Ribbands and the Blue Ribbands at Constantinople were all as nothing compared with this battle of the Gothic and Palladian styles.'[31] In other words, it had all been a great fuss over nothing. That could be seen as disingenuous. If Palmerston had really thought the Battle of the Styles was simply one between Big-Endians and Little-Endians (the reference of course is to the Lilliputian wars in Swift's *Gulliver's Travels*, fought over which end one should attack a boiled egg), then he surely should not have minded which side won. But he did. This was why he fought the Goths so furiously – that claim of his to 'impartiality' was another characteristic piece of devilry – and to such great effect. Once he had won, however, he could afford to ridicule the whole thing. That harmed the Gothic side more than the Classical, because that was the side that seemed to be taking the issue most seriously. He must have known that.

On one level, however, perhaps the broadest, this was what the Battle of the Styles had been: a contest between those who thought architecture should be taken seriously, and those who – seriously – did not. The unserious were definitely the winners here. It is not a success that can be measured easily – a victory for apathy – but there are plentiful signs. The fact that the 'Battle' itself subsided is one, with nearly all the pamphleteers and so on downing their pens as soon as the Government Offices affair was decided, and no future architectural controversy – and there were some (like over the Law Courts) – displaying quite the same degree or breadth of passion as in that case. Public interest in architecture did not appear to have been boosted at all in the long or even the medium term by the 'Battle', which was a great disappointment; with the same old complaints continuing after 1861 about 'a public whose taste in all that concerns the building art is universally degraded' – still.[32] Even middle-class patrons of architecture, building houses for themselves, could not be persuaded to take the matter seriously. You *must* choose a style, the architect Robert Kerr recounted telling a typical customer in 1865; only to be met with:

> I would much rather not. I don't want any style at all. I want a plain, substantial, comfort-able, *Gentleman's House*; and, I beg leave to repeat, I don't want any *style* at all. I really would very much rather not have any; I dare say it would cost a great deal of money, and I should very probably not like it. Look at myself; I am a man of very plain tastes; I am neither Classical nor Elizabethan; I am not aware that I am Renaissance, and I am sure I am not Mediaeval; I belong neither to old England, France, or Germany, nor to Belgium or Italy; – I am very sorry, but if you would kindly take me as I am, and build my house *in my own style* . . .[33]

And that was (largely) the commissioning class. People like this were never likely to take to any particular architectural ideology, and least of all the more fundamen-talist Gothic versions, with what Kerr called their 'claim to universal domination . . . and destruction of all else, which is arrogant'.[34] Eastlake was well aware of this, and of the danger it posed to his cause. With all those 'fanatical devotees and over-zealous antiquaries' around, he wrote, 'it is no wonder that men who do not share the extreme views of either party should have become nauseated with the very name of Gothic.'[35] It was, of course, the 'Battle of the Styles' that had brought all this 'seriousness' to the fore.

Afterwards everyone calmed down. The question of 'style' was still debated, and especially the search for a 'style of the future' – one that would express 'modernity'; but less shrilly, and more open-mindedly than in the 1850s. T. G. Jackson's young backsliding architect colleagues, for example, did not abandon Gothic altogether, but only the more ideologically 'correct' versions of it, and the awful weight of moral and moralistic arguments that those versions had been burdened with. Compromise broke out on all sides. The most commonly proffered solution to the 'problem' (of the 'style of the future') now became some form of 'free' style, based perhaps on one of the two main historical contenders, but quite loosely: not 'seriously', therefore.[36] Robert Kerr anticipated the Battle of the Styles being resolved, ultimately, in the 'honourable and creditable' way that all such conflicts should be settled: 'namely, alliance', with the two styles 'approaching one common centre', or coalescing.[37] Eclecticism was now widely accepted; either as the final solution, or as a holding operation until the new style 'emerged'. For it seemed to be acknowledged now, as another architect put it, that 'if ever again we are to have a national style, we shall not get it for squalling [shrieking]. We must wait patiently until it develops of itself. A man can no more invent a new style than he can invent a new language.'[38] That allowed them to relax. 'Queen Anne' was another symptom of the same phenomenon; chosen by Norman Shaw for his famous New Zealand Chambers in Leadenhall Street, John Summerson claimed, '*because* of its lack of stylistic seriousness'.[39] Both architects and their clients had had their fill of architectural theory, especially treated as a branch of ethics. They yearned to get back to what they liked and (some of them) did best; which was to build buildings that looked good.

There were still recognizably Gothic and Classical buildings built after the 1870s – very many of them; but with marked and significant differences about them. For a start, Gothic, the more 'principled' style of the two, became *less* principled, less 'politically correct', to use a modern term; in particular, less firmly rooted in that perfect *point de départ* (the thirteenth century) which most of the leaders of the Gothic movement had insisted on in the 1850s. On the surface this appears to be a betrayal and a failure; what may be surprising, therefore, is how many of the older Goths seemed fairly reconciled to it, on the grounds that though the substance of their style might have altered, the spirit behind it endured. The argument was this – and it is one that was consistent with at least one strand of old Pugin's thinking: that before he had come along English building had been superficial, dishonest and dull; he and his followers had liberated it from that, and introduced his deeper principles – especially functional and structural 'truth' – into architecture, which had been inextricably tied to the Gothic style at the beginning, but were not so *in* principle. So, although the style (in its 'correct' forms) had lost ground, no architect could afterwards ignore those underlying principles, whatever other styles he might design in. It was on exactly this idea that the very forward-looking A.J. Beresford Hope in 1863 pinned his – what otherwise might seem somewhat optimistic – hope for the triumph of Gothic ultimately.

> [I]t is not for me to conjecture whether the Architecture of 1963 will be the Architecture either of the Gothicists or the Classicists of 1863. But I say that in 1963 whatever Architecture then prevails will have drawn much of its life-blood from our teaching, and from the principles on which that teaching is based, than from the antagonistic school.[40]

So the body might die, but the soul would keep marching on. At the very least, this was a comforting thought for the mourners. It was a fairly common view at the time,[41] and has been taken up by modern historians since.[42] If the Battle of the Styles had helped establish these principles more firmly, then maybe it had not all been for naught.

What is interesting is to see the effect that this liberation from ideology had on the particular *forms* of Gothic that were chosen during this period – the final quarter of the nineteenth century; now, that is, that architects no longer needed to adhere to the style or styles that were considered most 'correct'. The most common response was a return to the previously much despised Perpendicular, which was where of course the serious Gothic Revival had started (with the Palace of Westminster) before the despising began; was where the historians and the 'low' Anglicans of the neo-Gothic movement would have felt more comfortable even in the 1850s;[43] and was the 'stage' of Gothic that several of the movement's later chroniclers – not fully understanding the ideological imperatives of the age, perhaps – thought in retrospect would have made a better starting point.[44] (It is interesting to speculate how the Revival might have fared ultimately if it had been.) So, what Basil Clarke called 'the foreign Gothic craze' ebbed;[45] to be supplanted by more narrowly English models, like the Perpendicular, in spite of its incorrectness. 'It was suddenly declared,' wrote Goodhart-Rendel in 1924, 'that early French was all a mistake. Gothic ought to be English, and as late as you pleased.'[46] It was noted in an earlier chapter how few of the Gothic entries in the Government Offices competition of 1857 had been in Perpendicular, despite its obvious selling points: its unambiguous English credentials, for example; the fact that it was the last of the old Gothic styles, and so the logical place, surely, to resume the tradition; and the glory – to unbiased eyes – of its surviving monuments. Now all that changed. Most neo-Gothic churches built in England from the 1870s onwards, right through to *Giles* Gilbert Scott's great Liverpool Anglican cathedral, started around 1910 but only completed in 1978, are more recognizably 'Perp' than anything else. Luckily for their peace of mind, all the architectural ideologues of the mid-nineteenth century, including Scott *grand-père*, were dead by then.

In part this was a switch from ideology to 'taste': from valuing the 'associations' of architecture, that is, to simply liking how it looked. To many people's taste the new Gothic buildings, especially the more original ones – those departing most from mediaeval precedents – just appeared 'ugly', and even, some suspected – and with reason, as we have seen – deliberately so.[47] But we cannot be confident that this was the only or even a main reason for the shift in styles: a growth of 'taste', and of reliance on taste; which incidentally none of the self-appointed guardians of 'taste' in the later nineteenth century – the *cognoscenti*, or *literati* – ever recognized among their more vulgar compatriots. What is more likely to have been happening is a switch *between* 'associations': from the principled, progressive and international ones we found to be dominant in the middle of the nineteenth century, to a more tribal kind. In the 1850s the emphasis on ideological 'correctness' had encouraged architects to look for models for those qualities elsewhere than in Britain: in northern France, Flanders and Lombardy, for example; and so to become cosmopolitan. (This incidentally seems to have been unique to Britain. When France held competitions for new Gothic cathedrals she insisted on French Gothic styles; and the same with German competitions for new city halls.) That no longer happened; or, at any rate, to the same extent. Principled cosmopolitanism in English architecture receded, to be replaced by 'Englishness'.

This may have reflected broader trends in contemporary British and European society. There are two possibilities here: one is that the English had always wanted it this way, even in the 1850s (there are hints of this, as we have seen), but that the architectural *élite* had defied them on this. In other words, 'culture', in this particular instance, did not reflect 'society'. The other is that the architectural debate *was* reflecting society, all through, and that from the 1870s that society changed. This is equally likely, and consistent with the broader evidence. For a general historian the idea of 'nationalism' and even 'imperialism' making a return to English architecture in the later nineteenth century, after an absence earlier, will come as no great surprise. The 1850s and early 1860s had been an unusual period in British history, distinguished (in part) by the self-confidence, sense of 'progress' and cosmopolitanism that were briefly described in Chapter 2 of this book as three of the main characteristics of that time, and which later chapters have shown to have been clearly reflected in its architectural discourse. But only briefly. From the 1870s onwards all three came to be quite fundamentally undermined, by – for example – economic depression; recidivist nationalism both in Europe and in Ireland; economic protectionism on the Continent; and extra-European colonial competition. The 1870s and 1880s were a different world, in perception at any rate, from the 1850s and 1860s. So we would expect it to be reflected differently in its public architecture.

That *might* explain, for example, the fading of that confident, 'progressive' streak in Gothic ideology after the Battle of the Styles, mirroring contemporary disillusionment with the dominant and similarly 'progressive' social and economic ideologies of the mid-nineteenth century; as well as the retreat from architectural 'cosmopolitanism', as the internationalist ideals of the earlier Victorians appeared to be failing in the wider world. Falling back on familiar, national styles (like

Perpendicular) is also explicable in terms of the need to assert England's, or Britain's, own nationality in the face of the extraordinary and really quite sudden increase in national feeling, nation-building and international tensions both abroad and across the Irish Sea. And then, when this turned in Britain's case into a self-conscious 'imperialism' towards the end of the century, it is equally unsurprising that a new architectural style should be found for that: in this case generally not Gothic,[48] but a heavy, monumental, Roman classicism, generally classified as 'Edwardian' (the new main front of Buckingham Palace, for example), which was very little like anything that had gone before, and *may* have reflected those changed times. (This needs more research in the written record of that period, before we can be sure.) By then – 50 years after the 'Battle' – English public architecture had become both more British, on one front, and more brutish, on another. Which only serves to throw into relief the distinctive character of *our* period, the 1850s, when it had been neither.

Conclusion

The Victorians never did settle the question that was at the bottom of the Battle of the Styles: which was what their architecture ought to look like. At least, they did not settle it to the satisfaction of most of them, which would have required the establishment of a single, characteristic style of building for nineteenth-century Britain, such as every nation and age (they believed) had had before. The lack of such a style was a matter of concern to many of them, convinced as they were of the greatness of their age, and consequently disturbed by the fact that it did not appear to have an architecture that expressed this; or alternatively, in a few cases, worried that this might indicate that their age might not be so great after all. At the time the Battle broke out, two historic styles were competing for this honour; or rather, one of them was strictly competing, with the other merely defending its patch. By then Gothic had cornered ecclesiastical and collegiate, Classic most of the urban secular market. But the Goths wanted all of it. The Foreign Office, as the greatest urban secular building project of the time, was the great bastion they needed to storm on the way to achieving this. If they won that, they would shortly have their one 'Victorian' style. Hence the significance, in architectural historical terms, of this debate.

In many ways it was curiously one-sided, though the side that made the most noise in it was, in the event, the one that lost. This explains the concentration of this book on the Gothic side of the argument, simply because the Goths had far more to say for themselves, and argued their case with more originality and depth.[1] The Classicists, being on the defensive, tended at first to take their style for granted, and then simply to address – in order to demolish – their rivals' points. They made few new ones of their own. So there is less to get one's analytical teeth into here. This, however, gives a distorted impression of the picture on the ground in Victorian England, where most of the buildings actually erected – rather than talked about – were Classical. This is apparently true of every part of the nineteenth century, including this middle period, when Gothic was most on the offensive.[2] Gothic buildings were outnumbered by English Renaissance, Italianate, French Second Empire, Greek and even Roman ones (if you lump them all together); and not only outnumbered but also sometimes out-designed. But the latter have usually seemed less interesting to write about, by both contemporaries and modern authors, than the brash, noisy and spiky Gothic, which was bound to stand out more, and still does, in many present-day cities and towns.

Nor were the Classicists always as conservative as the Goths liked to paint them, with some remarkable and even startling developments taking place, albeit more quietly, in neo-Classical architecture at this time. By the 1860s many Classicists had travelled at least as far from their archaeological roots as the most original of the Goths had from theirs, and along some of the same paths. There was a High Victorian Classic as well as a High Victorian Gothic, as Robert Furneaux Jordan points out, both of them characterized by 'hardness . . . brashness', and 'uninhibited richness'; which description may not do complete justice to either, but makes a fair point: that both styles were similarly 'High'.[3] (To me that word conjures up overripeness, which may not be thought to be inapt.) The tower of Barry's Halifax Town Hall, for example, mentioned in the previous chapter, has quite a lot in common even with Scott's roughly contemporary Albert Memorial; more, at any rate, than either has with its original mediaeval or Renaissance model. This is why we – or at least those of us who think we have an eye for architecture – can nearly always tell a 'Victorian' building from one of any other period: Exeter College Chapel from the *Sainte-Chapelle*, for example; or the Reform Club from the Banqeting Hall (to choose comparisons which seem superficially fairly close). Seen from the hindsight of more than a century later, there is a recognizably 'Victorian' quality to them all; a patina of 'Victorianism' which it is possible for us to recognize, though less easy to define or describe (it is not simply a question of 'hardness' and 'brashness'), and which contemporaries tended not to see, probably because they stood too near to it.

If they had seen it, they might have taken some comfort. There they were, desperately seeking an architecture characteristic of their age; and all the time they *had* it, without realizing it. It was expressed not in uniformity of style, as they had supposed it must be, but in the uniform way all their styles were handled by the architects and builders of the day. It can also be said to have been expressed, perversely, by that *lack* of a uniform style, the very thing that made contemporaries feel they *had* no common and characteristic architecture: the 'babel' of their styles, as Summerson called it;[4] which stretched, as we have seen, not only from Classic to Gothic but also between different and competing varieties of Classic and Gothic; through exoticisms of other kinds; to 'styles of the future' (but previewed in the present) which allegedly owed nothing to any previous style; and sheer 'eclectic' rag-bags of everything. Our 'Battle' illustrates vividly the pain and frustration that this confusion caused to so many of the combatants; but not, as it happens, to quite everyone at the time. We have met a number of contemporaries who, able to step back from the immediate fray, and from the partisanship that seemed to be required of it, actually rejoiced in the variety of styles that their age had thrown up, which for them indicated the freedom, choice and even democracy of that age by contrast with previous ones, when stylistic unity had only been possible because it had been imposed on them, or because their peoples were too ignorant of other styles to know that they had a choice. The moderns were happy, were they not, that their society had progressed from that kind of stage to the new liberal-capitalist one? Well, this was the price they had to pay for that, in terms of architecture. *Or*, by another way of looking at it, its glorious expression. On this question, writes J. Mordaunt Crook today, the Victorians 'judged themselves too harshly. Where the Victorians saw failure ... we see instead a plethora of achievement. Where they saw unrelieved chaos, we see today the rich, productive chaos of an age of eclecticism.'[5] For – adds Furneaux Jordan – 'the greatness of the Victorian Age is of a different kind from the greatness of other periods'.[6] The real problem for Victorian architects and architectural writers was that they could not see that yet. They were still striving, in this Battle of the Styles, for a kind of 'greatness' that was already anachronistic and out of their grasp when the Battle began.

'Culture' is often assumed to reflect the society around it; indeed, this is one of the justifications that cultural scholars often give for studying it, to give their work a deeper significance than the 'merely' artistic. It is certainly true that no work of art can ever be divorced from its social context, however much that needs to affect our judgement of its intrinsic worth (the greatest obviously transcend their immediate surroundings and purposes), and one of the purposes of this book has been to show how the Battle of the Styles related to *its* broader historical environment. But it has also shown, I think, that that relationship was complex, not to be 'read' simply and straightforwardly from the cultural artefacts we are studying, but dependent on some knowledge – the more the better – of both the broader history of the times and the particular circumstances that gave rise to (in this case) the building that is the main focus of this study: the Foreign and Commonwealth Office in Parliament Street. What our particular enquiries showed (in Chapter 1) was that that building, or at least the style that was chosen for it, cannot have greatly reflected the society of the time in any direct way – in other words, cannot be 'read' very usefully – simply because of its 'accidental' genesis: the extraordinary politicking that resulted in a building that no one was happy with, not even its patron (Palmerston) or its architect (Scott), or the people who came to work in it, or – so far as we can ascertain their feelings – the general public. At the very least, this must weaken any case that might be made that the building itself reflected any of the dominant discourses of the day. Of course the politicking surrounding it may have done – it may have reflected, for example, the corruption of the time. But not that pile in Whitehall.

It was for this reason that we then passed on to the public controversy surrounding it, which, representing as it did so much broader a range of early Victorian opinion, is bound to have mirrored rather more of the mores of that place and time. There we found a number of discourses that bore on people's preferences over this question of style, each with a social situation and history behind it; of which a couple were *weaker* than is sometimes assumed, and than may even seem self-evident; and others more powerful. Patriotism and imperialism are the two 'disappointments' here, with imperialism, by any reasonable definition of that slippery word, scarcely being a factor at all, certainly overtly; and 'national identity' generally being considered a secondary consideration, by comparison with others.

Of those others, 'modernity' appears to have been the major one, though it may only appear so because of the efforts that had to be put into establishing both styles' 'modern' credentials in the face of obvious appearances. Closely following were 'moral' considerations; the term being used here very broadly, to embrace, for example, functional 'truth', honesty in the use of materials, structural 'progressiveness', fidelity to nature, 'liberty' and a number of other perceived virtues that at that time were often described as 'masculine'. It was these two prime considerations – modernity and morality – that determined that both the Gothic and the Classic architecture of the 1850s and 1860s should *not* be narrowly nationalistic, or expansively imperial, but should transcend both these characteristics, which were seen as befitting an older, more backward stage of society than Britain had entered into then. It is here that a knowledge of that broader society and its peculiarities, compared not only with other nations' but also with Britain's own both before and afterwards, is necessary in order to understand how this can have been so. Very often cultural historians of the nineteenth century, when they do try to fill in the general backgrounds of their topics, tend to generalize across the whole hundred years. 'New Imperial' historians projecting the jingoistic 1890s back to the middle of the century is a fairly common example. It is this sort of thing, probably, that gave rise to the statement that this book opened with: that the FCO was 'built at the height of our Victorian imperial power,' 'specifically to impress foreigners', and in a style chosen 'to proclaim Britain's status in the world'; which we have shown to be so misleading. Different decades, different discourses; and all of them very mixed.

But we cannot stop there. Though the Battle over the building certainly reflects the societal concerns of its day better than the building alone does, it still only reflects them partially. Contemporary participants in the debate liked to think that they were speaking for the 'people' on this matter (on one side or the other), and some modern authors seem to have followed them in assuming this was a very 'public' debate, not simply confined to the experts. But this is mistaken. The evidence suggests that only a very small number of people took any interest at all in it, or had opinions on the question of whether and on what scale to build the new 'Government Offices'; and that even fewer – far fewer – had any feelings on the question of its *style*. Ignorance and apathy on these matters were widespread. The *cognoscenti* were always commenting on this, though we cannot always trust them, because they were snobs. But it is likely. Most people, if you had presented them with pictures of quintessentially Gothic and Classical buildings, could probably not have told you which was which. (I have no evidence for this, of course, apart from some of those recorded misreadings of the drawings exhibited at the 1857 Westminster Hall exhibition; a parliamentary committee member who asked Gilbert Scott in 1877 whether there was any Gothic in his new Foreign Office, now actually standing there before him;[7] and one or two middle-class friends of mine, frequent visitors to historic buildings, who have failed this very test. Those of us to whom this comes naturally should not assume it does to everyone.) It was the purpose of Chapter 8 to add this crucial dimension to the story, which must cast doubt on the idea that the Battle of the Styles necessarily reflected, even indirectly, anything at all about the really wider society of the time, outside the very narrow élite of people whose chattering is sometimes taken to be more representative than it was. If they could nonetheless be said to be speaking *for* the people, as their spokespersons, perhaps, there might be a case for linking their culture with the broader society of their time. But that is unlikely, in view of the vast social (and other) divisions that cut across Britain – that 'hybridity' – described in Chapter 2.

For the fact was – and probably still is – that architecture was a highly élite area both of practice and of interest, which may be surprising considering its ubiquity, for it is the art form that is least easy to avoid. In the seventeenth and eighteenth centuries it had been mainly under the control of rich patrons and the state, who still dominated the art to a great extent in the following century, albeit with the new 'profession' of architects taking its place alongside them. That is, if you defined 'architecture' as the designing only of large buildings, or buildings with an element of monumentality to them – churches, colleges, town halls, mansions – which by and large the Victorian architectural profession did; and which was the final thing that tended to alienate them and their works from the broader society around them, as we shall see. According to some Gothic ideologues, the revival of their style should have changed all that; the original Gothic having been, in their eyes, an intrinsically 'popular' style, born of the people, developed by ordinary crafts-men out of their own creativity, with the architect – or 'master mason' – very much in the background (indeed, often not identified), and responded to directly and affectionately by the people, who after all built in essentially the same way for themselves – in their great tithe barns, for example. Then, went the narrative, this was all overturned in Jacobean times (earlier in other countries) by a new alien style *imposed* on the people by their aristocratic oppressors, not involving the 'people' at all save as wage labourers, mechanically copying from architects' drawings or pattern books; which explained first why so much of it was bad, and second why ordinary people could not respond to it. Gothic was intrinsically more people-friendly; which is why, when it was revived in the nineteenth century, the people should have befriended it.

There is no evidence at all, however, that they did. One reason for this is undoubtedly that, whatever the situation *may* have been in the Middle Ages (the neo-Goths' version is highly dubious, of course), this new form of the style emphatically did *not* spring from the people, but was, as Michael Bright puts it, 'imposed by a small group every bit as élite as the aristocrats who introduced the classic into Renaissance England';[8] a different small group, of course, but equally unsympathetic (all that zealotry). With a few exceptions – the disgraced O'Shea brothers on the Oxford Museum, for example – and despite initiatives such as the Architectural Museum designed to encourage their creativity, builders were still treated as 'workers' rather than 'craftsmen', and degraded much as they had been under the Classical regime.[9] The great builders' strike of 1859 was a symptom of that.

Most crucially, the new Gothic style was controlled by *architects*, none of whom had ever been a mason himself; 'soft-handed "gentlemen"', as one contemporary critic sneeringly described them;[10] *aspiring* to be 'gentlemen', that is (it is what those double inverted commas signify): this aspiration, too, determined by the nature and ethos of the society that was described in Chapter 2, and fuelling, in the main, their drive to become recognized as a 'profession'. 'Professionalism' was also supposed to ensure standards, and a degree of control. It did not always work, with the Government Offices affair being a case in point; from the way he treated him it is obvious that Palmerston did not recognize Scott as a 'gentleman', or the rights his professional status should have given him over the way he carried out his work. A second aspiration, which did not always sit easily with the first, was to be accepted as 'artists'. All this had implications for the sort of work they took on, which set them apart both from their mediaeval predecessors and from their own society. One was that they only did – or at least preferred to do – work in which they could gain social prestige, or shine as artists: 'show off', as another contemporary put it.[11] Generally this meant 'monumental' buildings. (Another factor behind this may have been that it was usually the 'monuments' that had survived from the past.) Another implication was their anxiety to distance themselves from the engineers, who were not at all 'gentlemen'; and even, in many cases, from the latter's favoured material, iron. A third was their studied avoidance of ordinary domestic buildings, with the exceptions of the occasional suburban villa and parsonage; and definitely of large-scale domestic architecture: terraces, estates, blocks of apartments and so on, for ordinary people; while at the same time looking down sniffily on the 'speculative builders' who took up what they had left. These preferences all arose from their social situation in nineteenth-century Britain, and owed nothing at all – so far as we can see – to their mediaeval *point de départ*.

But they also set them *against* their times in certain ways. (This, incidentally, applies to Classical architects too.) One of the biggest trends of those times – though not the only one, as used to be thought – was the growth of democracy in Britain, which is conventionally supposed to have begun in 1832, and was much in the political air in the 1840s and 1850s, before receiving further boosts in 1867 and 1884; to which the concerns of the architectural profession at this time seemed deeply irrelevant in two ways. The first, of course, was its avoidance of social housing. The second was its resistance, in the main, to the principle of 'competition', which in theory should have made architects more answerable to the democracy, though in the case of the Foreign Office it turned out to be only to a tiny group of hand-picked amateurs, and ultimately to Palmerston alone. One can see why the *profession* of architecture did not think much of that. (In 1867 Street suggested that the council of the RIBA lodge a protest against the whole competition system, which he claimed was 'founded upon the idea that all architects are reckless gamblers, & not artists or gentlemen.')[12] Its third 'irrelevance' derived from its emphasis on monumental buildings. But democracies – as Sir John Summerson pointed out in 1949 – did not need monumental architecture. Monuments were for societies dominated by gods, kings or nobles. 'Today, to endeavour to be monumental is to be untrue to our own times.'[13]

Summerson's time was not Scott's and Street's and Barry's, of course; but there were signs even then of the way the wind could blow. One was an article published in 1861 arguing that monumentality in church architecture was actually putting large sections of the populace off. 'Stately spires and pointed window frames without, elegant shafts with arches and corbels within, frighten away the classes whom we are desirous of bringing under the influence of religious training.' The solution to this, suggested the author, was to suspend church architecture entirely, and hold services in plain schoolrooms instead.[14] Another straw in the wind was the turn taken in the 1870s onwards, and noted already, towards domestic building (albeit wealthy domestic), and a softer style of architecture, in the works of Philip Webb, Norman Shaw, Charles Voysey and the like. Peter Collins credits this with undermining 'the old idea that architecture was essentially something to do with temples and churches', and in this way 'broke through the archaeological barrier which in England [had] separated architecture from life.'[15] It also, incidentally, laid the foundation of probably the most internationally influential style of architecture that has ever originated in Britain, notwithstanding all those Magdalen College towers on American campuses.

All this makes the Battle of the Styles appear anachronistic, or rapidly approaching anachronistic; but then anachronisms are of course a part of any society. The Victorian age in fact doted on them: historical novels, Pre-Raphaelitism, invented traditions, mediaeval tourneys, statues of modern statesmen in togas (there are some of those in the Foreign Office),[16] and of course *all* their architectural 'revivals'; for it is the sheer number of these, as Peter Collins comments, again, that gives the Victorian age its 'singularity'. (Previous ages – for example the Renaissance – had revived one style at a time.)[17] The assumption is often made that these plunges back into the past indicated some kind of dissatisfaction with the present, which we have seen is true in certain instances (Pugin, most notably), but obscures two other important factors. The first is the rational, modern and 'progressive' claims that were made for both styles, but Gothic in particular, including by Pugin; not entirely unconvincingly. The second is that this question of 'style' was a genuine problem, with no obvious solution, but only a number of possible ones, of which reviving one or other 'historic' style was as reasonable as any.

Of course you first had to agree that the old Classic style was no longer adequate for the times; but that was not difficult, in view of the poor showing it had made (in England, at any rate) in recent years. The question then was how to improve it, or replace it. And that in fact was the crux of the problem: the fact that it *was* a question; a *choice*, therefore, which was almost unprecedented in the history of architecture, as a number of contemporary theorists pointed out. Earlier styles had either developed naturally and incrementally (the Egyptian, Graeco-Roman, Romanesque, Gothic, Hindu, Inca and 'Saracenic') or been unilaterally imposed (the Renaissance). In most cases, people had not known enough about other architectures to realize that they had a choice. That was the other 'singularity' of the Victorian age: that it had eaten from the tree of knowledge, and so could no longer be as happily innocent, architecturally speaking, as earlier times. It says much for the perspicacity of our Victorian architects and theorists that they jumped to this quite early, as we have seen, and realized the difficulties it posed. It was beneath them simply to copy a style of the past; and none of our mid-nineteenth-century architects was in any way a copyist, in fact, though they were often accused of it. So, accepting that one had to move forward, how was that to be done? A 'style of the future' was unlikely to emerge 'naturally', when one had all those other styles in front of one. A kind of proto-functionalism, and styles based on iron, were some of the ideas that were mooted, but they were not obvious choices yet. (For a start, the new materials, like iron and concrete, were not yet advanced enough to bear a new style; and why should it be assumed that 'modernism' had to be as plain and undecorated as it later became?) So it was difficult, if not impossible, to start afresh. That being so, it made sense to return to one of those other styles for a *point de départ*; but which one? In view of all this – given these choices – there were bound to be arguments. The Battle of the (historic) Styles was one of these, at what was considered to be a crucial time.

Of course both sides failed ultimately, but not without leaving some legacies. One is a corpus of often truly striking and even beautiful buildings, though the Government Offices may not qualify as one of these; and some even more wonderful projects, sadly unconsumated, among which a few of us may wish to include one or other of Scott's alternative Foreign Office designs. Another was a body of underlying principles – form expressing function, and so on – that the Battle enabled to be presented before a slightly wider audience than might otherwise have been aware of them, and to be honed in vigorous debate. That percolated through, the argument goes, into modern, functionalist architecture. A third legacy is a tradition of neo-Gothic and neo-Classical building in Britain which did not in fact disappear with the victory of 'modernism', which was mainly confined to public and monumental architecture, but which hardly affected at all the tastes of, for example, ordinary people who could afford to build houses for themselves. Hence the new fake-Tudor villas and pseudo-Classical mansions that continue to be built today, a century and a half after the great ideological battle between those two architectural traditions, albeit drained of the passion and the principle that had informed both styles then. In this way the Battle – or at least the rivalry – still lives on, albeit under the radar of the architectural establishment; in much the same way as the neo-Goths claimed their style had survived the imposition of Classicism by another élite in early modern times. Lastly, from the nineteenth-century historian's point of view, the legacy of the Battle is the uniquely rich and concentrated picture it presents to us of one particular aspect of mid-Victorian élite culture, and of its relation to some parts of the society of the time, in a way that is bound to illuminate our understanding of the nature – and especially the complexities and ambivalences – of each.

So: what does any of this *matter*? Historians generally like to write about events that are important, not just fun to work on, as this one was; but it is difficult to find much of broader significance in the Battle of the Styles. I did not realize this at the beginning of my researches, but it turns out that it did not really represent the opinions or feelings of more than a tiny minority of the British population; may not, even in an indirect way, have mirrored the mainstream culture or society of the time; did not influence the future course of English architecture greatly; and had hardly any impact, even, on the ultimate shape of the building it was supposed to be centred on. The impression one early reader of this book gained from it, as he reported back to me, was that it was in fact no more than 'a very elaborate dance on the head of a pin, activating contemporaries into passionate and furious statements, and yet ultimately more enervating than creative'. Why then, he asked me, bother with it? (Though he was glad I had.)[18] I have to say, this was a question that often and increasingly occurred to me too as I was working on the book. I found it unsettling, as I am not used to writing about things that don't 'matter', or that I cannot persuade myself do. More and more, I felt I was simply indulging in research for pleasure's sake; which went right against the early Protestant upbringing that clearly informs my research ethic still.

Brooding on it now, however, after completing my research, I think it may have been worthwhile, in three ways. First, using the Battle as a kind of focus for studying the society and culture of this specific period of British history has I feel enabled me to reveal some important things about it, even if I have had to go beyond that focus occasionally – refer to what the Battle did *not* show up – in order to do this faithfully. I don't think this has been done in quite this way before. Concentrating on a particular issue – not narrowly, but launching off in other directions occasionally, partly in order to get a perspective view of it, before always coming back to it – can give one a special kind of perception and appreciation of, in this case, the variegated character of mid-nineteenth-century English society: what I called its 'hybrid' class structure, its inconsistencies, conflicts, interactions, hopes and fears, shifting nature even within a short time frame; all this reflected *in part* by the Battle; in some (not all) of its great creative richness. If we go beyond the strict battle lines of this controversy, as we have done, to take on board 'modernistic', 'exotic', 'eclectic', 'speculative' and 'slum' building, too, we get a pretty vivid impression of the times. Readers must emerge from this, as I have, with a more knowledgeable but also *complex* notion of Victorian England than they probably had before, which may be uncomfortable, but is all to the good. It is (I believe) one of the main functions and duties of the historian to *confuse*. Many of our perceptions of nineteenth-century England tend to be partial, simplified, overgeneralized, too dominated by overarching 'theories'; all in order to make it more readily grasped, intellectually controllable – but only by doing violence to the far more messy realities. Hopefully this account will shine a new light, or rather several new lights, on the mess. This was always its main purpose; or, at least, the purpose I was most confident of fulfilling.

I also hope (secondly) that it may be useful to architectural historians, although – not being a member of the mystery myself – I am a little less confident of this. For them, what I am providing here is *context* for one of the great building enterprises of the mid-nineteenth century, and by extension for others. They can make what use they want of that. Some – I cited one in my Preface – apparently think that too much emphasis can be placed on 'context', which I'm sure is true: it's a very diminishing ideology, I believe, that seeks to explain every feature of any work of art in terms of its social, political or even cultural environment; but most of the architectural historians I have read do allow 'context' some role. Those who do will surely want to get it right. This book may help. That it is needed is proved by one of the quotations I began this book with, explaining the new Foreign Office building in terms of the 'imperialism' of the 1850s – others have jumped to this conclusion too – which I tried to show in my Chapter 5 is an oversimplification at the very least, and possibly substantially wrong. I have noticed other similar misreadings of general history in other works of architectural history (though I hasten to add that most, especially about the 'Gothic Revival', are pretty sound). This is surely the historian's second main function: to correct ignorant readings of the past; which is, to be honest, a full-time job. Another, in this case, may be to introduce architectural historians to aspects of the context surrounding their particular subject that they may not be aware of, so suggesting possible new interpretations. In my own specialist area, I am often stimulated greatly by learning new things from *its* contexts, however distant they might seem. I find it hard to believe that architectural history cannot be cross-fertilized in similar ways. Again, however, it is up to the architectural historians to decide precisely how.

My third reason for thinking this book may 'matter' is the bearing it has on the more general question of the relationship between what are called 'culture' (meaning, in this context, 'high' culture) and 'society'. One thing it has shown, I think, is that in the particular case of our 'Battle' that relationship was uneven and complex, even tenuous; so that dominant social discourses cannot simply be read from (or between) the stones of the new Foreign Office, in the way that 'cultural studies' scholars often try to do, in the parallel cases of literature and the other arts. Whether architecture is a special case here I don't know – it seems unlikely, in view of its very public profile; or even whether the Foreign Office was somehow different from other contemporary buildings in this regard – which would be less surprising, in view of what we know about its particular genesis. But there may be a general lesson to be drawn here, for the study of 'culture' more broadly. The way any cultural artefact expresses or reflects the dominant social discourses of its time depends on a number of factors: which only solid historical digging, in the ground around those artefacts, can reveal. I'm sorry if this reads like a self-interested plug for my own discipline and approach; but there it is.

In the final analysis, however, this book *has* been a piece of self-indulgence on my part, and its main interest to readers will probably have lain in its account of a lively, profound, high-minded, low-minded, rude, sometimes risible but always truly Victorian row, representing a profusion of contemporary interests, motives, ideologies and prejudices, and involving some curious, eccentric and even villainous characters; over a building on which great hopes were originally placed, but then sadly disappointed: however much it may, in the outcome, have 'mattered' or not.

Notes

Notes to the Preface

1   'The Great Offices of State: II: A Palace of Dreams', produced by Michael Cockerell, and broadcast on BBC4 on 19 February 2010. The David Miliband quotation, above, comes from the same programme.

2   See Michael J. Lewis, *The Politics of the German Gothic Revival* (1993), pp. 246–55. George Gilbert Scott submitted a design for that too, illustrated on p. 250: Gothic but with domes.

3   Kristian Hvidt, trans. Siff Pors, *Copenhagen City Hall: The Building and its Activities Through 100 Years* (Copenhagen: Københavns Kommune, 2005), pp. 34–5.

4   See Ronald Hyam, *Britain's Declining Empire: the Road to Decolonisation, 1918–1968* (Cambridge: Cambridge University Press, 2008), pp. 21–2. Sir Edwin Lutyens was the Classicist here, dismissing Mughal pointed arches on the grounds that 'God had not made a pointed rainbow'. If only Palmerston had thought of that!

5   Incidentally: when I write 'English', I mean 'English'. Scotland, Ireland and Wales have significantly different architectural and also political and social histories from England. It so happens, too, that none of these nations appears to have displayed as much interest in the debate over the new Government Offices as the English. It would be wrong, therefore, to use a term, like 'Britain', which implies that all its national constituents were the same.

6   The most substantial accounts are Ian Toplis, *The Foreign Office: An Architectural History* (1987) and his 'Gilbert Scott and the Foreign Office Affair', in Roger Dixon (ed.), *Sir Gilbert Scott and the Scott Dynasty* (1980); David Brownlee, 'That "Regular Mongrel Affair": GG Scott's Design for the Government Offices', in *Architectural History*, vol. 28 (1985), pp. 159–97; M. H. Port, 'Pride and Parsimony: Influences Affecting the Development of the Whitehall Quarter in the 1850s', in *London Journal*, vol. 2 (1976), and chapter 13 of his *Imperial London: Civil Government Building in London, 1851–1915* (1995); T. Armour, 'Four Attempts to Rebuild the Foreign Office; 1839 to 1869', unpublished history dissertation, Architectural Association School of Architecture, 1978; and a private report compiled by Cecil Denny Highton & Partners, Chartered Architects, *A History of the Building containing the India Office, the Foreign and Commonwealth Office and the Home Office* (March 1983), in the Foreign Office Library (my thanks to Professor Patrick Salmon, the FCO historian).

Notes to Chapter 1: The Battle Joined

1   The *Report from the Select Committee on Foreign Office Reconstruction*, 13 July 1858, gave as an example of this the rise in the amount of correspondence received and sent by the Foreign Office: 6,193 'despatches, &c.' in 1821; 19,006 in 1839; and 59,703 in 1857. PRO WORK 12–84/1, p. iii.

2   House of Commons, 10 August 1857; *Hansard*, 3rd series, vol. 147, cols 1305–6.

3   *The Times*, 18 August 1857, pp. 2–3. See plate 1.

4   See, for example, Sir William Molesworth, paper on 'Downing Street Improvement and
     Public Offices Extension', [November 1854], in PRO WORK 12–84/1 f.2; Molesworth
     and Lord Palmerston in the House of Commons, 31 July 1855: *Hansard*, 3rd series, vol.
     139, cols 1575–6; and, for the Malmesbury story, Lord Granville in House of Lords, 15 June
     1855: *Hansard*, 3rd series, vol. 139, col. 2015; and Geoffrey Tyack, *Sir James Pennethorne and
     the Making of Victorian London* (1992), p. 246.

5   *The Times*, 7 October 1856, p. 6.

6   See *The Times*, 6 August 1856, p. 6, which used an odd simile to describe the situation:
     comparing the Secretary of War to 'an old fogie performing his toilet – a wig out of this
     box, half a dozen teeth out of that, here the colour for the cheek, and there the padding
     for his manly chest.' See also Ian Toplis, *The Foreign Office: An Architectural History* (1987),
     p. 28.

7   *Report from the Select Committee appointed to consider plans for certain Public Offices proposed to
     be erected in Downing Street*: PP 1839 (466.) xiii; *Report on Downing Street Improvement and
     Public Offices Extension*, [November 1854], in PRO WORK 12–84/1 1854.

8   This is in the RIBA Drawings Collection, ref. PB 201/WYTH [18] (1–2). See plate 7.

9   *The Times*, 6 August 1856; and cf. the *Morning Advertiser*, 5 and 7 May 1857. Later Henry
     Cole suggested this as 'an honourable solution' of Scott's difficulties (of which more later):
     letter in *Builder*, 3 September 1859, p. 589.

10   This was in answer to criticisms by a parliamentary committee, reported in the *Architect*,
     1 September 1877, p. 110. Two of the other original prize-winning designs seem to me to
     owe something to the Banqueting Hall: Banks and Barry's (2nd) and Bellamy's (5th).

11   Two of Pennethorne's designs for the Government Offices, from April and September 1855,
     are reproduced in Tyack, *Sir James Pennethorne*, pp. 250 and 252; and here, plate 8.

12   This is preserved in the RIBA Drawings Collection, DR 12/4; and was pictured in *Builder*,
     December 1854, p. 643. Tarring (1806–75) is listed in Alison Felstead *et al.*, *Directory of
     British Architects 1834–1900* (3 vols, 1993) (which wonders whether he might have been
     related to Thomas Crapp Tarring, who died in 1859); but in no more selective biographical
     dictionary of architects. There are mentions of 'an offer . . . made to the Government by
     a private company to build all the public offices that were required at Whitehall' by Lord
     Malmesbury in the Lords, 15 June 1855: *Hansard*, 3rd series, vol. 138, col. 2017; and by Lord
     Redesdale in the Lords, 2 August 1855: *Hansard*, 3rd series, vol. 139, cols 1623–4 – which
     may be references to this. The *Saturday Review*'s comment is in its issue of 17 November
     1857, p. 48. See plate 6.

13   E.g. Redesdale in Lords, 2 August 1855: *Hansard*, 3rd series, vol. 139, cols 1622–3; *The Times*
     6 August 1856, p. 6.

14   See, for example, Lord Granville in the Lords, 15 May 1857: *Hansard*, 3rd series, vol. 145,
     col. 294; and Sir George Trevelyan, who may have been the one who first used the word
     'Palace' ('of Whitehall') to describe his own grandiose vision: see Toplis, *The Foreign Office*,
     p. 26. For Palmerston's alarm, see his letters to George Cornewall Lewis, 20 August and 7
     October 1856, in Palmerston Papers, GC/LE/74 and 191.

15   This is *The Times*, 1 August 1855, p. 8; précising somewhat freely the arguments of MPs like
     Bankes and Sir Francis Baring in a Commons debate, 31 July 1855: *Hansard*, 3rd series, vol.
     139, cols 1575–6. Bankes did make the point about ministers using their own homes.

16   *The Times*, 1 August 1855, pp. 3–4.

17   See my *The Refugee Question in Mid-Victorian Politics* (Cambridge: Cambridge University
     Press, 1979).

18   E.g. Macartney in Commons, 13 July 1857: *Hansard*, 3rd series, vol. 146, col.1421; Briscoe in Commons, 24 July 1857: *Hansard*, 3rd series, vol. 147, col. 364; *Daily News*, 4 May 1857: 'We have spent too much in demolishing Sebastopol . . . to have much left for beautifying London'; Coningham and Bentinck in Commons, 11 February 1859: *Hansard*, 3rd series, vol. 152, cols 270, 273, both urging parsimony while there was a war *looming*; and for Palmerston, see his letters to Lewis and to Hall, 25 August 1856, in BL Add. MS 48580, ff. 127–30, insisting that 'works and fortifications connected with the Defence of the Country' should be given higher priority. At this stage he seems to have thought the old Foreign Office could be patched up.

19   Passed on 31 July 1855, as the first instalment on a total sum estimated then at £585,000. *Hansard*, 3rd series, vol. 139, col. 1574–8.

20   Geoffrey Tyack has done a great job of rescuing and rehabilitating him, in his *Sir James Pennethorne and the Making of Victorian London* (1992).

21   See *ibid.*, pp. 134–5. A few years before, Pennington's predecessor Robert Smirke's chances of being appointed architect of the new Palace of Westminster in the 1830s had been undermined by exactly the same prejudice, against government patronage. See W. J. Rorabaugh, 'Politics and the Architectural Competition for the Houses of Parliament, 1834–1837,' in *Victorian Studies*, vol. 17 (1973), p. 161.

22   See, for example, *Saturday Review*, 17 November 1855, p. 48: 'The fact is, Mr Pennethorne is an inheritance from the Georgian era . . .'

23   The old Public Record Office in Chancery Lane is his leading Gothic (or Tudor-*ish*) work. See Tyack, *Sir James Pennethorne*, p. 160. In the 1830s he had also submitted a design for the Palace of Westminster in Gothic, which he had described then as 'the most congenial [style] to our climate and feelings, and essentially NATIONAL.' *Ibid.*, p. 33.

24   Pennethorne to Sir Benjamin Hall, 26 May 1856; PRO WORKS 122–84/1, f. 125.

25   David Brownlee, 'That "Regular Mongrel Affair": GG Scott's Design for the Government Offices', in *Architectural History*, vol. 28 (1985), p. 161.

26   Tyack, *Sir James Pennethorne*, p. 253; and see Roger H. Harper, *Victorian Architectural Competitions: An Index* (1983).

27   On the professional debate over competitions, see Barrington Kaye, *The Development of the Architectural Profession in Britain: A Sociological Study* (1960), p. 88; and Frank Jenkins, 'The Victorian Architectural Profession', in Peter Ferriday (ed.), *Victorian Architecture* (1963), pp. 43–4.

28   *Building News*, 2 March 1860, p. 162. See also (for the debate on architectural competitions generally) Anon., 'The Present State of Architecture', *Quarterly Review*, vol. 95 (September 1854), p. 340; *Building News*, 20 February 1857, p. 177; *Building News*, 8 May 1857, pp. 441, 449; *Builder*, 9 May 1859, p. 261; J. H. Stevens in *Builder*, 7 November 1857, p. 639; *Scotsman*, 17 December 1857; *Builder*, 19 June 1858, p. 418, and 26 June 1858, pp. 429–31; *Daily News*, 26 August 1858; Tite in *Civil Engineer*, December 1859, pp. 395–6. On 'gendered' references, see below, pp. 82–3.

29   Tyack, *Sir James Pennethorne*, p. 253.

30   See *Report from Select Committee . . . upon the Re-Construction of the Foreign Office*, 13 July 1858, p. iv, in PRO WORK 12–84/1; and *The Times*, 7 October 1856, p. 6.

31   It is hard to tell exactly why, though we know that some architects scorned competitions on principle; or a sense of grievance may have been a factor. He protested the decision, especially in view of the work he had been put to; Hall, however, replied that he had not wanted or expected him to furnish elaborate drawings, only rough sketches. Tyack, *Sir James Pennethorne*, p. 254.

32   Detailed specifications and rules are to be found in PRO WORKS 12–86/1, ff. 9–31.

33   No. 24 in Anon., *Designs for the Public Offices: A Hand-Book Guide for Visitors* (1857), p. 11.

34   See *Building News*, 17 July 1857, p. 739; *Saturday Review*, 1 August 1857, p. 105.

35   *Report* of the 1858 select committee, p. v para 7: PRO WORK 12–84/1.

36   So far as we know the competitors were all men, although the *Building News*, 15 May 1857, p. 474, speculated that one of the designs, or at least part of it – 'the forcible element' – might be by a woman. What its evidence for this was, or whether it was meant seriously, I have no idea.

37   See Tite at a council meeting of the RIBA, 3 May 1858, reported in 'General Meetings – Minutes', in RIBA Archive, 1.c.2; and *Report* of the 1858 select committee, pp. v–vi, para. 8: PRO WORK 12–84/1.

38   These were M.A. Crepinet, who came first in the 'block plan' section, and M.A. Botrel, who was awarded the second premium for the War Office – both Parisians. *Report of the Judges*, 27 June 1857, pp. 13–14: PRO WORK 12–86/3. An invitation to enter the competition had been published in *Le Moniteur*. Hammond to secretary, Board of Works, 1 November 1856, in PRO WORKS 12–86/4, f. 6.

39   Crepinet's ground plan, for example, featured a 'Place du Gouvernement'. Anon., *Designs for the Public Offices: A Hand-Book Guide for Visitors*, p. 8.

40   Objections to admitting foreign entries were referred to in Anon., *Designs for the Public Offices*, p. iv; expressed by certain members of a deputation of architects to Sir Benjamin Hall in August 1856; and reported in *Builder*, 30 August 1856, p. 468; and in the *Building News*, 29 May 1857, p. 541. For Beresford Hope, however, the fact that a Frenchman had won one of the prizes 'speaks volumes for the honesty and impartiality of the judges, and must satisfy our neighbours that they can have justice and impartiality from English gentlemen': Commons, 2 July 1857: *Hansard*, 3rd series, vol. 146, col. 795.

41   See, for example, a letter from the Architectural Association, 6 November 1856, in PRO WORK 12–86/4, f. 12; a letter in the *Building News*, 18 April 1857, p. 546; another in *Builder*, 6 June 1857, p. 313; an editorial in *Builder*, 23 May 1857, p. 281; and the Latin motto attached to one of the entries: *'Tempus defuit'*: *Building News*, 12 June 1857, p. 597. The later deadline for foreign entrants (5 days) is mentioned in a letter from the Board of Works to J. Hopkins, 6 February 1857, in PRO WORKS 1/53, f. 284.

42   This is reported in *Reynolds's Newspaper*, 24 May 1857, p. 7.

43   For example, Habershon and Buxton, who won 6th prize with their 'Renaissance' Foreign Office design, hedged their bets with a 'Flamboyant Gothic' alternative.

44   The Royal Archive contains one letter from Albert relating to the competition, but with no indication of any stylistic preferences. From other clues (Osborne House, for example) it seems he might have favoured German 'Rundbogenstil'. How many designs in this style there were at the exhibition is hard to tell. There was a great deal of xenophobic prejudice against Albert in Britain at this time, so any preference he might have expressed would probably have been counter-productive. Henry-Russell Hitchcock speculates that this may have been a motive for his keeping a low profile over the affair. Hitchcock also characterizes his wife as 'entirely philistine', which is, indeed, her general reputation: *Early Victorian Architecture in Britain* (1954), p. 9. Albert died just after the question of the style for the Offices was settled, in December 1861.

45   On the numbers who came, see below, p. 112.

46   *Morning Advertiser*, 4 May 1857, p. 3.

47   E.g. *Observer*, 10 May 1857, p. 5.

48   For complaints along these lines, see 'Nemo' in *Builder*, 28 March 1857, p. 178; *Building News*, 8 May 1857, p. 445 and 449; *Builder*, 9 May 1857, p. 261.

49   Any architectural elevation can of course be made to look better by clever 'shading'. As William Burges once wrote of G. E. Street: 'What a pity that he cannot build his cross-hatching'. Quoted in Georg Germann, trans. Gerard Onn, *Gothic Revival in Europe and Britain* (1972), p. 127.

50   Anon., *Designs for the Public Offices*, p. 22; and see *Builder*, 25 April 1857, p. 230. Scott (1811–78) is the major actor in the drama about to unfold in this chapter. He was the most famous, the most prolific and also the most vilified architect of his age. He was also the first to pen an autobiography, published posthumously (and in a slightly censored form) as *Personal and Professional Recollections* (1879). Gavin Stamp's reissue of this book (1995) restored the cuts made by his son; he writes about this in 'Sir Gilbert Scott's Recollections', in *Architectural History*, vol. 19 (1976), and about other aspects of Scott's life and work elsewhere. There is a sound biography of Scott by David Cole, *The Work of Sir Gilbert Scott* (1980); and an interesting essay on his life by Julian Litten in Roger Dixon (ed.), *Sir Gilbert Scott and the Scott Dynasty* (1980).

51   For example, the aforementioned *Designs for the Public Offices: A Hand-Book Guide for Visitors*, published by H. G. Clarke & Co. in May 1857. This covers every entry, though some of them very peremptorily (e.g. '4. A design in the Italian style.'), and the others with quotations from reviews that had already appeared in the newspapers.

52   The following newspapers began reviewing the entries systematically, but then stopped, usually after a single issue: the *Observer*, 3 May 1857; the *Daily News*, 4 May; the *Globe*, 4 May; the *Morning Advertiser*, 4–5 May; the *Morning Post*, 4 May; the *Saturday Review*, 23 May; and the *Illustrated London News*, 9 May. Most of these picked up the question again when the winners were announced, with reviews (and in the *ILN*'s case engravings) of the premiated designs.

53   The *Building News* began reviewing the entries on 8 May, and completed its survey on 19 June; *Builder* began on 9 May, and finished on 11 July.

54   This is in marked contrast to the Palace of Westminster competition, whose judges were announced at the start, so that contestants could tailor their designs to their tastes; and was probably to avoid what were remembered to have been the disadvantages of that. See W. J. Rorabaugh, 'Politics and the Architectural Competition for the Houses of Parliament', p. 167.

55   As the *Daily Scotsman* inevitably pointed out: 9 December 1857, p. 4.

56   See, for example, *Globe*, 12 May 1857; letter in *Builder*, 16 May 1857, p. 272; 'A Practical Man', *Remarks on the Designs Proposed for the New Government Offices* (1857), pp. 42–3.

57   See W. J. Rorabaugh, 'Politics and the Architectural Competition' p. 168.

58   Predictably, the membership of the RIBA got quite hot under their collars about this. See the report of their council meeting, 3 May 1858, in 'General Meetings – Minutes', RIBA Archive, 1.c.2.

59   It is now demolished, according to Nikolaus Pevsner, *The Buildings of England: The Cities of London and Westminster* (3rd edn, 1973), p. 544; but there is a picture of it, taken from the *Illustrated London News*, 1864, on the internet at http://en.wikipedia.org/wiki/Montagu_House,_Whitehall (accessed 2 December 2010).

60   According to the *Report from the Select Committee* of 13 July 1858, PRO WORK 12–84/1 p. iv, they were 'prevented from acting'.

61   *The Times*, 11 May 1857.

62   1858 *Report from the Select Committee*, PRO WORK 12–84/1, p. iv; Angell and Pownell, letter to the judges, 12 June 1857, in PRO WORK 12–86/3; *Athenaeum* 16 May 1857, p. 629.

63   The ones I have looked in are Dora Ware, *A Short Dictionary of British Architects* (1967); Roger Dixon and Stefan Muthesius, *Victorian Architecture* (1978), appendix; and Howard Colvin, *A Biographical Dictionary of British Architects 1600–1840* (1997). They do, however, appear in Felstead *et al.*, *Directory of British Architects* (1993), which appears to list every practising architect, however minor.

64   *Saturday Review*, 30 May 1857, p. 496.

65   See Toplis, *The Foreign Office*, p. 37.

66   See, for example, his *Remarks on Secular and Domestic Architecture, Present and Future* (1857).

67   See, for example, Anon., 'The National Style and its Critics', in *Gentleman's Magazine*, January 1860, p. 21.

68   On Tite, see below, p. 12 and p. 157, n. 133

69   The original row was reported in the *Daily News*, 5 November 1855, p. 2; *Builder*, 17 November 1855, p. 550; and its continuation in the RIBA's 'Reporter's Notes of General Meetings', in the RIBA Archive: entries for 26 February and 16 June 1856.

70   Reverend Boutell, reported in *Builder*, 23 May 1857, p. 284, col. 1, suggested Ruskin, who of course wouldn't have done at all, and James Fergusson, who might: he was later brought in by Palmerston to advise on one of Scott's designs, though he seems not to have given the advice Palmerston wanted. See below, p. 13; and, on Fergusson, pp. 69–71. The *Builder*, probably overestimating the degree of interest in the issue among cultivated people (see below, Ch. 8), believed that finding impartial judges would be 'impossible, unless we go to Lord R. Cecil's Peasantry': 25 April 1857, p. 230.

71   *Builder*, 11 July 1857, p. 383.

72   Report of the Judges, in PRO WORK 12–86/3, p. 15: 'We desire to express our great admiration of the unprecedented collection of designs submitted to us', whose 'artistic genius . . . reflects the highest credit upon the architects'.

73   The winners were first listed in the 'Judges' Report' of 27 June 1857: PRO WORK 12–86/3, pp. 13–14; and reached the professional press early the next month: see *Builder*, 11 July 1857, p. 383. The more general press mainly neglected the results, apart from the *Saturday Review*, 1 August 1857, pp. 105–6; and the *Illustrated London News*, which illustrated all the premiated entries between 29 August and 26 December 1857. The *Belfast News-Letter*, 2 July 1857, was quick off the mark with the news that one of its own, the Ulsterman Hastings, had come second in the 'block plan' competition.

74   The *Daily Scotsman*, 9 December 1857, p. 4, broke them down thus: Italian 77, Palladian 12, Roman 6, Renaissance 26, Gothic 20, Venetian 7, Castellated 1, various 14, block plans 55. Tite, on the other hand, counted only 10 Gothic designs: Commons, 11 February 1859, in *Hansard*, 3rd series, vol. 152, cols 260–3. Because most of the original designs have disappeared, and the descriptions of them in the press are so unreliable, we cannot check these figures.

75   See the *Building News*, 9 October 1857, p. 1049 ('But where then were the Goths?'); and below, p. 8.

76   Anon., *Designs for the Public Offices*, p. 22.

77   This is William Burges, quoted in Charles Handley-Read, 'William Burgess', in Peter Ferriday (ed.), *Victorian Architecture* (1963), p. 190.

78   Frank Jenkins quotes an RIBA report of 1838 which claimed that judging committees were all too easily and falsely 'captivated by the meretricious allurements of the artist': 'The Victorian Architectural Profession', p. 43. Later on, Thomas Hardy has one of his characters say, in *A Laodicean* (1881): 'Nowadays, 'tis the men who can draw pretty pictures who get recommended, not the practical men'; quoted in Michael Bright, *Cities Built to Music:*

Aesthetic Theories of the Victorian Gothic Revival (1984), p. 260. Hardy knew his architecture, being apprenticed to an ecclesiastical architect at this very time (the 1850s).

79 This is my reading of Cuthbert Brodrick's fifth-placed entry for the War Office, pictured in *Illustrated London News*, 3 October 1857, p. 349, and here as plate 24.

80 In the Foreign Office category the winners were Henry Coe and Henry Hofland (a joint design, in Classical), followed, in this order, by Banks and Barry (Classical); Scott (Gothic); Deane and Woodward (Gothic); Bellamy (Classical); and Buxton and Habershon (Classical); with Street (Gothic) bringing up the rear at number seven. For the War Office Henry Garling (Classical) came first, followed by Boitrel d'Hazeville (Classical); Rochead (Classical); Pritchard and Seddon (Gothic), and Brodrick (*really* Classical). The list is in 'Designs for the Government Offices', PRO WORK 12–86/3. They are all pictured here, in plates 5, 14–26.

81 Toplis finds it 'difficult to understand the award, unless it was the impressiveness of Coe's presentation that swayed the lay judges': *The Foreign Office*, p. 48.

82 See E. B. Denison letter to *The Times*, 2 December 1858, p. 9; Tite at the RIBA council meeting of 3 May 1858, reported in 'General Meetings – Minutes', in RIBA Archive, 1.c.2; Tite in the Commons, 11 February 1859, in *Hansard*, 3rd series, vol. 152, cols 260–3; letter signed 'At Spes Non Fracta' in *The Times*, 4 December 1858, p. 7; and Beresford Hope in Commons, 11 February 1859: *Hansard*, 3rd series, vol. 152, col. 267. Also, compounding this, the design that was widely touted as the public's favourite, no. 112, by Robert Kerr, which *Builder* characterized, perceptively, as a Classical building striving after Gothic (i.e. picturesque) effect, was originally long-listed but then dropped, possibly because it was considered to be too expensive. See *Morning Advertiser*, 4 May 1857, p. 3; *Builder*, 20 June 1857, p. 346, 11 July 1857, p. 383, and 1 August 1857, p. 431; and Anon., *Designs for the Public Offices*, pp. 21–2. This is the only *non*-premiated design that was illustrated in the press: in *Builder*, 26 September 1857. See plate 9.

83 Henry Hofland's letter of protest to Lord John Manners over this, 25 September 1858, is in PRO WORK 12–86/4, ff. 69–70.

84 Brownlee, 'That "Regular Mongrel Affair"', p. 165.

85 See below, pp. 38–9.

86 Scott's letter to *The Times*, 26 August 1857, p. 9; E. B. Denison letter to *The Times*, 2 December 1858, p. 9; Beresford Hope in Commons, 11 February 1859, *Hansard*, 3rd series, vol. 152, col. 267.

87 See Scott's letter to *The Times*, 26 August 1857, p. 9. He was supported in his 'two seconds make a first' argument by E. B. Denison in *The Times*, 2 December 1858, p. 9. Scott was a great self-publicist; a characteristic which probably indicates his middle-class roots, and so prejudiced his social 'betters' (like Palmerston) against him; and may have something to do with his enduring poor reputation among even pro-neo-Gothic architectural historians since: see below, pp. 126–7.

      This incidentally was not his first Gothic–Classical 'battle'. A similar row had broken out – pamphlets flying, and so on – over his (German) Gothic design for the new Nikolaikirche in Hamburg, pitted against a Greek plan, which Scott famously won. See David Cole, *The Work of Sir Gilbert Scott*, p. 36.

88 See Beresford Hope and Bentinck in Commons, 10 August 1857: *Hansard*, 3rd series, vol. 147, cols 1299 and 1311; *The Times*, 12 August 1857, p. 9.

89 *Building News*, 21 August 1857, p. 875. The word 'palace' does appear to have grated with many people; in 1857, for example, Lord Malmesbury spoke out against those who seemed to wish to turn London into 'a city of palaces': House of Lords, 15 May 1857: *Hansard*, 3rd

series, vol. 145, col. 291. Some objected to the use of this 'magniloquent' word even for the parliament building; for example, Colonel Salwey in the Commons, 24 May 1850: *Hansard*, 3rd series, vol. 111, col. 343.

90 See Gladstone in Commons, 13 July 1857: *Hansard*, 3rd series, vol. 146, cols 364–65; and Russell in Commons, 10 August 1857: *Hansard*, 3rd series, vol. 147, cols 1302–3.

91 *The Times*, 12 August 1857, p. 9. Cf. the *Morning Advertiser*'s strictures on 'the feverish and heated suggestions generally represented in the designs': 5 May 1857, p. 3.

92 See Commons debate, 10 August 1857: *Hansard*, 3rd series, vol. 147, cols 1295–312; *Report from the Select Committee* (1858), p. v: in PRO WORK 12–84/1.

93 Manners in Commons, 11 February 1859: *Hansard*, 3rd series, vol. 152, col. 263.

94 This is mentioned in Ellen K. Morris, 'Symbols of Empire: Architectural Style and the Government Offices Competition', in *Journal of Architectural Education*, vol. 32 (1978), pp. 9–10. Barry's design is preserved in the RIBA Drawings Collection, reproduced here as plate 10. It seems to me a brilliant way of solving the '*genius loci*' problem that a number of people raised in connection with the Government Offices: that is, should they blend with the Gothic or with the Classical ends of Whitehall – the abbey or the Banqueting Hall? The style chosen reflects Inigo Jones's building, but on a larger scale, and with a series of repeated columns which fit very well with the Palace of Westminster's rows of buttresses.

95 The petition, to the Commissioner of the Board of Works and dated 25 March 1858, is to be found in PRO WORK 12–86/4. Sir Benjamin Hall, Palmerston's First Commissioner of Works from February 1855 to February 1858, made it known that *he* was opposed to appointing Pennethorne in any case; as he wrote to the Treasury on 5 November and 28 December 1857, as it would make a mockery of the whole principle of competitions: PRO WORK 2/18 (Letter Books), pp. 96–9 and 205–6.

96 *Building News*, 14 August 1857, p. 851, and 25 February 1859, p. 176; and see G. G. Scott, *Personal and Professional Recollections* (1995 reprint), p. 180.

97 Toplis, *The Foreign Office*, p. 63; and David Cole, *The Work of Sir Gilbert Scott*, p. 75; according to which he got Beresford Hope to intercede via the two professional assessors.

98 It was confirmed by Sir George Lewis and Palmerston in the House of Commons, 18 February 1859: *Hansard*, 3rd series, vol. 152, cols 521 and 523. Palmerston said he still liked Pennethorne's design best. For the full Pennethorne story, see Tyack, *Sir James Pennethorne*, ch. 8.

99 G. G. Scott, *Explanatory Remarks upon the Designs for the New Government Offices* (1857), pp. 20–1, 25, 30.

100 1858 select committee evidence, reported in *Saturday Review*, 25 September 1858, p. 305.

101 Belvoir Castle, Leicestershire, remodelled in the early nineteenth century by James Wyatt. Manners had been Commissioner of Works previously, in 1852.

102 *Select Committee Report* (1858).

103 Reported in, for example, *Daily News*, 29 November 1858, and *Leeds Mercury*, 30 November 1858.

104 The correspondence on this, between Scott, Wyatt and Lord Stanley (secretary of state for India), is in the India Office papers: IOL L/SUR/6/1; IOL L/SUR/5/8; and IOL L/SUR/2/3–4.

105 *Ecclesiologist*, vol. 19 (December 1858), p. 396. On its spat with Scott, see the latter's *Personal and Professional Recollections*, p. 134 *et passim*; and James F. White, *The Cambridge Movement: The Ecclesiologists and the Gothic Revival* (1962), pp. 126–7. The row was sparked by his having designed a heretical – that is, Lutheran – church (in Hamburg).

106 Burges to Scott, 29 November 1858: in RIBA ScGGS/4/2/ f. 14.

107   11 February 1859: *Hansard*, 3rd series, vol. 152, cols 270–3; 18 February 1859: *Hansard*, 3rd series, vol. 152, cols 523–4.

108   [Edward Freeman], 'The Foreign Office: Classic or Gothic', in *National Review*, vol. 10 (January 1860), p. 39. Others to blame Palmerston's line simply on 'party politics' were 'EJ', 'Neither Gothic nor Classical', in *Building News*, 19 August 1859, p. 748; 'The New Foreign Office', in *Civil Engineer*, March 1859, p. 75; and the *Derby Mercury*, 24 August 1859. [Frederick Capes], 'Palmerston on Architecture', in the *Rambler*, November 1859, p. 90, thought it smelled of 'jobbery'.

109   The Palmerston Papers, GC/DO/4, contain a letter of 4 August 1859 from Donaldson, enclosing 'some sensible remarks by a practical man' along these lines. Attached to this in the archive is another long memorandum, undated, probably by E. B. Lamb, usually classed as a 'rogue' (that is, highly original) architect, giving a broad philosophical analysis of the contemporary architectural situation which leans towards Gothic. And at the same time Scott was explaining his views to him both verbally and in a couple of long letters: Scott to Palmerston, 23 July and 22 August 1859: GC/SC/18 and 20. David Cole claims that another of his 'Classical' coaches was William Tite: *The Work of Sir Gilbert Scott*, pp. 75, 78. Brownlee adds, however, that 'Palmerston . . . was capable of making most aesthetic decisions without advice': 'That "Regular Mongrel Affair"', p. 170. Donaldson may have had a personal interest in the Government Offices affair. In March 1856 he asked if he might be included among the architects 'invited' to design the new Government Offices: letter to Benjamin Hall, forwarded to Palmerston, in Palmerston Papers, GC/HA/16. Whether he entered the *open* competition is not known.

110   Much of this was based on the assumption that Gothic windows had to be casement, and could not be double-sash. That too is nonsense. (My own Victorian terrace house has sash windows pointed at the top.)

111   Scott, *Personal and Professional Recollections*, p. 182; Scott, *Explanatory Remarks* (1860 version), p. 10; *Report from the Select Committee* (1858), p. vi, para 10: PRO WORK 12–84/1.

112   'I quite admit', he said in 1859, 'that you can get as much light as you please, and that one style of architecture does as well as another in that respect'; switching then to another argument, that 'the Italian would be cheaper'. *Builder*, 6 August 1859, p. 517; and see below, p. 159, n. 145.

113   Palmerston in Commons, 4 August 1859: *Hansard*, 3rd series, vol. 155, col. 931; and see below, p. 55.

114   Palmerston in Commons, 8 July 1861; *Hansard*, 3rd series, vol. 164, col. 537.

115   Palmerston in Commons, 11 February 1859: *Hansard*, 3rd series, vol. 152, col. 270.

116   Manners in Commons, 18 February 1859: *Hansard*, 3rd series, vol. 152, col. 518.

117   This is Lord Elcho heading a deputation of 'Goths' to Palmerson, 29 July 1859, reported in *Builder*, 6 August, p. 515; and cf. [Frederick Capes], 'Palmerston on Architecture', in the *Rambler*, vol. 25 (November 1859), p. 88: 'Here we have the real fountain of parliamentary ill-will to Gothic'; and Elcho (again) in the Commons, 8 July 1861: *Hansard*, 3rd series, vol. 164, col. 511.

     The Palace of Westminster was still under construction in the 1850s (see plate 2), but was already deeply unpopular among many MPs; their complaints aired, for example, in Commons debates of 24 May 1850: *Hansard* 3rd series, vol. 111, cols 328–60; and 22 June 1857: *Hansard*, 3rd series, vol. 145, cols 149–64. See also Anon., 'Strictures on a Pair of Public Structures', in *Fraser's Magazine*, vol. 42 (August 1850), pp. 165–70: 'we are already tired of it before it is finished' (p. 165); *Builder*, 6 June 1857, p. 317; Palmerston in the Commons, 11 February 1859: 'it was a great mistake . . . to make them Gothic': *Hansard*, 3rd series, vol. 152, col. 272; the *Globe*, 12 February 1859, p. 2: 'the selection of the style of the reign of Henry VII for the Houses of Parliament in the reign of Victoria was an aesthetic mistake'; William Coningham in the Commons, 18 February 1859: *Hansard*, 3rd series, vol. 152, col. 523; *Daily Telegraph*, 22 February 1859, p. 4; *The Times*, 9 July 1861, p. 9; and a leading article in the *Liverpool Mercury*, 12 July 1861, which refers unfavourably to the Westminster Palace precedent three times. And see Palmerston, February 1859: 'Dined at Speaker's in his new official House [in the Victoria Tower]: detestably Gothic – dark, inconvenient, and gloomy': quoted in Brownlee, 'That "Regular Mongrel Affair"', p. 170.

Among practical objections to it (apart from the ventilation, below) were its spiralling costs, which many critics attributed to the style – i.e. Gothic was dearer than classical: e.g. H. Shepherd Rosen, letter to the *Morning Post*, 7 May 1857, p. 2; the *Morning Post*, 14 February 1859, p. 4; and its apparent impermanence, with its stone 'crumbling' already (apparantly a too-soft stone had been selected in preference to London's more traditional and durable Portland stone): *Building News*, 22 July 1859, p. 663.

Another precedent that was supposed to undermine the 'Gothic' case (in addition to the architect's credentials) was Pennethorne's new Public Record Office in Chancery Lane. See, for example, *Saturday Review*, 17 November 1855, p. 49: 'a nightmare reminiscent of . . . Barry's Westminster Palace'; and Capes in *Rambler*, November 1859, p. 88.

118   Disgusting accounts of the 'abominable stench' coming off the Thames on hot days, from the sewers running into it, carrying not only ordure but also 'dead cats, dead dogs, and he believed occasionally . . . a dead human being', can be found in the speeches of Earl Granville in the Lords and Sir Benjamin Hall in the Commons, 15 May and 2 July 1857, in *Hansard*, 3rd series, vols 145, col. 292, and vol. 146, col. 803. The *Building News* jocularly suggested that this afforded 'means of intimidation, if not of corruption' to governments which, for example, 'if they have reason to apprehend the consequences of a debate, or to fear the eloquence of an opposition orator', could simply adjust the ventilation so that 'the uncorrected atmosphere of the Thames' could be 'wafted through': *Building News*, 22 July 1859, p. 663. Interestingly enough, when the building of a new Palace of Westminster was debated in the 1830s, a few MPs argued for its relocation for this reason, albeit in vain against the majority who felt that the 'glorious historical associations' of the existing site compensated for any insalubrity. Commons debate of 9 February 1836, in *Hansard*, 3rd series, vol. 31, cols 236–7, 242, 243; and Col Davies in Commons, 14 June 1838, in *Hansard*, 3rd series, vol. 43, cols 695–705.

119   E. A. Freeman was one of those who made the point that the Palace of Westminster should not be taken as a precedent for the Government Offices. It was 'not a good Gothic building', having been designed 'by an architect whose real bent was towards Classical architecture . . . Now Gothic architecture is far better understood.' Letter to *The Times*, 19 October 1859, p. 10; and see his 'The Foreign Office: Classic or Gothic', in *National Review*, vol. 10 (January 1860), pp. 26–7, 37–8. Similar criticism of the palace for its 'un-Gothicness' appears in *Building News*, 20 February 1857, p. 181; G. G. Scott's *Explanatory Remarks* of 1857, pp. 23–4 (repeated personally to Palmerston in a letter of 23 July 1859, in Palmerston Papers, GC/SC/18); Beresford Hope in the Commons, 2 July 1857: *Hansard*, 3rd series, vol. 146, cols 799–800; E. B. Denison letter to *The Times*, 25 August 1859, p. 9; [Frederick Capes], 'Palmerston on Architecture', in the *Rambler*, vol. 25 (November 1859), p. 88; W. J. Cockburn Muir, *Pagan or Christian* (1860), pp. 215–16; Francis E. Scott, *Shall the New Foreign Office be Gothic or Classic?* (1860), pp. 43–5; Buxton in the Commons, 8 July 1861: *Hansard*, 3rd series, vol. 164, col.. 516. We shall come on to the question of Perpendicular's perceived stylistic (as opposed to practical) deficiencies later, p. 91.

But no, replied Tite in the final debate in the 'Battle': 'the faults of that House' were not the architect's (Barry's), but 'incidental' (meaning intrinsic) 'to the style': Commons, 8 July 1861: *Hansard*, 3rd series, vol. 164, col. 525.

120 See, for example, the *Guardian*, 15 February 1859, p. 3; *Punch*, 13 August 1859, p. 72.

121 Kenneth Clark is unusual in regarding Palmerston's arguments as 'humorous' and 'unscrupulous', but also 'sensible', and 'containing nothing but good sense'. *The Gothic Revival* (1928), p. 169.

122 For example, the *Saturday Review*, 30 July 1859, p. 129; *Builder*, 6 August 1859, p. 514, and 13 August 1859, p. 535; *Building News*, 26 August 1859, pp. 767–8; *Civil Engineer*, August 1859, p. 249; the *Guardian*, 9 August 1859, p. 2. One dissentient was a correspondent to the *Building News*, 2 September 1859, p. 803, who disagreed that the new designs showed 'any real progress', dismissing them as mere 'copy and guess'. *Builder*, 13 August 1859, p. 537, and 10 September 1859, p. 601, carried engravings of them.

123 Palmerston to Scott (copy), 26 July 1859: in BL Add. MS 48581, ff. 13–14; David Cole, *The Works of Sir Gilbert Scott*, p. 79; and Brownlee, 'That "Regular Mongrel Affair"', pp. 172–3. It is possible that Palmerston did genuinely feel that the external style of a building was no great matter, rather like what coat one wore. He was clearly satisfied with Scott's interior plan. See Toplis, *The Foreign Office*, p. 97.

124 See Jopling letter on 'this stir which Lord Palmerston has produced amongst architects', in *Building News*, 2 September 1859, p. 803.

125 *Belfast News-Letter*, 2 August 1859. The *Belfast News-Letter* was anti-Gothic.

126 There is an authoritative account of the meeting in *Builder*, 6 August 1859, pp. 515–17. Palmerston's speech in the Commons, 4 August 1859: *Hansard*, 3rd series, vol. 155, cols 930–6, repeated most of the same arguments.

127 Scott, *Explanatory Remarks*, p. 30. His actual words, in explanation of his principled decision to stick with Gothic despite the impediments he suspected had been pre-erected against it, were that 'I feel a deeper interest' on 'the great question of style . . . than on that of my own success.'

128 Stirling and Manners in Commons, 4 August 1859: *Hansard*, 3rd series, vol. 155, cols 929 and 937; and cf. [E. A. Freeman], 'The Foreign Office: Classic or Gothic', in *National Review*, vol. 10 (January 1860), p. 52.

129 Francis E. Scott, *Shall the New Foreign Office be Gothic or Classic?* p. 45.

130 *Building News*, 26 August 1859, p. 767.

131 *The Times*, 6 August 1859, p. 9. Its main ground for this was that because Scott was not trained as a Classicist any Classical building he designed 'will be a failure'.

132 Gladstone to Scott, 30 August 1859: in Gladstone Papers, BL Add. MS 44530, ff. 67–8.

133 Tite in the Commons, 4 August 1859: *Hansard*, 3rd series, vol. 155, col. 924.
Tite is best known for his London Royal Exchange of 1841–4, which is Classical; but he also designed churches and even railway stations in Perpendicular, and one church (St James, Gerrards Cross, 1858–9) in 'uncompromisingly strident Byzantine', according to his entry in the *Oxford Dictionary of National Biography*, vol. 54, pp. 844–6. Twitted over this in parliament, he made it clear that his main objections to Scott's Gothic design were not anti-Gothic *per se*, but related to this particular case. First, he said, although Gothic was suited to churches 'and probably also to domestic buildings' – a large concession – it did not easily adapt to great public buildings, mainly because of the window problem. Second, Gothic could not be made to *look* like offices. Third, Scott's *sort* of Gothic was 'different in character to what we were generally acquainted with in London': i.e. was not Perpendicular. Indeed, it was not even English, but 'Lombardo-Veneto'. And fourth, for that very reason it was incongruous in that place, clashing as violently – for those who liked to employ the '*genius loci*' argument

(below, p. 47) – with the Palace of Westminster as with Inigo Jones's Banqueting Hall. For exactly the same reason Tite also objected to some of the more florid Italian and French Renaissance designs among the winners. For this, see his other Commons interventions: on 10 August 1857, 11 and 18 February 1859 and 8 July 1861: *Hansard*, 3rd series, vol. 147, cols 1309–10; vol. 152, cols 260–3 and 251–2; and vol. 164, cols 524–7. These seem to me to be reasonable arguments. Unfortunately they may have been devalued by Tite's reputation: see below, this page.

134   The *Daily News*, 20 August 1859, and *Building News*, 26 August 1859, pp. 774–5, carry full reports.

135   *Building News*, 26 August 1859, pp. 767–8; and cf. similar attacks by G. E. Street in *Builder*, 24 September 1859, pp. 637–68; by Freeman in *National Review*, January 1860, pp. 50–3; by Edward Freeman, 'The Foreign Office: Classic or Gothic', in *National Review*, vol. 10 (January 1860), pp. 52–3; and Anon., *Shall Gothic Architecture be Denied Fair Play* (1860), *passim*. On this episode, see Toplis, *The Foreign Office*, pp. 103–6.

136   The story is that he had not originally entered for the competition himself, but had been appointed to its panel of judges; which then, however, awarded the commission to him, over the head of Cockerell, whose entry would otherwise have won. *Oxford Dictionary of National Biography*, vol. 12, p. 845. The affair was much discussed in the first volume of *Builder*. According to David Cole, another unsuccessful (and therefore cheated) entrant in that competition was Gilbert Scott's early partner, William Moffatt: *The Work of Sir Gilbert Scott*, p. 13.

137   Tite, 'On the Progress and Present State of Architecture and its Future Prospects', in *Civil Engineer*, vol. 22, December 1859, pp. 395–6.

138   This was reported in the *Caledonian Mercury*, 16 April 1860, which attributed it to his conduct over this matter. In answer to an enquiry, the archivist of the Athenaeum, Jennie De Protani, kindly confirmed to me that on 13 February 1860 the membership rejected the application made on his behalf by a massive 192 votes to 42. No reasons are preserved in the Athenaeum's archive, and the vote, of course, was secret. Other reasons for Tite's rejection may have been memories of that earlier professional 'scandal'; or his middle-class origins – his father had been a merchant, and he had attended very 'ordinary' schools. 'I inherited a fortune, married a fortune and made a fortune', he is reported to have told Prince Albert: quoted in Peter Ferriday, 'The Revival: Stories Ancient and Modern', in *Architectural Review*, vol. 121 (1957), p. 155; it could have been the last of those 'fortunes' that stuck in the Athenians' craw. Tite was, however, knighted in 1869.

139   Gladstone to Scott, 30 August 1859: in Gladstone Papers, BL Add. MS 44530, ff. 67–8. Scott's original motive for writing to Gladstone was probably to enlist his support in Palmerston's cabinet – which he had just joined as chancellor of the exchequer – for his original designs. Scott and Gladstone knew each other, with the former having been given the job of restoring the church on Gladstone's Hawarden estate in 1857 after a fire; it will have been this that led Scott – understandably – to see him as 'a champion of Gothic architecture'. Scott to Gladstone, 2 August and 23 August 1857, in BL Add. MS 44392, ff. 103–4, 139–48; and see Brownlee, 'That "Regular Mongrel Affair"', p. 171. The latter's reply will not have been what Scott wanted.

The computerized catalogue of Gladstone's original book collection ('GLADCAT') at St Deiniol's Library, Hawarden, Flintshire, carries several works on Gothic architecture, including by Parker, Pugin and Fergusson; together with Scott's *Explanatory Remarks* on his Government Offices design, though none of his other works. The catalogue, however, is not complete.

140 *Saturday Review*, 28 July 1860, pp. 110–11; *Athenaeum*, 28 July 1860, p. 131.

141 *Gentleman's Magazine*, vol. 209 (September 1860), p. 306.

142 Scott, *Personal and Professional Recollections*, p. 194.

143 See Scott, *Explanatory Remarks* (1860 version), p. 14.

144 Scott, *Personal and Professional Recollections*, p. 197.

145 Even, now, in the case of Gothic. 'The Speaker complains that his windows [in the Gothic Palace of Westminster] are so constructed that there cannot be any shutters put to them; and when he goes to bed at 3 o'clock in the morning . . . there is the sun pouring full into his bedroom, and he has no chance of repose except what a green baize curtain can afford him.' This is Palmerston, quoted in *Builder*, 6 August 1859, p. 517. 'Further than this,' Charles Eastlake commented, 'inconsistency could scarcely be carried': *A History of the Gothic Revival* (1872), p. 311.

146 *Saturday Review*, 28 July 1860, p. 111. These designs were exhibited in the Commons Library in August 1860: see *Builder* 11 August 1860, p. 515; and Scott, *Explanatory Remarks* (1860 version). See plate 27.

147 Scott, *Explanatory Remarks* (1860 version), p. 18.

148 David Cole, *The Work of Sir Gilbert Scott*, p. 80.

149 Buxton in House of Commons, 8 July 1861: *Hansard*, 3rd series, vol. 164, col. 523. See plate 28.

150 H. S. Goodhart-Rendel, 'Victorian Public Buildings', in Peter Ferriday (ed.), *Victorian Architecture*, p. 96.

151 This was the maximum for that day; taken from 'Daily Results from Royal Observatory, Greenwich, July 1861', kindly found for me by Glyn Hughes, assistant archivist at the Meteorological Office's National Meteorological Archive. July 8 was in fact the hottest day of that month.

152 See Scott, *Personal and Professional Recollections*, p. 273.

153 8 July 1861: 'Elchos motion against Italian architecture for Foreign Office. Good debate. I spoke. Motion rejected' (punctuation added): Palmerston Papers, D/21.

154 Elcho in House of Commons, 8 July 1861: *Hansard*, 3rd series, vol. 164, col. 513.

155 See Buxton and Layard in House of Commons, 8 July 1861: *Hansard*, 3rd series, vol. 164, cols 516, 522–3.

156 Elcho in House of Commons, 8 July 1861: *Hansard*, 3rd series, vol. 164, cols 508, 510.

157 Cowper and Tite in House of Commons, 8 July 1861: *Hansard*, 3rd series, vol. 164, cols 518, 525.

158 Palmerston in House of Commons, 8 July 1861: *Hansard*, 3rd series, vol. 164, col. 546. His actual words were: 'It may not be a splendid and magnificent piece of architecture, but it is handsome enough for the purpose, and I am quite sure it will be constructed at less cost than any of the other elevations.'

159 Quoted in Toplis, *The Foreign Office*, p. 128.

160 Scott, *Explanatory Notes* (1860 version), esp. p. 17.

161 In his *Personal and Professional Recollections* (1879; 1995 reprint), p. 199, he claims that a study he made of the Louvre just previously 'recovered some of my lost feelings for the style', but clearly not much. Scott was in a difficult situation, of course, not wishing to further undermine his credit with the Gothicists by professing too great a love for Classical.

162 *Ibid.*, p. 200. This appears on the dust wrapper of the present book.

163 *Ibid.*, p. 272.

164 *Ibid.*, p. 477. This passage was edited out of the original edition by Scott's son.

165 *Ibid.*, pp. 199–201.

166 E.g. *ibid.*, pp. 273, 374, 449.

167 See *Remarks on Secular and Domestic Architecture* (1857), p. 188 *et passim*. Much of *Personal and Professional Recollections* is devoted to criticizing the 'ideological' Goths: e.g. p. 372. See also 'On the Present and Future Prospects of the Revival of Gothic Architecture', published in *Associated Architectural Societies Reports and Papers*, vol. 4 (1857–8), p. 82.

168 *Remarks on Secular and Domestic Architecture*, pp. 192–5. On the other hand he might seem to contradict himself here a little later, where he rejects the idea that English public buildings could be 'copied . . . from the works of certain Italian architects of the fifteenth and sixteenth centuries' (p. 201). The operative word here is probably 'copied'; and the crucial point whether his final Government Offices design can be seen as a 'copy' or as simply drawing on ideas from the Italian Renaissance.

169 'If it should turn out that the Premier's obstinacy would not submit to a Pointed design, many of Mr Scott's friends . . . felt that an Italianizing design from a Pointed architect would be a better thing than a mere Palladianism': *Saturday Review*, 28 July 1860, p. 111.

170 Charles Eastlake, *A History of the Gothic Revival*, p. 312. Scott was still alive when he wrote this.

171 *The Times*, 9 July 1861, p. 9.

172 *Ecclesiologist*, vol. 22, August 1861, pp. 221–2.

173 *Belfast News-Letter*, 1 November 1859.

174 For example, *Building News*, 12 July 1861, p. 582; *Blackwood's Magazine*, March 1862, pp. 289, 298; *Liverpool Mercury*, 12 July 1861; and in parliament, Elcho, Buxton and Manners in House of Commons, 8 July 1861: *Hansard*, 3rd series, vol. 164, cols 510, 516 and 528–9.

175 George L. Hersey, *High Victorian Gothic: A Study in Associationism* (1972), pp. 199, 208.

176 On the India Office, see John Cornforth, 'The Old India Office', in *Country Life*, Nov. 1987.

177 PRO FO 366/378 and PRO WORK 12–46/2 contain many of these complaints, from 1867 to 1880; and Scott's responses: PRO WORK 12–46/2, ff. 468–71.

178 See below, pp. 125–6.

179 *Report* to the First Commissioner of Works *on new Home Office and Colonial Office Plans*, by C. E. Trevelyan, W. H. Stephenson and J. Ferguson, 27 February 1869: PRO WORK 12–96/2, f. 59. This particular comment relates to the Foreign and India Offices.

180 Hammond to Scott, 27 September 1867: in PRO FO 366/378.

181 See below, p. 126.

Notes to Chapter 2: A Hybrid Society

1 Figures, for 1851 and 1871, taken from the summary of census reports in Chris Cook and Brendan Keith, *British Historical Facts 1830–1900* (London: Macmillan, 1975), p. 232.

2 *Ibid.*, p. 234.

3 John Summerson, *The London Building World of the Eighteen-Sixties* (1973), pp. 7–8.

4 The story is told of his office's once receiving a telegram from him at a Midlands station: 'Why am I here?' David Cole, *The Work of Sir Gilbert Scott* (1980), p. 86, taken from W. R. Lethaby, *Philip Webb and His Work* (1935), p. 66. Charles Eastlake thought Scott's work suffered from being spread so wide and thinly: *A History of the Gothic Revival* (1872), p. 222.

5 The best-known examples are Dickens's descriptions of his fictional 'Coketown', in *Hard Times* (1854).

6 James Stevens Curl, *Victorian Architecture* (1990), p. 21.

7 Robert Furneaux Jordan, *Victorian Architecture* (1966), pp. 18, 110.

8   Pevsner, 'Victorian Prolegomena', in Peter Ferriday (ed.), *Victorian Architecture* (1963), pp. 23–8 (italics added).

9   This is elaborated in my *Britannia's Burden: The Political Evolution of Modern Britain 1851–1990* (London: E. Arnold, 1994), pp. 22–3.

10 See Christopher Hill, 'The Norman Yoke', in *Puritanism and Revolution*, ed. Christopher Hill (London: Secker and Warburg, 1958).

11 For example, James Fergusson, *The Illustrated Handbook of Architecture* (1855), part 2, book 8, ch. 3. For a modern work that pays proper but unusual attention to the early neo-Gothic movement in Scotland and the north of England, see James Macaulay, *The Gothic Revival 1745–1845* (1975).

12 So far as can be ascertained from the available catalogues and press reports of the Westminster Hall exhibition of 1857. No. 150 was called 'Sassenagh go bragh', but that was a ground plan only.

13 See Gavin Stamp, *Alexander 'Greek' Thomson* (1999).

14 See E. R. Norman, *Anti-Catholicism in Victorian England* (London: George Allen & Unwin, 1968), and D. G. Paz, *Popular Anti-Catholicism in Mid-Victorian England* (Stanford, CA: Stanford University Press, 1992).

15 The 'Revivalist' movement is well summarized in K. Theodore Hoppen, *The Mid-Victorian Generation 1846–1886* (Oxford: Clarendon Press, 1998), pp. 457–60.

16 S. Lang, in 'The Principles of the Gothic Revival in England', in *Journal of the Society of Architectural Historians*, vol. 25 (1966), p. 240, makes the interesting claim that 'English seems to be the only language which has a word for revival'. I have checked in several foreign dictionaries, and found equivalents for the word 'revival' in all of them; but these may be in other senses than the one meant here.

17 John Stuart Mill, for example, whose *Principles of Political Economy* was one of the key texts of early Victorian capitalism, added to its second edition (London: John W. Parker, 1849) the observation that, if the free market did not lead to a substantial reduction of the gap between rich and poor, he for one would prefer 'Communism'; though he was confident enough in the egalitarian tendencies of capitalism to think it would never come to that. Book 2, chapter 1, section 3.

18 See Barrington Kaye, *The Development of the Architectural Profession in Britain: A Sociological Study* (1960); and Frank Jenkins, 'The Victorian Architectural Profession', in Peter Ferriday (ed.), *Victorian Architecture* (1963).

19 John Summerson, *The Architecture of Victorian London* (1976), p. 66.

20 See Cobden's Manchester speech of 15 January 1846, printed in his *Speeches on Public Policy* (eds) John Bright and Thorold Rogers (London: Macmillan, 1870), vol. 2 pp. 315–16; looking forward a time when 'the motive for large and mighty empires; for gigantic armies and great navies . . . will die away', and with them the need for *nationalities*. There are similarities here with certain idealistic (and I would say naïve) modern notions about the benefits of 'globalization'. In both cases the real 'imperial' or dominating implications of them tended to be hidden from their aficionados.

21 Alfred Tennyson, 'Locksley Hall', *Poems*, vol. 2 (London: Edward Moxon, 1842).

22 See, for example, *Chambers's Information for the People* (1841–2), vol. 1, p. 635, on the 'Duties which the people of one country owe to those of another'.

23 Anyone who has studied diplomatic history will be aware of this; my own introduction to it came from my work on international negotiations over the 'refugee question' in the 1850s, where it was clear that British ambassadors empathized with the outlook of the Continental European courts far more than with that of the British 'democracy'. See my *The Refugee*

Question in mid-Victorian Politics (Cambridge: Cambridge University Press, 1979).

24 Expressed in Prince Albert's address at a pre-Exhibition banquet in the Mansion House, 21 March 1850, summarized in Jeffrey A. Auerbach, *The Great Exhibition of 1851: A Nation on Display* (1999), p. 60.

25 For a further elaboration of this, see my *Britain, Europe and the World 1850–1982: Delusions of Grandeur* (London: Allen & Unwin, 1983), ch. 1.

26 'As to the War Office', said Lord Ellenborough in the House of Lords on 15 May 1857, 'every day the accommodation wanted there was less and less, for every day the noble Lord at the head of that department was diminishing the army': *Hansard*, 3rd series, vol. 145, col. 305. Not that Ellenborough approved of this; rightly in view of the outbreak of the Indian 'Mutiny' at precisely that time.

27 The 1861 census recorded 84,090 foreigners living in England and Wales in March that year. Charles Anthony Coke, 'Foreigners in England and Wales', *Census of the British Empire, 1861* (London: Harrison, 1864), vol. 2, p. 181.

28 See Henry Weisser, *British Working-Class Movements and Europe, 1815–48* (Manchester: Manchester University Press, 1975).

29 By prosecuting an accessory to the 'Orsini' bomb plot, and 'truckling' to the latter's intended victim, Louis Napoleon, in other ways. See my *The Refugee Question*, ch. 6.

30 Francis Fukuyama, *The End of History and the Last Man* (1992).

31 Leader in *The Times* shortly after the outbreak of the revolution in Paris, 15 April 1848, p. 4.

32 House of Commons, 1 April 1852, in *Hansard*, 3rd series, vol. 119, cols 511–12.

33 See my *The Refugee Question*, pp. 86–9.

34 Bernard Porter, '"Monstrous Vandalism": Capitalism and Philistinism in the Works of Samuel Laing (1780–1868)', in *Albion*, vol. 23 (1991).

35 Tristram Hunt, *Building Jerusalem: The Rise and Fall of the Victorian City* (2004), pp. 263–74 *et passim*.

36 See my *The Lion's Share: A Short History of British Imperialism, 1850–2004*, 4th edn (London: Pearson Longman, 2004), pp. 23–6.

37 That is, in Piedmont-Sardinia under Cavour.

38 Generally called 'informal' or, for this period, 'free-trade' imperialism.

39 Carlyle coined it in his essay *Chartism* of 1839.

40 To be found at the start of chapter 5.

41 Jeremy Bentham's famous idea, though I don't think a strict 'panopticon' was ever built in England. Prisons with *corridors* extending out from a control point or hub are not 'panopticons' if the warders cannot see inside every cell from their central point.

42 G. G. Scott, *Remarks on Secular and Domestic Architecture* (1857), p. 238.

43 Anon., *Remarks on a National Style in Reference to the Proposed Foreign Office* (1860), pp. 11–12. And cf. 'Verax' in *Builder*, 28 November 1857, p. 692: 'There was neither learning, arts, nor commerce' in the Middle Ages. 'The lower orders were actually slaves.'

44 See Rosemary Jann, 'Democratic Myths in Victorian Mediaevalism', in *Browning Institute Studies*, vol. 8 (1980), p. 135; and the rest of this article, which is well worth reading on this whole topic.

45 The historian Henry Hallam (1818) believed the Norman interregnum had actually toughened the libertarian tradition in England, through the resistance it had provoked, which had 'invigorated the whole national system' and so 'stimulated the growth of freedom'. Quoted in Jann, 'Democratic Myths', p. 135.

46 E. A. Freeman, *The Growth of the English Constitution from the Earliest Times* (1872), quoted in *ibid.*, p. 140.

47 See H. S. Goodhart-Rendel, 'Rogue Architects of the Victorian Era', in *Journal of the Royal Institute of British Architects*, 3rd ser., vol. 56 (1949); and Nikolaus Pevsner, 'Victorian Prolegomena', in Peter Ferriday (ed.), *Victorian Architecture* (1963), p. 34.

48 See Hunt, *Building Jerusalem*, ch. 5, section iv.

Notes to Chapter 3: Early Skirmishes

1 The name 'Gothic' was problematical, and nearly every contemporary book on architecture carries a discussion of the term. It originated in the idea that the style came with the tribes – 'Goths and Vandals' – that had sacked Rome in the seventh century, which of course it did not; which also brought with it, at least early on, strong connotations of barbarity. Common alternatives designed to avoid this were 'Pointed' and 'Christian', both of which, however, were equally problematical: see E. A. Freeman, *A History of Architecture* (1849), pp. 298–9. William Hosking was unusual in restricting his use of the 'g'-word to the Romanesque stage of mediaeval building, after which it became 'Pointed': see his entry on 'Architecture' in *Encyclopaedia Britannica*, 7th edn (1830–42); Bishop Heber eccentric in the opposite direction, using it for anything with pointed arches, including, for example, Muslim mosques: Freeman, *op. cit.*, p. 301.

2 The great work on this is Nikolaus Pevsner, *The Englishness of English Art* (London: Architectural Press, 1956).

3 All the histories of the early Gothic Revival in England start with this; and cf. James Macaulay, drawing attention to a 'continuous lairdly tradition of castle dwelling' in *Scotland*; in *The Gothic Revival 1745–1845* (1975), p. 46.

   The distinction between a 'survival' and a 'revival', however, is largely a semantic one. Chris Brooks claims that the many examples of seventeenth-century Gothic cannot be classed as 'survivals' because they were not natural continuations of the earlier style, but deliberate harkings back: *The Gothic Revival* (1999), pp. 20, 27. On the other hand, H. S. Goodhart-Rendel refused to use the word 'Revival', on the grounds that 'the Gothic style in England' had never 'become a corpse': 'English Gothic Architecture of the Nineteenth Century', in *Journal of the RIBA*, vol. 31 (1924), p. 321. The solution might be to coin another term for this kind of conscious and artificial *prolongation* of a style.

4 Anon., 'Fair Play for Gothic Architecture!' (an anti-Gothic piece), in *Building News*, 29 June 1860, p. 511. It was G. K. Chesterton who remarked that the early nineteenth century saw the Middle Ages 'by moonlight': quoted in James F. White, *The Cambridge Movement: The Ecclesiologists and the Gothic Revival* (1962), p. x.

5 For example, Horace Walpole, Ann Radcliffe and Matthew Lewis.

6 'I am almost as fond,' wrote Horace Walpole, the builder of Strawberry Hill, 'of Sharawaggi, or Chinese': quoted in S. Lang, 'The Principles of the Gothic Revival in England', in *Journal of the Society of Architectural Historians*, vol. 25 (1966), p. 250. See also, on the Gothic/Oriental point, Geoffrey Scott, *The Architecture of Humanism* (1914), pp. 42–3; Basil Clarke, *Church Builders of the Nineteenth Century* (1938), p. 14; Henry-Russell Hitchcock, *Early Victorian Architecture in Britain* (1954), p. 13; Peter Collins, *Changing Ideals in Modern Architecture 1750–1950* (1965), pp. 35–6; James Macaulay, *The Gothic Revival 1745–1945* (1975), pp. 38, 168–9; and Michael McCarthy, *The Origins of the Gothic Revival* (1987).

7 See Chris Brooks, *Gothic Revival*, p. 100. The main reason for this was that eighteenth-century churches were still predominately 'preaching halls' rather than sites of ritual. We see that this sparked a debate later on.

8 See Henry-Russell Hitchcock, *Early Victorian Architecture*, pp. 16–17, and Chris Brooks,

Gothic Revival, pp. 186–8. Hitchcock thought very little of 'Jacobethan', which did not express what the Victorians were, but only what they liked, and 'maintained only a sort of vegetable existence' throughout the nineteenth century.

9   John Britton's *The Architectural Antiquities of Great Britain*, vol. 5 (1826), ch. 1, listed no fewer than 66 early theories of the origin of the Gothic arch; according to Charles Eastlake's count, in *A History of the Gothic Revival* (1872), pp. 132–3, which selects the leading half dozen. Rev John Milner, *A Treatise on the Ecclesiastical Architecture of England during the Middle Ages* (3rd edn, 1835), p. ii, favoured intersecting round arches. The 'wickerwork' theory is illustrated, extraordinarily, in Sir James Hall, *Essay on the Origin, History, and Principles of Gothic Architecture* (1813), frontispiece.

10   'Aunt Elinor', *Aunt Elinor's Lectures on Architecture: Dedicated to the Ladies of England* (1843), p. 19. 'Aunt Elinor' was a serious Goth. For her, Strawberry Hill represented the superficial and irreligious side of the Revival.

11   A recent book that makes it seem worthy of study is Chris Brooks' masterly *The Gothic Revival* (1999), covering a longer period but concentrating on this 'Gothick' one. It is part of Brooks's argument (pp. 52, 58–64) that, whatever its stylistic failings, the spirit behind the style was not at all superficial, carrying as it did important political messages; to which we shall return: below, Ch. 4.

12   Chris Brooks, *The Gothic Revival*, p. 59.

13   Nicholas Taylor, 'The awful sublimity of the Victorian City', in H. J. Dyos and Michael Wolff (eds), *The Victorian City: Images and Realities* (1973), vol. 2, p. 432.

14   See E. A. Smith, *George IV* (New Haven, CT: Yale University Press, 1999), chs 3 and 21; and Terence Davis, *John Nash: The Prince Regent's Architect* (London: Country Life, 1966), pp. 71, 82–8.

15   G. G. Scott, *Remarks on Secular and Domestic Architecture* (1857), p. 197. On the poor National Gallery, see Anon., 'The British School of Architecture', in *Blackwood's Edinburgh Magazine*, August 1838, p. 237, who reckoned its 'vitiated taste . . . makes all Englishmen blush'; and Anon., 'Hamilton, &c. on Architecture', in *Quarterly Review*, vol. 58 (February 1837), p. 79: 'we, at least, have never heard a single word uttered in favour of the building'. Later on even Palmerston, defending Classical, admitted that the National Gallery was 'certainly not one of the most favourable specimens' of the style in London: Commons, 4 August 1859, in *Hansard*, 3rd series, vol. 155, col. 933. Henry-Russell Hitchcock claims it 'ruined his [Wilkins's] reputation': *Architecture, The Nineteenth and Twentieth Centuries* (1958), p. 108. And Nash's new front for Buckingham Palace – since replaced by its present heavy Edwardian one – was dubbed a 'monstrous architectural abortion' by the *Architectural Magazine*: quoted in W. J. Rorabaugh, 'Politics and the Architectural Competition for the Houses of Parliament, 1834–1837', in *Victorian Studies*, vol. 17 (1973), p. 158.

16   *Chambers's Information for the People* (1842), vol. 2, p. 683.

17   *Quarterly Review*, vol. 58 (February 1837), p. 75.

18   Freeman, *History of Architecture*, p. 449. Almost. He exempted one or two secular buildings 'of the most sumptuous character'.

19   [William Hosking], 'Architecture', in *Encyclopaedia Britannica*, 7th edn (1830–42); and cf. entry for 'London', in *Penny Cyclopaedia* (1833–43), p. 113.

20   John Summerson, 'London, the Artifact', in Dyos and Wolff (eds), *The Victorian City*, vol. 1, p. 313. Any tributes to modern English architecture from this period are rare, and usually conscious that they are written against the grain. The only one I have found before 1850 is a piece in *Blackwood's Magazine*, August 1838, pp. 227–8, claiming that architecture was the *only one* of the arts in which Britain stood 'unrivalled'.

21 Later examples are the *Quarterly Review*, vol. 95 (September 1854), p. 354, condemning the 'prosaic' buildings of Belgravia; the *Saturday Review*, 17 November 1855, p. 48, referring to 'the bare architecture of bricks and oblong windows' that had characterized the Georgian era; 'ERH' in the *Building News*, 29 May 1857, p. 547: 'people are tired of buildings which look as if they had no roofs, which do not harmonise with our scenery'; a letter to *Builder*, 20 June 1857, describing the latter as an age 'of intense darkness as far as regards architecture in England'; J. L. Petit's references in *Builder*, 1 June 1861, p. 372, to 'the cold formality' of most recent Greek Revivalist architecture, and 'the feeble, unmeaning, uninteresting character which prevails in so much of our work that claims a derivation from the Roman' – and this from a Classicist!; Frederick Capes's castigation of just about every recent Classical building in London (the National Gallery, the British Museum, King's College) on the same grounds: dullness; in the *Rambler*, November 1859, p. 89: these are just a few examples, deliberately avoiding the views of ideological Goths, who might be thought to be prejudiced.

    Again there are one or two exceptions; for example, an article in *Builder*, 9 May 1857, p. 262, bravely asserting that the Westminster Hall exhibition proved that, whatever the general opinion, British architects *could* stand the comparison with foreigners. Some newspaper reports were also impressed with the exhibition, but they were usually penned by ignoramuses. E.g. the *Observer*, 3 May 1857, p. 5; *Daily News*, 4 May 1857; the *Globe*, 4 May 1857, p. 4; and *Morning Advertiser*, 4 May 1857, p. 3.

22 John Summerson, *Heavenly Mansions* (1949), p. 173.

23 Kenneth Clark, *The Gothic Revival* (1928), p. 67.

24 John Summerson, *Architecture in Britain 1530–1830* (1953), p. 409.

25 The chapel and library sides of the Corpus New Court are particularly successful.

26 See J. H. Parker, *An Introduction to the Study of Gothic Architecture* (1849), pp. 186–7, and Charles Eastlake, *History of the Gothic Revival*, pp. 4–5.

27 See H. S. Goodhart-Rendel, *English Architecture since the Regency: An Interpretation* (1953), p. 58.

28 Robert Furneaux Jordan, *Victorian Architecture* (1966), pp. 62–4; and cf. S. Lang, 'The Principles of the Gothic Revival in England', p. 267: the Renaissance came 'very late' to England, 'and never settled as firmly here as the Baroque and Neoclassicism in France or the Baroque in Germany'.

29 See, for example, S. Bradley, 'The Englishness of Gothic: Theories and Interpretations from William Gilpin to JH Parker', in *Architectural History*, vol. 45 (2002); and J. M. Frew, 'Gothic is English: John Carter and the Revival of the Gothic as England's National Style', in *Art Bulletin*, vol. 64 (1982).

30 Scott, *Remarks on Secular and Domestic Architecture*, p. 188.

31 On the building of the Palace of Westminster, see W. J. Rorabaugh, 'Politics and the Architectural Competition for the Houses of Parliament, 1834–1837', in *Victorian Studies*, vol. 17, no. 2 (1973); M. H. Port, 'The Houses of Parliament Competition', in Port (ed.), *The Houses of Parliament* (1976); and Alexandra Wedgwood, 'The New Palace of Westminster', in Christine and Jacqueline Riding, *The Houses of Parliament: History, Art, Architecture* (2000). Rorabaugh is especially good on the politics of the affair, which favoured the eventual winner of the competition, James Barry, because of his intimate Whig links. Smirke, the front runner at the start, was the architect of the British Museum and University College, London. The case for 'Classic' came from two directions: the old architectural élite, whose mouthpieces were W. R. Hamilton in his *Letters . . . to the Earl of Elgin, on the new Houses of Parliament* (1836–7), and Lord Brougham in the House of Lords, 18 April 1837, in *Hansard*,

3rd series, vol. 37, col. 1390; and from Radicals like Joseph Hume, who had been advocating a semicircular chamber on the lines of the French and American legislatures for years: see, for example, the Commons debate of 7 March 1833, with Hume and Warburton advocating a semicircular chamber, and Sir Robert Inglis opposing it on the grounds of its Yankee 'vulgarity': *Hansard*, 3rd series, vol. 16, cols 37–76.

32   Rorabaugh, 'Politics and the Architectural Competition', p. 155. On its contemporary popularity both in Britain and abroad, see the *Building News*, 12 June 1857, p. 498; Denison in *Builder*, 2 January 1858, p. 154; and Lord Elcho in *ibid.*, 6 August 1859, p. 515.

33   This was J. Alfred Gotch, responding to a paper by H. R. Goodhart-Rendel, reported in the *Journal of the RIBA*, vol. 31 (1924), p. 339. Later, Peter Fleetwood-Hesketh claimed it ranked 'high among the world's greatest architectural groups'; and this despite Barry's 'questionable taste': 'Sir Charles Barry', in Peter Ferriday (ed.), *Victorian Architecture* (1963), p. 132.

34   Reginald Turnor, *Nineteenth Century Architecture in Britain* (1950), pp. 36, 55. Turnor was an extraordinarily bad choice for this Batsford book, whose main purpose, the dust wrapper tells us, was to 'understand how architecture came to take the "wrong turning"' in Victorian times.

35   Clark, *Gothic Revival*, p. 104.

36   Above, p. 10.

37   John Summerson, 'London, the Artifact', p. 314.

38   On Pugin generally see Rosemary Hill's outstanding *God's Architect: Pugin and the Building of Romantic Britain* (2007).

39   This is my opinion. I really cannot understand why Pugin is admired as a draftsman, by, for example, H. S. Goodhart-Rendel, 'English Gothic Architecture', p. 327; Reginald Turnor, *Nineteenth Century Architecture*, p. 56; Charles Handley-Read, 'William Burges', in Ferriday (ed.), *Victorian Architecture*, p. 190; and Chris Brooks, *Gothic Revival*, p. 207; and, in his own time, by the *Ecclesiologist*, vol. 5 (1846), p. 11. Others of his contemporaries were less generous; such as *Fraser's Magazine*, vol. 28 (1843), p. 603, which referred to his 'harsh and scratchy' drawing style, which in my view describes it exactly. One plate from *Contrasts* is reproduced as plate 30 in this book.

40   Basil Clarke, *Church Builders of the Nineteenth Century* (1938), p. 49.

41   Below, p. 52–3.

42   Goodhart-Rendel called them 'invaders' of Classical's 'peculiar province': 'English Gothic Architecture', p. 333.

43   Summerson, 'London, the Artifact', pp. 312–16. 1857 marks the start of the 'phase of intense conflict'.

44   This point is made by Henry-Russell Hitchcock, 'Early Victorian Architecture', pp. 11, 13; Summerson, 'London, the Artifact', pp. 315–16; Nicholas Taylor, 'Awful Sublimity', p. 432; James Stevens Curl, *Victorian Architecture* (1990), p. 19; and Collins, *Changing Ideals*, p. 98.

45   This was one of the chief explanations given for the 'failure' of that building: for example, by E. A. Freeman, letter to *The Times*, 19 October 1859, p. 10: the problem he said was that it had been designed 'by an architect whose real bent was towards Classical architecture'; and also, for example, of what were thought at that time to be Wren's west towers (actually Hawksmoor's) for Westminster Abbey: Coningham, letter to *The Times*, 11 August 1859, p. 7. More modern Gothic 'failures' were accounted for in the same way: by the fact that their builders had been 'trained in Classic and Renaissance', as G. E. Street put it, 'and had found themselves unequal to rise above early prejudices': *Builder*, 19 May 1860, p. 308. Too much modern Gothic architecture, Professor J. H. Chamberlain told a meeting of the Midlands Archaeological Association in 1861, 'suffered at the hands of the various pretenders, who

had contrived to graft themselves upon it for their own profit only': this reported in *Jackson's Oxford Journal*, 28 September 1861. More generally, G. E. Street claimed in 1860 that 'since the creation no school has been successful that has worked in more than one [style]': *Builder*, 19 May 1860, p. 308.

46   Pugin's *An Apology for the Revival of Christian Architecture* (1843) makes the case for Gothic's adaptability to secular uses; as does – by implication – John Ruskin's *The Stones of Venice* (1851–53). These were followed by G. E. Street's *An Urgent Plea for the Revival of True Principles of Architecture in the Public Buildings of the University of Oxford* (1853); T. Hudson Turner, *Some Account of Domestic Architecture in England* (3 vols, 1851–59), covering the Middle Ages only, and designed to show (this is in vol. 3, p. iv) 'that with fair and proper development and adaptation it [Gothic] is still the most suited to meet the various requirements of the present time'; and culminated with Scott's, *Remarks on Secular and Domestic Architecture, Present and Future* (1857) (see plate 31), and dozens of pamphlets and articles making the case for secular Gothic at the time of the Government Offices competition. By 1872 Charles Eastlake thought that the case for adapting Gothic to secular purposes had been conclusively demonstrated, and was now 'probably a strong plea in its favour': *History of the Gothic Revival*, p. 129.

Notes to Chapter 4: A Grand and National Work

1   Duke of Newcastle in Lords, 10 April 1856; *Hansard*, 3rd series, vol. 141, col. 770.
2   *Morning Advertiser*, 4 May 1857, p. 3.
3   *Ecclesiologist*, August 1857, p. 236.
4   A. J. Beresford Hope, *Public Offices and Metropolitan Improvements* (1857), p. 12. On Beresford Hope, who was the leader of the Gothic forces in the House of Commons, see Chris Brooks, 'The Stuff of a Heresiarch', in Christopher Webster and John Elliott (eds), *'A Church as it Should Be': The Cambridge Camden Society and its Influence* (2000).
5   *Building News*, 20 February 1857, p. 178.
6   Hope in the Commons, 2 July 1857; *Hansard*, 3rd series, vol. 146, col. 799.
7   *Blackwoods Magazine*, August 1836, p. 228.
8   'A Cambridge Man', *The New Palaces of Administration* (1857), p. 17.
9   Benjamin Hall in House of Commons, 10 August 1857, *Hansard*, 3rd series, vol. 147, col. 1306.
10   Scott, *Explanatory Remarks upon the Designs for the New Government Offices* (1857), p. 21.
11   Leeds, W. H. 'An Essay on Modern English Architecture', in Charles Barry, *The Traveller's Club* (privately printed, 1839), p. 3.
12   See, for example, [Lascelles Wraxall], 'Imperial Paris', in *Bentley's Miscellany*, vol. 43 (1858); and 'Supplement – 1853' to the 'Architecture' entry (by William Hosking), in *Encyclopaedia Britannica*, 8th edn (1852–60), p. 496.
13   'A Looker-on', in *Building News*, 19 June 1857, p. 642.
14   For example: when we visit Paris or St Petersburg, 'we feel as if, coming from London, we had passed from the works of pygmies to those of giants.' The British School of Architecture', in *Blackwood's Edinburgh Review*, vol. 40 (August 1836), p. 235.
15   See M. H. Port, *Imperial London* (1995), p. 14; and John Pudney, *The Thomas Cook Story* (1953).
16   Report of a meeting of the RIBA, reported in *Daily News*, 9 November 1855.
17   W. M. Thackeray, *The Book of Snobs* (1848), ch. 21; and cf. 'A Practical Man', *Remarks on the Designs Proposed for the New Government Offices* (1857), p. 4, on the 'lucubrations of those

enthusiastic admirers of everything out of their own country – those systematic depreciators of almost everything in it'.

18 Montague House, the Duke of Buccleugh's new residence in Whitehall, was an example: now demolished, but illustrated at http://www.londonancestor.com/views/montague-house.jpg (accessed 2 December 2010).

19 Such judgements are of course subjective; but among my suggestions would be C. R. Cockerell, the elder Barry, the Scot Alexander 'Greek' Thomson, and even poor Pennethorne among the Classicists; plus three or four of the leading Goths; and possibly Paxton from outside both camps. None of the Classicists listed here appears to have entered for the Government Offices competition. (We cannot be certain because not all *noms de plume* were penetrated.)

20 *Blackwood's Magazine*, March 1862, p. 284.

21 *Building News*, 4 September 1857, p. 928; and cf. *ibid.*, 8 May 1857, pp. 441–2; and Ellice in *Builder*, 6 August 1859, p. 516.

22 John Summerson, *Architecture in Britain 1530–1830* (1953), pp. 523–4; and cf. Nikolaus Pevsner, 'Victorian Prolegomena', in Peter Ferriday (ed.), *Victorian Architecture* (1963), p. 35.

23 Robert Furneaux Jordan, *Victorian Architecture* (1966), p. 140.

24 Above, p. 40.

25 [Coventry Patmore], 'London Street Architecture', in *National Review*, July 1857, pp. 44–6, and 'Gothic Architecture – Present and Future', in *North British Review*, vol. 28 (May 1858), p. 348 *et passim*; and Beresford Hope, *Public Offices and Metropolitan Improvements* (1857), p. 4.

26 For example, *Blackwood's Magazine*, August 1836, pp. 235–6 (nothing is built 'unless it promises a good dividend'); *Fraser's Magazine*, November 1843, p. 595; Huggins in *Builder*, 15 May 1858, p. 333; G. G. Scott, *Remarks on Secular and Domestic Architecture* (1857), p. 7 *et passim*; *Builder*, 4 December 1858, p. 809; and the digs at 'speculative builders' scattered throughout the professional journals.

27 Patmore in *North British Review*, May 1858, pp. 372–4.

28 See W. J. Rorabaugh, 'Politics and the Architectural Competition for the Houses of Parliament, 1834–1837', in *Victorian Studies*, vol. 17 (1973), p. 162, quoting Sir Edward Cust in 1835 blaming this factor specifically from the 'poverty of taste' shown in all public buildings of the period; and, 20 years later, *Saturday Review*, 17 November 1855, p. 49; and the *Building News*, 17 May 1861, p. 403, claiming that private enterprise would never have made as much of a mess over the new Government Offices (and also the planned 1862 Exhibition building) as the Government had.

29 G. G. Scott, 'On the Present Position and Future Prospects of the Revival of Gothic Architecture', in *Associated Architectural Societies Reports and Papers*, vol. 4 (1857–58), pp. 71, 78; and see Michael Bright, *Cities Built to Music: Aesthetic Theories of the Victorian Gothic Revival* (1984), p. 216.

30 *Quarterly Review*, vol. 95 (September 1854), p. 351.

31 *Ibid.*, *loc. cit.*

32 Edward Buckton Lamb, *Studies of Ancient Domestic Architecture* (1846), p. 2 (italics added). 'A Foreigner' in *Builder*, 27 June 1857, p. 359, also blamed the low status accorded to architects in England.

33 John Ruskin, *The Stones of Venice* (1853; abridged edn, 1965), p. 204; and cf. Edward Freeman, *A History of Architecture* (1849), pp. 426–7.

34 G. G. Scott, *Secular and Domestic Architecture*, p. 5.

35 [Lascelles Wraxall], 'Imperial Paris', in *Bentley's Miscellany*, vol. 43 (1858), p. 627. As M. H. Port puts it: 'London differed from all those cities' – Vienna, Berlin and St Petersburg as well as Paris – 'in that it was ungoverned'. *Imperial London: Civil Government Building in London 1850–1915* (1995), p. 5; and also his 'Government and the Metropolitan Image: ministers, parliament and the concept of a capital city, 1840–1915', in D. Arnold (ed.), *The Metropolis and its Image: Constructing Identities for London, c. 1750–1950* (1999).

36 See above, p. 10.

37 Quoted in Edward Bottoms, 'The Royal Architectural Museum in the Light of New Documentary Evidence', in *Journal of the History of Collections*, vol. 19 (2007), p. 117.

38 *Daily Telegraph*, 29 August 1859, p. 2.

39 See Frank Jenkins, 'The Victorian Architectural Profession', in Peter Ferriday (ed.), *Victorian Architecture*, p. 46.

40 Bottoms, 'The Royal Architectural Museum', p. 116. Most of these lectures are to be found reproduced or reported in the pages of *Builder* and the *Building News*. See also Paul Thompson, *William Butterfield* (1971), p. 60.

41 *Ibid.*, pp. 116, 120.

42 Barrington Kaye, *The Development of the Architectural Profession in Britain: A Sociological Study* (1960), p. 88.

43 Scott, *Personal and Professional Recollections* (1879), p. 168.

44 James Fergusson, *On a National Collection of Architectural Art* (1857), p. 15.

45 This is a complicated story, rather simplified here. For a full account, see Bottoms, 'The Royal Architectural Museum', *passim*; and Isabelle Flour, '"On the Formation of a National Museum of Architecture": the Architectural Museum versus the South Kensington Museum', in *Architectural History*, no. 51 (2008). Fergusson held the post of general manager of the Crystal Palace Company from 1856 to 1858. His 1857 lecture (quoted above) was delivered in that capacity.

46 These are reported in the *Derby Mercury*, 22 August 1860; and in the RIBA Council Minutes, vol. 4, entries of 25 February, 18 and 25 March, 8 April and 6 May, 1861.

47 Fergusson's works appeared in numerous different arrangements and editions, and under different titles, which can be confusing. The chief ones extant in our period (in their earliest versions) were *The Illustrated Handbook to Architecture*, vol. 1 (1855), mainly on Eastern styles; vol. 2, *Christian Architecture* (1855), covering pre-Renaissance European building; and *A History of the Modern Styles of Architecture* (1862), on post-Renaissance. Three other popularizers of the time were F. A. Paley, *A Manual of Gothic Architecture* (1847); E. A. Freeman, *History of Architecture*; and J. H. Parker, *An Introduction to the Study of Gothic Architecture* (1849).

48 These include *Chambers's Information for the People* (1842), vol. 2, no. 93; *The Pictorial Gallery of the Arts*, vol. 2, *Fine Arts* (1847), book 1; and the *Penny Cyclopaedia* (1833–43), under 'Architecture'.

49 E.g. *Building News*, 29 May 1857, p. 542.

50 The *Building News* went on about this interminably, protesting for example regarding one of the exhibits at the Westminster Hall exhibition that 'of Blake, Marlborough, Nelson, and Wellington we see nothing, but there are Roman warriors with the short sword in all kinds of lively attitudes': 22 May 1857, p. 501. 'Why ... should we bother ourselves about the combats of the Lapithae and the Centaurs,' he wrote later, 'when we have the combats of heroes with French and Russians in many a hard-fought field?': 12 June 1857, p. 597. He also objected to inscriptions in the language of Cicero, rather than of Shakespeare: *ibid.*, 29 May 1857, p. 542. He, however, was difficult to please; one frieze that did celebrate 'the war history of the empire' got on to the wrong foot for him by starting with the British

fighting the Romans, when in fact the British then, as he pointed out, were not English at all but Celts. 'If the building were within a Welsh empire, such an illustration would be relevant'; but it was not: *Building News*, 19 June 1857, p. 626. See also John P. Seddon, lecture on 'Ancient and Modern Architectural Ornament', reported in the *Building News*, 29 January 1858, p. 112; and G. G. Scott's *Explanatory Remarks* (1857 version), p. 28, where he was pleased to say that all *his* statues were of Brits.

51 For example, most of *Building News*'s suggestions were of military men and monarchs (above, p. 169, n. 50). For Mr S. Huggins of the Liverpool Architectural Society, however, the 'demi-Gods of English history' who deserved to be memorialized in this way were 'the Spencers, Bacons, Cromwells, Newtons'. Lecture reported in *Builder*, 15 May 1858, p. 333. (Cromwell of course could be taken both ways.)

52 Peel in Commons, 4 June 1838, in *Hansard*, 3rd series, vol. 43, col. 707.

53 For example, Scott in his *Explanatory Remarks* (1857), pp. 9–10; 'A Cambridge Man', *The New Palaces of Administration* (1857), pp. 6–7; A. J. Beresford Hope, *Public Offices and Metropolitan Improvements* (1857), pp. 5, 18–19; and many others. When Manners was quizzed in the House of Commons on 18 February 1859 on why he had favoured Scott's design over the two that had beaten it in the competition, he replied that '*genius loci*' had been the deciding factor: *Hansard*, 3rd series, vol. 152, col. 519.

54 *Building News*, 18 February 1859, p. 153 (italics added).

55 Elcho in Commons, 4 August 1859; in *Hansard*, 3rd series, vol. 155, col. 923. Gilbert Scott also argued against the assumption that 'perfect uniformity of character were essential to beauty' in *Remarks on Secular and Domestic Architecture*, p. 190. Of course, the Goths needed to establish this more than the Classicists, otherwise, with most street architecture of that time being Classical, they would never squeeze in.

56 On the 'Saracens', see below, p. 69.

57 *Michael J Lewis, The Politics of the German Gothic Revival* (1993), pp. 30, 75–8, 80, 83–4.

58 The most authoritative disputants in this controversy in the 1850s were the historians J. H. Parker: e.g. paper delivered to the Oxford Architectural Society, 9 February 1859, reported in *Gentleman's Magazine*, vol. 206 (1859), pp. 275–80; and letter in *ibid*., pp. 284–8; and E. A. Freeman: letter to *The Times*, 19 October 1859; and 'The Foreign Office: Classic or Gothic', in *National Review*, vol. 10 (January 1860), pp. 25, 44–8, 53.

59 J. H. Parker, *An Introduction to the Study of Gothic Architecture* (1849; repr. 1861), pp. 189–90; and cf. [William Hosking], 'Architecture', in *Encyclopaedia Britannica*, 2nd series (1830), pp. 422, 453; 'Bm Wr' in *Building News*, 30 November 1860, p. 910; and 'WP' in *Builder*, 31 October 1857, p. 624. We find the same argument in Germany, once the Germans had reluctantly ceded primacy to France: 'perhaps Germany did not have the first Gothic buildings, but she had the best' – i.e. Cologne Cathedral. Lewis, *Politics of the German Gothic Revival*, p. 78.

60 On 'Teutons', see Freeman, 'The Style of the New Foreign Office', in *Ecclesiologist*, vol. 20 (December 1859), p. 368; Anon., *Shall Gothic Architecture be Denied Fair Play?* (1860), p. 12; and A. J. Beresford Hope, *The Common Sense of Art* (1858), p. 6. One should not, incidentally, assume that any 'racism' attached to this; at this level of debate, 'Teutons', and likewise 'Germanics' and 'Saxons', were nearly always distinguished from others by their social and political institutions, environmentally determined, rather than by their genes.

61 John Henry Parker, for example, regretted the 'fashion at present to run down the Perpendicular style because it is exclusively English' in favour of 'what is Venetian, or at least foreign': *An Introduction*, p. 183. It is interesting that the two academic historians involved in the controversy – the other was E. A. Freeman, *History of Architecture*, p. xiv – were both

much more favourable to Perpendicular than the bulk of architectural and ecclesiological theorists; as were popular works like the *Penny Cyclopaedia* (1833–43, entry on 'Gothic Architecture', p. 325).

62 [Coventry Patmore], 'London Street Architecture', in *National Review*, vol. 5 (July 1857), p. 53.

63 G. E. Street, *An Urgent Plea for the Revival of True Principles of Architecture in the Public Buildings of the University of Oxford* (1853), p. 13.

64 Street, Lecture on 'Gothic Architecture and Domestic Buildings', reported in *Builder*, 19 May 1860, pp. 308: 'in Classic Buildings the window is an inconvenience. In Gothic it is the principal feature'; A. J. Beresford Hope, *Public Offices and Metropolitan Improvements* (1857), p. 20; and J. T. Jeffcock, lecture on 'Gothic Architecture, a National Style', in *Ecclesiologist*, vol. 18 (August 1857), p. 245.

65 Edward Freeman, *History of Architecture*, p. 47; and his 'The Style of the New Foreign Office', p. 368.

66 [Scott, G. G.], *The Gothic Renaissance: Its Origin, Progress, and Principles* (1860), p. 7; and cf. Scott, *Remarks on Secular and Domestic Architecture*, p. 199.

67 'A Cambridge Man', *The New Palaces of Administration* (1857), p. 22.

68 'Lord Palmerston and the Designs for the Foreign Office', in *Gentleman's Magazine*, vol. 207 (November 1859), p. 472 (original capital initials).

69 E. A. Freeman, 'The Foreign Office: Classic or Gothic', in *National Review*, vol. 10 (January 1860), p. 41; and cf. G. G. Scott, *Remarks on Secular and Domestic Architecture* (1857), p. 5; Francis Scott, *Shall the New Foreign Office be Gothic or Classic?* (1860), pp. 21, 32, 60–2; and much of Pugin. Again, we find the same argument in Germany: Lewis, *Politics of the German Gothic Revival*, p. 159.

70 See, for example, Freeman, *History of Architecture*, p. 29.

71 See J. T. Jeffcock, paper on 'Gothic Architecture, a National Style', reported in *Ecclesiologist*, vol. 18 (August 1857), p. 245–7.

72 Palmerston in Commons, 8 July 1861: *Hansard*, 3rd series, vol. 164, col. 537. Cf. Cowper in the same debate, col. 519, claiming that the best examples of the original British style extant then were 'Stonehenge' and 'Irish cabins'. The *Globe*, 12 February 1859, makes the same point about Jones and Wren; and Anon., 'Classic, or Pseudo-Gothic', in *Building News*, 27 July 1860, p. 593, the same point about the capacity of Renaissance architecture to become 'naturalized' generally.

73 Anon., *The Gothic Renaissance*, p. 4.

74 Review of Francis Scott, *Shall the New Foreign Office be Gothic or Classic?* (1860), in *Building News*, 10 August 1860, p. 618. Palmerston made much the same point in his response to the 'Gothic' deputation of 29 July 1859, reported *Builder*, 6 August 1859, pp. 516–17. For the 'Saracen' origin of Gothic, see below, p. 179, n. 40.

75 See, for example, letter from 'A' to *The Times*, 1 November 1859, p. 10; Tite, 'On the Progress and Present State of Architecture', in *Civil Engineer*, December 1859, pp. 393–4; and Anon., *Remarks on a National Style* (1860), pp. 5–8.

76 The two contemporary architectural pamphlets which argue this case most fully are Francis Scott, *Shall the New Foreign Office be Gothic or Classic?* (1860): see esp. pp. 4, 46–50, 62, 67; and W. J. Cockburn Muir, *Pagan, or Christian?* (1860), pp. vii, viii, x, 186–7, 218.

77 Chris Brooks, *The Gothic Revival* (1999), pp. 41–4.

78 E. A. Freeman suggested one way in which this stylistic separation might reflect certain political differences in the two countries, viz.: 'the English clustered pillar ... typifies the union of many powers in the state under a constitutional monarch; while the single pillar, so

often retained in France, typifies the French tendency to the *unité du pouvoir*'. He hastened to add, however, that he was not putting this idea forward seriously. 'The Foreign Office: Classic or Gothic?', in *National Review*, vol. 10 (January 1860), p. 47.

79 Freeman, *History of Architecture*, p. 423.

80 For example (one of many), in Charles Dickens's *A Child's History of England* (1853).

81 See Francis Scott, *Shall the New Foreign Office be Gothic or Classic?*, pp. 21, 32, 60–2.

82 See the review of Sir Francis Scott's *Shall the New Foreign Office be Gothic or Classic?* in *Building News*, 20 July 1860, p. 566: 'That was a mere coincidence'.

83 W. J. Cockburn Muir, *Pagan or Christian? Or Notes for the General Public on our National Architecture* (1860), pp. 232, 273–4.

84 On this, see Anon., 'Hamilton &c on Architecture', in *Quarterly Review*, vol. 58 (February 1837), p. 69; Anon., 'Gothic Art: John Ruskin', in *London Quarterly Review*, vol. 7 (January 1857), pp. 489–90; 'FAM', letter to *Builder*, 26 December 1857; G. E. Street, lecture on 'Gothic Architecture and Domestic Buildings', reported in *Builder*, 19 May 1860, p. 308; Francis E. Scott, *Shall the New Foreign Office be Gothic or Classic?*, p. 25. August Reichensperger had a similar image of mediaeval building in Germany: see Lewis, *The Politics of the German Gothic Revival*, p. 47.

85 Scott reported in *Builder*, 18 February and 3 March 1860, pp. 100, 132 (original italics); and [Scott, G. G.], *The Gothic Renaissance*, pp. 25–6 (quoting G.G. Scott); and cf. Francis Scott, *Shall the New Foreign Office be Gothic or Classic?*, pp. 34, 39, 69.

86 In *News from Nowhere* (1890), and in his early (c. 1877–84) lectures on Art and Society, in A. L. Morton (ed.), *Political Writings of William Morris* (London: Lawrence & Wishart, 1973).

87 Meeting reported in *Builder*, 24 July 1858, pp. 497–9.

88 Tite in *Civil Engineer*, December 1859, p. 396.

89 Reported in *Builder*, 5 November 1855, p. 549.

90 James Anderson, 1800, quoted in Pat Anderson, 'The Other Gothic Revival', in *Canadian Journal of History*, vol. 22 (1987), p. 5.

91 Thomas Rickman, *An Attempt to Discriminate between the Styles of English Architecture, from the Conquest to the Reformation* (1817); and cf. Reverend John Milner, *A Treatise on the Ecclesiastical Architecture of England during the Middle Ages* (3rd edn, 1835), pp. vi–vii. Milner's book was a direct response to those who condemned Gothic for being 'destitute of orders, rules, and proportions'.

92 See Pat Anderson, 'The other Gothic Revival: Contemporary Ideals in English Revivalism, 1730–1840', in *Canadian Journal of History*, vol. 22 (April 1987).

93 Petit, 'On the Revival of Styles', in *Builder*, 1 June 1861, p. 372.

94 Francis E. Scott, *Shall the New Foreign Office be Gothic or Classic?*, p. 69.

95 See John Summerson, *The London Building World of the Eighteen-Sixties* (1973), p. 20.

96 As Edward Garbett argued in 1850: see below, pp. 106–7.

97 Scott, *Remarks on Secular and Domestic Architecture*, pp. 187, 201, 269, 274.

98 On this, see Peter Collins, *Changing Ideals in Modern Architecture 1750–1950* (1965), p. 69.

99 See Suzanne Marchand, 'Arnold Böcklin and the Problem of German Modernism' (unpublished paper), describing German 'anxiety in the face of too much diversity' at this time. For a '"style-less" age, it was agreed, could not be a great one.'

100 Above, p. 13.

101 Above, pp. 40–1.

102 Brooks, *Gothic Revival*, p. 300.

103 For example, E. A. Freeman, *History of Architecture*, pp. 2, 27–8, 299–300; and G. E. Street, 'The True Principles of Architecture', in *Ecclesiologist*, vol. 13 (June 1852), p. 256.

104 Below, pp. 85–90.

105 'Fanatical' is justified; see, for example, his articles in the *Dublin Review*, vols 10 and 12, May 1841 and February 1842, attacking the Church of England quite viciously: 'these are not times for compromise' (February 1842, p. 140); and *Some Remarks on the Articles which have recently appeared in the "Rambler" relative to Ecclesiastical Architecture and Decoration* (1850), p. 24: 'It' – the task of re-Gothicizing England – 'is not inferior to the rescuing of the Holy Land from the Infidels'.

106 A. W. N. Pugin, 'Ecclesiastical Architecture in England', in *Dublin Review*, vol. 12 (February 1842), p. 181.

107 See Anon., 'Architectural Revivalism and Puginism', in *Fraser's Magazine*, vol. 28 (November 1843), p. 603, which claimed that this was Pugin's 'frank' intention. It is strongly implied, I think, in certain of his works; including the article on 'Ecclesiastical Architecture' just cited, pp. 160–1 and 182–3; and his *An Apology for the Revival of Christian Architecture* (1843).

108 Anon., 'Architectural Revivalism and Puginism', in *Fraser's Magazine*, vol. 28 (November 1843), p. 603.

109 'Verax' in *Builder*, 28 November 1857, p. 692. 'No wonder', he added, unkindly, 'his mind gave way'.

110 E. A. Freeman, 'The Foreign Office: Classic or Gothic', in *National Review*, January 1860, pp. 25, 30.

111 Charles Eastlake, *A History of the Gothic Revival* (1872), p. 218.

112 Basil Clarke, *Church Builders of the Nineteenth Century* (1938), p. 64.

113 Quoted in Eastlake, *A History of the Gothic Revival*, pp. 167–8 (italics added).

114 See, for example, Tite, 'On the Progress and Present State of Architecture', in the *Civil Engineer*, December 1859, p. 395, making the point that Gothic was unsuitable for what he called 'intellectual' worship; a letter to *Builder* from 'A Competitor', 13 June 1857, p. 337, claiming that Gothic was unsuited to 'the pure Christianity of the Gospel', as opposed (it is implied here) to the Catholics' impure kind; a letter from George Wightwick in *Builder*, 9 January 1858, p. 25; a lecture by Mr S. Huggins, reported in *Builder*, 15 May 1858, p. 332; Thomas Goodchild, letter to *Builder*, 7 February 1857, p. 81; and J. H. Stevens in *Builder*, 7 November 1857, p. 638. And as Christopher Wren put it: 'It is enough if they' – the 'Romanists' – hear the murmur of the Mass and see the Elevation of the Host, but ours [Protestant churches] are fitted as auditories.' Quoted in Basil Clarke, *Church Builders of the Nineteenth Century*, p. 5.

115 'Fopperies' is Goodchild in *Builder*, 7 February 1857; 'mummeries' is Anon., 'Architectural Revivalism and Puginism', in *Fraser's Magazine*, vol. 28 (November 1843), pp. 604–5.

116 Rev Francis Close, *Church Architecture, Scripturally Considered* (1844), quoted in Gareth Atkins, 'Rebuilding the Reformation': paper read to NAVSA Conference in Cambridge, 2009.

117 This is (allegedly) the Reverend J. H. (later Cardinal) Newman, quoted (but unsourced) in Peter Ferriday, 'The Revival: Stories Ancient and Modern', in the *Architectural Review*, vol. 121 (1957), p. 156.

118 See E. A. Freeman, 'The Foreign Office: Classic or Gothic', in *National Review*, January 1860, pp. 25, 29; Ernest W. Bacon, *Spurgeon: Heir of the Puritans* (1967), pp. 64–5; and Clyde Binfield, 'Architects in Connexion: Four Methodist Generations', in Jane Garnett and Colin Matthew (eds), *Revival and Religion since 1700* (1993), pp. 167–9.

119 See Palmerston in Commons, 4 August 1859: *Hansard*, 3rd series, vol. 155, col. 931; and, correcting his Jesuit 'blunder', Francis Scott, 1860 pamphlet, pp. 4, 65, 67; Layard in Commons, 8 July 1861, *Hansard*, 3rd series, vol. 164, col. 522: 'Everybody knew that the Gothic, instead of being the style of the Jesuits, was the very style which the Jesuits destroyed'; *Derby Mercury*,

24 August 1859; *Daily Telegraph*, 29 August 1859; and *Liverpool Mercury*, 12 July 1861, p. 2, which claimed that Palmerston was being much 'ridiculed' by the *literati* over this.

On the other hand, some Jesuits did employ – by that time anachronistic – Gothic details in their otherwise Classical churches:'pointed' window tracery, for example; which, if he had known about it, might have helped Palmerston argue back. See Chris Brooks, *Gothic Revival*, p. 24.

120 This went right back to Pugin's emergence on to the scene. Examples – from both Classicists and Goths – are the *Quarterly Review*, vol. 58 (February 1837), p. 65; *Fraser's Magazine*, November 1843, pp. 595ff. (one of the only ones to dare to criticize his 'scratchy' drawing style); the (very pro-Gothic) *Ecclesiologist*, 1846; a satirical poem published in *Builder*, 1 August 1857, p. 440;Tite in *Civil Engineer*, December 1859, p. 393; Prof Donaldson quoted in *Building News*, 30 November 1860, p. 905; and Tarbuck in *Building News*, 5 April 1861, p. 285.

121 A contributor to *Blackwood's Magazine*, vol. 91 (March 1862), p. 297, commended Scott for having 'succeeded in making the exclusively Roman Catholic bigotry of Pugin bend to Protestant principles.' In the case of Ruskin, Charles Eastlake, who found most of his theories 'absurd', gave him credit for this 'one good service': to have prised the Revival away from the papist associations that the 'extreme Protestant party' saw 'lurking in every pointed arch, and . . . peeping from behind every Gothic pillar'. Eastlake, *History of the Gothic Revival*, p. 266.

122 See, for example, Lord John Manners in the Commons, 4 March 1859: *Hansard*, 3rd series, vol. 152, col. 941; William White, 'So-Called Mediaeval *v.* So-Called Classic', in *Builder*, 14 February 1857, p. 90; and E. A. Freeman, letter to *The Times*, 19 October 1859; p. 10. Stefan Muthesius, *The High Victorian Movement in Architecture 1850–1870* (1972), p. 153, and Rosemary Hill, *God's Architect*, pp. 398–9, point out how anti-Gothic the great English Catholic leader Cardinal Newman was.

123 Anon., *Remarks on a National Style* (1860), p. 9;'Verax' in *Builder*, 28 November 1857, p. 692.

124 In E. M. Forster's novel *A Room with a View* (1908), the middle-class Mr Emerson makes the same point to his radical son George during a visit to the *duomo* in Florence; George initially can only see the building's Catholicism, which he despises, until his father presents it to him in this more democratic way.

125 This is broadly E. A. Freeman's argument in a letter to *The Times*, 19 October 1859, p. 10, and in 'The Foreign Office: Classic or Gothic', in the *National Review*, vol. 10 (January 1860), pp. 29–31. Others distinguished between – and claimed that Pugin had confused – 'Catholic' architecture (in the broadest sense) with 'Papist': e.g. W. Sewell, 'Principles of Gothic Architecture', in *Quarterly Review*, vol. 69 (December 1841), pp. 144–5; and William White, 'So-Called Mediaeval *v.* So-Called Classic', in *Builder*, 14 February 1857, p. 90.

126 Contemporary reactions to All Saints, Margaret Street, are summarized in Charles Eastlake, *A History of the Gothic Revival* (1872), pp. 252–5.

127 Above, pp. 22–3.

128 Anon., 'Architectural Revivalism and Puginism', in *Fraser's Magazine*, vol. 28 (November 1843), pp. 604–5.

129 The nineteenth-century meaning of the word 'enthusiasm' seems to have been stronger than it is today, closer to 'zeal', 'fanaticism' or even 'possession'. See the *Shorter Oxford English Dictionary*, and one particular 1841 example quoted there:'Everywhere the history of religion betrays a tendency to enthusiasm'.

130 Gareth Atkins, 'Rebuilding the Reformation: History, Architecture and National Identity, c. 1830–1850', paper read at the 10th Annual Conference of the British Association for

Victorian Studies, Churchill College, Cambridge, July 2009, and cited with his permission. I am greatly indebted to Mr Atkins for alerting me to this particular branch of the Gothic Revival; exemplified for example in two Cambridge churches: Christ Church, Newmarket Road (1837–9), and St Paul, Hills Road (1841), both by Ambrose Poynter.

131   Below, p. 91.

132   See James Parker, lecture on 'English Domestic Architecture', reproduced in the *Gentleman's Magazine*, vol. 206 (1859), p. 276; and A. E. Freeman, 'The Foreign Office: Classic or Gothic', in the *National Review*, vol. 10 (January 1860) p. 35. By the 1850s this problem was coming to be addressed, by the publication of, for example, T. Hudson Turner, *Some Account of Domestic Architecture in England from the Conquest to Henry VIII* (4 vols, 1851–9).

133   The full motto, from Horace's *Ars Poetica*, runs: 'Nec minimum meruere decus uestigia Graeca ausi desere et celebrare domestica facta'; which can be translated as: 'it is worthy of no little praise to have dared to abandon the footsteps of the Greeks, and to celebrate the achievements of our own country.' Ellen K. Morris's translation, in 'Symbols of Empire', in *Journal of Architectural Education*, vol. 32 (1978), pp. 8–13.

134   See, for example, Parker in *Builder*, 1 January 1859, p. 5.

135   And one trade route in particular: 'through the English provinces in the west of France, in as direct a line as possible through the northern parts of Normandy and Brittany, along the line of hills through Limoges and Perigueux, and skirting the foot of the Pyrenees, and by the Mediterranean port of Aiges Mortez, now blocked up, the sea having receded in the past'; but giving a wide berth to Lombardy. Freeman, letter to *Builder*, 1 January 1859, p. 6. G. E. Street thought this was silly: letter to *Builder*, 8 January 1859, pp. 23–4.

136   For example, 'Honesty' in *Building News*, 3 July 1857, p. 697; letter to *The Times*, 1 December 1858, p. 12; William Tite in the House of Commons, 11 February and 4 August 1859, in *Hansard*, 3rd series, vol. 152, col. 262 and vol. 155, col. 925; leader in *Daily News*, 20 August 1859; and, with regard to the 'Byzantine' design, *Builder*, 11 August 1860, which reports C. Bentinck, MP, asking if photos of certain buildings in Venice could be exhibited along with these in the Commons, to show where Scott got his ideas.

137   *Building News*, 27 July 1860, p. 593; and cf. 'Verax' in *Builder*, 28 November 1857, p. 892: 'if it be the architecture of our forefathers, why throw it aside for continental forms?'; and Fergusson, *On a National Collection of Architectural Art*, p. 6: by choosing 'the bastard Gothic of the Italians', men like Ruskin and Scott were 'abandoning their strongest ground of the style being our own national type', and cutting us 'again loose in the sea of styles'. Charles Eastlake later referred to this 'strong party who felt that in resigning the nationality of their art they' – that is, the Revivalists around this time generally – 'would yield a point which had long been considered a strong one in its favour': Eastlake, *History of the Gothic Revival*, p. 334. Peter Collins would appear to go along with this: that 'the great weakness of the English architects' claim to be resurrecting an indigenous style was their disinclination to base their designs on national prototypes': *Changing Ideals*, p. 101.

138   Anon., 'Lord Palmerston and the Designs for the Foreign Office', in *Gentleman's Magazine*, vol. 207 (November 1859), pp. 473–4. Palmerston and Tite both made great play with this: Palmerston in the Commons, 11 February 1859, *Hansard*, 3rd series, vol. 152, col. 272, and Tite in the Commons, 4 August 1859, *Hansard*, 3rd series, vol. 155, col. 925. Other complaints at Scott's exoticisms included 'Honesty', 'The Great Gothic Failure', in *Building News*, 3 July 1857, p. 697; 'Mercutio', 'The Deputation to the Premier', in *ibid.*, 9 September 1859, p. 826; and *Builder*, 4 July 1857, p. 371. A suggestion made in response to this in the *Building News*, 26 August 1859, p. 768, that Venice and Belgium could have imported these features from England originally, cannot have convinced anyone.

139   Letter from 'Forward' to *Builder*, 30 May 1857, p. 304. The press illustrations of the prize-winning entries confirm this. The most 'English' is also the dullest (Buxton and Habershon's sixth-prize design for the Foreign Office); the others are all dominated by Flemish and Venetian features (with a touch of Siennese in Street's seventh-placed Foreign Office). See *Illustrated London News*, 12 September to 24 October, 1857.

140   Above, p. 24.

141   Burges, *Art Applied to Industry* (1865), pp. 111–12. Burges claimed that 'nearly all our faults in modern architecture may be traced to the misuse of Italian examples', which he attributed to this.

142   *Seven Lamps of Architecture*, preface to the 1st edn.

143   Below, Ch. 7.

144   Street, letter to *Builder*, 8 January 1859, p. 24.

145   See, for example, his paper on 'The True Principles of Architecture, and the Possibility of Development', reported in the *Ecclesiologist*, vol. 13 (June 1852), pp. 247–62. And cf. S. Huggins, lecture on 'The Question of Styles', reported in *Builder*, 15 May 1858, p. 333; and the 'Eclectics' mentioned below, p. 106.

146   Clarke, *Church Builders*, p. 121. French Gothic was the stipulated style for Lille. Several English architects entered for the competition, including William Burges, whose design won it, but was never built.

147   See below, p. 132.

148   This is August Reichensperger, quoted in Michael J. Lewis, *The Politics of the German Gothic Revival*, p. 40.

149   When English neo-Gothic architects designed buildings for abroad, it was nearly always in the local indigenous styles. Scott's famous (but now demolished) Nikolai Church in Hamburg, and his later design for the Rathaus there, are examples.

Notes to Chapter 5: Worthy of our Imperial City

1   Among works that could be regarded as precursors of *Culture and Imperialism* is Martin Green, *Dreams of Adventure, Deeds of Empire* (New York: Basic Books 1979).

2   He does, however, mention (pp. 123–5) Ruskin, and his famous (or notorious) first Slade Lecture at Oxford in January 1870; which was supposed to be about art, but began with a remarkable, even eccentric, diatribe in favour of British imperial expansion. Said claims that this 'frames nearly everything in Ruskin's copious writings on art', though without saying how exactly it could be said to 'frame' (whatever that means) *The Stones of Venice* and *The Seven Lamps*. (It is not obvious.) In fact Ruskin's views on art and imperialism were highly confused; see below, p. 121.

3   Exceptions are F. Driver and G. Gilbert (eds), *Imperial Cities: Landscape, Display and Identity* (1999): this is in Mackenzie's series); M. H. Port, *Imperial London: Civil Government Building in London, 1851–1915* (1995); and George L. Hersey's brief but interesting discussion of Gothic as an 'imperial' style in *High Victorian Gothic: A Study in Associationism* (1972), pp. 48, 73–83. Chris Brooks also touches on this briefly in *The Gothic Revival* (1999), p. 65, when he suggests that the tall towers of some eighteenth-century neo-Gothic castles 'imply an extension into the illimitable prospects – both vistas and opportunities – of the Empire that beckons beyond the horizon.' 'Imply' is a slippery word for a historian.

4   The exceptions are E. K. Morris, 'Symbols of Empire: Architectural Styles and the Government Offices Competition', *Journal of Architectural Education*, vol. 32 (1978), pp. 8–13; and G. Alex Bremner, 'Nation and Empire in the Government Architecture of mid-

Victorian London: The Foreign and India Office Reconsidered', *Historical Journal*, vol. 48, no. 3 (2005), pp. 703–42; both of which carry some fascinating and original arguments, but whose central 'imperial' claims are based on a very narrow range of sources, selectively and sometimes misleadingly used; and with very little understanding of the broader political and social context of the 1850s and 1860s.

5   E.g., me. See my *The Absent-Minded Imperialists: Empire, Society and Culture in Britain* (Oxford: Oxford University Press, 2004), ch. 7.

6   Trevelyan's evidence to the 1856 committee, quoted in Ian Toplis, *The Foreign Office: An Architectural History* (1987), p. 27.

7   See my *Absent-Minded Imperialists*, pp. 42–3.

8   'At one end' of the great range of buildings he envisioned, 'we should have the ancient Palace of Westminster bringing down historical associations from the times of the early Saxon kings, and at the other we should have the Palace of Whitehall carrying them on to the revolution'; with, as he continued later, the whole complex giving 'the honour due to the focus of all our liberties, [and] of that regulated freedom which we hope will overspread the world.'

9   'A Cambridge Man', *The New Palaces of Administration* (1857), p. 5.

10 *Leeds Mercury*, 9 October 1856.

11 'Civis Britannicus', in *The Times*, 12 May 1857, p. 5. The *nom de plume*, clearly referring to Palmerston's famous 'Civis Britannicus sum' speech over the *Don Pacifico* affair (1850), situates the writer in the Palmerstonian camp.

12 *Illustrated London News*, 9 May 1857, p. 424; and cf. *ibid.*, 26 December 1857, p. 636.

13 For example, early on *Blackwood's Magazine*, vol. 40 (August 1836), p. 232, refers to London as 'capital of half the world', asking what 'durable monuments' it has to show for this. During the Battle itself there are occasional references to, for example, this 'great imperial plan': Beresford Hope in the Commons, 2 July 1857, *Hansard*, 3rd series, vol. 146, col. 797; and to London as the 'centre' or 'focus' or 'heart' of an empire: e.g. 'A Practical Man', *Remarks on the Designs Proposed for the New Government Offices* (1857), p. 9; *The Times*, 12 August 1857, p. 9; and the *Building News*, 8 May 1857, p. 442. The *Building News*, 30 November 1860, p. 909, thought it was shaming that a nation 'upon whose possessions the sun could never set', could be so indifferent to its architectural legacy. [Coventry Patmore], 'London Street Architecture', in the *National Review*, vol. 5 (July 1857), p. 52, commented on the prospects for the Palace of Westminster's enduring 'as long as the British Empire'. And when the Battle was over *Blackwood's Magazine*, vol. 91 (March 1862), p. 286, reminded its readers how much had rested on it: a building capable of 'disgracing or adorning the capital of the empire'. Another take on this was provided by one W. Glover, in a lecture reported in the *Building News*, 12 July 1861, p. 589, where he expressed the hope that they would erect buildings fine enough – and in the Classical style – to remind future generations of Britain's greatness 'when her banner as mistress of the seas shall be given to another, when her colonies have released themselves from her grasp, and her name only be known as belonging to the past'.

14 See Beresford Hope in the Commons, 10 August 1857: *Hansard*, 3rd Series, vol. 147, cols 1299, 1311; *The Times*, 12 August 1857, p. 9; and *Building News*, 14 August 1857, p. 851.

15 See, for example, the contemporary W. F. Collier's *History of the British Empire* (London: T. Nelson and Sons, 1858), 95 per cent of which is devoted to the British Isles. The 'imperial' in that title was meant to indicate that it included – unusually – Scotland, Wales and Ireland as well as England.

16 See T. S. R. Boase, 'The Decoration of the New Palace of Westminster, 1841–63', in *Journal of the Warburg and Courtauld Institutes*, vol. 17 (1954).

17 See above, p. 3.

18 For example: 'this great and wealthy metropolis', Beresford Hope's favourite phrase: in the Commons, 2 July 1857: *Hansard*, 3rd series, vol. 146, col. 798; and in *Public Offices and Metropolitan Improvements* (1857), p. 4.

19 It is Patrick Brantlinger's intriguing idea, in *Rule of Darkness: British Literature and Imperialism, 1830–1914* (Ithaca, NY: Cornell University Press, 1988), that the less imperial attitudes were openly expressed at this time, the more thoroughly assimilated it proves them to have been.

20 'A Practical Man' *Remarks on the Designs Proposed for the New Government Offices* (1857), pp. 4, 9.

21 A. J. Beresford Hope, *Public Offices and Metropolitan Improvements* (pamphlet, 1857), pp. 33–4 (italics added).

22 *The Times*, 12 August 1857, p. 9.

23 Port, *Imperial London*, p. 198.

24 On the India Office building, see G. Alex Bremner, 'Nation and Empire in the Government Architecture of Mid-Victorian London', *loc. cit.*; M. C. C. Seton, *The India Office* (1926); Lavinia Handley-Read, 'Legacy of a Vanished Empire: The Design of the India Office', in *Country Life*, July 1970; D. Williams, *The India Office, 1858–1869* (Hoshiapur, 1983); and John Cornforth, 'The old India Office', in *Country Life*, November 1987. Much later (1874) a Colonial Office was added to the complex, and adorned with imperial statuary.

25 *Saturday Review*, 15 January 1859, p. 68.

26 Below, p. 88.

27 So far as I have been able to find. I have come across just one, very early, example of Classic's being positively championed because of its Roman imperial associations; this is the seventeenth-century diarist John Evelyn, quoted by W. Sewell, 'Principles of Gothic Architecture', in *Quarterly Review*, vol. 69 (December 1841), p. 111.

28 See above, p. 49.

29 For example, Bremner, 'Nation and Empire', p. 710, which refers to the 'oft-alluded correlation between the British empire and that of ancient Rome', but without furnishing evidence from this period.

30 Whether one leaned to the Greeks or to the Romans could well serve as an indication of one's contemporary political views. See Quentin Broughall, 'A Careful Hellenism and a Reckless Roman-ness: The Gladstone v. Disraeli Rivalry in the Context of Classics': paper read to the Gladstone Bicentennial Conference, Hawarden, September 2009.

31 Above, p. 37.

32 Coventry Patmore, 'London Street Architecture', in *National Review*, July 1857, pp. 44, 66–8.

33 Above, p. 52.

34 See below, pp. 69–71.

35 Fergusson, *An Historical Enquiry into the True Principles of Beauty in Art, More Especially with Reference to Architecture* (1849), p. 8; and compare his *The Illustrated Handbook of Architecture* (1855), vol. 1, p. 296, where the imperial Roman period is presented as 'the last act in the great [Classical] drama, the gorgeous but melancholy catastrophe by which all these [previous] styles of architecture were collected in wild confusion in Rome, and perished beneath the luxury and crimes of that mighty people'. The historian E. A. Freeman characterized the Romans as 'about the best builders in the world and about the worst architects': letter

to *The Times*, 19 October 1859, p. 10 – rather like the English, in fact. He makes the same point in his *History of Architecture* (1849), p. 26.

36 Below, p. 120.

37 See above, p. 20.

38 Ellen K. Morris, 'Symbols of Empire', p. 10.

39 In *The Absent-Minded Imperialists*, pp. 6–12.

40 This idea in fact goes back a long way – at least to Wren, who thought Gothic 'ought properly and truly to be *named* Saracenic Architecture, refined by Christians, which first of all began in the East': quoted in Basil Clarke, *Church Builders of the Nineteenth Century* (1938), pp. 7–8. In Wren's case this was probably meant to be disparaging. This, however, changed later. See John Britton, *The Architectural Antiquities of Great Britain*, vol. 5 (1826), p. 53; and R. Willis, *Remarks on the Architecture of the Middle Ages* (1835), p. v; William Hosking's 'Architecture' entry in *Encyclopaedia Britannica*, 7th edn (1830–42), p. 420; and *Penny Cyclopaedia* (1833–43), under 'Gothic Architecture'. The idea then was that the Crusaders brought the pointed arch back from the Holy Land. For its continued prevalence in the 1850s, see G. G. Scott's letter in *Builder*, 5 December 1857, p. 706, and his Royal Academy lecture of 28 January, 1858, reported in *Builder*, 20 February 1858; J. L. Petit reported in *Builder*, 1 June 1861; Edward Tarbuck in *Building News*, 16 November 1860, p. 875; a review of 'Sir FE Scott on Gothic Architecture', in *Building News*, 10 August 1860, p. 618; and Anon., 'Classic or Gothic: The Battle of the Styles', in *Blackwood's Edinburgh Magazine*, vol. 91 (1862), pp. 295–6. All these are happy to hypothesize, at any rate, a 'Saracenic' origin. Fergusson, who greatly admired Islamic architecture (see below, and his encomium to it in *The Illustrated Handbook of Architecture*, vol. 1, 1855, pp. 469–70), believed it was the origin of the pointed arch in southern Europe (coming via Sicily), but not in northern Europe, whose builders had hit on the idea independently: *Illustrated Handbook*, vol. 2, pp. 815–16, 824, 839.

41 This is 'Verax', 'Pointed Architecture and its Worst Enemies', in *Builder*, 28 Nov 1857, p. 692. 'The fact is that pointed Architecture is neither Christian, [nor] Germanic ... It is Moslem – it is Saracenic ... It was brought over by the Crusaders'. But that, he thinks, was Gothic's undoing; subjected to this 'hot-bed of Islamism', the style 'lasted scarce a century [longer] in chilly Europe, and then faded, became degraded and debased, and died.' A good example, this – albeit a rare one in this field – of the fear of 'Oriental' seduction.

Edward Freeman's take on the 'Saracenic' issue was to acknowledge that Islam used the pointed arch before the Goths, but 'without any trace of its pervading spirit.' 'They made a systematic use of the pointed arch, but they never made it part of a system.' So it was 'a sort of dead end Gothic'. *History of Architecture*, pp. 27, 301.

42 Fergusson has a three-page entry in the *Oxford Dictionary of National Biography* (2004). See also Maurice Craig, 'James Fergusson', in John Summerson (ed.), *Concerning Architecture* (1968); Nicholas Pevsner's chapter on him in *Some Architectural Writers of the Nineteenth Century* (1972); Robert Elwall, 'James Fergusson (1808–1886): A Pioneering Architectural Historian', in *Royal Society of Arts Journal*, vol. 139 (May 1991); John Mackenzie, *Orientalism* (1995), pp. 95–6; Mark Crinson, *Empire Building: Orientalism and Victorian Architecture* (1996), pp. 42–8; and Thomas R. Metcalf, 'Architecture in the British Empire', in Robin W. Winks, *Oxford History of the British Empire*, vol. 5, *Historiography* (1999), pp. 584–7. Perhaps surprisingly, Fergusson does not feature in Edward Said's *Orientalism* (1978).

43 Listed above, p. 169, n. 47.

44 This is also reproduced in John Physick and Michael Darby, '*Marble Halls': Drawings and Models for Victorian Secular Buildings* (Victoria and Albert Museum, exhibition catalogue,

1973), p. 41, and as plate 11 here. The motto under which it was entered in the competition – 'Dulcius ex Asperis' – is mangled in the (unofficial) catalogue of the Westminster Hall exhibition to read 'Dulcis exeas peria'; and the catalogue's longer description, taken from the *Morning Advertiser*, does not seem to fit the drawing exactly.

45 Fergusson was one of a 'committee' of three (the others were the Classical architects C. R. Cockerell and William Burn) whom Palmerston called in to advise him on the design, hoping they would hate it: but they didn't. *Saturday Review*, 28 July 1860.

46 James Fergusson, *Illustrations of the Rock-Cut Temples of India* (London: John Weale, 1845); *Picturesque Illustrations of Ancient Architecture in Hindustan* (London: Hogarth, 1847).

47 Thomas Metcalf regards his belief in the 'decline' of Indian architecture since the (European) Middle Ages as a typically 'Orientalist' trope, which it certainly was; but Fergusson thought this of European architecture too. Metcalf, 'Architecture in the British Empire', p. 585.

48 Fergusson, *Archaeology in India, with Reference to the Works of Babu Rajendralala Mitra* (London: Trübner & Co.,1884), p. vi; and cf. *A History of Indian and Eastern Architecture* (1876, but mainly re-worked from his *Illustrated Handbook*, 1855), vol. 1, pp. 350–1; vol. 2, pp. 176, 287 (on 'the ruthless barbarism of our rule'), 312.

49 This is in *Archaeology in India* (1884). Fergusson had previously suggested that the Hindus – like some Middle Eastern nations – might have got the idea of using stone for their buildings from the Greeks. Mitra grotesquely misrepresented this as arguing that Indians were living in mud huts before the Europeans taught them to build in a civilized way: i.e. that they needed European influence to 'civilize' them. This is emphatically not what Fergusson wrote, and, indeed, goes right against his fundamental views of Indian architecture: which were that its styles were entirely indigenous, and superior to Western ones, but, early on, were carried out in wood, which was a better material for their purposes, and probably productive of the most glorious buildings, which had, however, perished because wood was less permanent. That was the advantage of stone. Whether the Indians got the idea of using stone from the Greeks was unimportant, and he was not at all dogmatic about it. One can understand Fergusson's irritation at Mitra's misrepresentation here; unfortunately, however, his response went way beyond the measured reply it seemed to call for. Attributing Mitra's libels to his nationalism, he used the incident to launch an attack on the Ilbert Bill, of all things (which would have allowed Europeans to be tried by Indian magistrates); it was no wonder, he argued, that Britons were worried about being judged by Bengalis when the latter could behave as Mitra had to him. Mitra's charge is in *Proceedings of the Asiatic Society*, January 1871, p. 17; Fergusson's response in the *Indian Antiquary*, January 1873, pp. 28–9.

50 Fergusson, *Rude Stone Monuments in All Countries: Their Ages and Uses* (London: John Murray, 1872).

51 From his appendix to *The Modern Styles of Architecture* (1862).

52 *Illustrated Handbook*, vol. 1 (1855), p. 130.

53 See below, p. 105.

54 *The Study of Indian Architecture* (1867), paper read to the Society of Arts, December 1866, pp. 14, 22.

55 These were the famous brothers O'Shea, sculptors, who, however, fell out of favour with the Oxford authorities by carving monkeys and cats on the corbels, and then – when told off for this – giving them the faces of members of Convocation.

56 Edward Bottoms, 'The Royal Architectural Museum in the Light of New Documentary Evidence', in *Journal of the History of Collections*, vol. 19 (2007), p. 123.

57 Tim Barringer, *Men at Work: Art and Labour in Victorian Britain* (2005), ch. 5. On this, see also Metcalf, 'Architecture in the British Empire', p. 591.

58 Fergusson, *A History of Indian and Eastern Architecture* (1876), vol. 1, pp. 418–19; vol. 2, pp. 163, 181, 324. The quotation is from vol. 2, p. 181.

59 Magdalen College, Oxford, that is. Christ Church Episcopal church in New Haven (1898) – not strictly a part of Yale University, but surrounded by it – and Mitchell Tower in Chicago (1903), are close copies, though slightly shorter. Yale and Chicago also both have versions of the 'Boston Stump' in Lincolnshire: Harkness Memorial Tower at Yale (1921) and the Victor Lawson Tower at Chicago (1928). These are all extraordinarily late, of course.

60 See below, p. 120.

61 The most celebrated of his Continental European buildings was the Nikolaikirche in Hamburg, begun in 1846, but destroyed in World War II.

62 D. C. McCaskie, 'Cultural Encounters: Britain and Africa in the Nineteenth Century', Andrew Porter (ed.), *Oxford History of the British Empire*, vol. 3, *The Nineteenth Century* (1999), p. 665.

63 The literature on British colonial architecture is fairly extensive, and includes Jan Morris with Simon Winchester, *Stones of Empire: The Buildings of the Raj* (1983); Jan Morris and R. Fermor-Hesketh (eds), *Architecture of the British Empire* (1986); Thomas Metcalf, *An Imperial Vision: Indian Architecture and the British Raj* (1989); and Mark Crinson, *Empire Building: Orientalism and Victorian Architecture* (1996).

64 Also to link it to French libertarianism – its has many French features – and to distinguish it from Washington imperial.

65 Metcalf, 'Architecture in the British Empire', p. 590.

66 Probably since Britain declared her independence from *them* by joining the European Common Market in the early 1970s. The 'colonial subject' myth has gained ground powerfully, however; I have an Australian friend who is convinced that 'we' (the British) are to blame for the fact that she was only able to study British history at school, whereas in fact, of course, it was the Australians' own choice. On this, see James Belich, *Replenishing the Earth: The Settler Revolution and the Rise of the Angloworld* (Oxford: Oxford University Press, 2009), pp. 462ff.

67 W. J. Cockburn Muir, *Pagan or Christian? Notes for the General Public on Our National Architecture* (1860), p. 242.

68 *Building News*, 16 September 1859, p. 834. (Reporting a lecture by one John Bell.)

69 In this connection the *Ecclesiologist* magazine made the interesting suggestion in the 1840s that the version of Gothic translated to New Zealand should be the Norman, on the grounds that its simplicity, massiveness and 'grotesque' sculpture would suit 'native' tastes better; the implications being that 'native' – presumably Maori – society could be considered on the same level as English eleventh–twelfth century; and that 'in course of time the natives would develop a First and Second Pointed style' from that. See Basil Clarke, *Church Builders*, p. 81.

On the other hand it has to be said that leading English architects of the mid-nineteenth century often seem to have taken offence when colonial clients of theirs dared to adapt their – metropolitan-produced – designs in accordance with local needs or tastes. Butterfield for example was continually scrapping with the Melbourne church authorities over his great St Paul's Cathedral there: though in that case one cannot help wishing he had been given his way a little more, especially with the western towers, eventually completed in a style totally incongruous with the rest. And Scott was reported to have told one of his New Zealand correspondents 'with many bitter complaints, that his plans for churches in the colonies were constantly altered'. See Jonathan Mane-Wheoki, 'Colonial Brick and Marble: High Victorian Gothic in the Antipodes', in *Victorian Gothic: Papers Delivered at the Australian Victorian Association Conference held at the University of Sydney, February 1992*, p. 159.

70 The plans and elevations for this, designed by W. Slater, are reproduced in the Ecclesiological Society's *Instrumenta Ecclesiastica*, vol. 2 (1858) (pages unnumbered). Henry-Russell Hitchcock claims that this whole project was stymied when the English bishops refused to consecrate the churches, but provides no precise reference for this: *Architecture: Nineteenth and Twentieth Centuries* (1958), p. 188. On the use of iron more generally, see below, pp. 102–3.

71 George L. Hersey, *High Victorian Gothic: A Study in Associationism* (1972), p. 48.

72 Tim Barringer, *Men at Work*, p. 276.

73 See Preeti Chopra (University of Wisconsin-Madison), 'Decoding Victorian Bombay: The Construction of Meaning by the City's Local Inhabitants'; unpublished paper delivered to the NAVSA Conference on the Arts and Culture in Victorian Britain, November 2008, and reproduced with her permission.

74 Chris Brooks, *The Gothic Revival* (1999), p. 377.

75 On the first of these possibilities, I am familiar with and I think sensitive to, 'coded' references, and have found hardly any of them. In fact the only reason why people might have used codes in this connection would be that imperialism was a matter of controversy: certainly not 'accepted without saying', therefore.

76 Morris, 'Symbols of Empire', p. 12.

77 This refers to T. E. Collcutt's Imperial Institute in South Kensington, 1887–93 (now demolished apart from the tower); and to the 'Imperial Monumental Halls and Tower' that were designed by J. P. Seddon and E. B. Lamb in 1904, to stand in Westminster, but never erected. Examples of 'Edwardian Baroque' are Selfridges store in west London, and the George V Galleries of the British Museum. On the first two, see G. Alex Bremner, '"Some Imperial Institute": Architecture, Symbolism, and the Ideal of Empire in Late-Victorian Britain, 1887–93', *Journal of the Society of Architectural Historians*, vol. 62 (2003); and '"Imperial monumental halls and tower": Westminster Abbey and the Commemoration of Empire, 1854–1904', in *Architectural History*, vol. 347 (2004), pp. 251–82.

78 The only examples I have found are later, such as the (present) Royal College of Organists (1870) near the Albert Hall, in an Egyptian style. Orientalisms were used, we know, for venues of cheap entertainment, like the very 'Saracenic' Royal Panopticon in Leicester Square (1854); which says volumes about the popular perception of them, and explains why so few of them survive. See John MacKenzie, *Orientalism: History, Theory and the Arts* (1995), ch. 4; and John Sweetman, *The Oriental Obsession: Islamic Inspiration in British and American Art and Architecture 1500–1920* (1988), ch. 5.

79 Below, Ch. 8.

Notes to Chapter 6: The Lamp of Morality

1 'Earnestness' is Henry-Russell Hitchcock's word, in *Early Victorian Architecture in Britain* (1954), p. 13.

2 'You are to be in all things regulated and governed by fact. . . . You must discard the word Fancy altogether. You must have nothing to do with it. You are not to have, in any object of use or ornament, what would be a contradiction in fact. You don't walk upon flowers in fact; you cannot be allowed to walk upon flowers in carpets. You don't find that foreign birds and butterflies come and perch upon your crockery; you cannot be permitted to paint foreign birds and butterflies upon your crockery': Charles Dickens, *Hard Times* (1854; 1907 Everyman edn), p. 6. On real-life Gradgrinds, see Robert Gilmour, 'The Gradgrind School: Political Economy in the Classroom', in *Victorian Studies*, vol. 2 (1967), pp. 207–24.

3   Pugin, *The True Principles of Pointed or Christian Architecture* (1841), p. 59.

4   Ruskin, *The Stones of Venice* (1852), abridged version, ed. J. G. Links (2001), 215–21.

5   See my '"Monstrous Vandalism": Capitalism and Philistinism in the Works of Samuel Laing (1780–1868)', in *Albion*, vol. 23 (1991), pp. 253–68.

6   *Blackwood's Magazine,* August 1836, p. 352. It should be noted, however, that Ruskin was not absolutely against 'pleasure', so long as it was earned: *The Seven Lamps of Architecture* (2nd edn, 1880), p. 119, and *Stones of Venice*, pp. 25–6; and felt comfortable with 'fantasy', insofar as it was a product of the 'imagination', and not of deceit: *Stones of Venice*, p. 64, and *Seven Lamps*, pp. 32–3.

7   Reginald Turnor, *Nineteenth Century Architecture in Britain* (1950), p. 63.

8   Henry-Russell Hitchcock, 'High Victorian Gothic', in *Victorian Studies*, vol. 1 (1957), p. 50.

9   G. E. Street, 'The True Principles of Architecture', in *Ecclesiologist*, vol. 13 (June 1852), p. 252; and cf. A. W. N. Pugin, *An Apology for the Revival of Christian Architecture* (1843), p. 4.

10   See Geoffrey Scott, *The Architecture of Humanism* (1914; repr. 1961), p. 33; and Kenneth Clark, *The Gothic Revival*, pp. 102, 192.

11   Early in his career Scott produced a few Classical buildings – some conventional Georgian terraces, for example, and several severely Classical workhouses; but that was before he had seen the light. See David Cole, *The Work of Sir Gilbert Scott* (1980), pp. 6, 12.

12   Above, p. 11.

13   Edward Freeman was a partial exception; a passionate Goth, yet insisting that one's choice *among* Gothic variants was 'surely a matter of taste', and that acknowledgement of Gothic's superiority did not require rejecting all non-Gothic buildings, including even the much despised St Paul's Cathedral (London), which he held to be 'a great work', albeit mainly because of its mediaeval features, like its plan. *A History of Architecture* (1849), pp. xiv, 10, 446.

14   Above, p. 39

15   Above, p. 10.

16   Below, p. 91.

17   J. H. Parker, lecture to the Oxford Architectural Society, 9 February 1858, reprinted in *Gentleman's Magazine*, vol. 206 (1859), p. 278; and cf. E. A. Freeman at a meeting of the Oxford Architectural Society, 18 June 1857, reported in the *Ecclesiologist*, vol. 18 (August 1857), p. 246: 'He spoke of the Houses of Parliament as so many walls erected according to Palladian rules and on a Palladian plan, with pieces of Gothic stolen from Henry VII's chapel nailed on to them.' The 'Classicism' of the building can be read, presumably, in its horizontal lines, and the symmetry of its river front, which Pugin – Barry's collaborator – is supposed then to have merely decorated; but these are dramatically offset by the towers and spires, one of which, the famous clock tower (housing 'Big Ben'), was almost certainly designed in outline by Pugin. See Rosemary Hill, *God's Architect: Pugin and the Building of Romantic Britain* (2007), pp. 481–2.

18   For example Anon., 'The Architecture of the Palaces of Administration', in *Building News*, 20 February 1857, p. 181; and William Tite, address to the RIBA reported in the *Daily News*, 9 November 1855, p. 2.

19   It was while working at Covent Garden that he got his future first wife pregnant, possibly in one of the boxes where he sometimes slept while working late (speculates Hill, in *God's Architect*, p. 93); and probably contracted syphilis (*ibid.*, p. 151). He may have sired another illegitimate child a few years later, in 1843 (*ibid.*, pp. 278–9).

20   James Fergusson, *History of the Modern Styles of Architecture* (1862), p. 318, fn.

21   J. H. Parker, in *Gentleman's Magazine*, vol. 206 (1859), p. 278.

22   In the *Building News*'s survey of the various competition entries in its issue of 15 May 1857, p. 474, there is the suggestion that one of the French entries, no. 162, a ground plan, was 'partly the work of a lady, who may have contributed the forcible element in the union' (!); but the only evidence offered for this is 'the handwriting of the motto'. I think I can detect humour here; or maybe it is a reference to the French*man's* femininity – a common stereotype.

23   See plate 12.

24   Reported in *Builder*, 24 July 1858, p. 499.

25   *Builder*, 2 January 1858, p. 154.

26   *Building News*, 29 June 1860, p. 511; *Builder*, 24 July 1858, p. 499.

27   *Building News*, 29 June 1860, p. 511; and G. E. Street lecture reported in *Builder*, 19 May 1860, p. 308.

28   On the gendered associations of architecture generally, see George L. Hersey, *High Victorian Gothic: A Study in Associationism* (1972), pp. 48–50; and Chris Brooks, *The Gothic Revival* (1999), p. 319.

29   Above, p. 3.

30   In the eighteenth century 'Gothic' had widely been regarded as 'emotional' and 'sensual', conventionally seen as 'feminine' qualities; Classic as 'rational' and 'intellectual'. See Peter Collins, *Changing Ideals in Modern Architecture 1750–1950* (1965), p. 40. Maybe the new insistence on Gothic's 'masculinity' was an attempt to counter that.

31   Examples of the use of the 'm'-word to celebrate Gothic architecture are Rev J. L. Petit, lecture on 'Originality of Design in Architecture', reported in *Jackson's Oxford Journal*, 31 March 1855; 'ERH', 'Classic or Gothic', in *Building News*, 29 May 1857, p. 547; Anon., 'The Great G.O. Affair', in *Building News*, 21 August 1857, p. 875; G. G. Scott, 'On the Present Position and Future Prospects of the Revival of Gothic Architecture', in *Associated Architectural Societies Reports and Papers*, vol. 4 (1857–58), p. 75; 'A Cambridge Man', *The New Palaces of Administration* (1857), p. 19; A. F. B. Beresford Hope, *The Common Sense of Art* (1858), p. 21, and a lecture on this subject reported in *Builder*, 11 December 1858, pp. 830–1; Parker letter in *Builder*, 1 January 1859, p. 5; W. J. Cockburn Muir, *Pagan or Christian?* (1860), p. 277.

      'Manliness' had different meanings and associations in the nineteenth century from today. Here is one definition, by Dean Church of St Paul's, from a little later in the century. 'Under the virtues of *Manliness* I mean those that belong to a serious estimate of the uses, the capacities, the call of human life; the duty of hard work; the value and jealousy for true liberty; independence of soul, deep sense of responsibility, and strength not to shrink from it, steadiness, endurance, perseverance; the power of sustaining cheerfully disappointment and defeat; the temper not to make much of trifles, whether vexations or pleasures. I include that great self-commanding power, to which we give the name of moral courage, which makes a man who knows and measures all that his decision involves not afraid to be alone against numbers; not afraid, when he knows that he is right, of the consciousness of the disapprobation of his fellows, of the face, the voice, the frown, the laugh, of those against him; moral courage, by which a man holds his own judgement, if reason and conscience bid him, against his own friends, against his own side, and of which, perhaps, the highest form is that by which he is able to resist, not the sneers and opposition of the bad, but the opinion and authority of the good.' It comes from W. R. W. Stephens (ed.), *The Life and Letters of Edward A Freeman*, vol. 2 (London: MacMillan, 1865), p. 463; to which I was led by J. Mordaunt Crook, *The Architect's Secret* (2003), p. 73.

32   For example, Ruskin, *The Stones of Venice*, abridged edn (2001), pp. 142, 145, 169; and *Seven Lamps of Architecture* (1880 edn), p. 171.

33   *Stones of Venice*, p. 71.

34   Ruskin, *The Stones of Venice*, abridged edn (2001), p. 142.

35   David Cole, *The Work of Sir Gilbert Scott* (1980), p. 42.

36   Beresford Hope, *The Common Sense of Art*, p. 20.

37   Ruskin, *Stones of Venice*, pp. 57, 61.

38   E.g. Anon., 'The New Houses of Parliament', in *Edinburgh Review*, April 1837, pp. 175, 177; *Building News*, 20 February 1857, p. 177; and Reverend Charles Boutell, lecture on the 'Government Buildings Competition', reported in *ibid.*, 12 June 1857, p. 597; J. H. Parker, 'The New Foreign Office', in *Gentleman's Magazine*, vol. 206 (February 1859), pp. 175, 199; and Anon., 'Lord Palmerston and the Designs for the Foreign Office', in *ibid.*, vol. 207 (November 1859), p. 473

39   A point made by Papworth at a meeting of the RIBA, 23 February 1857: *Papers Read at the Royal Institute of British Architects, Session 1856–7* (1857), p. 101.

40   See 'FAM', 'The Gothic Controversy', in *Builder*, 26 December 1857, p. 761; and cf. Montalembert quoted at the beginning of ch. 2 of Pugin's *Contrasts* (2nd edn, 1841), p. 8.

41   As Geoffrey Scott fairly pointed out, 'We may doubt whether the inspired Gothic craftsmen of that socialist Utopia ever existed in the Middle Ages. No historical proof of his existence is advanced.' *The Architecture of Humanism*, p. 141.

42   A. W. Pugin, *Contrasts* (1841 edn), the fourteenth full-page illustration (which are unnumbered), reproduced here, as plate 30. Indeed, the 'contrast' was starker than that, with the modern poorhouse resembling a Benthamite 'panopticon', and the mediaeval version more like an Oxford college.

43   Ruskin, *Stones of Venice*, pp. 213, 221, 223–4; and cf. his *Crown of Wild Olive* (1866), lecture 2.

44   Pugin, *True Principles*, pp. 21, 33.

45   Quoted in Peter Ferriday, 'The Revival: Stories Ancient and Modern', in *Architectural Review*, vol. 121 (1957), p. 155.

46   For examples of anti-industrial capitalism, see Pugin, *Contrasts*, pp. 48–50; Ruskin, *Seven Lamps*, pp. 11, 21, 210–11: the last passage recommending a return to craftsmanship as a solution to the problem of unemployment.

47   Ruskin, *Seven Lamps*, pp. 148, 165, 169, 173; *Stones of Venice* (abridged), pp. 152, 156–7; and cf. Rev Thomas Hugo, lecture on 'The Application of Gothic Architecture to Civil and Domestic Purposes', reported in *Builder*, 7 February 1857, p. 76.

48   G. E. Street, 'The True Principles of Architecture', lecture printed in *Ecclesiologist*, vol. 13 (June 1852), p. 262. And cf. Ruskin, *Seven Lamps*, pp. 145–6 and 155, which come close to this; and p. 24, fn.: 'No rascal will ever build a pretty building'; and Basil Clarke, *Church Builders of the Nineteenth Century* (1938), p. 69.

49   Looking at bad buildings, by contrast, encouraged 'improbity, sensuality, and falsehood'. [Coventry Patmore], 'London Street Architecture', in *National Review*, vol. 5, July 1857, p. 69.

50   This of course was the old traditional picture of the Middle Ages, indicated by the frequent use of words like 'barbarism' and the 'dark ages' to describe them, which are too many to require citing, but which can be found, for example, in nearly all Palmerston's speeches on this issue. A good contemporary elaboration of it can be found in Anon., *Remarks on a National Style in Reference to the Proposed Foreign Office* (1860), pp. 10–11.

51   E.g. Coningham, in House of Commons, 4 August 1859, in *Hansard*, 3rd series, vol. 155, col. 941.

52   *Edinburgh Review*, vol. 65 (April 1837), p. 175; and cf. *Fraser's Magazine*, vol. 42, August 1850, p. 173; Thomas Goodchild, 'Gothic and Classic', in *Builder*, 10 January 1857, p. 25; and see above, p. 37.

53   Lecture by Kerr, quoting one Villalpanda, reported in *Builder*, 12 May 1860, p. 293.

54   Wightwick, letter in *Builder*, 9 January 1858, p. 25. This is the only example of this argument I have found.

55   See below, p. 99.

56   Lecture by Hugo (who was not an out-and-out anti-Goth) reported in *Builder*, 7 February 1857, p. 77.

57   *Fraser's Magazine*, vol. 28 (November 1843), p. 600. In fairness it should be pointed out that Pugin was just as scathing about 'castellated mansions', for example in *True Principles* p. 58, which carries a deliberately ridiculous sketch of one.

58   *Chambers's Edinburgh Journal*, vol. 9 (1848), p. 234.

59   *Building News*, 26 June 1857, p. 652.

60   Thomas Goodchild, 'Gothic and Classic', in *Builder*, 10 January 1857, p. 25. Sedilia were seats for the clergy.

61   For example, the *Ecclesiologist*, 1846, pp. 11–13.

62   Michael Bright, *Cities Built to Music: Aesthetic Theories of the Victorian Gothic Revival* (1984), p. 103.

63   'Trickery and dishonesty', however, comes in the previous chapter, p. 24.

64   G. G. Scott, *Remarks on Secular and Domestic Architecture* (1857), p. 235.

65   Pugin, *True Principles*, p. 8. He objected even more to the huge brick cone between the two domes, which is entirely hidden.

66   Of course it could be argued that Classical could reflect function too. Tite, for example, as a member of the 'Classical' deputation that waited on Palmerston in August 1859, claimed that a Classical palace looked essentially more palace-*like* than a Gothic one ever could: reported in *Daily News*, 20 August 1859; and an anonymous piece in the *Building News*, 20 February 1857, p. 180, maintained that the sizes of the windows in Palladian villas expressed the purposes of the rooms behind them perfectly, with tiny attic ones, for example, denoting 'servants'.

67   *Building News*, 20 February 1857, p. 180.

68   Nikolaus Pevsner quotes some precedents in *The Sources of Modern Architecture and Design* (1968), pp. 9–10.

69   The very early origins of this idea are discussed in Pat Anderson, 'The Other Gothic Revival: Contemporary Ideals in English Revivalism, 1730–1840', in *Canadian Journal of History*, vol. 22 (April 1987), pp. 1–8. The earliest convincing example cited there (p. 6) is an article by the antiquarian James Anderson, published in 1800.

70   Pugin, *True Principles*, p. 1; and cf. Edward Buckton Lamb, *Studies of Ancient Domestic Architecture* (1846), p. 9.

71   Number two in *The Seven Lamps*. Cf. G. E. Street, 'The Principles of Architecture', in *Ecclesiologist*, vol. 13 (June 1852), p. 248: 'There is . . . one grand principle at the foundation of art . . . and this principle, or law, is that of truth.'

72   Ruskin, *Seven Lamps*, p. 66. Ruskin credits Robert Willis's *Remarks on the Architecture of the Middle Ages* (1835) with making the decisive breakthrough here. Pat Anderson, 'The Other Gothic Revival', cites other early nineteenth-century precedents.

73   See above, p. 36.

74   Charles Eastlake credited this 'discovery', of the connection between style and structure
     in Gothic, to A. Bartholomew, in *On the Decline of Excellence in the Structure and Science of
     Modern English Buildings* (1842); cited in Eastlake, *A History of the Gothic Revival* (1872),
     pp. 214–15.

75   Ruskin, *Stones of Venice* (abridged), p. 149; Ruskin's italics.

76   E.g. *Building News*, 16 September 1859, p. 834, and 3 February 1860, p. 161; E. A. Freeman
     letter to *The Times*, 19 October 1859; and a lecture by Street reported in *Builder*, 19 May
     1860, p. 308.

77   See, for example, Pugin in the *Dublin Review*, May 1841, p. 318, and February 1842, p. 137;
     Reverend Thomas Hugo, 'The Application of Gothic Architecture to Civil and Domestic
     Purposes', in *Builder*, 7 February 1857, p. 76; 'A Cambridge Man', *The New Palaces of
     Administration* (1857), pp. 19, 21; Anon., *The Gothic Renaissance* (1860), pp. 15, 18; Francis E.
     Scott, *Shall the New Foreign Office be Gothic or Classic?* (1860), p. 16; and, for 'common sense',
     J. P. Seddon lecture reported in *Building News*, 29 January 1858, pp. 109, 112; Scott reported
     in *Builder*, 11 February 1860, p. 83; and (though he did not claim this quality for Gothic
     exclusively) James Fergusson, *History of the Modern Styles of Architecture* (1862), pp. 30, 299,
     329, 417, 490.

78   Reported in *Builder*, 11 February 1860, pp. 82–5, 18 February 1860, pp. 99–100, and 3
     March 1860, pp. 131–2. These lectures give the fullest account of the 'structural' explanation
     and justification for the Gothic style; fuller and better argued than in, for example, Pugin.
     'Occult' appears on p. 83.

79   On symmetry, see Ruskin, *Stones of Venice* (abridged), p. 149.

80   See, for example, Pevsner, *The Sources of Modern Architecture*, ch. 1. The other major 'Gothic'
     influence is supposed to have been the far more 'rationalist' (that is, secular) French Gothic
     theorist, Eugène-Emmanuel Viollet-le-Duc; on whom see John Summerson, 'Viollet-le-
     Duc and the Rational Point of View', in *Heavenly Mansions* (1949).

81   See, for example, Gilbert Scott's definition, quoted in the *Oxford English Dictionary*:
     'Architecture, as distinguished from mere building, is the decoration of construction.' Cf.
     also Ruskin, *Seven Lamps*, pp. 8–9, and *Stones of Venice*, p. 21; and James Fergusson, *On A
     National Collection of Architectural Art* (1857), p. 7. Fergusson's definition, however, does give
     a place to sheer proportion. 'Any building … may become an object of architecture by a
     slight rearrangement or grouping of its parts so as to give some evidence of design, and by
     the addition of ornament.' One assumes that the 'and' there is crucial. And Edward Freeman
     hints occasionally at a non-decorative definition; for example: 'building and architecture are
     totally distinct … the one is a matter of bricks and mortar, strains and pressures; the other
     of grace, harmony, and proportion': *A History of Architecture* (1849), p. 6.

82   See Bright, *Cities Built to Music*, p. 252.

83   Pugin, *True Principles*, p. 42.

84   Ruskin, *Seven Lamps*, pp. 184–5; and see above, [Ch. 4].

85   '[A]ll noble ornamentation was the expression of man's delight in God's work': Ruskin,
     Stones of Venice, p. 83.

86   See Bright, *Cities Built to Music*, p. 161, on the peculiarity of the nineteenth-century idea
     of 'nature'.

87   G. E. Street, *An Urgent Plea for the Revival of True Principles of Architecture in the Public Buildings
     of the University of Oxford* (1853), p. 12.

88   Fidelity to 'nature' is one of the main themes of Ruskin's *Modern Painters* (5 vols, 1843–60),
     and an inspiration to the Pre-Raphaelite Brotherhood, which may not have been give the
     prominence in the present book it deserves.

89   Cole, *The Work of Sir Gilbert Scott*, p. 55.

90   Michael Bright, *Cities Built to Music*, p. 252 (citing 'pigs' snouts'); and Basil Clarke, *Church Builders*, p. 138 (suggesting 'entrails').

91   Ruskin, *Seven Lamps*, pp. 106, 108.

92   Ruskin has a long passage on colour in architecture in the *Seven Lamps*, pp. 138–42. According to him it was okay if it was natural stone (or other materials) that provided the colour; and if it were used without reference to the sculptural forms it incorporated; which would fit most of Butterfield's and Street's stripey work.

93   Ruskin, *Seven Lamps*, pp. 49–50. Scott devotes a chapter (ch. 11) of *Remarks on Secular and Domestic Architecture* to these problems, using roughly the same formula as Ruskin: what matters is 'the *intention to deceive*' (p. 242; original italics).

94   Ruskin, *Seven Lamps*, pp. 196–7. Cf. John W. Papworth, 'On Beauty in Architecture and its Alliance with the Past', lecture of 23 February 1857, reported in *Papers Read at the Royal Institute of British Architects, Session 1856–7* (1857), p. 95.

95   Much of Scott's *Recollections*, but especially ch. 9, discusses his restoration work, seeking to rebuff the charges – usually of *over*-restoration – made against him, and which have largely lasted to the present day, though many of them are unfair, as Cole argues in his *Work of Sir Gilbert Scott*. The most unfair was probably William Morris's comment on Bradford on Avon church: 'scraped to death by G. Scott the (happily) dead dog'. In fact Scott had had nothing to do with this. *Ibid.*, p. 180.

96   More than half of ch. 2 of the *Seven Lamps* is spent wrestling with these problems, ingeniously.

97   For example, William Tite, 'On the Progress and Present State of Architecture and its Future Prospects', in the *Civil Engineer*, vol. 22 (December 1859), p. 394.

98   E.g. Pugin, 'Ecclesiastical Architecture in England', in *Dublin Review*, vol. 10 (1841), p. 302; and Ruskin, *Lectures on Architecture and Painting* (1854), in E. T. Cook and Alex Wedderburn (eds), *The Complete Works of John Ruskin*, vol. 12 (1904), p. 45.

99   Scott's second Royal Academy Lecture, reported in *Builder*, 3 March 1860, p. 131 (original italics).

100   A Mr Bell, quoted in *Building News*, 16 September 1859, p. 834. Cf. E. W. Godwin in *Builder*, 31 January 1857, p. 60, and again in *Builder*, 28 March 1857, p. 176; Wightwick in *Builder*, 4 July 1857, p. 373; and 'FAM', 'The Gothic Controversy', in *Builder*, 26 December 1857.

101   This is implied in Pugin's emphasis on structure and function, rather than directly stated. See his *Apology*, p. 22; Hill, *God's Architect*, pp. 280–2; and Phoebe B. Stanton, 'Pugin: Principles of Design *versus* Revivalism', in *Journal of the Society of Architectural Historians*, vol. 13 (1954). Alf Bøe speculates that, had he lived, these principles might have led him to beat 'a completely new track', away from Gothic: *From Gothic Revival to Functional Form* (Oslo, 1957), p. 18.

      Ruskin did not go this far. He was equally insistent that the 'spirit' of the style was an essential feature, but could never conceive of that divorced from the pointed arch. See *Stones of Venice*, pp. 141, 158–9. Edward Freeman also thought pointed arches were a *sine qua non* of Gothic: *History of Architecture*, p. 302.

102   *The Times*, 6 August 1859. And cf. 'A Cambridge Man' [A. J. Beresford-Hope], *The New Palaces of Administration: An Earnest Appeal to the Competitors, the Public and the Committee* (1857), p. 191; Coventry Patmore, 'Gothic Architecture: Present and Future', in *North British Review*, May 1858, pp. 357, 360; Pugin, *An Apology*, pp. 37–9.

103   See below, p. 91.

104   J. P. Seddon, 'Ancient and Modern Architectural Ornament Contrasted', in *Building News*, 29 January 1858, p. 112.

105 See Robert Macleod, *Style and Society: Architectural Ideology in Britain 1835–1914* (1971), pp. 19–21

106 The anti-spying ethos is exemplified in my *Plots and Paranoia: A History of Political Espionage in Britain 1790–1988* (London: Unwin Hyman, 1989), ch. 5.

107 That is, the English (by which he may have meant the British), French, Germans and Danes (which was probably intended to cover all Scandinavians). Ruskin, *Seven Lamps*, p. 34; *Stones of Venice*, pp. 150, 155.

108 Ruskin, *Seven Lamps*, p. 35.

109 See J. H. Parker's letter in *Builder*, 1 January 1959, p. 5; and lecture on 'English Domestic Architecture', delivered to the Oxford Architectural Society, 9 February 1859, and reported in *Gentleman's Magazine*, vol. 206 (1859), p. 279; Rev Boutell lecture reported in *Builder*, 23 May 1857, p. 283; E. A. Freeman, letter to *The Times*, 19 October 1859, and article in *National Review*, January 1860, pp. 26, 34–6.

110 Ruskin, *Stones of Venice, passim*; Street, *An Urgent Plea for the Revival of True Principles of Architecture* (1853).

111 Muir, *Pagan or Christian?* p. 235.

112 Capes in *Rambler*, November 1859, p. 88.

113 [Coventry Patmore], review of Scott's *Remarks on Secular and Domestic Gothic*, in *North British Review*, vol. 28 (May 1858), p. 352.

114 Quoted in *Fraser's Magazine*, August 1850, pp. 165–6.

115 G. E. Street, *An Urgent Plea*, p. 16.

116 Scott's advocacy of 'Middle Pointed' is to be found in his 'On the Present Position and Future Prospects of the Revival of Gothic Architecture', in *Associated Architectural Societies Reports and Papers*, vol. 4 (1857–8), pp. 82–3, and *Remarks on Secular and Domestic Gothic* (1857) pp. 14, 16–17. Pugin and Ruskin, though they started from different positions (Perpendicular and Venetian) originally, both ended up in the thirteenth century eventually (see Hill, *God's Architect*, p. 227; Ruskin, *Seven Lamps*, p. 208); and a majority of the leading Goths stayed there for at least a couple of decades afterwards. See, for example, Beresford Hope quoted in the *Ecclesiologist*, vol. 7 (March 1847), p. 88; G. E. Street, *An Urgent Plea for the Revival of the True Principles of Architecture* (1853), *passim*; J. H. Parker, letter to *Builder*, 1 January 1859, p. 5; E. A. Freeman, letter to *The Times*, 19 October 1859, p. 10; and W. J. Cockburn Muir, *Pagan or Christian?* (1860), p. 249.

117 [Richard Simpson], 'The Development of Gothic Architecture', in *Rambler*, vol. 24, May 1859, p. 80. He probably got this from Ruskin, *Stones of Venice*, p. 207.

118 Street, 'How is the Revival to be Pursued?', in *Builder*, 8 January 1859, p. 24.

119 Ruskin paper delivered at the Architectural Museum, 13 January 1858, reported in *Builder*, 16 January, p. 46.

120 Peter Collins, *Changing Ideals in Modern Architecture 1750–1950* (1965), pp. 208, 212.

121 Bright, *Cities Built to Music*, p. 70.

122 *Building News*, 16 September 1859, p. 834; and see above, p. 00.

123 William White in *Builder*, 14 February 1857, p. 90. It is clear from the context that he means 'Catholic' in the basic, not sectarian, sense.

124 Above, pp. 74–5.

125 *Builder*, 16 January 1858, p. 46 (italics added).

126 Above, p. 32.

127 For example, G. G. Scott, 'On the Present Position and the Future Prospects of the Revival of Gothic Architecture', paper published in *Associated Architectural Societies Reports and Papers*, vol. 4 (1857–8), p. 81, and his *Remarks on Secular and Domestic* (1857) pp. viii, 17, 21–2; [E. A.

Freeman], 'The Foreign Office, Classic or Gothic', in *National Review*, vol. 10 (January 1860), p. 32; and W. J. Cockburn Muir, *Pagan or Christian?* (1860), pp. 230–7.

128   'Verax' in *Builder*, 28 November 1857, p. 693.

129   See Palmerston in House of Commons, 11 February 1859, in *Hansard*, 3rd series, vol. 152, cols 271–2, and in a letter to Scott, 26 July 1859, BL Add. MS 48581, ff. 13–14. The same point (roughly) was made by Coningham in the House of Commons, 18 February 1859, *Hansard*, 3rd series, vol. 152, col. 522; *Builder*, 4 July 1857, p. 371; the architect Robert Smirke as a member of the notorious 'Classical' delegation to Palmerston, reported in the *Daily News*, 20 August 1859; and the *Globe*, 12 February 1859: 'where is all this to stop?'

130   *Daily Telegraph*, 22 February 1859.

131   Joseph Jopling letter in *Building News*, 2 September 1859, p. 803.

Notes to Chapter 7: An Architecture for our Age

1   Donaldson addressing a meeting of the Architectural Association, quoted in John Summerson, *Heavenly Mansions* (1949), p. 195. Donaldson was emeritus professor of architecture at University College, London.

2   In House of Commons, 4 August 1859: *Hansard*, 3rd series, vol. 155, col. 931; and his reply to a Gothic deputation, reported in *Builder*, 6 August 1859, p. 516.

3   William Tite, 'On the Progress and Present State of Architecture, and its Future Prospects', in *Civil Engineer and Architect's Journal*, vol. 22 (December 1859), p. 396.

4   *Household Words*, 15 June 1850, pp. 265–7. Pugin dismissed this as 'a stale trick to raise a temporary laugh among fools at the expense of the advocates of Catholic antiquity, but', he went on, 'it is too hollow to elicit a grin from any but a fool': *Some Remarks on the Articles which have recently appeared in the "Rambler" relative to Ecclesiastical Architecture and Decoration* (1850), p. 7.

5   *Building News*, 26 June 1857, p. 652.

6   *Building News*, 9 November 1860, p. 855.

7   *Building News*, 16 November 1860, p. 876.

8   Scott, *Remarks on Secular and Domestic Architecture* (1857), p. 188.

9   House of Commons, 8 July 1861; *Hansard*, 3rd series, vol. 164, col. 521; and cf. Col Davies in the debates over the new Palace of Westminster 20 years earlier: was it not 'singular', he observed, 'that we, who are giants in all improvements, and have advanced in such a manner, should be pigmies in the erection of our public edifices'? Commons, 14 June 1838, in *Hansard*, 3rd series, vol. 43, col. 705.

10   G. G. Scott, *Remarks on Secular and Domestic Architecture* (1857), p. 188.

11   See above, p. 40. On earlier 'progressive' arguments for Gothic, see Pat Anderson, 'The Other Gothic Revival: Contemporary Ideals in English Revivalism, 1730–1840', in *Canadian Journal of History*, vol. 22 (April 1987).

12   See above, p. 91.

13   Scott, *Remarks on Secular and Domestic Architecture*, p. 202.

14   See, for example, Beresford Hope, quoted in *Ecclesiologist*, March 1847, p. 90; G. E. Street, writing in the *Ecclesiologist*, June 1852, pp. 249–50, 262; Viollet-le-Duc quoted in Anon., *The Gothic Renaissance* (1860), pp. 21–2; E. W. Godwin in *Builder*, 31 January 1857, p. 60; letter to *Builder*, 23 May 1857, p. 284; and Gilbert Scott, *Personal and Professional Recollections* (1879), p. 156.

15   Quoted in Georg Germann, *Gothic Revival in Europe and Britain: Sources, Influences and Ideas* (1972), pp. 124–5, 186. Others, looking back from later, have placed the 'take-off' at other

times. Butterfield's All Saints, Margaret Street (completed in 1859), is a popular candidate. Robert Furneaux Jordan credits Butterfield and Scott together with snapping the umbilical cord between the Middle Ages and neo-Gothic, so enabling 'something new – a Victorian style, a "modern" style, to be born': *Victorian Architecture* (1966), p. 137. H. S. Goodhart-Rendel thought the key building was Street's All Saints, Clifton (1868): 'English Gothic Architecture of the Nineteenth Century' in *Journal of the RIBA*, vol. 31 (1924), p. 335.

16 E.g. Pugin quoted in Hill, *God's Architect*, p. 341; and 'Ecclesiastical Architecture in England', in *Dublin Review*, vol. 10 (May 1841), p. 342; Ruskin, *Stones of Venice* (abridged), p. 225; G. E. Street, 'The True Principles of Architecture', paper published in *Ecclesiologist*, vol. 13 (June 1852), p. 250, and 'How is the Revival to be Pursued?', in *Builder*, 8 January 1859, p. 24; and Beresford Hope in *Ecclesiologist*, March 1847, p. 90.

17 Scott, 'On the Present Position and Future Prospects of the Revival of Gothic Architecture', lecture printed in *Associated Architectural Societies Reports and Papers*, vol. 4 (1857–8), p. 83.

18 See above, p. 40; and David Cole, 'Sir Gilbert Scott', in Peter Ferriday (ed.), *Victorian Architecture* (1963), p. 180.

19 See his letter to *The Times*, 14 February 1859, appealing to 'reformist' MPs on these grounds; and his evidence to a select committee of the House of Commons, cited in the *Building News*, 26 August 1859, p. 767.

20 Buxton in House of Commons, 4 August 1859; *Hansard*, 3rd series, vol. 155, col. 929.

21 For Palmerston's objections to Gothic windows, see above, p. 10. In 1860 Scott spent a good half of his second Royal Academy lecture on this theme: *Builder*, 18 February 1860, pp. 99–100; as well as much of the second version of his *Explanatory Remarks on the Designs for the New Foreign Office* (1860, after the battle had been lost); before returning to it much later in his *Recollections*, pp. 182 *et passim*.

22 Paxton in House of Commons, 4 August 1859; *Hansard*, 3rd series, vol. 155, cols 939–40. Paxton's judgement, as 'a practical man', greatly impressed the *Caledonian Mercury*, 10 August 1859.

23 *Building News*, 25 February 1859, p. 175.

24 Scott, *Remarks on Secular and Domestic Architecture*, p. 270.

25 *Building News*, 12 August 1859, pp. 723–4.

26 Although one needs to bear in mind that for every great cathedral crossing tower still standing, probably one other, at least, was half-built and then collapsed. It was a very 'trial-and-error' system.

27 G. E. Street, 'The True Principles of Architecture and the Possibility of Development', paper read to the Oxford Architectural Society, 18 February 1852, and reproduced in *Ecclesiologist*, June 1852, pp. 249–50; and *An Urgent Plea for the Revival of the True Principles of Architecture in the Public Buildings of the University of Oxford* (1853), p. 4.

28 [Coventry Patmore], review of Scott's *Remarks on Secular and Domestic Architecture*, in *North British Review*, vol. 28 (May 1858), p. 350 (italicized in the original); and cf. his 'London Street Architecture', in *National Review*, vol. 5 (July 1857), pp. 51, 62. In fact it was difficult to deny the superiority of Gothic to Renaissance architecture on these particular (structural engineering) grounds. Geoffrey Scott, for example, the great post-Victorian scourge of the neo-Gothic style, did not try to, simply arguing that this was irrelevant: *The Architecture of Humanism* (1914), p. 99. Among architectural historians I have found only one who downplayed the structural convenience of the pointed arch, claiming that it gave only marginally more strength than the round one: John Summerson, *Heavenly Mansions* (1949), pp. 12–13.

In fact the Goths were wrong, as Thomas Harris (below, p. 102) was one of the few contemporaries to point out. He predicted that the advent of new materials would mean that 'any further development will be towards a trabeated style'; which is what happened. Dudley Harbron, 'Thomas Harris', in *Architectural Review*, vol. 92 (1942), p. 66.

29 Patmore, 'London Street Architecture', in *National Review*, July 1857, p. 71. Patmore, in common with most other architectural writers of his time, seems to have been unaware that Riddarholmskyrkan in Stockholm – where Sweden's royalty are buried – already boasted a cast-iron Gothic spire, erected in 1838–41 to the designs of the sculptor E. G. Göthe, after the original tower had burned down in 1835. The height of that spire is 90 metres (295 feet). See E. W. M. Schürer von Waldheim, *Riddarholmskyrkan* (Stockholm, 1897), pp. 12–14. Rouen Cathedral's 151-metre (495-foot) cast-iron Gothic spire dates from 1876.

There is an interesting essay by Andrew Saint on the application of iron to English neo-Gothic buildings in Jan de Maeyer and Luc Verpoest (eds), *Gothic Revival: Religion, Architecture and Style in Western Europe 1815–1914* (2000); later elaborated in his *Architecture and Engineer: A Study in Sibling Rivalry* (2008).

30 *Ecclesiologist*, vol. 17 (October 1856), pp. 349–52; and see Michael J. Lewis, *The Politics of the German Gothic Revival* (1993), pp. 4 *et passim*.

31 Paul Thompson, 'Architecture: The Problem of Ugliness', in Victorian Society, *The High Victorian Cultural Achievement*, Second Conference Report, (1965), p. 14.

32 Nikolaus Pevsner's coinage, in 'Victorian Prolegomena', in Peter Ferriday (ed.), *Victorian Architecture* (1963), p. 33.

33 *Building News*, 26 June 1857, p. 652 (original italics). See also *Builder*, 23 May 1857, p. 28.

34 *Building News*, 19 August 1859, p. 751 (original italics). All this of course was 'mere' semantics. One of Gilbert Scott's counters to it was to employ the common academic use of the word 'modern', in contradistinction to 'ancient' – 'Gothic' thereby falling in the former category, and 'Classical' in the latter. *Remarks on Secular and Domestic Architecture*, p. 189.

35 *Builder*, 4 July 1857, p. 371. Cf. *Building News*, 27 July 1860, p. 593, and 2 November 1860, p. 835.

36 *Building News*, 5 April 1861, p. 286.

37 *Builder*, 2 January 1848, p. 1.

38 Scott, *Explanatory Remarks* (1860), p. 15.

39 Ian Toplis, *The Foreign Office: An Architectural History* (1987), p. 82.

40 E. M. Dodd, 'Charles Robert Cockerell', in Peter Ferriday (ed.), *Victorian Architecture* (1963), pp. 112–18.

41 Thomas Goodchild, 'Gothic and Classic', in *Builder*, 10 January 1857, p. 25. See also letter from 'Z' in *ibid.*, 17 January 1857, p. 38; George Wightwick, 'Architecture in General, and the Gothic Sect', in *ibid.*, 9 January 1858, p. 25; and E. B. Lamb, quoted in *Building News*, 26 August 1859, p. 775.

42 For example, W. R. Hamilton, *Letter . . . to the Earl of Elgin, on the New Houses of Parliament* (1836), includes Roman with Greek as 'perfect' styles; and Anon., 'The New Houses of Parliament', in *Edinburgh Review*, vol. 65 (1837), p. 175, refers to the Roman as a 'pure' style – while admitting that the Greek was 'yet chaster'.

43 Except in Scotland: see J. Mordaunt Crook, *The Greek Revival* (1972). The best-known Greek Revival building in London, St Pancras Parish Church (H. W. and W. Inwood, 1819–22), stands almost directly opposite Scott's Gothic St Pancras Station Midland Hotel.

44 For example, G. G. Scott, *Explanatory Remarks* (1857), p. 23; Lord John Manners in the Commons, 8 July 1861: *Hansard*, 3rd series, vol. 164, cols 530–1.

45 S. Huggins, reported in *Builder*, 15 May 1858, p. 333.

46 Address to the Midlands Archaeological Association, reported in *Jackson's Oxford Journal*, 26

September 1861. As early as 1840 the *Ecclesiologist* was complaining of the same thing in relation to Pugin, who was not following 'his own early lessons' about 'development', and so on, but still merely copying. Anon., 'The Artistic Merits of Mr Pugin', in *Ecclesiologist*, vol. 5 (1846), pp. 11, 14–16.

47 John Ruskin, *The Seven Lamps of Architecture* (1880 edn), pp. 35, 39–41, 56–7, 174.

48 [Coventry Patmore], 'Gothic Architecture – Present and Future', in *North British Review*, vol. 28 (May 1858), pp. 247–8; above, p. 101. The 1858 article is a generally critical review of Scott's *Remarks on Secular and Domestic Architecture*, which advocated iron.

49 *Ecclesiologist*, vol. 13 (June 1852), p. 248; *Builder* 19 May 1860, p. 308. Those who more consistently favoured the use of iron in modern Gothic architecture included Ambrose Poynter, 'On the Effects which Should Result to Architectural Taste . . . from the General Introduction of Iron . . .', in *Civil Engineer and Architect's Journal*, September 1843, pp. 291–6; Beresford Hope, *Public Offices and Metropolitan Improvements* (1857), pp. 16–17, 22–4, and *The Common Sense of Art* (1858), p. 13; G. G. Scott, 'On the Present Position and Future Prospects of the Revival of Gothic Architecture' (1857), p. 77, and his *Explanatory Remarks* (1857), p. 28; 'Mr Skidmore of Coventry', lecture to Oxford Architectural Society, printed in *Gentleman's Magazine*, vol. 206 (April 1859), pp. 401–2; G. N. Burnell lecture reported in *Building News*, 30 September 1859, p. 881; and (moderately favourable) W. J. Cockburn Muir, *Pagan or Christian? Notes for the General Public* (1860), pp. 260–3.

50 See Barrington Kaye, *The Development of the Architectural Profession in Britain* (1960).

51 See Simon Bradley, *St Pancras Station* (2007).

52 'High Victorianism' is best represented at this time (and indeed, probably for all time) by William Butterfield's All Saints, Margaret Street. There is a modern theory that architects like Butterfield set out to build 'ugly' on purpose; originating in the celebrated review of this building in the *Ecclesiologist*, vol. 20 (1859), pp. 184–9, referring (approvingly) to its 'deliberate ugliness'. See John Summerson, 'William Butterfield, or the Glory of Ugliness', in *Heavenly Mansions* (1949); Paul Thompson, 'The Problem of Ugliness': Victorian Society, on *The High Victorian Cultural Achievement* (1965); Nicholas Taylor, 'The Awful Sublimity of the Victorian City', in H. J. Dyos and Michael Wolff (eds), *The Victorian City: Images and Realities* (1973), vol. 2, esp. p. 434; James Stevens Curl, *Victorian Architecture* (1990), p. 27; and George L. Hersey, *High Victorian Gothic: A Study in Associationism* (1992), pp. xviii, 114. (Hersey calls it 'sado-masochism'.)

53 Anon., 'Classic or Gothic: The Battle of the Styles', in *Blackwood's Magazine*, vol. 41 (March 1862) pp. 287–9.

54 *Builder*, 19 February 1859, p. 125.

55 Anon., 'Philosophy of Architecture', in *Chambers's Journal*, vol. 3 (June 1855), p. 344.

56 This question will be taken up again, however, in Chapter 9.

57 Quoted in Georg Germann, *Gothic Revival*, p. 9.

58 This is mentioned in Michael Bright, *Cities Built to Music: Aesthetic Theories of the Victorian Gothic Revival* (1984), pp. 13–14. See also Pevsner, 'Victorian Prolegomena', pp. 28–9.

59 Peter Collins, *Changing Ideals in Modern Architecture 1750–1950* (1965), pp. 69, 130.

60 Ruskin, *The Seven Lamps of Architecture*, book 8, quoted in Nikolaus Pevsner, 'Victorian Prolegomena', p. 30.

61 Scott, *Remarks on Secular and Domestic Architecture*, pp. 258, 200–1.

62 Thomas Hope, *An Historical Essay on Architecture* (1835), p. 561 (original italics). This book was published after Hope's death in 1831. Nikolaus Pevsner cites some even earlier examples in *Sources of Modern Architecture and Design* (1968), p. 9; and James Stevens Curl some contemporary ones in *Victorian Architecture* (1990), ch. 6, 'New Materials and New Challenges'.

63 Thomas Harris, *Victorian Architecture* (1860), pp. 3–5. On Harris, see Dudley Harbron, 'Thomas Harris', in *Architectural Review*, vol. 92 (1942). He was born in 1830.

64 Jeffrey Auerbach's (otherwise excellent) *The Great Exhibition of 1851* (1999) only has a couple of pages on the building itself (pp. 48–50). It burned down in 1936; but an idea of it can be got from the superb interior of the Museum of Childhood in Bethnal Green, originally built as a temporary 'Victoria and Albert Museum' in the immediate aftermath of the Great Exhibition, and out of its profits, and very reminiscent of the 'Crystal Palace', though smaller. (Information from the museum.)

65 One example is the German architect Gottfried Semper, who was just then living as a political refugee in London, where he developed a new theory of artistic style based on materials, before (much later) building the present, and rather conventional, Dresden Opera House. See Nikolaus Pevsner, *Sources of Modern Architecture and Design*, p. 10. Pevsner also mentions in this context a short-lived *Journal of Design and Manufactures* he was involved with, which essentially advocated 'functionalism' in building. The Crystal Palace also received surprising endorsements from one or two neo-Goths, like Beresford Hope, who regarded it as 'an offshoot of the Gothic Revival': James Stevens Curl, *Victorian Architecture*, p. 210; and Wyatt: Nikolaus Pevsner, *Matthew Digby Wyatt* (1950), pp. 19–20.

66 *Building News*, 19 August 1859, p. 748. Compare the architect George Aitchison's advocacy five years later of mere 'purity of outline and elegance of proportion, with an almost total absence of ornament'; which advice, however, he did not abide by in his own work, and reneged on later. J. Mordaunt Crook, *The Architect's Secret: Victorian Critics and the Image of Gravity* (2003), p. 19. For King's Cross Station, see plate 33.

67 Anon., *Classic or Pseudo-Gothic: A Reply to a Pamphlet entitled 'Shall Gothic Architecture be Denied Fair Play?'* (1860), p. 20.

68 See below, p. 105.

69 See above, Ch. 5.

70 See Lawrance Hurst, 'Concrete and the Structural Use of Cement in England before 1890', in James Sutherland *et al.* (eds), *Historic Concrete: Background to Appraisal* (2001). Forms of concrete had been used for building since Roman times. From the 1860s or 1870s, however, the 'Concrete Building Company' was active in employing it for whole buildings, mainly workers' dwellings (for cheapness), but also including Anerley New Church in south London, close to the relocated Crystal Palace (1883): *ibid.*, p. 59.

71 This is Thomas Harris. See Harbron, 'Thomas Harris', p. 66.

72 Letter from Pickett in the *Ecclesiologist*, vol. 17 (1856), pp. 280–1; which goes on to to accuse the design of dishonesty and of outraging 'decency'. In its original version the letter was so insulting that the *Ecclesiologist*'s editors found it necessary to take certain 'strong epithets' out. On Slater's iron church, see above, p. 182, n. 70.

73 Pickett's main works are *A New System of Architecture* (c. 1845), and *New Forms in Architecture* (1849). Contemporary articles about him include anonymous reviews in the *Westminster Review*, vol. 51 (1849), pp. 104–45, and in the *Edinburgh Review*, vol. 116 (1862), pp. 204–37; and a chapter in John Scoffern *et al.*, *The Useful Metals and their Alloys* (1857), pp. 479–90. There are also modern articles by Peter Collins, 'Metallurgic Architecture 1844', in *Architectural Review*, October 1961, pp. 267–8; and Pedro Guedes, 'William Vose Pickett's Written Architecture', in A. Leach and G. Matthewson (eds), *Celebration: Proceedings of the 22nd Annual Conference of the Society of Architectural Historians, Australia and New Zealand* (2005), pp. 147–53.

74 See the illustrations in Harbron, 'Thomas Harris', pp. 64–5.

75 Anerley New Church, for example, mentioned above (p. 194, n. 70), is described by

Lawrence Hurst, 'Concrete and the Structural Use of Cement in England before 1890', p. 59, as 'neo-Gothic'; and what is probably the last surviving concrete domestic house from this period, in Southwark, dating from 1873, and recently saved from demolition (see *Guardian*, 19 February 2009), looks positively Ruskinian.

76   H. S. Goodhart-Rendel, 'The Victorian Home', in Peter Ferriday (ed.), *Victorian Architecture*, p. 76.

77   Pevsner, 'Victorian Prolegomena', pp. 27–8; and cf. *Sources of Modern Architecture and Design*, p. 18.

78   Summerson, 'London, the Artifact', in Dyos and Wolff (eds), *The Victorian City*, vol. 1 p. 314.

79   Pevsner, *Matthew Digby Wyatt*, p. 24.

80   Robert Furneaux Jordan, 'Sir Joseph Paxton', in Ferriday (ed.), *Victorian Architecture*, p. 161.

81   Henry-Russell Hitchcock, *Architecture: The Nineteenth and Twentieth Centuries* (1958), pp. 169, 186, 189.

82   Peter Collins, *Changing Ideals*, pp. 128, 196–7.

83   [E. A. Freeman], 'The Foreign Office: Classic or Gothic', in *National Review*, vol. 10 (January 1860), p. 41.

84   Kerr lecture, reported in *Builder*, 12 May 1860, p. 294; and cf. the architect John Savage much earlier: 'It is said that every [architectural] thing is already invented; that the age of invention is passed': though he disagreed. This is from his *Observations on Style in Architecture* (1836), p. 27, quoted in Georg Germann, *Gothic Revival*, p. 9.

85   John Stuart Mill, however, had a similar idea about music: that shortly the stock of available melodies would be exhausted. See his posthumous *Autobiography* (1873), ch. 5; in Max Lerner, ed., *Essential Works of John Stuart Mill* (New York: Bantam, 1961), pp. 89–90.

86   Anon., 'The National Style and its Critics', in *Gentleman's Magazine*, vol. 208 (1860), pp. 25–6.

87   Very little was written or known about native American architecture in the 1850s. Fergusson's *Illustrated Handbook of Architecture*, vol. 1 (1855), carries a few pages on it, acknowledging that it was 'an art wholly indigenous and original', and regretting, therefore, that that there were too few surviving examples of it (as he thought) for proper study: p. 144.

88   *An Historical Enquiry into the True Principles of Building in Art* (1849), p. 161. And see his *History of the Modern Styles of Architecture* (1862), p. 488; and cf. Anon., *The Gothic Renaissance* (1860), p. 22.

89   *On a National Collection of Architectural Art* (1857), p. 11. It took the same number of years, he claimed, for the Corinthian capital to evolve from the Egyptian.

90   For example, *Observations of the British Museum, National Gallery and National Record Office* (1849), pp. 39, 66, recommending Marshall's Flax Mill in Leeds in particular.

91   In his *History of the Modern Styles of Architecture* (1862), p. 329, he recommends 'as a "*tertium quid*", a style which, for want of a better name, is sometimes called the Italian, but should be called the common-sense style'. Later he proposed the new (Classical) Palais de Justice in Brussels as a model: 'The Proposed new Cathedral for Liverpool', in *Nineteenth Century*, vol. 16 (1884), pp. 905–6.

92   See above, p. 69.

93   For example, E. B. Lamb: 'by continuing the same spirit which marked the works of preceding ages, we should in a short time work out a style accommodated to our actual requirements, and at the same time marked by aesthetic quality': *Studies of Ancient Domestic Architecture* (1846), p. 5.

94   For example, W. H. Leeds, *An Essay on Modern English Architecture* (1839), which is illustrated
      with drawings of Barry's new Travellers Club; Thomas Harris, *Victorian Architecture*: see above,
      p. 102; and T. Mellard Reade, *On the Foundation of a New Style of Architecture* (n.d.; c. 1862),
      accompanied by drawings of four-square Classical buildings with the occasional Gothic
      tracery in some windows.

95   'Astylism' is common; it is used in many of the descriptions of the Westminster Hall exhibits,
      for example. 'Latitudinarianism' is the word used by *Builder*, 12 May 1860, p. 294, to describe
      W. H. Leeds's approach (which he calls simply 'latitude'), in *An Essay on Modern English
      Architecture* (1839); and by Sir John Summerson, 'London, the Artifact', p. 316. Another
      contemporary term for it was 'the Mixed Style': Pevsner, 'Victorian Prolegomena', p. 31.
      James Stevens Curl, *Victorian Architecture*, pp. 29–31, cites some earlier eclecticists.

96   See Pevsner, 'Victorian Prolegomena', p. 31.

97   See his Hull City Hall, now demolished but illustrated in the *Building News*, 26 September
      1862: mainly Renaissance but topped with a little 'Hindoo' cupola, saved from the original
      building and now standing in a park at the end of my road. This is probably how Fergusson
      saw his '*tertium quid*': Italian Renaissance but with features of other styles added; 'It can use
      either pillars or pinnacles as may be required. It can either indulge in plain walls, or pierce
      them with innumerable wondows. It knows no guide but common sense; it owns no master
      but true taste': *History of the Modern Styles*, p. 329.

98   See, for example, 'Bm Wr' in *Building News*, 30 November 1860, p. 909; and Allom's paper
      reported in *ibid.*, 25 January 1861, p. 77.

99   See his *The Common Sense of Art* (1958); and J. Mordaunt Crook, *The Architect's Secret*, ch. 3.
      Hope owned the *Saturday Review*, and had bankrolled All Saints, Margaret Street.

100 For example, W. H. Leeds, *An Essay on Modern English Architecture;* T. Mellard Reade, *On
      the Foundation of a New Style of Architecture*, and 'A New Style: How can it be Formed?' in
      Builder, 26 July 1862, pp. 537–8; Samuel Huggins, *The Course and Current of Architecture*
      (1863); and Robert Kerr, *The Gentleman's House* (1865). The Gothicist Beresford Hope
      also recommended what he called 'eclecticism' in a lecture at the Architectural Museum
      in December 1858, albeit as a stage they must pass through before they arrived at a new
      common ground: *Builder*, 11 December 1858, pp. 830–1; and see the *Saturday Review*, 22
      January 1869, pp. 96–7.

101 A. W. N. Pugin, *An Apology for the Revival of Christian Architecture* (1843), p. 5.

102 Street reported in *Builder*, 19 May 1860, p. 308.

103 W. J. Cockburn Muir, *Pagan or Christian? Notes for the General Public* (1860), pp. 164, 213

104 Robert Kerr, *The Gentleman's House* (1865), p. 342.

105 *Builder*, 4 July 1857, p. 370.

106 Summerson, *Heavenly Mansions* (1949), p. 198.

107 For 'Queen Anne' see Mark Girouard, *Sweetness and Light: The Queen Anne Movement,
      1860–1900* (New Haven, 1984). This style is generally dated back to the 1870s; but it was
      recommended as early as 1861, as the foundation for a new 'English' architecture, by the
      Reverend J. L. Petit, in a lecture reported in the *Building News*, 24 May 1861, p. 438.

108 W. J. Cockburn Muir, *Pagan, or Christian?* (1860), p. 165.

109 E. L. Garbett, *Rudimentary Treatise on the Principles of Design in Architecture* (1850),
      pp. 248–50.

110 Reported in *Caledonian Mercury*, 3 April 1860.

111 J. Henry Stevens, 'The Revivalists and the Vernacular Architecture', in *Builder*, 7 November
      1857, p. 639.

112 S. Huggins, lecture on 'The Question of Styles', reported in *Builder*, 15 May 1858, pp. 332–3.

113 Bright, *Cities Built to Music*, p. 52.

114 S. Huggins, 'The Question of Styles', pp. 332–3.

115 Robert Kerr, *The Gentleman's House* (1865; 1872 edn, reprinted 1972 with an introduction by J. Mordaunt Crook), p. 342.

116 Henry-Russell Hitchcock, *Early Victorian Architecture in Britain* (1954), pp. xi, 22.

117 David Hume's great, but now largely forgotten, *History of England from the Invasion of Julius Caesar to the Revolution in 1688* (1754–61) is an early precursor.

118 Charles Dickens's popular *A Child's History of England* (1853) can perhaps stand for the rest; many of which are listed in the bibliography to my *The Absent-Minded Imperialists* (2004), pp. 434–7.

119 *Origin of Species* was published in 1859.

120 See Herbert Butterfield, *The Whig Interpretation of History* (London: G Bell & Sons, 1931); J. W. Burrow, *A Liberal Descent* (Cambridge: Cambridge University Press, 1981).

121 Anon., 'Fair Play for Gothic Architecture!', in *Building News*, 29 June 1860, p. 512.

122 Anon., 'Architectural Revivalism and Puginism', in *Fraser's Magazine*, November 1843, pp. 600–1.

123 Cited (and argued against) by the historian E. A. Freeman, in *National Review*, vol. 10 (January 1860), p. 31; and cf. letter in *Builder*, 13 June 1857, p. 337.

124 James Fergusson, *History of the Modern Styles of Architecture* (1862), p. 489.

125 *Building News*, 26 June 1857, p. 652.

126 Anon., 'Architectural Revivalism and Puginism', in *Fraser's Magazine*, vol. 28 (November 1843), p. 593.

127 G. G. Scott, *Remarks on Secular and Domestic Architecture* (1857), pp. 259–60.

128 William Burges, *Art Applied to Industry* (1865), p. 8.

129 Viollet-le-Duc in 1858, quoted in Germann, *Gothic Revival*, p. 11.

130 Eastlake, *A History of the Gothic Revival* (1872), pp. 2–4.

131 See above, p. 105.

132 In the same sense as Francis Fukuyama's *End of History* (1992): of History – that is, in the Marxist sense – of progress through stages.

133 See my '"Monstrous Vandalism": Capitalism and Philistinism in the Works of Samuel Laing (1780–1868)', in *Albion*, vol. 23, no. 2 (Summer 1991).

Notes to Chapter 8: Not the Most Interesting Public Question of the Day

1 Probably. Attendances were never recorded in *Hansard*, and I have found no indication of them in press reports. The small numbers who spoke and voted, however; the unpopular hours at which most of the debates took place; and the lack of any of the usual references to 'crowded Houses' and the like, suggest small numbers.

2 M. H. Port, *Imperial London* (1995), p. 199.

3 The main Goths were Lord Elcho, A. J. Beresford Hope and Lord John Manners; the main Classical debaters, apart from Palmerston, were William Coningham, Sir Benjamin Hall and Sir William Tite. As well as these, the following made brief interventions which indicated their stylistic preferences: H. A. Bruce, Charles Buxton, Sir Edward Colebrooke, R. A. Cross, Dudley Fortescue, Austen Layard, Joseph Paxton and W. Stirling for the Goths, and W. F. Cowper, W. D. Seymour and a Sir J. V. Shelley for the Classicists. In addition, 54 other MPs (of both Houses) participated in the debates from 1855 to 1861, but without touching at all on the question of 'style', and usually (again) very briefly indeed – sometimes with only a question or an interjection. Most of their contributions related to the practical

necessity or otherwise of the buildings; the cost; or the procedures followed.

4   *Art-Journal*, no. 80, August 1861, p. 237.

5   The Palmerston Papers at Southampton University appear to contain little on this issue, apart from a very brief correspondence with Scott. At the time of the 'Battle' Palmerston seemed more interested in the discussions over a monument to or statue of the Duke of Wellington, which were taking place at the same time. An exhibition of designs for that immediately succeeded the 'Government Offices' one in Westminster Hall.

6   Russell to Gladstone, 6 January 1860, in BL Add. MS 44291, ff. 316–17 (emphases in the original). By April that year he had 'give[n] up all idea of fine architecture Gothic or Grecian'. Russell to Gladstone, 26 April 1860, in Russell Papers, PRO 30/22/31, f.30.

7   *The Times*, 6 August 1859, p. 9.

8   They are the following: four anonymous pamphlets: '*Nec minimum meruere decus, vestigial Graeca*' (1857); *Shall Gothic Architecture Be Denied Fair Play?* (1860); *Classic or Pseudo-Gothic* (1860); and *Remarks on a National Style, in Reference to the Proposed Foreign Office* (1860); three by A. J. Beresford-Hope: *Public Offices and Metropolitan Improvements* (1857); *The Expense of the Government and of Mr. Beresford-Hope's Plan of Public Offices Compared* (1857); and, under the pseudonym 'A Cambridge Man', *The New Palaces of Administration* (1857); plus W. J. Cockburn Muir, *Pagan or Christian? Or Notes for the General Public on our National Architecture* (1860); Sir Francis E. Scott, *Shall the New Foreign Office be Gothic or Classic?* (1860); and G. G. Scott (the architect), *Explanatory Remarks upon the Designs for the New Government Offices*, in two versions (1857 and 1860). Fuller titles and details will be found in the Bibliography. I hope I've not missed any.

9   *The Times* carried 11 leading articles on the issue from 1855 to 1861, and around two dozen letters (some from Scott). No other daily newspaper approached this number. *The Times* has sometimes been taken to be more representative of British opinion, or at least of the opinion of the political classes, than it really was. In fact it had a circulation of only 40,000 (but possibly a readership of four times that). The importance placed on it by researchers in the past may have something to do with the fact that it is the only daily newspaper that had an index, making it comparatively easy, therefore, to search for particular items. Going through the huge dusty volumes of other newspapers without such guidance can be a Herculean task; I know, having done it on several occasions. Now with the digitalization of several scores of British newspapers by the British Library, and by some of the newspapers themselves (like the *Manchester Guardian*), this is much easier; and reveals how atypical *The Times* in fact was.

10 This is the *Saturday Review*, owned and edited by James Beresford Hope.

11 Examples of gentle mockery are to be found in the *Manchester Guardian*, 15 February 1859; the *Belfast News-Letter*, 12 August 1859; *Punch*, 13 August 1859, p. 72; and the *Daily Telegraph*, 20 and 31 August 1859.

12 *Reynolds's Newspaper* carried regular parliamentary reports, which covered the debates of 11 February and 4 August 1859, but with 'architectural' considerations marginalized. A typical example is its report of 7 August 1859 (p. 4): 'After a long discussion, principally on the question of architecture, the vote was agreed to'; and cf. *ibid.*, 20 February 1859, p. 4. That was the only mention 'style' got.

13 See Tristram Hunt, *Building Jerusalem: The Rise and Fall of the Victorian City* (2004), ch. 5. Nearly every newspaper carried reports of this, including *Reynolds's*. The most extensive (of course) are in the *Manchester Guardian*, 1–13 May, *passim*; where they elbow out nearly all mention of the Westminster show. See plate 13.

14 *Ibid.*, p. 190.

15 The *Building News*, 8 May 1857, p. 447, estimated 9,000 for the first day, and 7,000 for the second; *Builder*'s guesses ('believed to be'), 9 May 1857, p. 261, were 10,000 for the first day, approaching 7,000 for the second, and then back to 10,000 for the third. Estimating numbers of crowds is always unreliable, depending largely on what you would like the figure to be: take, for example, police and protestors' guestimates of political demonstrations; in this case a figure indicating a widespread interest in architecture would probably suit the professionals better than a smaller one.

16 None of the non-professional press reports (that I have seen) attempted to put a number to it. The *Observer*, 10 May 1857, p. 5, claimed the hall was 'thronged'; the *North Wales Chronicle*, 9 May, claimed the number was 'considerable'; and *The Times*, 11 May, wrote of 'thousands'.

17 *Observer*, 10 May 1857; *Building News*, 8 May 1857, p. 441, and 12 June 1857, p. 598.

18 *Building News*, 8 May 1857, p. 449. *Builder*, 16 May 1857, p. 269, pleaded for the opening hours to be extended (after 6 p.m.) so that craftsmen could attend after work.

19 'A Practical Man', *Remarks on the Designs proposed for the New Government Offices* (1857), pp. 10–13, 43.

20 *Building News*, 12 June 1857 p. 599.

21 See above, p. 92. Apart from the obvious suspects – Scott and Street on the Gothic side, Tite on the Classical – few practising architects joined in the debate in print.

22 Stefan Muthesius, *The High Victorian Movement in Architecture 1850–1870* (1972), p. 162; and cf. Eve Blau, *Ruskinian Gothic* (1982), pp. 93–4.

23 Peter Ferriday, 'The Revival: Stories Ancient and Modern', in *Architectural Review*, vol. 121 (1957), p. 155.

24 Halsey Ricardo, 'John Francis Bentley', in Peter Ferriday (ed.), *Victorian Architecture* (1963), pp. 291–2.

25 Kenneth Clark, *The Gothic Revival* (1924), p. 167. Clark won't have known much about 'ordinary men'.

26 Blau, *Ruskinian Gothic*, p. 94.

27 *Building News*, 19 August 1859, p. 751.

28 *Punch*, 13 August 1859, p. 72.

29 Francis E. Scott, *Shall the New Foreign Office be Gothic or Classic?* (1860), pp. 66–7. Coningham was MP for Brighton, and pro-Classical.

30 *Building News*, 12 July 1861, pp. 580–2.

31 E.g. *Building News*, 25 Feb 1859, pp. 175–6; *Civil Engineer*, March 1859, p. 75; and see above, p. 9.

32 Above, p. 12.

33 Quoted in the *Building News*, 26 August 1859, p. 767. Another example of bad 'tone' is the Tite–Scott exchange of November 1855, cited above, p. 6.

34 See 'Forward' in *Builder*, 30 May 1857, p. 304; George Wightwick in *ibid.*, 9 January 1858, p. 25; S. Huggins reported in *ibid.*, 15 May 1858, pp. 332–2; 'Classic or Gothic: The Battle of the Styles', in *Blackwood's Magazine*, vol. 91 (March 1862), p. 283; and, defending the Goths against the charge of 'monomania', Scott letter to *The Times*, 14 February 1859, and the *Globe*, 12 February 1859, p. 2.

35 Though we saw (above, p. 54) that Spurgeon was zealous *against* Gothic when it came to architecture.

36 *Building News*, 26 August 1859, p. 768.

37 See above, p. 8.

38 John Summerson, *The London Building World of the Eighteen-Sixties* (1973), p. 23. And on the

'economists', see M. H. Port, 'Pride and Parsimony: Influences Affecting the Development of the Whitehall Quarter in the 1850s', in *London Journal*, vol. 2 (1976).

39   Quoted in Geoffrey Tyack, *Sir James Pennethorne and the Making of Victorian London* (1992), p. 121.

40   Renamed the 'Durbar Court' in 1902: Anthony Seldon, *The Foreign Office* (2000), p. 55.

41   The builders were campaigning for a nine-hour working day. This is reported prominently in *Reynolds's Newspaper* throughout the summer; see, for example, its issues of 2 May, 14 August and 9 September 1859.

42   That of Dr Thomas Smethurst, sentenced to be hanged for the poisoning of his wife, then pardoned after a press campaign over the forensic evidence, only to be convicted later of bigamy.

43   Thompson and Bentinck in the Commons, 11 February 1859, reported in *Hansard*, 3rd series, vol. 152, cols 270 and 273; and cf. McCartney in the Commons, 13 July 1857, in *Hansard*, 3rd series, vol. 146, col. 1421. Palmerston had himself used a similar argument earlier, albeit privately; see Palmerston to Benjamin Hall, 25 August 1856, in BL Add. MS 48580 (Palmerston's Copy-Books), ff. 129–30.

44   See, for example, *Observer*, 3 May 1857; *Morning Advertiser*, 4 May 1857.

45   See *Saturday Review*, 21 February 1857, p. 174; and *Builder*, 26 February 1859, p. 158.

46   Above, pp. 5–6.

47   See *Building News*, 12 June 1857, p. 597; E. L. Garbett in *Builder*, 27 June 1857, p. 360; and G. G. Scott, 'On the Present Position and Future Prospects of the Revival of Gothic Architecture', in *Associated Architectural Societies Reports and Papers*, vol. 4 (1857–8), p. 77.

48   Rev Boutell, reported in *Builder*, 23 May 1857, p. 283.

49   'Gaping cockneys' is E. L. Garbett, 'Mr Wightwick and the Classicists', in *Builder*, 27 June 1857, p. 360.

50   'The majority of the journals have abandoned the subject in sheer despair of it': *Builder*, 23 May 1857, p. 281.

51   For example, entry no. 14 is described as 'Italian' in the *Observer*, 3 May 1857, but as 'German Gothic' by *Builder*, 16 May 1857, p. 269 (and as 'simply hideous' by the *Daily News*, 4 May 1857); no. 30 was described as 'Anglo-Saxon' by the *Observer*, 3 May 1857, but as 'Italian' by the *Building News*, 29 May 1857, p. 541. In each of these cases one of the descriptions must be mistaken – probably the daily newspaper one, though it of course impossible to be sure without seeing the drawings. But then, as *Builder* pointed out, 23 May 1857, p. 281, one could not expect journalists to master the art of architecture in just a few hours.

52   The 'popular choice', according to *Builder*, 1 August 1857, p. 431, was no. 112, an ornate Classical design by Robert Kerr, which it carried an engraving of, 28 September 1857, p. 551. It was certainly the *Morning Advertiser*'s choice, 4 May 1857. The *Daily News*, 4 May 1857, picked no. 141, perhaps because it came with the largest number of drawings; and the *Illustrated London News*, 9 May 1857, p. 424, no. 147. See plate 9.

53   *Building News*, 15 March 1861, p. 219.

54   *Edinburgh Review*, April 1837, p. 177 (italics added).

55   *Quarterly Review*, vol. 95 (September 1854), p. 342.

56   *Gentleman's Magazine*, November 1859, p. 469.

57   Francis Scott, *Shall the New Foreign Office be Gothic or Classic* (1860), pp. 9–10.

58   Freeman, *A History of Architecture* (1849), pp. 2, 13–14.

59   Charles Eastlake, *A History of the Gothic Revival* (1872), p. 298. This seems an odd argument, in view of the fact that you did not need to go into galleries to see buildings

60   See above, pp. 37–8.

61   Coventry Patmore, 'London Street Architecture', in *National Review*, July 1857, p. 48.

62   G. G. Scott, 'On the Present Position and Future Prospects of the Revival of Gothic Architecture', pp. 77–8.

63   Above, pp. 45–6.

64   *Chambers's Journal*, 1848, p. 232; and, on *Chambers's Information for the People*, see above, p. 169, n. 48.

65   The best and most accessible was probably J. H. Parker, *An Introduction to the Study of Gothic Architecture* (1849).

66   See above, p. 169, n. 47.

67   *Daily Telegraph*, 29 August 1859, p. 2.

68   Fergusson, *History of the Modern Styles of Architecture* (1862), p. 35.

69   *Ibid.*, p. 244. Later on Fergusson blamed this on the elevated status the public schools gave to (Greek and Roman) *literature*, in whose shadow architecture appears as a mere 'corpus vile': Fergusson, 'Rawlinson on Ancient Architecture', in *Fortnightly Review* (January 1868), p. 43.

70   *Blackwood's Magazine*, August 1836, pp. 236–7.

71   Fergusson, *An Historical Enquiry into the True Principles of Beauty in Art, More Especially with Reference to Architecture* (1849), introduction, part 1. *True Principles* was an early work on aesthetics generally.

72   Nikolaus Pevsner, *Matthew Digby Wyatt* (1950), pp. 5–6; and cf. 'Victorian Prolegomena', in Peter Ferriday (ed.), *Victorian Architecture* (1963), p. 35. The same élitist point is made by Geoffrey Scott, *The Architecture of Humanism* (1914), p. 33; and Kenneth Clark, *The Gothic Revival* (1924), p. 132.

73   Such as Samuel Laing the elder, referred to below, p. 120.

74   W. J. Cockburn Muir, *Pagan or Christian?* (1860), pp. 204–5.

75   S. Huggins reported in *Builder*, 15 May 1858, p. 333.

76   Above, p. 87.

77   This was Lieutenant-Colonel F. P. Dunne in the House of Commons, 24 May 1850, *Hansard*, 3rd series, vol. 111, col. 358. Others who took this 'economy' line included G. Bankes in the Commons, 24 May 1850 and 31 July 1855: *Hansard*, 3rd series, vol. 111, cols 244–6 and vol. 139, col. 1575; Bernal Osborne in the Commons, 24 May 1850 and 8 July 1861: *Hansard*, 3rd series, vol. 111, cols 328–32, and vol. 164, cols 534–5; and G. W. P. Bentinck in the Commons, 10 August 1857 and 11 February 1859: *Hansard*, 3rd series, vol. 147, cols 1311–2, and vol. 152, col. 273.

78   *Daily News*, 5 May 1857 (italics added).

79   E.g. Beresford Hope, *Public Offices and Metropolitan Improvements* (1857), p. 12.

80   'A Practical Man', *Remarks on the Designs Proposed for the New Government Offices* (1857), pp. 3, 9, 17, 23.

81   Baring in Commons, 31 July 1855: *Hansard*, 3rd series, vol. 139, col. 1576 (italics added).

82   *Morning Advertiser*, 5 May 1857, p. 3. The *Advertiser* favoured – as several MPs did – extending Inigo Jones's 'simple' but 'majestic' Banqueting Hall.

83   M. H. Port, *Imperial London* (1995), p. 16.

84   See above, p. 8.

85   Geoffrey Tyack. *Sir James Pennethorne and the Making of Victorian London* (1992), p. 310.

86   *Liverpool Mercury*, 12 July 1861, pp. 1–2 (italics added).

87   Fergusson, *True Principles*, pp. 9–12.

88   E.g. Scott's *Remarks on Secular and Domestic Architecture* (1857), p. 7 *et passim*; *Builder*, 2 January 1858, pp. 1–2; and *Builder*, 4 December 1858, p. 809

89　G. E. Street in the *Ecclesiologist*, June 1852, pp. 247–8.

90　Anon., 'Classic or Gothic', in *Blackwood's Magazine*, March 1862, p. 289; S. Huggins reported in *Builder* 15 May 1858, p. 333.

91　Anon., 'The British School of Architecture', in *Blackwood's Magazine*, vol. 48 (1836), pp. 235–7.

92　See above, p. 44.

93　Beresford Hope, reported in *Building News*, 3 May 1861, p. 377.

94　Charles Kingsley, *Westward Ho! Or the Voyages and Adventures of Sir Amyas Leigh* (Cambridge: MacMillan & Co., [1855] 1893), p. 230.

95　Carlyle, Thomas. *Past and Present* (London: Chapman & Hall, [1843] 1895), p. 196.

96　On Laing, whose ideas about art are inconveniently scattered among five travel books he published between 1836 and 1852, see my '"Monstrous Vandalism": Capitalism and Philistinism in the Works of Samuel Laing (1780–1868)', in *Albion*, vol. 23 (1991), pp. 253–68.

97　*Ibid.*, p. 265.

98　Ruskin, lecture (untitled) delivered at the Opening Meeting of the Architectural Museum at Brompton, 13 January 1858, reported in *Builder*, 16 January, pp. 45–6; and reprinted as Lecture I, 'The Deteriorative Power of Conventional Art over Nations', of *The Two Paths* (1859).

99　Schmitz, Oskar A. H. *Das Land ohne Musik: englische Gesellschaftsprobleme* (Munich: G. Müller, 1914). In fact the book isn't about music, but the title became a common description of the English musical scene. A case can be made for the presence of music in England between Purcell and Elgar, relying mainly on church and perhaps popular music; but no one would claim that Cipriani Potter, Samuel Wesley, William Sterndale Bennett or William Crotch (probably the best of the nineteenth-century ones before Stanford, Parry and Elgar) were a patch on even – say – Hummel.

100　Palmerston in the Commons, 1 June 1863, quoted in Tyack, *Sir James Pennethorne*, p. 139.

101　Henry-Russell Hitchcock, *Early Victorian Architecture in Britain*, vol. 2 (1954), carries illustrations of most of these. Again, for reasons explained in the Preface, I have limited this list to English examples. Scotland was also building energetically at this time. The National Gallery of Scotland in Edinburgh and Queen Victoria's Balmoral Castle in Aberdeenshire are two examples from the 'Battle' period.

102　I hope so. I live in one.

103　Above, pp. 79–80.

104　Martin J. Wiener, *English Culture and the Decline of the Industrial Spirit 1850–1980* (1981).

105　Above, p. 28.

106　James Fergusson, *On a National Collection of Architectural Art* (1857), p. 13 (italics added).

107　Information supplied by Kate Crowe of the FCO.

108　Tyack, *Sir James Pennethorne*, p. 269. The 'tragedy' for him is that they were preferred over Pennethorne's designs, which in his view – which seems a reasonable one, judging by the elevations reproduced in his book – were, if you were going to have a 'Classical' building, far better.

Notes to Chapter 9: A Change for the Worse

1　Scott's evidence to the 1877 select committee on 'The Annual Expenditure on Public Offices and Buildings', reported in *The Architect*, 1 September 1877, p. 110.

2　For example, in the *Art-Journal*, vol. 7 (1868), pp. 224–5.

3   See, for example, the evidence given to the 1877 select committee, *loc. cit.*; [J. Kaye], 'The House that Scott Built', in *Cornhill Magazine*, vol. 16 (1867), pp. 358, 369; and above, p. 16.

4   Scott's evidence to the 1877 select committee, in *The Architect*, 1 September 1877, p. 109.

5   *Ibid., loc. cit.*

6   *Ibid.*, p. 110. The TV series alluded to here is Michael Dobbs's *House of Cards*, featuring the (fictional) Conservative chief whip Francis Urquhart, whose 'You might well say that; I couldn't possibly comment' became a popular political catchphrase thereafter.

7   This comes from a minute by the FCO's Donal McCarthy, 27 December 1968, quoted in Keith Hamilton, 'Accommodating Diplomacy: The Foreign and Commonwealth Office and the Debate over Whitehall Redevelopment', in *Contemporary British History*, vol. 18 (2004), pp. 205–6. On the lavatories Oliver Wright, chief of administration at the Foreign Office, minuted on 20 July 1970 that 'I am told the one near the canteen in the basement is particularly revolting': *ibid.*, p. 210.

8   See Gavin Stamp, 'The Nation's Drawing-Room: Restoring the Foreign Office', in *Apollo*, July 1992.

9   See Hamilton, 'Accommodating Diplomacy', p. 218.

10 John Summerson, 'London, the Artifact', in H. J. Dyos and Michael Wolff (eds), *The Victorian City* (2 vols, 1973), p. 327. Even Scott's biographer acknowledges that it 'has seldom been regarded as great architecture', and quotes Sir Reginald Bloomfield's dismissal of it as 'one of the most boring buildings in London, of vast size, but petty in conception': David Cole, *The Work of Sir Gilbert Scott* (1980), p. 81.

11 This is Reginald Turnor, *Nineteenth Century Architecture in Britain* (1950), p. 85; and was also roughly the judgement of H. S. Goodhart-Rendel, in *English Architecture since the Regency: An Interpretation* (1953, but written in 1934), p. 117; and of Henry-Russell Hitchcock, who, however, thought it would have worked better in French Second Empire style: 'High Victorian Gothic', in *Victorian Studies*, vol. 1 (1957), p. 64. Christopher Hussey in 1964 was more positive towards it, but he had an agenda – to save it from demolition: 'Foreign Office's Threatened Glory', in *Country Life*, 6 February 1964, p. 272.

12 See, for example, Alexander 'Greek' Thompson's ferocious onslaught on Scott's Glasgow University designs, delivered to the Glasgow Architectural Society in 7 May 1866, and published in *Builder*, 19 May, pp. 368–71; with an editorial comment, however, suggesting that Thompson was merely piqued that a Scottish architect had not been asked to tender. Scott refers to other attacks on him in his *Personal and Professional Recollections* (1879), *passim*. For St Pancras, see plate 32.

13 Joseph Kinnard, 'GE Street, the Law Courts and the "Seventies"', in Peter Ferriday (ed.), *Victorian Architecture* (1963), p. 229.

14 Quoted in Gavin Stamp's 1995 edited reprint of Scott's *Recollections*, p. 388.

15 Kenneth Clark, *The Gothic Revival* (1928), p. 161. And there was worse. For example: 'we forget one great difference between Gilbert Scott and ourselves: he believed that he built very good Gothic, we that he built very bad' (p. 166); and Clark's dismissal of the Albert Memorial as 'the expression of pure philistinism' (p. 172), appealing only 'to the class of people who like a monument to be large and expensive-looking, and to show much easily understood sculpture, preferably of animals' (p. 173).

16 Goodhart-Rendel, *English Architecture since the Regency*, pp. 95–6.

17 Basil Clarke, *Church Builders of the Nineteenth Century: A Study of the Gothic Revival in England* (1938), p. 172.

18 Reginald Turnor, *Nineteenth Century Architecture*, p. 80.

19 Henry-Russell Hitchcock, 'High Victorian Gothic', p. 52.

20 Other modern put-downs include Martin Briggs, who thought Scott's work was smug, pompous, self-satisfied and sanctimonious at worst, and no more than 'industrious' and 'ambitious' at best, in *Goths and Vandals: A Study of the Destruction, Neglect and Preservation of Historical Buildings in England* (1952), p. 170; and Robert Macleod, who focused on his 'spectacular rise . . . the savage smugness of his restoration work, and, not least, his eye for the main chance', rather than his art; in *Style and Society: Architectural Ideology in Britain 1835–1914* (1971), p. 18.

21 Palmerston in the Commons, 8 July 1861: *Hansard*, 3rd series, vol. 164, col. 535.

22 According to the *West Riding* volume in the Pevsner *Buildings of England* series (1959, 2nd edn, 1967, p. 231), Halifax's spire 'defeats period categorising'.

23 Charles Eastlake, *A History of the Gothic Revival* (1872), p. 333.

24 *Ibid.*, pp. 72, 129, 132.

25 T. G. Jackson, *Modern Gothic Architecture* (1873), p. 2.

26 Goodhart-Rendel, *English Architecture Since the Regency*, p. 154.

27 For example, John Summerson, *Heavenly Mansions, and Other Essays on Architecture* (1949), p. 173: 'Quite suddenly, around 1870, taste was again established', and his *Victorian Architecture: Four Studies in Evaluation* (1970), p. 4; Turnor, *Nineteenth Century Architecture in Britain*, p. 95; Henry-Russell Hitchcock, 'High Victorian Gothic', p. 49; Nikolaus Pevsner, 'Prologomena', in Peter Ferriday (ed.), *Victorian Architecture*, p. 25; James Stevens Curl, *Victorian Architecture* (1990), p. 109.

28 H. S. Goodhart-Rendel, 'English Gothic Architecture of the Nineteenth Century', in *Journal of the Royal Institute of British Architects*, vol. 31 (1924), p. 337.

29 Kinnard, 'GE Street, the Law Courts and the "Seventies"', p. 231. See plate 34.

30 John Summerson, 'London, the Artifact', p. 320.

31 Palmerston in Commons, 8 July 1861: *Hansard*, 3rd series, vol. 164, col. 535.

32 [J. T. Emmett], 'The State of English Architecture', in *Quarterly Review*, vol. 132 (April 1872), p. 298.

33 Robert Kerr, *The Gentleman's House* (1865; 3rd edn, 1872), p. 341 (original italics).

34 *Ibid.*, p. 368.

35 Eastlake, *History of the Gothic Revival*, p. 232.

36 See, for example, T. Mellard Reade, 'A New Style: How Can it be Formed?' in *Builder*, 26 July 1862, pp. 537–8; Samuel Huggins, *The Course and Current of Architecture* (1863), final chapter, 'The Style of the Future'.

37 Kerr, *The Gentleman's House*, p. x.

38 J. T. Micklethwaite, *Modern Parish Churches* (1874), p. 251.

39 See John Summerson, 'London, the Artifact', p. 317 (italics added).

40 A. J. B. Beresford Hope, *The Condition and Prospects of Architectural Art* (1863), p. 14.

41 See, for example, T. G. Jackson, *Modern Gothic Architecture* (1873), p. 22; J. T. Micklethwaite, *Modern Parish Churches* (1874), p. 253; and Thomas Harris, *Three Periods of English Architecture* (1894), p. 51.

42 See H. S. Goodhart-Rendel, *English Architecture Since the Regency*, p. 189, on Philip Webb's essential functionalism: 'and if all that is not to be Gothic, what is?'; Henry-Russell Hitchcock, *Architecture: Nineteenth and Twentieth Centuries*, pp. 154–5; Georg Germann, trans. Gerald Onn, *Gothic Revival in Europe and Britain* (1972), p. 172.

43 See above, pp. 55–6.

44 For example Kenneth Clark, *The Gothic Revival*, p. 155; and Basil Clarke, *Church Builders of the Nineteenth Century*, pp. 78–9.

45 Clarke, *Church Builders*, p. 176.

46 Goodhart-Rendel, 'English Gothic Architecture of the Nineteenth Century', p. 337.

47 On 'ugliness', see, for example, Robert Kerr, *The Gentleman's House*, p. 368; and above, p. 193, n. 52.

48 An exception here, though it was never built, was the projected Gothic 'Imperial Monumental Halls and Tower' designed for Westminster by J. P. Seddon and E. B. Lamb in 1904; which is the subject of G. Alex Bremner's article, '"Imperial Monumental Halls and Tower": Westminster Abbey and the Commemoration of Empire, 1854–1904', in *Architectural History*, vol. 47 (2004).

Notes to the Conclusion

1 Of the dozen 'Battle' pamphlets listed above (p. 198, n. 8), for example, only two – *Remarks on a National Style* (1860), and *Classic or Pseudo-Gothic* (1860), both by the same (anonymous) author – are by Classicists.

2 Many authorities assert this, although so far as I know no one has ever taken a census of nineteenth-century buildings to prove it. That would of course be almost impossible; for a start, demolished buildings would need to be included as well as surviving ones. Among general works to emphasize this point are Henry-Russell Hitchcock, *Early Victorian Architecture in Britain* (1954), pp. 11, 13–14, 22; John Summerson, *The Architecture of Victorian London* (1976), pp. 5, 33; and James Stevens Curl, *Victorian Architecture* (1990), pp. 73–5. Others do it implicitly, by covering the Classical legacy of the nineteenth century as fully as the Gothic one.

3 Robert Furneaux Jordan, *Victorian Architecture* (1966), pp. 137, 148.

4 John Summerson, 'London, the Artifact', in H. J. Dyos and Michael Wolff (eds), *The Victorian City* (2 vols, 1973), vol. 1, p. 311.

5 J. Mordaunt Crook, *The Architect's Secret: Victorian Cities and the Image of Gravity* (2003), p. 6.

6 Robert Furneaux Jordan, *Victorian Architecture*, p. 169.

7 Reported in *The Architect*, 1 September 1877, p. 111. Scott could have mentioned the Locarno Room: above, p. 123.

8 Michael Bright, *Cities Built to Music: Aesthetic Theories of the Victorian Gothic Revival* (1984), p. 101.

9 See [J. T. Emmett], 'The State of English Architecture', in *Quarterly Review*, vol. 132 (April 1872), pp. 304–13.

10 *Ibid.*, p. 305.

11 J. T. Micklethwaite, *Modern Parish Churches* (1874), p. 265.

12 Street to J. P. Seddon, 15 April 1867, in RIBA Papers, LC/4/11/14; and see [Emmett], 'The State of English Architecture', p. 297.

13 John Summerson, *Heavenly Mansions, and Other Essays on Architecture* (1949), pp. 203–4.

14 George Magoun, 'Church Architecture and the Masses', in *Congregational Quarterly*, vol. 4 (Boston, 1863), p. 29, quoting Anon., 'Spiritual Destitution in the Metropolis', in the *London Quarterly*, April 1861, pp. 216–41: which, however, I have been unable to find in the UK edition of that journal (it may have been carried by a US version; or the reference may be wrong).

15 Peter Collins, *Changing Ideals in Modern Architecture 1750–1950* (1965), pp. 122–3.

16 Brought along from the old Foreign Office, so not contemporary with the new one.

17 *Ibid.*, p. 62.

18 This was the perceptive John Mackenzie.

Bibliography

This list is confined to the works bearing more or less directly on the 'Battle'. Others are cited in the endnotes, together with details of files, etcetera, consulted.

MANUSCRIPT SOURCES

OFFICIAL

Public Record Office

Office of Works: WORK 1/52–70; 2/16; 6/12; 6/307; 11/9; 12/84; 12/86; 12/90; 12/96; 17/16; 22/8; 30/898–902, 979, 6140, 6281–2, 6331–2; 38/431.
Crown Estates: CRES 35/2239.
Foreign Office: FO 366/378 and 415; 366/415; FO 391 (Hammond Papers).
MR 1/2004.

British Library

India Office Library (IOL): L/SUR/2/3–4; L/SUR/5/8; L/SUR/6/1; C/1.

PRIVATE PAPERS

Public Record Office

Russell Papers: PRO 30/22/30–1.

British Library

Gladstone Papers: BL Add. MSS 44271, 44291, 44389, 44291, 44389–90, 44392, 44530–1.
Palmerston's Copy-Books: BL Add. MS 48580–1.

Victoria and Albert Museum

Royal Institute of British Architects: RIBA Archive 1.c.2–4; RIBA Archive 18.c.3; RIBA LC/4/11/14.
Scott Papers (ScGGS): boxes 1–5.

Southampton University

Palmerston Papers (BP): GC/F1/8A; GC/HA/16; GC/LE/74–5, 78, 189, 191–2; GC/SC/18–20; D/17–21.

GOVERNMENT PRINTED PAPERS

Parliamentary Papers

'Downing Street Improvement and Public Offices Extension' [November 1854]. In PRO WORK 12–84/1 f.2.

BPP xi (1857–8), *Report from the Select Committee on Foreign Office Reconstruction* . . . Also in PRO WORK 12–84/1.

BPP xlviii (1857–8), 'Copy of Any Correspondence . . . between the First Commissioner of Works and the Treasury . . .'

BPP 2s. xv (1859), 'Copies of the Official Letters by Which Mr Scott was Appointed . . .'

Parliamentary Debates (Hansard)

3rd series: vols 111, 138–9, 141, 144–7, 152, 155, 164.

CONTEMPORARY BOOKS, PAMPHLETS AND SUBSTANTIAL ARTICLES

'A. M.', 'Lord Palmerston and Mr Scott', *Gentleman's Magazine*, vol. 207 (1859).

[Alison, A.], 'The British School of Architecture', *Blackwood's Edinburgh Magazine*, vol. 40 (1836).

Anon., Review of 'Report from the Select Committee on the House of Commons Buildings', *Westminster Review*, vol. 22 (1835).

Anon., 'Architecture', *Penny Cyclopaedia* (London: Society for the Propagation of Useful Knowledge [SPUK], 1833–43).

Anon., 'Hamilton &c on Architecture', *Quarterly Review*, February 1837.

Anon., 'The New Houses of Parliament', *Edinburgh Review*, vol. 65 (April 1837).

Anon., 'Ecclesiastical Architecture in England', *Dublin Review*, vol. 10 (May 1841).

Anon., 'Architecture', in *Chambers's Information for the People*, vol. 2 (1842).

Anon., 'Catholic Church Architecture, and the Church of England', *Christian Remembrancer*, vol. 2 (c. 1842).

Anon., 'Styles of Church Architecture', *Christian Remembrancer*, vol. 4 (c. 1843).

Anon., 'Architectural Revivalism and Puginism', *Fraser's Magazine*, vol. 28 (November 1843).

Anon., 'Danger in Downing Street', *Punch*, 4 August 1844.

Anon., 'Church Architecture in England', *Sharpe's London Magazine*, vol. 1 (1846).

Anon., 'The Artistic Merit of Mr Pugin', *Ecclesiologist*, vol. 5 (1846).

Anon., 'Symbolism of Pointed Architecture', *Eclectic Review*, vol. 78 (c. 1846).

Anon., 'Architecture', *The Pictorial Gallery of Arts* (Chas Cox, 1847).

Anon., 'Mr Hope's Essay on the Present State of Ecclesiological Science in England', *Ecclesiologist*, vol. 7 (March 1847).

Anon., 'Popular Architecture', *Chambers's Edinburgh Journal*, vol. 9 (1848).

Anon., 'Architecture: Adaptation of Iron', *Westminster Review*, vol. 51 (April 1849).

Anon., 'Old Lamps for New Ones', *Household Words*, 15 June 1850.

Anon., 'Strictures on a Pair of Public Structures', *Fraser's Magazine*, vol. 42 (August 1850).

Anon., 'Styles and Examples of Modern Architecture', *Christian Remembrancer*, vol. 18 (c. 1850).

Anon., 'History and Styles of Architecture', *Christian Remembrancer*, vol. 18 (c. 1850).

Anon., 'Mr Pugin and "The Rambler"', *Ecclesiologist*, vol. 10 (April 1850).

Anon., 'The Present State of Architecture', *Quarterly Review*, vol. 95 (June–September 1854).

Anon., 'Philosophy of Architecture', *Chambers's Journal*, vol. 3 (June 1855).

Anon., 'Gothic Art: John Ruskin', *London Quarterly Review*, vol. 7 (January 1857).

Anon., *Designs for the Public Offices: A Hand-Book Guide for Visitors* (H. G. Clarke, 1857).

Anon., '*Nec minimum meruere decus, vestigial Graeca*' (privately printed, 1857).

Anon., 'The Competition for Government Offices in Westminster Hall', *Ecclesiologist*, June 1857.

Anon., 'The Coming Competition', *Saturday Review*, 21 February 1857.

Anon., 'The Judges of the Public Offices' Competition', *Saturday Review*, 16 May 1857.

Anon., 'The New Government Offices', *Athenaeum*, 16 May 1857.

Anon., 'The Prizes for the Public Offices', *Saturday Review*, 1 August 1857.

Anon., 'The Award in the Government Offices Competition', *Ecclesiologist*, vol. 18 (August 1857).

Anon., 'The Question of Architectural Style for the New Public Offices', *Saturday Review*, 25 September 1858.

Anon., 'The New Foreign Office', *Ecclesiologist*, vol. 19 (December 1858).

Anon., 'Onward', *Saturday Review*, 15 January 1859.

Anon., 'The Common Sense of Art', *Saturday Review*, 22 January 1859.

Anon., 'The New Foreign Office', *Ecclesiologist*, vol. 20 (April 1859).

Anon., 'The New Foreign Office', *Saturday Review*, 30 July 1859.

Anon., 'Palladian Palmerston', *Punch*, 13 August 1859.

Anon., 'Fine Arts: Fine-art Gossip', *Athenaeum*, 13 August 1859.

Anon., 'Fine Arts: Fine-art Gossip', *Athenaeum*, 28 July 1860.

Anon., 'Lord Palmerston and the Designs for the Foreign Office; or, Classical *versus* Gothic', *Gentleman's Magazine*, vol. 207 (November 1859).

Anon., 'The National Style and its Critics', *Gentleman's Magazine*, vol. 208 (January 1860).

Anon., 'Progress of Architecture in 1859', *Gentleman's Magazine*, vol. 208 (March 1860).

Anon., 'The New Foreign Office and Lord Palmerston', *Saturday Review*, 28 July 1860.

Anon., *Remarks on a National Style, in Reference to the Proposed Foreign Office* (1860).

Anon., *Shall Gothic Architecture be Denied Fair Play? Thoughts Suggested by Reading a Pamphlet Entitled 'Remarks on a National Style, in Reference to the Proposed Foreign Office'* (1860).

Anon., *Classic or Pseudo-Gothic: A Reply to a Pamphlet Entitled 'Shall Gothic Architecture Be Denied Fair Play'* (Bell & Daldy, 1860).

Anon., 'Lord Palmerston's Dictatorship', *Saturday Review*, 22 September 1860.

Anon., Review of Francis E. Scott's *Shall the New FO be Gothic or Classic?*, *Gentleman's Magazine*, vol. 209 (September 1860).

Anon., 'The New Foreign Office: "The Battle of the Styles"', *Art-Journal*, vol. 80, August 1861.

Anon., 'Classic or Gothic: The Battle of the Styles', *Blackwood's Edinburgh Magazine*, vol. 91 (March 1862).

Anon., 'Iron – its Uses and Manufacture', *Edinburgh Review*, vol. 116 (July 1862).

Anon., *Examples of London and Provincial Architecture of the Victorian Age: A Monthly Review of the World's Architectural Progress* (1 May 1862).

Anon., 'The New Foreign Office', *Art-Journal*, vol. 7 (1868).

Anon., 'New Courts-of-Justice Designs', *Belgravia*, vol. 2 (1868).

Ashpitel, Arthur, *Treatise on Architecture* (Edinburgh: A & C Black, 1867).

[Beresford-Hope, A. J.], 'The Rebuilding of the Public Offices', *Saturday Review*, 17 November 1855.

[Beresford-Hope, A. J. P.] 'A Cambridge Man', *The New Palaces of Administration: An Earnest Appeal to the Competitors, the Public and the Committee* (Cambridge: Macmillan, 1857).

Beresford-Hope, A. J., *Public Offices and Metropolitan Improvements* (London: James Ridgway, 1857).

Beresford-Hope, A. J., *The Expense of the Government and of Mr. Beresford-Hope's Plan of Public Offices Compared, with a Plan* (London: James Ridgway, 1857).

[Beresford-Hope, A. J.], 'The Competition for the Public Offices', *Saturday Review*, 23 May 1857.

[Beresford-Hope, A. J.], 'The Competition for the Public Offices', *Saturday Review*, 30 May 1857.

[Beresford-Hope, A. J.], 'The Prizes for the Public Offices', *Saturday Review*, 1 Aug 1857.

Beresford-Hope, A. J., *The Common Sense of Art* (London: John Murray, 1858).

Beresford-Hope, A. J., *The Condition and Prospects of Architectural Art* (London: 1863).

Beresford-Hope, A. J., *The Art Workman's Position* (London: 1864).

Britton, John, *The Architectural Antiquities of Great Britain*, 5 vols (London: Longman, 1804–26).

Brougham, H., 'The New Houses of Parliament', *Edinburgh Review*, vol. 65 (1837).

Burges, William, *Art Applied to Industry* (Oxford: J. H. and J. Parker, 1865).

[Capes, Frederick], 'Palmerston on Architecture', *Rambler*, vol. 25 (November 1859).

Carlyle, Thomas, *Past and Present* (London: Chapman & Hall, [1843] 1895).

Caverno, D. H., 'The Gothic', in *University Quarterly* (New Haven), vol. 1 (October 1860).

Chambers's Information for the People, 2 vols (Edinburgh: 1841–2).

Clarke, H. G., *A Critical and Descriptive Catalogue of the Competition Designs for the Public Offices now on View in Westminster Hall* (London: 1857).

Cobden, Richard, *Speeches on Public Policy*, John Bright and Thorold Rogers (eds.) (London: MacMillan, 1870).

Coke, Charles Anthony, 'Foreigners in England and Wales', *Census of the British Empire, 1861* (London: Harrison, 1864), vol. II, p. 181.

Collier, W. F., *History of the British Empire* (London: T. Nelson and Sons, 1858).

Darwin, Charles, *On the Origin of Species by Means of Natural Selection* (London: John Murray, 1859).

Dickens, Charles, *A Child's History of England*, 2 vols (New York: Harper and Brothers, 1853).

Dixon, Richard Watson, 'Gothic Art – John Ruskin', *London Quarterly Review*, vol. 7 (January 1857).

[Eastlake, Charles], 'Third Report of the Commissioners of the Fine Arts', *Art-Union*, September 1844.

Eastlake, Charles L., *A History of the Gothic Revival* (London: Longmans, Green & Co., 1872).

'Elinor, Aunt', *Aunt Elinor's Lectures on Architecture: Dedicated to the Ladies of England* (London: 1843).

[Emmett, J. T.], 'The State of English Architecture', *Quarterly Review*, vol. 132 (April 1872).

Encyclopaedia Britannica, 7th edn (London: 1830–42); 8th edn (London: 1852–60).

Fergusson, James, *Illustrations of the Rock-Cut Temples of India* (London: John Weale, 1845).

Fergusson, James, *Picturesque Illustrations of Ancient Architecture in Hindustan* (London: Hogarth, 1847).

Fergusson, James, *An Historical Enquiry into the True Principles of Beauty in Art, More Especially with Reference to Architecture* (London: 1849).

Fergusson, James, *Observations on the British Museum, National Gallery, and National Record Office; with Suggestions for their Improvement* (London: 1849).

Fergusson, James, *The Illustrated Handbook of Architecture*, 2 vols (London: John Murray, 1855).

Fergusson, James, *On a National Collection of Architectural Art* (London: 1857).

Fergusson, James, *History of the Modern Styles of Architecture* (London: John Murray, 1862).

Fergusson, James, *Rude Stone Monuments in All Countries: Their Ages and Uses* (London: John Murray, 1872).

Fergusson, James, *A History of Architecture in All Countries: From the Earliest Times to the Present Day*, 4 vols (London: John Murray, 1865–7, 1874, 1893).

Fergusson, James, 'Architectural Art', *American Journal of Education*, vol. 6 (1871).

Fergusson, James, 'The New Law Courts', *Macmillan's Magazine*, vol. 25 (January 1872).

Fergusson, James, 'St Paul's Cathedral', *Contemporary Review*, vol. 24 (June/November 1874).

Fergusson, James, *A History of Indian and Eastern Architecture* (London: John Murray, 1876).

Fergusson, James, *Archaeology in India, with Reference to the Works of Babu Rajendralala Mitra* (London: Trübner & Co., 1884).

Fergusson, James, 'The Proposed New Cathedral in Liverpool', *Nineteenth Century*, vol. 16 (December 1884).

Fergusson, James, 'The Restoration of Westminster Hall', *Nineteenth Century*, November 1885.

Freeman, E. A., *A History of Architecture* (London: Joseph Masters, 1849).

Freeman, E. A., 'The Style of the New Foreign Office', *The Times*, 19 October 1859, and in *Ecclesiologist*, vol. 20 (December 1859).

[Freeman, E. A.], 'The Foreign Office: Classic or Gothic', *National Review*, January 1860.

Garbett, Edward Lacy, *Rudimentary Treatise on the Principles of Design in Architecture as Deducible from Nature* (London: 1850).

Hall, Sir James, *Essay on the Origin, History, and Principles, of Gothic Architecture* (London: 1813).

Hamilton, W. R., *Letter[s] from WR Hamilton to the Earl of Elgin, on the New Houses of Parliament* (London: 1836–7).

Harris, Thomas, *Victorian Architecture: A Few Words to Show that a National*

Architecture Adapted to the Wants of the Nineteenth Century is Attainable (London: Bell & Daldy, 1860).

Harris, Thomas, *Three Periods of English Architecture* (London: Batsford, 1894).

Hosking, William, 'Architecture', in *Encyclopaedia Britannica*, 7th edn (1830–42).

Hope, Thomas, *An Historical Essay on Architecture* (London: Murray, 1835).

Huggins, Samuel, *The Course and Current of Architecture* (London: Weale, 1863).

Jackson, T. G., *Modern Gothic Architecture* (London: H. S. King, 1873).

Jeffcock, J. T., 'Gothic Architecture: A National Style', *Ecclesiologist*, vol. 18 (August 1857).

[Kaye, J.], 'The House that Scott Built', *Cornhill Magazine*, vol. 16 (September 1867).

Kerr, Robert, *The Gentleman's House* (London: 1865).

Kerr, Robert, 'Ruskin and Emotional Architecture', *Journal of the Royal Institute of British Architects*, 3rd ser., vol. 7 (1899–1900), 181–8.

Kingsley, Charles, *Westward Ho! Or the Voyages and Adventures of Sir Amyas Leigh* (Cambridge: MacMillan & Co., [1855]1893).

Lamb, Edward Buckton, *Studies of Ancient Domestic Architecture* (London: 1846).

Leeds, W. H., 'An Essay on Modern English Architecture', in Charles Barry, *The Traveller's Club* (private published, 1839).

'Lucius', 'Vulcanian Architecture', *Athenaeum*, 8 June 1844.

Magoun, Rev George F., 'Church Architecture and the Masses', *Congregational Quarterly* (Boston), vol. 4 (1863).

Micklethwaite, J. T., *Modern Parish Churches: Their Plan, Design, and Furniture* (London: Henry S. King, 1874).

Milner, Rev John, *A Treatise on the Ecclesiastical Architecture of England during the Middle Ages*, 3rd edn (London: Weale, 1835).

Muir, W. J. Cockburn, *Pagan or Christian? Or Notes for the General Public on our National Architecture* (London: Richard Bentley, 1860).

O'Connell, James, 'Natural History of Architecture', *London Review*, vol. 13 (October 1859).

Paley, M. A., *A Manual of Gothic Architecture* (London: 1847).

Papworth, John W., 'On Beauty in Architecture and its Alliance with the Past'. *Papers read at the Royal Institute of British Architects, Session 1856–7* (1857).

Parker, John Henry, *An Introduction to the Study of Gothic Architecture* (Oxford: J. A. and Jas Parker, 1849).

Parker, J. H., 'English Domestic Architecture', lecture to the Oxford Architectural Society, *Gentleman's Magazine*, vol. 206 (1859).

Parker, J. H., 'The New Foreign Office', *Gentleman's Magazine*, vol. 206 (1859).

Parker, J. H., 'The New Government Offices: The Application of Gothic to Domestic Purposes', *Gentleman's Magazine*, vol. 206 (1859).

Parker, J. H., 'The Earliest Gothic Buildings, and the Revival of Gothic for Domestic Purposes', *Gentleman's Magazine*, vol. 206 (1859).

Parker, John Henry, 'On the English Origin of Gothic Architecture', *Archaeologia*, vol. 43 (1871).

[Patmore, Coventry], 'London Street Architecture', *National Review*, vol. 5, July 1857.

[Patmore, Coventry], 'Gothic Architecture – Present and Future', *North British Review*, vol. 28 (May 1858).

Penny Cyclopaedia (London: 1833–43).

Pickett, William Vose, *To the President . . . of the Royal Academy* (privately printed, 1843).

Pickett, William Vose, *A New System of Architecture* (London: Longmans, 1845).

Pickett, William Vose, *New Forms in Architecture* (London: 1849).

Pickett, William Vose, 'Mr Vose Pickett's New System of Iron Architecture', ch. 24 of Scoffern, John, *et al.*, *The Useful Metals and their Alloys* (London: 1857).

Pictorial Gallery of the Arts, The, 2 vols (London: 1847).

Poynter, Ambrose, 'Of the Effects which should Result to Architectural Taste, with Regard to Arrangement and Design, from the General Introduction of Iron in the Construction of Buildings', *Civil Engineer and Architect's Journal*, September 1843.

'Practical Man, A'. *Remarks on the Designs Proposed for the New Government Offices: More Particularly on Those for the Block Plans and the Approaches to the New Palace at Westminster* (London: J. Ridgway, 1857).

Pugin, A. W. N., *A Letter to AW Hakewill, architect, in answer to his reflexions on the style for rebuilding the Houses of Parliament* (Salisbury: W. B. Brodie, 1835).

Pugin, A. W. N., *Contrasts: or, A Parallel between the Noble Edifices of the Fourteenth and Fifteenth Centuries, and Corresponding Buildings of the Present Day; Shewing the Present Decay of Taste* (London: Charles Dollman, 1837).

Pugin, A. W. N., *The True Principles of Pointed or Christian Architecture* (London: John Weale, 1841).

Pugin, A. W. N., 'The Present State of Ecclesiastical Architecture in England', *Dublin Review*, vols 10, 12 (May 1841 and February 1842).

Pugin, A. W. N., *An Apology for the Revival of Christian Architecture* (London: John Weale, 1843).

Pugin, A. W. N., *The Present State of Ecclesiastical Architecture in England* (London: 1843; first published 1841–2 in *Dublin Review*).

Pugin, A. W. N., *Some Remarks on the Articles which have recently appeared in the "Rambler" relative to Ecclesiastical Architecture and Decoration* (London: Charles Dolman, 1850).

Reade, T. Mellard, *On the Formation of a New Style of Architecture, Specially Adapted to Civic Purposes* (London & Liverpool, [1862]).

Reichensperger, A., 'The Spire and Roof of Cologne Cathedral', and editorial response, *Ecclesiologist*, vol. 17 (October 1856).

Rickman, Thomas, *An Attempt to Discriminate between the Styles of English Architecture, from the Conquest to the Reformation* (London: Longman, 1817).

Ruskin, John, *The Seven Lamps of Architecture* (Orpington: G Allen, 1849).

Ruskin, John, *The Stones of Venice* (London: 1853).

Ruskin, *Lectures on Architecture and Painting* (London: Smith & Elder, 1854).

Ruskin, John, *The Two Paths* (London: Smith & Elder, 1859).

Scoffern, John, Truran, William and Clay, William, *et al.*, *The Useful Metals and their Alloys* (London: Houlston and Wright, 1857).

Scott, Sir Francis E., *Shall the New Foreign Office be Gothic or Classic? A Plea for the Former: Addressed to Members of the House of Commons* (Bell & Daldy, 1860).

Scott, G. G., *Remarks on Secular and Domestic Architecture, Present and Future* (London: John Murray, 1857).

Scott, G. G., 'On the Present Position and Future Prospects of the Revival of Gothic Architecture', lecture published in *Associated Architectural Societies Reports and Papers*, vol. 4 (1857).

Scott, G. G., *Explanatory Remarks upon the Designs for the New Government Offices and its Approaches, &c* (London: George Barclay, 1857).

Scott, G. G., *A Plea for the Faithful Restoration of Our Ancient Churches* (London: 1859).

[Scott, G. G.], *The Gothic Renaissance: Its Origin, Progress, and Principles* (London: Saunders, Otley & Co., 1860).

Scott, G. G., *Explanatory Remarks on the Design for the New Foreign Office Now Laid before the House of Commons* (London: Strangeways & Walden [1860]).

Scott, G. G., 'On the Rationale of Gothic Architecture', Royal Academy Lectures, *Builder*, 11, 18 February and 3 March 1860.

Scott, G. G., *Lectures on the Rise and Development of Mediaeval Architecture*, 2 vols (London: Murray, 1878).

Scott, George Gilbert, *Personal and Professional Recollections* (London: Sampson Lowe, 1879; 1995 reprint, Paul Watkins publ., edited and with an introduction by Gavin Stamp).

Sewell, W., 'Principles of Gothic Architecture', *Quarterly Review*, vol. 69 (December 1841).

[Simpson, Richard], 'The Development of Gothic Architecture', *Rambler*, vol. 24 (May 1859).

Skidmore, Mr, 'Ancient Metalwork Applied to Domestic Purposes, and the Uses of Iron in Reference to the New Museum', lecture to the Oxford Architectural Society, *Gentleman's Magazine*, vol. 206 (1859).

Stephens, W. R. W. (ed.), *The Life and Letters of Edward A Freeman*, vol. II (London: MacMillan, 1865).

Street, G. E., 'The True Principles of Architecture and the Possibility of Development', *Ecclesiologist*, vol. 13 (June 1852).

Street, G. E., *An Urgent Plea for the Revival of True Principles of Architecture in the Public Buildings of the University of Oxford* (Oxford: J. H. Parker, 1853).

Street, G. E. 'Mr Street on German Pointed Architecture', *Ecclesiologist*, vol. 18 (June 1857).

Street, A. E., *Memoir of George Edmund Street, RA, 1824–1881* (London: John Murray, 1888).

Stuart Mill, John, *Principles of Political Economy*, 2nd edn (London: John W. Parker, 1849)

Tennyson, Alfred, 'Locksley Hall', in *Poems*, vol. 2 (London: Edward Moxon, 1842).

Thackeray, W.M. *The Book of Snobs* (London: *Punch* Office, 1848).

Tite, W., *On the Progress, Position and Future of Architecture* (privately printed, 1859; also printed in *Civil Engineer and Architect's Journal*, vol. 22 (December 1859).

Turner, T. Hudson, *Some Account of Domestic Architecture in England from the Conquest to Henry VII*, 4 vols (Oxford: J. H. Parker, 1851–9).

Willis, R., *Remarks on the Architecture of the Middle Ages, Especially of Italy* (Cambridge: 1835).

Willson, E. J., *Introduction* to A Pugin (*père*), *Examples of Gothic Architecture*, 2nd edn (London: Bohn, 1838).

Wraxall, Lascelles, 'Imperial Paris', in *Bentley's Miscellany*, vol. 43 (June 1858).

Wyatt, M. Digby, *The Industrial Arts of the Nineteenth Century* (London: Day, 1851).

CONTEMPORARY PERIODICALS AND NEWSPAPERS

Academy
All the Year Round
Archaeologia
Architect
Art-Journal
Art Union Monthly Journal of the Fine Arts
Associated Architectural Societies Reports and Papers
Athenaeum
Belfast News-Letter
Belgravia
Bentley's Miscellany
Birmingham Daily Post
Birmingham Daily Press
Bristol Mercury
Blackwood's Edinburgh Magazine
Builder
Building News
Caledonian Mercury

Chambers's Edinburgh Journal
Christian Remembrancer
Civil Engineer and Architects' Journal
Congregational Quarterly (Boston)
Cornhill Magazine
Daily News
Daily Scotsman
Daily Telegraph
Derby Mercury
Dublin Review
Ecclesiologist
Eclectic Review
Economist
Edinburgh Review
Era
Examiner
Express
Fraser's Magazine
Freeman's Journal
Gentleman's Magazine
Glasgow Herald
Globe
Hampshire Telegraph and Sussex Chronicle
Hull Morning Telegraph
Hull Packet and East Riding Times
Household Words
Illustrated London News
Ipswich Journal
Jackson's Oxford Journal
Journal of the Franklin Institute (Philadelphia)
Leeds Intelligencer
Leeds Mercury
Literary Gazette
Liverpool Daily Post
Liverpool Mercury
Lloyd's Weekly Newspaper
London [Quarterly] *Review*
Macmillan's Magazine
Manchester Guardian
Manchester Weekly Examiner & Times / Times & Examiner
Month: A Literary and Critical Journal
Morning Advertiser
Morning Chronicle

Morning Herald
Morning Post
National Review
Newcastle Courant
North American Review
North British Review
North Wales Chronicle
Northern Daily Times
Northern Daily Express
Observer
Preston Guardian
Punch
Quarterly Review
Rambler
Reynolds's Newspaper
Royal Institute of British Architects: Proceedings
Saturday Review
Sharpe's London Magazine
Sheffield Daily Telegraph
Sheffield Daily News
Standard
Sun
The Times
Trewman's Exeter Flying Post
University Quarterly (New Haven)
Western Daily Press
Westminster Review

SECONDARY SOURCES

Aldrich, Megan, *Gothic Revival* (London: Phaidon, 1994).

Anderson, Pat, 'The Other Gothic Revival: Contemporary Ideals in English Revivalism, 1730–1840', *Canadian Journal of History*, vol. 22 (1987).

Armour, T., 'Four Attempts to Rebuild the Foreign Office; 1839 to 1869', unpublished history dissertation, Architectural Association School of Architecture, 1978.

Arnold, D (ed.), *The Metropolis and its Image: Constructing Identities for London, c. 1750–1950* (Oxford: Blackwell, 1999).

Atkins, Gareth, 'Rebuilding the Reformation: History, Architecture and National Identity, c. 1830–1850', paper read at the 10th Annual Conference of the British Association for Victorian Studies, Churchill College, Cambridge, July 2009.

Auerbach, Jeffrey A., *The Great Exhibition of 1851: A Nation on Display* (New Haven: Yale University Press, 1999).

Barker, Felix and Hyde, Ralph, *London as it Might Have Been* (London: John Murray, 1982).

Barringer, Tim, *Men at Work: Art and Labour in Victorian Britain* (New Haven: Yale University Press, 2005).

Bayley, Stephen, *The Albert Memorial* (London: Scolar, 1981).

Belich, James. *Replenishing the Earth: The Settler Revolution and the Rise of the Angloworld* (Oxford: Oxford University Press, 2009).

Binfield, Clyde, 'Architects in Connexion: Four Methodist Generations', in Jane Garnett and Colin Matthew (eds), *Revival and Religion since 1700* (London: Hambledon, 1993).

Bingham, N. R., 'Victorian and Edwardian Whitehall: Architecture and Planning, 1869–1918', PhD Thesis, Bedford College, London, 1985.

Blau, Eve, *Ruskinian Gothic: The Architecture of Deane and Woodward, 1* (Princeton: Princeton University Press, 1982).

Boase, T. S. R., 'The Decoration of the New Palace of Westminster, 1841–1863', *Journal of the Warburg and Courtauld Institutes*, vol. 17 (1954).

Bøe, Alf, *From Gothic Revival to Functional Form: A Study in Victorian Theories of Design* (Oslo: Oslo University Press, and Oxford: Blackwell, 1957).

Bottoms, Edward, 'The Royal Architectural Museum in the Light of New Documentary Evidence', *Journal of the History of Collections*, vol. 19 (2007).

Bradley, S., 'The Englishness of Gothic: Theories and Interpretations from William Gilpin to JH Parker', *Architectural History*, vol. 45 (2002).

Bradley, Simon, *St Pancras Station* (London: Profile Books, 2007).

Brantlinger, Patrick. *Rule of Darkness: British Literature and Imperialism, 1830–1914* (Ithaca, NY: Cornell University Press, 1988).

Bremner, G. A., '"Some Imperial Institute": Architecture, Symbolism, and the Ideal of Empire in Late-Victorian Britain, 1887–93', *Journal of the Society of Architectural Historians*, vol. 62 (2003).

Bremner, G. A., '"Imperial Monumental Halls and Tower": Westminster Abbey and the Commemoration of Empire, 1854–1904', *Architectural History*, vol. 347 (2004).

Bremner, G. Alex, 'Nation and Empire in the Government Architecture of mid-Victorian London: the Foreign and India Office reconsidered', *Historical Journal*, vol. 48, no. 3 (2005).

Briggs, Asa, *Victorian Cities* (London: Odhams, 1963).

Briggs, Martin S., *Goths and Vandals: A Study of the Destruction, Neglect and Preservation of Historical Buildings in England* (London: Constable, 1952).

Bright, Michael, *Cities Built to Music: Aesthetic Theories of the Victorian Gothic Revival* (Columbus: Ohio State University Press, 1984).

Brooks, Chris, *The Gothic Revival* (London: Phaidon, 1999).

Brooks, Chris, '"The Stuff of a Heresiarch": William Butterfield, Beresford

Hope, and the Ecclesiological Vanguard', in Christopher Webster and John Elliott (eds), *"A Church as it Should Be": The Cambridge Camden Society and its Influence* (Stamford: Shaun Tyas, 2000).

Brownlee, David B., *Law Courts: The Architecture of George Edmund Street* (Cambridge, MA: MIT Press, 1984).

Brownlee, David B., 'That "Regular Mongrel Affair"': GG Scott's Design for the Government Offices', *Architectural History*, vol. 28 (1985).

Burrow, J. W., *A Liberal Descent* (Cambridge: Cambridge University Press, 1981).

Butterfield, Herbert, *The Whig Interpretation of History* (London: G Bell & Sons, 1931).

Carrott, Richard, *The Egyptian Revival* (Berkeley: University of California Press, 1978).

Cecil Denny Highton & Partners, Chartered Architects, *A History of the Building containing the India Office, the Foreign and Commonwealth Office and the Home Office* (March 1983), in the Foreign Office Library.

Chopra, Preeti, 'Decoding Victorian Bombay: The Construction of Meaning by the City's Local Inhabitants', paper delivered to the NAVSA Conference on the Arts and Culture in Victorian Britain, Yale University, November 2008.

Clark, Kenneth, *The Gothic Revival: An Essay in the History of Taste* (London: Constable, 1928; revised edn, 1962).

Clarke, Basil F. L., *Church Builders of the Nineteenth Century: A Study of the Gothic Revival in England* (revised edn, Newton Abbott: David & Charles, 1969).

Cole, David, *The Work of Sir Gilbert Scott* (London: Architectural Press, 1980).

Collins, Peter, 'Vose Pickett: A New System of Architecture', *Architectural Review*, October 1961, pp. 267–8.

Collins, Peter, *Changing Ideals in Modern Architecture 1750–1950* (London: Faber & Faber, 1965).

Colvin, Howard, *A Biographical Dictionary of British Architects 1600–1840* (London: J. Murray, 1997).

Cook, Chris and Keith, Brendan, *British Historical Facts, 1830–1900* (London: Macmillan, 1975).

Cornforth, John, 'The Old India Office', *Country Life*, November 1987, pp. 164–9.

Craig, Maurice, 'James Fergusson', in Summerson, John (ed.), *Concerning Architecture: Essays on Architectural Writers and Writing Presented to Nikolaus Pevsner* (London: Allen Lane, 1968).

Crew, Sarah (ed.), *Visionary Spires* (London: Waterstone, 1986).

Crinson, Mark, *Empire Building: Orientalism and Victorian Architecture* (London: Routledge, 1996).

Crook, J. Mordaunt, *The Greek Revival* (Feltham: Country Life Books, 1972).

Crook, J. Mordaunt, *The Dilemma of Style* (London: Murray, 1987).

Crook, J. Mordaunt, *The Architect's Secret: Victorian Critics and the Image of Gravity* (London: John Murray, 2003).

Curl, James Stevens, *The Egyptian Revival* (London: Allen & Unwin, 1982).

Curl, James Stevens, *Victorian Architecture* (Newton Abbot: David & Charles, 1990).

Curl, James Stevens, *Book of Victorian Churches* (London: Batsford, 1995).

Curl, James Stevens, *Victorian Architecture, Diversity and Invention* (Reading: Spire, 2007).

Davis, Terence, *John Nash: The Prince Regent's Architect* (London: Country Life, 1966).

Dellheim, Charles, *The Face of the Past* (Cambridge: Cambridge University Press, 1982).

Denslagen, Wim, *Architectural Restoration in Western Europe: Controversy and Continuity* (Amsterdam: Architectura & Natura Press, 1994).

Dixon, Roger (ed.), *Sir Gilbert Scott and the Scott Dynasty* (London, Polytechnic of the South Bank, Department of Architecture 1980).

Dixon, Roger and Muthesius, Stefan, *Victorian Architecture* (London: Thames & Hudson, 1978).

Driver, F. and Gilbert, G. (eds), *Imperial Cities: Landscape, Display and Identity* (Manchester: Manchester University Press, 1999).

Dyos, H. J. and Wolff, Michael (eds), *The Victorian City: Images and Realities*, 2 vols (London: Routledge, 1973).

Elwall, Robert, 'James Fergusson (1808–86): A Pioneering Architectural Historian', *RSA Journal*, vol. 139, no. 5418 (May 1991).

Felstead, Alison, Franklin, Jonathan, and Pinfield, Leslie (eds), *Directory of British Architects 1834–1900* (London: Mansell, 1993).

Ferriday, Peter (ed.), *Victorian Architecture* (London: Jonathan Cape, 1963).

Ferriday, Peter, 'The Revival: Stories Ancient and Modern', *Architectural Review*, vol. 121 (1957).

FCO, *A History of the Building Containing the India Office, the Foreign and Colonial Office and the Home Office*: report prepared by Cecil Denny Highton & Partners, March 1983.

FCO, *Foreign & Commonwealth Office*, 3rd edn (London: HMSO, 1996).

Fisher, Geoffrey, Stamp, Gavin and Heseltine, Joanna (eds), *Catalogue of the Drawings Collection of the Royal Institute of British Architects: The Scott Family* (London: RIBA, 1991).

Flour, Isabelle, '"On the Formation of a National Museum of Architecture": the Architectural Museum versus the South Kensington Museum', *Architectural History*, no. 51 (2008).

Frew, J. M., 'Gothic is English: John Carter And the Revival of the Gothic as England's National Style', *Art Bulletin*, vol. 64 (1982).

Germann, Georg, trans. Gerald Onn, *Gothic Revival in Europe and Britain: Sources, Influences and Ideas* (London: Lund Humphries, 1972).

Girouard, Mark, *The Victorian Country House* (New Haven: Yale University Press, 1979).

Girouard, Mark, *Sweetness and Light: The Queen Anne Movement, 1860–1900* (New Haven: Yale University Press, 1984).

Girouard, Mark, *Alfred Waterhouse and the Natural History Museum* (London: British Museum, 1981).

Goodhart-Rendel, H. S., 'English Gothic of the Nineteenth Century', *Journal of the Royal Institute of British Architects*, vol. 31 (1924).

Goodhart-Rendel, H. S., 'Rogue Architects of the Victorian Era', *Journal of the Royal Institute of British Architects*, 3rd ser., vol. 56 (1949).

Goodhart-Rendel, H. S., *English Architecture since the Regency: An Interpretation* (London: Century, 1954).

Green, Martin, *Dreams of Adventure, Deeds of Empire* (New York: Basic Books 1979).

Guedes, Pedro, 'William Vose Pickett's Written Architecture: Celebrating Invention Without Convincing Delineation', in A. Leach and G. Matthewson (eds), *Celebration: Proceedings of the 22nd Annual Conference of the Society of Architectural Historians, Australia and New Zealand* (2005).

Keith Hamilton, 'Accommodating Diplomacy: The Foreign and Commonwealth Office and the Debate over Whitehall Development', in *Contemporary British History*, vol. 18, no. 3 (Autumn 2004).

Handley-Read, Lavinia, 'Legacy of a Vanished Empire: The Design of the India Office', *Country Life*, July 1970.

Harbron, Dudley, 'Thomas Harris', *Architectural Review*, vol. 92 (1942).

Harper, Roger H., *Victorian Architectural Competitions: An Index to British and Irish Architectural Competitions in the Builder 1843–1900* (London: Mansell, 1983).

Hersey, George L., *High Victorian Gothic: A Study in Associationism* (Baltimore: Johns Hopkins University Press, 1972).

Heseltine, Joanna (ed.), *Catalogue of the Drawings Collection of the Royal Institute of British Architects: The Scott Family* (London: RIBA, 1981).

Hill, Christopher, 'The Norman Yoke', in *Puritanism and Revolution*, ed. Christopher Hill (London: Seeker and Warburg, 1958).

Hill, Rosemary, *God's Architect: Pugin and the Building of Romantic Britain* (London: Penguin/Allen Lane, 2007).

Hitchcock, Henry-Russell, 'Victorian Monuments of Commerce', *Architectural Review*, vol. 105 (1949), pp. 61–74.

Hitchcock, Henry-Russell, *Early Victorian Architecture in Britain*, 2 vols (London: Architectural Press, 1954).

Hitchcock, Henry-Russell, 'High Victorian Gothic', *Victorian Studies*, vol. 1 (1957).

Hitchcock, Henry-Russell, *Architecture: The Nineteenth and Twentieth Centuries*, 2nd edn (London: Penguin, 1963).

Hoppen, K. Theodore, *The Mid-Victorian Generation, 1846–1886* (Oxford: Clarendon Press, 1998).

Hunt, Tristram, *Building Jerusalem: The Rise and Fall of the Victorian City* (London: Weidenfeld, 2004).

Hurst, Lawrence, 'Concrete and the Structural Use of Cement in England before 1890', in James Sutherland, *et al.* (eds), *Historic Concrete: Background to Appraisal* (London: Thomas Telford, 2001).

Hussey, C., 'Foreign Office's Threatened Glory', *Country Life*, February 1964.

Hvidt, Kristian, trans. Siff Pors, *Copenhagen City Hall. The Building and its Activities Through 100 Years* (Copenhagen: City of Copenhagen, 2005), pp. 34–5.

Hyam, Ronald, *Britain's Declining Empire: the Road to Decolonisation, 1918–1968* (Cambridge: Cambridge University Press, 2008)

Jann, Rosemary, 'Democratic Myths in Victorian Medievalism', *Browning Institute Studies*, vol. 8 (1980).

Jordan, Robert Furneaux, *Victorian Architecture* (Harmondsworth: Penguin, 1966).

Kaye, Barrington, *The Development of the Architectural Profession in Britain: A Sociological Study* (London: Allen & Unwin, 1960).

Lang, S., 'The Principles of the Gothic Revival in England', *Journal of the Society of Architectural Historians*, vol. 25 (1966).

Lerner, Max (ed.), *Essential Works of John Stuart Mill* (New York: Bantam, 1961).

Lewis, Michael J., *The Politics of the German Gothic Revival: August Reichensperger* (New York: Architectural History Foundation, 1993).

Lewis, Michael J., *The Gothic Revival* (Thames & Hudson, 2002).

Macaulay, James, *The Gothic Revival 1745–1845* (Newcastle: University of Newcastle-upon-Tyne, 1975).

McCarthy, Michael, *The Origins of the Gothic Revival* (New Haven: Yale University Press, 1987).

Mace, Angela, *The Royal Institute of British Architects: A Guide to its Archive and History* (London: RIBA, 1986).

Mackenzie, John, *Orientalism: History, Theory and the Arts* (Manchester: Manchester University Press, 1995).

Macleod, Robert, *Style and Society: Architectural Ideology in Britain 1835–1914* (London: RIBA Publications, 1971).

Madsen, Stephen Tschudi, *Restoration and Anti-Restoration* (Oslo: Universitetsforlaget, 1975).

Maeyer, Jan de and Verpoest, Luc (eds), *Gothic Revival: Religion, Architecture and Style in Western Europe 1815–1914* (Leuven: Universitaire Pres, 2000).

Mane-Wheoki, Jonathan, 'Colonial Brick and Marble: High Victorian Gothic in the Antipodes', in Penny Gay and Judith Johnston (eds), *Victorian Gothic* (Sydney: Australian Victorian Studies Association, 1992).

Metcalf, Thomas R., *An Imperial Vision: Indian Architecture and the British Raj* (London: Faber, 1989).

Metcalf, Thomas R., 'Architecture in the British Empire', in Robin W. Winks,

Oxford History of the British Empire, vol. 5, *Historiography* (Oxford: Oxford University Press, 1999).

Mignot, Claude, *Architecture of the 19th Century* (Fribourg: Evergreen, 1983).

Morris, Ellen K., 'Symbols of Empire: Architectural Styles and the Government Offices Competition', *Journal of Architectural Education*, vol. 32 (1978).

Morris, Jan, with Simon Winchester, *Stones of Empire: The Buildings of the Raj* (Oxford: Oxford University Press, 1983).

Morris, Jan and Fermor-Hesketh, R. (eds), *Architecture of the British Empire* (London: Weidenfeld, 1986).

Morton, A. L. (ed.), *Political Writings of William Morris* (London: Lawrence & Wishart, 1973).

Muthesius, Stefan, *The High Victorian Movement in Architecture 1850–1870* (London: Routledge, 1972).

Norman, E. R., *Anti-Catholicism in Victorian England* (London: George Allen & Unwin, 1968).

Oxford Dictionary of National Biography (Oxford: Oxford University Press, 2004).

Parker, C. J. W., 'The Failure of Liberal Racialism: The Racial Ideas of EA Freeman', *Historical Journal*, vol. 24 (1981), pp. 825–46.

Paz, D. G., *Popular Anti-Catholicism in Mid-Victorian England* (Stanford, CA: Stanford University Press, 1992).

Pevsner, Nikolaus, *The Englishness of English Art* (London: Architectural Press, 1956).

Pevsner, Nikolaus, *Matthew Digby Wyatt: The First Cambridge Slade Professor of Fine Art* (Cambridge: Cambridge University Press, 1950).

Pevsner, Nikolaus, *The Sources of Modern Architecture and Design* (London: Thames & Hudson, 1968).

Pevsner, Nikolaus, *Ruskin and Voillet-le-Duc: Englishness and Frenchness in the Appreciation of Gothic Architecture* (London: Thames & Hudson, 1969).

Pevsner, Nikolaus, *Some Architectural Writers of the Nineteenth Century* (Oxford: Clarendon Press, 1972).

Pevsner, Nikolaus, *The Buildings of England: The West Riding*, 2nd edn (Harmondsworth: Penguin, 1967).

Pevsner, Nikolaus, *The Buildings of England: The Cities of London and Westminster*, 3rd edn (Harmondsworth: Penguin, 1973).

Physick, John and Darby, Michael, *'Marble Halls': Drawings and Models for Victorian Secular Buildings* (exhibition catalogue) (London: Victoria and Albert Museum, 1973).

Port, M. H. (ed.), *The Houses of Parliament* (New Haven: Yale University Press, 1976).

Port, M. H., 'Pride and Parsimony: Influences Affecting the Development of the Whitehall Quarter in the 1850s', *London Journal*, vol. 2 (1976).

Port, M. H., *Imperial London: Civil Government Building in London, 1851–1915* (New Haven: Yale University Press, 1995).

Port, M. H., 'Government and the Metropolitan Image: Ministers, Parliament, and the Concept of a Capital City, 1840–1915', D. Arnold (ed.), *The Metropolis and its Image: Constructing Identities for London, c. 1750–1950* (Oxford: Blackwell, 1999).

Porter, Bernard, '"Monstrous Vandalism": Capitalism and Philistinism in the Works of Samuel Laing (1780–1868)', *Albion*, vol. 23 (1991).

Porter, Bernard, *Britain, Europe and the World, 1850–1982: Delusions of Grandeur* (London: Allen & Unwin, 1983).

Porter, Bernard, *Plots and Paranoia: A History of Political Espionage in Britain, 1790–1988* (London: Unwin Hyman, 1989).

Porter, Bernard, *Britannia's Burden: The Political Evolution of Modern Britain, 1851–1990* (London: E. Arnold, 1994).

Porter, Bernard, *The Absent-Minded Imperialists: Empire, Society and Culture in Britain* (Oxford: Oxford University Press, 2004).

Porter, Bernard, *The Lion's Share: A Short History of British Imperialism, 1850–2004*, 4th edn (London: Pearson Longman, 2004).

Pudney, John, *The Thomas Cook Story* (London: Michael Joseph, 1953).

Quinault, R., 'Westminster and the Victorian Constitution', *Transactions of the Royal Historical Society*, vol. 2 (1992).

Richardson, Douglas S., 'Gothic Revival Architecture in Ireland'. PhD Dissertation, Yale University, 1970.

Riding, Christine and Riding, Jacqueline (eds), *The Houses of Parliament: History, Art, Architecture* (London: Merrell, 2000).

Ritvo, H., 'Gothic Revival in England and America . . .', M. Bloomfield (ed.), *Allegory, Myth, and Symbol* (Cambridge, MA: Harvard University Press, 1981).

Rorabaugh, W. J., 'Politics and the Architectural Competition for the Houses of Parliament, 1834–1837', *Victorian Studies*, vol. 17 (1973).

Royal Commission on Historical Monuments, *An Inventory of the historical monuments in London*, vol. 2, *West London, Excluding Westminster Abbey* (London: HMSO, 1925).

Saint, Andrew, *Architect and Engineer: A Study in Sibling Rivalry* (New Haven: Yale University Press, 2008).

Schmitz, Oskar A. H., *Das Land ohne Musik: englische Gesellschaftsprobleme* (Munich: G. Müller, 1914).

Scott, Geoffrey, *The Architecture of Humanism: A Study in the History of Taste* (London: Constable, 1914).

Scruton, Roger, *The Aesthetics of Architecture* (Princeton: Princeton University Press, 1979).

Seldon, A., *The Foreign Office: An Illustrated History of the Place and its People* (London: HarperCollins, 2000).

Seton, M. C. C., *The India Office* (London: Putnam, 1926).

Simmons, Jack, *St Pancras Station* (London: Allen & Unwin, 1968).

Smith, E. A., *George IV* (New Haven, CT: Yale University Press, 1999).

Stamp, Gavin, *Alexander 'Greek' Thomson* (London: Laurence King, 1999).

Stamp, Gavin, 'Sir Gilbert Scott's Recollections', *Architectural History*, vol. 19 (1976).

Stamp, Gavin, 'Sir Gilbert Scott and the "Restoration" of Mediaeval Buildings', *AA Files*, vol. 1, no. 1 (1981–2).

Stamp, G., 'The Nation's Drawing-Room: Restoring the Foreign Office', *Apollo*, July 1992.

Stamp, Gavin, 'George Gilbert Scott and the Cambridge Camden Society', in Christopher Webster and John Elliott (eds), *"A Church as it Should Be": The Cambridge Camden Society and its Influence* (Stamford: Shaun Tyas, 2000).

Stamp, Gavin, and Amery, Colin, *Victorian Buildings of London 1837–87: An Illustrated Guide* (London: Architectural Press, 1980).

Stanton, Phoebe B., *The Gothic Revival and American Church Architecture: An Episode in Taste, 1840–1856* (Baltimore: Johns Hopkins University Press, 1968).

Stanton, Phoebe B., 'Pugin – Principles of Designs *versus* Mediaevalism', *Journal of the Society of Architectural Historians*, vol. 13 (1954), pp. 20–5.

Stein, Roger B., *John Ruskin and Aesthetic Thought in America, 1840–1900* (Cambridge, MA: Harvard University Press, 1967).

Summerson, John, *Heavenly Mansions and Other Essays on Architecture* (London: Cresset Press, 1949).

Summerson, John, *Architecture in Britain 1530–1830* (London: Penguin Books, 1953).

Summerson, John (ed.), *Concerning Architecture: Essays on Architectural Writers and Writing, Presented to Nikolaus Pevsner* (London: Allen Lane/Penguin, 1968).

Summerson, John, *Victorian Architecture: Four Studies in Evaluation* (New York: Columbia University Press, 1970).

Summerson, John, *The London Building World of the Eighteen-Sixties* (London: Thames & Hudson, 1973).

Summerson, John, 'London, the Artifact', in H. J. Dyos and Michael Wolff (eds), *The Victorian City: Images and Realities* (London: Routledge, 1973).

Summerson, John, *The Architecture of Victorian London* (Charlottesville: University Press of Virginia, 1976).

Sweetman, J., *The Oriental Obsession: Islamic Inspiration in British and American Art and Architecture, 1500–1921* (Cambridge: Cambridge University Press, 1988).

Thompson, Paul, 'The Problem of Ugliness', Victorian Society, *Second Conference Report*, on 'The High Victorian Cultural Achievement' (1965).

Thompson, Paul, *William Butterfield* (London: Routledge, 1971).

Toplis, Ian, 'Gilbert Scott and the Foreign Office Affair', in Roger Dixon (ed.), *Sir Gilbert Scott and the Scott Dynasty* (1980).

Toplis, Ian, *The Foreign Office: An Architectural History* (London: Mansell, 1987).

Turnor, Reginald, *Nineteenth Century Architecture in Britain* (London: Batsford, 1950).

Tyack, Geoffrey, *Sir James Pennethorne and the Making of Victorian London*
    (Cambridge: Cambridge University Press, 1992).
Victoria and Albert Museum, *Sir Gilbert Scott (1811–78), Architect of the Gothic
    Revival* (exhibition catalogue) (London:Victoria and Albert Museum, 1978).
Ware, Dora, *A Short Dictionary of British Architects* (London: Allen & Unwin,
    1967).
Webster, Christopher and Elliott, John (eds), *'A Church as it Should Be':The
    Cambridge Camden Society and its Influence* (Stamford: Shaun Tyas, 2000).
Weisser, Henry, *British Working-Class Movements and Europe, 1815–48*
    (Manchester: Manchester University Press, 1975).
White, James F., *The Cambridge Movement:The Ecclesiologists and the Gothic
    Revival* (Cambridge: Cambridge University Press, 1962).
Wiener, Martin J., *English Culture and the Decline of the Industrial Spirit,
    1850–1980* (Cambridge: Cambridge University Press, 1981).
Williams, D., *The India Office, 1858–1869* (Hoshiapur: 1983).
Yates, Nigel, *The Oxford Movement and Anglican Ritualism* (London: Historical
    Association, 1983).

Index